VOICES OF BALLARD AND BEYOND

Stories of Immigrants and their Descendants in the Pacific Northwest

Gordon Strand, Editor

A publication of
The Nordic American Voices
Oral History Project
of
The Nordic Heritage Museum

Funded in part by a grant from

CULTURE

The
Nordic American Voices Oral History
Project of the Nordic Heritage Museum

Cover image: Original oil painting,
Ballard Docks I by Signe Heggem Davis

Photo Credits: The images in this book were taken
by the interviewers, provided by the narrators,
or were obtained from the archives of
the Nordic Heritage Museum.

ISBN 0-9712413-2-9

Table of Contents

Dedicated to Lynn Moen, Editor of *Voices of Ballard: Immigrant Stories from the Vanishing Generation.*
Her participation in the creation of this new edition and the sharing of her expertise gained from the editing of several books was essential to this project.
Lynn's dedication to preserving her immigrant heritage was an inspiration to all who worked on this book.

Preface

The book *Voices of Ballard and Beyond* is the result of several years of collaborative work to capture the spirit and growth of the Nordic community in Seattle through recorded interviews. The stories presented in this book provide a glimpse of the extensive project, Nordic American Voices, consisting of more than 200 recorded interviews. These interviews have been transcribed and archived at the Nordic Heritage Museum where they serve as a rich resource for future research.

Prior to producing this book, the Nordic American Voices oral history project already has brought together hundreds of individuals: interviewers and interviewees, various committees and organizations. Though these stories arise from disparate groups and reflect experiences situated in places set apart by the Atlantic ocean, occurring in different periods and motivated by different reasons, the accounts in *Voices of Ballard and Beyond* offer profound messages for those concerned with the impact of the migration of emigrants from the Nordic countries on their communities in the United States. To many of the interviewees, going back and forth between the Nordic countries and the Northwest is part of life, not a distant dream of a utopian homeland.

Although a portion of the material of this book has been the subject of a previous publication, this book provides an opportunity to compare the stories of emigration from the Nordic countries to the Pacific Northwest from three different time periods in the 20th century. It also provides an opportunity to re-examine existing notions of the role of storytelling in cultures of displacement, even when such movement may have been voluntary.

The stories included in *Voices of Ballard and Beyond* encompass contradictions and ambivalence, consensus and clearcut direction. They speak of the dynamics of cultural differences in society at large and within a group. In this volume, diverse voices offer perspectives on the meaning of storytelling through transitions in the wake of emigration from the Nordic countries to the Pacific Northwest - or more precisely - to the Seattle area in the State of Washington, known for its industries, fishing and logging, and as the home of Swedish Hospital, Microsoft, Boeing, Amazon and Starbucks.

Just as many of the stories within this volume emerge from a partnership between the interviewee and the active listener, the book is a result of collaborative work of committee members and organizations, also over time. As such the book has a heritage of its own. The book builds on *Voices of Ballard: Immigrant Stories from the Vanishing Generation*, a 1999 joint effort of the Swedish Finn Historical Society, the Ballard Historical Society, and the Nordic Heritage Museum. The aim back then was to capture stories about Ballard's growth and change, a process of which many emigrants from the Nordic countries had been part; 123 interviews were carried out, transcribed and made available for future research. The 1999 project in turn was a result of previous oral history projects, including one by Leif Eie and Knut Karlsen in the 1990s. Eie and Karlsen's group recorded memories among Nordic residents of Ballard. These interviews became core material in the Nordic Heritage Museum.

The current book *Voices of Ballard and Beyond* may therefore best be understood as a window to the ongoing work within the Nordic American Voices project, but also as a recourse to past projects and as a prelude of those yet to come.

Voices of Ballard and Beyond brings together stories of individuals with the common focus to honor the first person narrative. The stories have been edited. Like the book itself, each section and even each chapter should be viewed as a window to a fuller story or as a piece in the evolving story of Nordic migration. The reader whose interest is piqued by a section or a particular story is urged to seek out the full transcripts and the recordings at the Nordic Heritage Museum.

We all know that oral language differs from written language. Spoken word tends to be more spontaneous and vivacious, but sometimes also repetitive, implied, or difficult to follow. The stories in *Voices of Ballard and Beyond* have been edited to make them more succinct without losing the unique voice of the narrator.

On behalf of the Nordic Heritage Museum, I am grateful to all the interviewees who generously shared their stories with us. I also wish to express my deepest gratitude to the group of volunteers whose passion for the project and for the museum is a stellar example of Nordic-American culture in action.

Varmaste tack till

Stig Andersen	Laila Lie
Brandon Benson	Kaisa London
Janice Bogren	Gary London
Rebecca Bolin	Saundra Magnussen Martin
Michelle Brodgen	Lynn Moen
Jette Bunch	Sandra Nestorovic
Julia Comstock-Ross	Paul Norlen
Laura Cooper	Lise Orville
Caitlin Cotter	Janet Rauscher
Syrene Forsman	Greta Roseberg
Shelby Gilje	Eric Schaad
Jon Halgren	Georgia Selfridge
Susan Haris	Affa Sigurdardottir
Nancy Hevly	Nedra Slauson
Mari-Ann Kind Jackson	Gordon Strand
Dan Kaylor	Peggy Sturdivant
Cristy Lake	Abigail Taplin
Mina Larsen	Lynn Tengbom
Solveig M. Lee	Marilyn Whitted

Lizette Gradén
Chief Curator, Nordic Heritage Museum

Editor's Notes

Voices of Ballard and Beyond includes all 97 stories from the original edition of *Voices of Ballard: Immigrant Stories from the Vanishing Generation* published in 2001 and edited by Lynn Moen. The title of this edition was changed to reflect the addition of 31 new stories culled from oral history interviews conducted since 2009 with the launch of the Nordic Heritage Museum's Nordic American Voices Oral History Project. The 2012 edition also has a slight change in focus. The original volume focused on stories from immigrants  and their families who lived and worked in Seattle's Ballard district and included Ballard residents of many ethnicities beyond the Nordics.

The interviews recorded since 2009 have also included individuals working and living outside the Seattle area. Volunteer teams have traveled to Everett, Auburn, Mount Vernon, Poulsbo and Stanwood to conduct interviews of first generation immigrants from the Nordic countries or their descendants who settled in the Puget Sound region. While the project has focused on documenting the lives of immigrants and their families in the Northwest it has also sought out individuals who lived in the Nordic countries during World War II. As a result, this new edition contains dramatic stories of daily life in occupied Norway and Denmark often from a child's perspective and includes accounts of participation in resistance activities against the occupiers. Postwar Finnish immigrants provide personal memories of the fierce stuggle to preserve Finnish sovereignty in the face of Soviet invasion and of the deliberate evacuation of 70,000 Finnish children to safety in neutral Sweden.

The book is divided into three sections: stories from immigrants coming to America before World War II; stories from immigrants coming to America after World War II and stories from the descendants of immigrants.

It is our hope this book will inspire young and old readers with first-hand accounts from one segment of the greatest migration in world history – the movement of more than forty-million from the old world to North America. These stories illuminate their struggles with language, the search for work, the desire for education and the need to create institutions that preserved their heritage and offered support in a new and strange environment.

Gordon Strand

COMING TO AMERICA: BEFORE WORLD WAR II

Immigration to the United States

1820-1860	5,062,414
1861-1880	5,127,015
1881-1900	14,061,192
1901-1920	14,531,197
1921-1939	4,564,884
TOTAL	43,346,702

- As transportation improved in the 1860s, mass emigration became common. Improvements in healthcare, the small pox vaccine and other factors produced a population explosion in the Nordic countries.

- In the mid 1800s the Danish population increased rapidly. Families were often large, so more and more children growing up in rural areas had little hope of owning a farm. Between 1820 and 1990 more than 375,000 Danes came to the United States.

- The number of Finnish immigrants remained small until the 1860s, when widespread economic depression led to massive emigration. Some 300,000 Finns settled permanently in the United States between 1864 and 1924.

- Between 1870 and 1914 between 16,000 and 20,000 Icelanders emigrated or 20-25% of the total population. Harsh weather and natural disasters in the latter half of the 19th century led to economic hardship. At the same time news was reaching Iceland of the mass movement of emigrants from Europe to North America.

- Between 1851 and 1930 about 1.2 million Swedes immigrated to the United States. About every fifth Swede around the year 1900 lived in the USA.

- Between 1815 and 1900 the population of Norway more than doubled. Norway was second only to Ireland in percentage of its population to immigrate. More than 85% of the 900,000 Norwegian immigrants to the US came between 1865 and 1930.

Herb and Ellen (Mestunis) Goodman

*"I retired from the waterfront in 1970.
I was 63. I could stay till I was 65, but
one morning I just got up and thought,
'Why should I go to work? I'll soon retire.'
So I did. And I've enjoyed every minute."*

H ERB: When I was about 15, I'd go down to Stimson's with a team of horses, to get slab cord wood which was pretty popular with people. The wood still had bark on it. I'd walk from Ballard to the stables at Golden Gardens and hook up my team of horses. I drove the team for the man who owned them, and they were pretty lively horses, too. They got them at Frye's Packing House.

One time we were coming down 59th onto 24th when those horses kicked over the tree and started off. And boy, did they go — I was on this wagon and with me was a kid or two. The kids liked to see those horses. I hung on to the reins the best I could, and I thought we were going to straddle a telephone pole. But I hung on and stopped them. They had different stables and barns for the horses around Ballard. The wagon I drove was pretty lengthy. I'd back that wood wagon into the driveway, and sometimes the women would come outside and raise Cain with me because the horses were eating up their roses. We got paid about 60 cents a load. We never stacked it much. We threw it outside, or in the drive, or in the window.

Well, then my mother remarried. I was about 21 or 22, I guess when I moved out. My step-dad was a longshoreman, and he was there in the '34 strike. He was Swedish, a real nice guy. He got me in on the waterfront in '34. Yeah, I was part of the strike. I wasn't even in the union at the time, but we'd go to the Hall and pick up extra work sometimes. It wasn't very agreeable jobs that we got. Sometimes it was loading animal skins.

Once I was in the Hall and we were told some guys were going to have a bunch of finks the following morning to a place where they made garbage cans. So we went down there, knowing they were going to have a strike. This was across Spokane Street, close to where the Hall is now. When we got there, we put locks on the doors. These finks came in and they didn't know we had them locked up. The door had glass that went all the way down. So I could see this fink sitting inside, holding a shotgun. I saw this guy's gun, and I bent down to pull it away from him, and I got the whole barrel in my leg. I was bleeding to beat hell. They took me right to the hospital on top of the hill on Spokane Street. I've got a lot of shotgun lead in my leg yet. I was in the hospital quite awhile. The union gave me, I think it was $500, quite a bit of money in those days. They took care of it in the union meetings. And I went into the union soon after that.

The work was all done by hand, we called it mucking. For instance, you'd have canned fish. That was all mucking. Then later they went into mechanization. Rather than take money, the union let mechanization go through and didn't fight it because they felt in lieu of wages, you're better off to have some money for medicines and medical purposes. That was in the '40s, I think.

Before the union came along we'd just go stand in front of the piers and someone would come out and call people to come in and work. It was a time when some guys working in there took a notion that they could steal things at midnight. One guy there was really a pig for packing stuff off the dock. So this night, he packed a whole big slab of bacon off the dock, and then went uptown to eat. He was going to get the package when he came back, but they were waiting for him and they grabbed him for stealing.

After the strike in '34, we went into the union hall. Had to be there at seven o'clock to shape up, then we'd peg in. Well, that's a pegboard system. If you were a guy that knew mechanization, they put you on the bull board. That's another machine that you drive, and you get extra money for knowing how. I was a bull driver. I drove one of the first bull driver bulls that came on that waterfront.

We had medical care. And we had a pension. And we used to get three weeks of paid vacation. You worked a number of months, then you didn't work for three weeks. I always saw to it that I got my required amount of time in, in order to get a chance to make a trip.

I retired from the waterfront in 1970. I was 63. I could stay till I was 65, but one morning I got up and thought, "Why should I go to work? I'll soon retire." So I did. And I've enjoyed every minute.

Herb and Ellen Goodman - 3

The wife and I made a trip to where my mother was born in Reykjavik, Iceland, quite a nice trip. We saw where my mother was born. She was born in the city, and she worked as a waitress.

ELLEN: Both my father and my mother are from Lithuania, and I speak Lithuanian fluently. They met in Lithuania, and then came here to America. I was born in Cumberland, Washington, close to Enumclaw. My dad was a coal miner. He married my mother, but they didn't last. He had a violent temper and Mama was scared of him. I was born March the 6th, 1912, and I was about four years old when my mom left my dad. I had three sisters and one brother. I was the baby of the family. My sisters were all quite a bit older than me.

Mama moved into South Seattle. She found a little house for $10 a month and she worked in the laundry for years. Supported us by working in the laundry room. After I got out of high school, I went to work in Bertha's Restaurant in Ballard for about ten years. And Bertha was real good to me. She let all the help live upstairs. No rent to pay and we got our free food from her. And then she paid us $10 a week salary. Lots of Ballard people came into the restaurant. Families came with their children, lunch people that worked around Ballard. And a lot of guys came alone. And they always liked Bertha's pies. Bertha was a good cook.

I met Herb at a dance downtown at the Sixth Avenue Dance Hall. We could get in there for 34 cents. And Herb'd say to me, "I could take you as far as your home, but that's all the money I got. I don't have gas money." I wanted to get married. My sister said, "Well you can get married at my house, and I'll pay for your wedding." And she gave the priest $10 for our marriage.

Herb was a strong union believer. He wanted everything honest and running. He's the guy that's 93 years old, and he's still honest. He never was thievy — he never wanted to steal from anybody. He never wanted to tell lies. He's a good guy. Too damn good.

Herb Goodman was born January 29, 1907 in Canada. His parents immigrated from Iceland. His father was a pharmacist, his mother a waitress. When he was six years old, he and his mother moved to Ballard. He attended Adams and Webster schools. He began working on the waterfront in 1934. Ellen (Mestunis) was born in Cumberland, Washington, March 6, 1912. Her parents were both immigrants from Lithuania. She had three older sisters and a brother. Her brother died when he was 11. In 1916 her mother left her father and came to Seattle with her children. Ellen and Herb have a son, Gerald (1942). Herb retired in 1970. He died in August, 2000.

4 - Herb and Ellen Goodman

Caroline Andersen Rolie Norman

**"I got two jobs as a cook, because
'All Norwegian girls were good cooks.'
But I never had cooked in my life.
So I was fired twice."**

I was born on an island in northern Norway. Like most of the people there, we lived off the sea. I was number two in the family — I was born in 1895. My brother Aslak was born in 1894, Josie, 1896. After that there was a little more time between each child, Dagny, 1898, Gundhild, 1900, Arngrim, 1903, Hansine, 1907 and Johannes in 1910. My father was fishing and he owned a two-story house and a big barn, and a place for our fuel for the winter. We had cows and sheep, a pig and horse and goats, and chickens. In the winter they had to stay in their house, because it was always snow up there — no light in the wintertime. And in the spring, they came out. And we sent the sheep and the cows out to the nearby hills to feed, so we could raise hay around the place for winter food for the animals. That's how we lived there, very comfortable. We raised the things we needed.

Anyway, in about 1908, some people decided to have a boat to bring the fish down to the southern part of Norway. My dad and a bunch of his cousins and friends went together, and they went good for the boat, in case of an accident — there was no insurance in those days. It went on until early 1910. Something happened then — the boat was completely lost. All the others had put all their homes in their sons' name, except my dad. So they came and took everything he had, the house and everything. Everything.

Papa came home one day, he packed his suitcase and said "I'm going to America." He had a niece over in Somers, Montana, and he went to Somers. It's a little town near Kalispell at the head of Flathead Lake. And he got a job right away. He had had asthma since he was 19, but he managed to work in a sawmill there, and made enough money. In 1911 he sent for his son, A.K. — Aslak Klaudius was his name. Then between the two of them, they sent money in 1913 for my sister Josie and I to come over.

Josie and I stopped in Bergen one night. Then we got on a boat over to England and then on a train across over to Liverpool. And that's where we entered the ship, an English steamer, to Quebec. We were four in a cabin. The two were from Sweden, but they were from the southern part of Sweden, and they were hard to understand.

Coming over on the train, they were loaded, so they put Josie and me in a smoking car. Our meals were paid for, but nobody told us where to go and get meals, and we didn't dare to move. There was a bunch of men in that car and they would give us fruit. Of course the fruit that we knew about, apples and bananas, we knew how to eat. And then they gave us each a peach and we had never seen a peach in our life. And, you know, you feel a peach? We couldn't bite into that. We got rid of it, but we didn't get any more fruit after that.

One place we stopped, I got off the train, and here was food. They had little buns and things on a plate inside the counter. And I wanted some of that, and somebody came and took me by my neck, and came "Come on, to the... ", he spoke English, of course, but I knew, I remember the "Come." If it hadn't been for Josie, they would have left me there. But she made such a racket about it that her sister wasn't on board. The girl behind the counter was a Swede. "Nu må du skynde dig" ["You have to hurry!"] Oh, my goodness, I can talk to someone. So I was going to take my time.

In Kalispell I got two jobs as a cook, because "All Norwegian girls were good cooks." But I never had cooked in my life. So I was fired twice. Then I got a job as a nursemaid, taking care of children. And I'd done that all my life, so there was nothing to it. They were very nice, those people. They sent me to school. The lady in the house [Mrs. Keith] had ten kids. And when any of them was sick, she had a room next to her bedroom where she put them during the night so she could tend to them. When I was sick, she put me there, too.

Gundhild and Dagny had come to Montana in 1915 and Arngrim next, and in 1918 Papa decided to move to Seattle. He and Gundhild left. I waited a few days so Arngrim would finish school. When we got here I looked at the green grass on the ground, I didn't believe it. It was in January, and in Kalispell, I had to hold something over my nose so I wouldn't freeze between the house and the train.

I came by train, but I knew how to find this place up on Fairview Avenue, and a Mrs. Vammer. It was nine o'clock in the evening, and I didn't know how to get in touch with A.K. and Papa, and my cousin who lived in Ballard. She said, "Well, my house is full." She rented out rooms to bachelors. She didn't feed them; they just had the rooms there. She said, "I can't let you go out this time of the night, so if you'll sleep

on the sofa and your brother sleep on the floor, you can stay overnight."
That was my first night in Seattle.

Papa took Arngrim and Gundhild and I got an apartment together.
And we went to "Stub Church," that's Immanuel Lutheran Church on
Pontius and Thomas with Pastor Hans Stub. That was our "home" in
Seattle. A.K. and Gundhild and I sang in the choir. And we sang there
three times on holidays. And then the last night, my sister had every one
of us in the choir in for chocolate and cookies.

I got a job to go gibbing herring in Alaska in 1919. It was really fun. I
felt like I just come to life. The herring station was at Warm Spring Bay
on Baranoff Island. Gibbing means that you take the guts and gills out of
the herring. As you work, you can feel what size they are, and you had
to put them in barrels for each size. And we salted them with a fine salt.
We had to know just how much salt to put on it. I'd never done it in my
life, but in five minutes I knew how to do it, and I was fast — I'd been
taught since I was small to use my hands, doing knitting. Sometimes we
worked day and night. They had to be done right away, or they wouldn't
be any good.

And this is my beginning in the United States. I loved it all.

Caroline Andersen was born April 27, 1895 in Bø i Vesterålen, Norway to Kaia (Olsen) and Kristoffer Andersen. She immigrated in 1913. She worked for a tailor sewing buttonholes in the flys in men's suits (before zippers). She married Chris Rolie in 1920. He was from Lurøy, Norway. Their children: Howard (1921) and Marilyn "Lynn" (1924). She worked at U.S. Plywood as a grader from 1941 to 1954, when she married Reidar Norman. She lived in Ballard from 1920. She was interviewed on November 30, 1990. She died June 1, 1999, age 104 years, 1 month, 4 days.

Lilly Helene Bjornstad

"And then I had one more job, just to learn to cook a little, because I was going to get married and I didn't know anything about cooking."

Well, I lived in a small place, Berger in Vestfold, Norway. And I always wanted to go to United States. My neighbors, the Bjornstads, were home in 1914. They came home to celebrate. It was a big year in Norway. I could go back to the United States with them when they were going back. But then the war started. And they had a hard time getting back to the United States. But I went with them on the *Hellige Olav.* It took us nine, probably ten days. I had a cabin — we were four people in there. They had the most wonderful food you ever wanted to eat. We landed in New York, at Ellis Island. We were put here and there, according to our nationalities. And a man came over to me and he talked Norwegian to me, and that's all I could talk at that time. And I didn't understand him. I was so confused. So many people, and so many nationalities.

I went to Eau Clair, Wisconsin with the two oldest Bjornstad boys and I lived there two years. A Bjornstad cousin was married to Dr. Milford. They had 11 children. So I worked there and took care of the children. And then I had one more job, just to learn to cook a little because I was going to get married, and I didn't know anything about cooking. I married Andrew, Andreas Bjornstad, November 11, 1916. He was a wonderful guy. He had a team of horses and worked in the woods. They hauled timber and things. And finally, after two years, we got married. It wasn't long before I was pregnant. Lucille, my first girl was born Oct, 16, 1917. Some of my husband's family lived out here in Seattle and they wanted us so to come out here. Lucille was seven months old when we left. It took nearly three days on the train. Oh, I loved Seattle. We came in June, and it wasn't too nice weather — you know how June is here, but I really loved Seattle.

Andreas started carpenter work, and it wasn't long before we had another little girl. Ruth was born in 1919. Ruth McCausland she is now.

It was almost impossible to get houses during the war time. We all lived in a great big house on 77th and Greenwood, while we were building our houses out on 101st. We had a very small house. We lived there about a year, and then we found a little house down by Fremont. Then my husband started to build our house on 86th, right off of 6th Avenue. And that's where I have lived until I came here to Norse Home. It was 639 West 86th, then it became Northwest 86th. I loved to garden. It wasn't big, but I had all kinds of different flowers, and carrots and peas and the corn we had in the fall.

Then my husband started in construction. He's been on a lot of the big, tall buildings down in Seattle. Most of the big buildings that they had at that time, he did work on a lot of them.

I was at home. I kept up everything at home, the garden and everything, and I did a lot of sewing dresses and quilting. And I worked for awhile. I worked at a company where we made dresses. I always sewed my clothes and the children's, even their coats, so I was always busy. I had a good Singer. At first I had a little sewing machine, then I had a treadle. For my material I went mostly downtown to Sears where they sold remnants.

My husband, he said, "You're the world's best cook, Lilly." He loved *lapskaus.* You know what *lapskaus* is? That's kind of stew made in small pieces, kind of diced like that, and fried brown, and then you do the same with the potatoes. Put them together and then cook it together. Oh, it was so good. And *får i kål* means lamb and cabbage. Those were two real steady Norwegian dishes. We were not very much on fish. My husband liked a lot of fish but my family would hardly eat fish.

We had some friends, two couples. They lived in Ballard and would come to visit. And we went out to Norway Hall a lot. We danced schottisches and polkas and a hambo. They had a guy that played the accordion. And we loved to dance. Sometimes, when it was a special program, then they would dress up — but you didn't see very many Norwegian costumes. They really had wonderful bazaars down there.

Oh, I have many happy memories.

Lilly Havre was born December 16, 1894 in Berger, Norway. She immigrated in 1914, married Andreas (Andrew) Bjornstad in 1916. Their children: Lucille (1917) and Ruth (1919). Andrew died 1973. Lilly died in 2003.

Thor B. Bjornstad

"You're busy when you work, then after you retire, you get busier yet, but you don't get paid for it."

My dad, Hans Olaus Hansen Bjornstad was born in 1855. Some of his brothers took the name of Hansen, but he took the name of Bjornstad after the farm. It was southeastern Norway in Idd, a community near Fredrikstad. They had 10 kids, and I was next to the youngest.

My mother's name was Eline Marie Grosvold Bjornstad. The Grosvold came from near Kongsberg. They never called her by name, they called her Mor Bjornstad, Mother Bjornstad. Anybody had any problem, they came to Mor Bjornstad. My parents met and married in Holmestrand, where the oldest two or three kids were born. They moved to Berger in Vestfold, where the rest of us were born.

In the wintertime we'd go skiing. Mostly ski jumping, because that was the Norwegian sport in the wintertime. In the summertime, you went fishing, not for commerce, but for family fish.

When I came to the United States I was 11, almost 12. My brothers and sisters egged my parents on, you might say. My dad had such a good job back home. He was well established and well liked. He came here, he couldn't speak a word of English, so he had to take menial labor jobs. That was 1919 and he must have been 60 or so.

We came directly to Seattle. Four brothers and the parents. We lived on 101st between Greenwood and Third Avenue, just south of Holman Road. It was farmland, divided into half-acre lots. The streetcar went up to 85th, the Seattle city limits at that time. Mother would walk there, and take the streetcar to the Public Market to buy groceries. Oftentimes the butcher'd give her meat for the dog. That dog never tasted that meat until we'd had at least one meal out of it. There was a little paved road, just 12 feet wide — Greenwood. It was paved because it went out to the Seattle Golf and Country Club. The Highlands. But that was the only road.

We had electricity, but not right away. We had lived in Norway with electricity for several years, because of the mill, and the electric power that it got from the dams. Here, we were back to oil lamps.

My oldest sister had a boy in the 2nd grade at Oak Lake School. They agreed to take me and let my nephew kind of lead me around, because I didn't know English. I was a 12-year-old in the second grade. It took me three and a half years to go from second grade through eighth grade. I'm not saying this to bolster myself, but this is actual fact. The state had written examinations for the kids. I took that and I had a hundred in arithmetic; a hundred in grammar, and all the rest of them were up in the nineties. I graduated as Valedictorian.

We walked down to Piper's Creek. On the north side was a little cleared area. On the south side there had been an old brick kiln in there. You could see piles of brick lying around so we called it the brickyard. It was a nice area to walk down, you know. Piper apparently worked for the city, so he must have got a little pull to get a road down there — a winding road, so it was a nice walk.

My dad died in 1927, from a ruptured appendix. I graduated from Ballard High School the same year and started at the University of Washington in Engineering. I got through the last year in 1931.

I got a job as a junior engineer with the Columbia Basin Commission, working in Denver under the Bureau of Reclamation in 1933. That was the first engineering job I had after graduating in '31. I think I was paid $145 a month. I was there four years.

I met my first wife, Dorothy Hvatum, at the Seattle Ski Club lodge. Her dad was prominent in the Norwegian colony. He sometimes took guests up there. One of those times, his daughter came along with him and I was a ski jumper, and so she met me up there. My mother said, "Don't get your hopes up. They're higher class than we are." But somehow it worked out, and in the summertime, we'd go swimming, camping and fishing. And when I got the job in Denver, I persuaded her to become engaged to me. I started in Denver in August. She came down and we got married on the 2nd of December, 1933. We had our first child in Denver in 1935, but both my wife and I wanted to get back to Seattle, so I resigned and took the job in Olympia in 1937.

I worked on the Tacoma Narrows Bridge — the one that fell down [Galloping Gertie]. I overheard a conversation between Eldridge, the State of Washington Bridge Engineer, and one of the consulting engineers. Eldridge said he was worried about that horizontal load. Well, the guy said, "Don't worry, just design for the stresses that come on there when it blows that hard, or deflects so much." But nobody at that time had used harmonic motion. So that's what developed. It was so light and it started swaying.

Thor Bjornstad - 11

I bought our house at 3515 Northwest 60th in 1942. It was built in 1940. I paid $7,000 for it and lived there for 49 years.

I was involved in the Norse Home, Norwegian Male Chorus, Knute Rockne, a Sons of Norway organization, and something like the Bergen and Seattle Sister Cities. The Norse Home organization started, the earliest that I can come up with is 1929. The Pacific coast lodges of the Sons of Norway met every year. They all agreed to have a retirement home for Norwegians, but couldn't agree to where it should be, so it was dropped. In 1931, it came up again. The meeting was in Seattle, and they got it located in the Puget Sound area. Then they started raising money. Every year they had bazaars and sales. They made a little money, but it didn't amount to much. Abraham Kvalheim, the first president of the organization, served two three-year terms. Next was Dr. Trygve Buschman. Paul Berg was the third for several years. I was the fourth president. My first term was in 1955, the year the building was started. I was Chairman of the Building Committee. They had found this site and bought it for $8,000 in 1938. There used to be a Ferris wheel and a merry-go-round just to the north, and a miniature golf course where the Norse Home is now. In 1955. And they hired an architect, Edward Mahlum, a Norwegian-American. We wanted to get started by the end of the year. We let the contract for roughly a million and a quarter. They money they raised was not enough. They took out a loan with the government. Norse Home was the first home of this kind to get this type of loan.

There was no actual rule or regulation about it, but to start with, it was mostly Norwegians [who lived here]. Later on, we made a count, and there was about 52 percent Norwegian, or of Norwegian ancestry. The president was under the 18-member Board of Trustees. They were elected for a term of three years. They could not serve more than a total of nine years. Except Paul Berg and I stayed on you might say forever. I served from 1955-1985, 30 years. Then the Board granted Paul Berg and me honorary president for life. We could join them anytime we wanted to.

The main problem was getting money to build it. That was the big project. People nowadays ask, "Why didn't you put air conditioning in?" No money. Why didn't you do this or that? No money. We had a tough time. But we made this loan. And that helped us out. And we paid that loan off. Now they're doing remodeling downstairs, but we made it clear, don't take out another mortgage.

Organizations that belong appoint representatives at their annual meetings, and those representatives elect the officers: Seattle Male Chorus, the Sons of Norway, [other Norwegian groups.]

The Sons of Norway lodges held their meetings in Norwegian. So the young people wanted to have them in English, so they organized this Knute Rockne. They were the first Norwegian lodge to have English-speaking meetings. I think it was founded in 1934.

My wife, June, was a charter member. Dorothy died in 1960. And I married June in 1962. I met her at meetings down at Norway Center. She said she would not marry me until all my three daughters would agree. They did, so we were married on December 22nd, 1962. We have no children by the second marriage. But she had two boys. One of them lives in Seattle now and we see him quite often. The other one is someplace up in Alaska.

I keep working for the Austin Company. The first 20 years, I worked as a structural designer. Then I became Assistant District Engineer, and then the last 20 years, I was District Engineer in the Northwest District. I had offices in — our scope was in Washington, Oregon, Montana, Idaho, and Alaska I retired January 1st, 1971.

Well, like I said, you're busy when you work, then after you retire, you get busier yet, but you don't get paid for it. So I've been active in different things.

I have a medal from the King of Norway [St. Olav Medal]. I had nothing to do with it. Somebody nominated me. And it went through the consul and right to Norway. And, next thing I knew, why they granted it. There are not very many that get it, so I felt very lucky. They get it for doing extra work for the benefit of Norway. So, I worked on Norse Home so long that that's helped me a lot.

Thor Bjornstad was born December 5, 1907 in Berger, Norway. He married Dorothy Hvatum in 1933. They had three daughters: Eline (1935), Catherine (1939-1987) and Barbara (1943). Dorothy died in 1960. Thor married June Haugen in 1962.

Holger Leander Berg

"You know, Ballard was the greatest place in the world to grow up. There were a million things to do and nobody was shooting one another."

Canada was a barren place as far as people were concerned, and they were anxious to get anybody who could work over there. Many who wanted to immigrate to the United States, if they weren't allowed because of quotas, would come to Canada, and after five years they could immigrate from there. It was probably in 1920 my family left Canada and came to Seattle. Aunt Sigrid and Arthur Carlson came first and met us and brought us to their house on Capitol Hill. Later my folks and the Carlsons found a house on Phinney Ridge between 60th and 65th. It was a huge house, and all the Carlsons lived upstairs and the Bergs lived downstairs. And newcomers that came into Seattle, came here, to find out which was a good logging company to work for, or who was hiring fishermen, and so on. We stayed at that house, and I went to John B. Allen School. Then we moved to Ballard, to just off 11th and 62nd. I was in about the third grade. It was quite a hike to West Woodland School, but it didn't seem to hurt us any.

When I was in the seventh grade, I met James Selly. We were talking at lunch time, and he said, "Holger, did you ever go trout fishing?" And I said, "No. I don't know even how to go about it." "Well," he said, "I have some common pins I bent into hooks. You want to go fishing?" I said "When?" He said, "Now." I thought, gosh, tomorrow morning we'll really catch it when we come back to school. "Ah," he says, "come on."

So we legged it out to Piper's Creek Canyon, running all the way, and we dug up some worms. I never had so much fun catching fish in all my life. I had a little paper bag full of fish, probably seven, eight inches long. So we finally said, "Hey, it's about time to go home; school has got to be out."

I came home with these fish, and my mother wanted to know where I got them. No use lying about it. I said, "This kid talked me into running away from school today to catch fish." I guess my dad didn't think too much of that, but he looked them over and said, "Well, there must be a lot of fish up there." I said, "There sure is."

Piper's Creek was a long way from 60th. We went straight out 8th Avenue Northwest, and at 85th, came to this cow pasture. There was no Holman Road there, and we just made a beeline. James knew exactly where to go, down into the canyon, and we fished way, way down till we thought we had enough.

Years ago the *P.I.* paper had free swimming classes. My mother decided my brother and I should learn to swim. I remember some bitter cold days in that water with the wind blowing. But after you got dunked a few times, it really wasn't that bad, but it was cold. We'd stay and have our dinner there. My father met us after work and took us home. I talk to my contemporaries, and I say, "You know, Ballard was the greatest place in the world to grow up. There were a million things to do and nobody was shooting one another."

My brother Håkan and I were always fascinated by logging locomotives. They just exuded power to us kids. On 15th Avenue Northwest, there was a single streetcar track that went from the Ballard Bridge to 85th. I wondered why they never ran streetcars on that track. It had the wire up in the air. Then a fellow told us, "They bring the freight train from Everett down this track every night about one a.m." I thought, a freight train coming down 15th? This, I gotta see. My brother and I talked to our folks and we walked the two blocks from our house to 15th and sat there and waited. Pretty soon here comes this electric train, with boxcars and log cars and cattle cars, everything you can imagine.

I could not figure out how they got to 15th Avenue. Later it was explained to me: they came on the interurban tracks from Everett. Then they had special turns behind buildings because you cannot take a freight train around a 90-degree curve. When the train got to the Ballard Bridge, a locomotive was waiting. The electric locomotive would unhook and get out of the way, and the steam train would take over. I don't know where it went from there, but to us — that was most fascinating.

At that time my father was longshoring. He would come home from work and say, "Well, boys, that silk train is going to leave about four o'clock tomorrow afternoon, and if you want to go see it — ." So, boy, we would jump on our bikes and go all the way over to Shilshole, park our bikes and sit there and wait. These trains, the Mikado, would really roll through there. They had baggage cars plus a combination car on the end had some U.S. marshals, 'cause the train was hauling raw silk skeins and they didn't want anybody hijacking it. This train beat the records going to the silk mills in Patterson, New Jersey. It took precedence over any train — mail, passenger, freight; they had to get out of the way. Several railroad companies had these silk trains. The silk came from Japan. The Nippon Yushon Keisha (NYK) Line had ships going into California, Oregon and Washington, and the silk needed to get to the mill fast.

After my Uncle Arthur passed away, my aunt married another Norwegian fisherman, who had his own boat. One time he saw a skiff floating, so he brought it home and gave it and a set of oars to my brother and me. Oh, we were top dogs, we had our own rowboat. So then, we were watching people out on the log booms peeling bark off the logs. You know, the bark used to be five, four, six inches thick? And you had to have a rope tied to your crowbar, because if you let go of it, you lost it. We would bring bark to the foot of 22nd Avenue and stack it up, and I'd run home and tell Dad, "We got a load of bark for us." We'd save it to burn in the heating stove,

There were all these mills. Seattle Cedar was the biggest, and there was Bolcom. I think Bolcom had these old chain-drive trucks, with a greyhound on the side of the cab, like the Greyhound Bus. And underneath it said, "speed gets 'em." That was their motto for delivering wood. That was pretty neat.

The folks bought what were called edgings, the trimmings off the logs. They were three to six inches thick, and 20 to 30 feet long. We'd get a load of those in summer, and my brother and I would stare at it and say, oh, boy, because we had a bucksaw and a crosscut saw. My dad wanted us to split the wood and fill the woodshed right up to the ceiling. I was glad to see when the last piece was cut. Oh, mercy! That took a lot of time, yes.

A man who had a grocery store at 61st and 8th Avenue Northwest came to our house and asked me to work for him. And I said sure. He told me after I got to the store he'd pay me $18 a week for six days a week.

My dad was still out of work so that's where my money went. I got to drive a brand new Ford V-8 panel delivery truck, pretty jazzy for a young guy. I picked up supplies from the wholesalers. I arranged the groceries in the truck in the order I would deliver them. I had my receipt book and cash to make change. Some people bought on a tab they paid weekly or monthly and then some paid cash. So I had to be writing receipts, too. That was a good job. I was there for some months, probably through the winter. Then here comes Dave Beck. You drive a truck; you have to belong to the Teamster's Union. It cost $50 to join the union and $12 a month in dues. No way could Mr. Nelson pay me that kind of money. And he had two ladies working there. At the end of the week, if the bananas didn't look too good, Mr. Nelson would say, "Why don't you and the ladies divide the bananas? They're getting a little over-ripe." So we each got a big bag of bananas. We got our groceries at cost, so this helped a lot. But when Dave Beck came, that was the end of that.

Holger Leander Berg was born December 29, 1916 in Espanola, a Finnish community in Ontario, Canada. His father, Conrad Leander Berg left Sideby, Finland about 1907 to escape conscription by the Russian Army. Holger's mother, Helmi Xenia Drugg, from Tarsund, a farming area in Finland, came on the *Lusitania,* around 1914 to Helmi's sister Sigrid in Espanola. Sigrid and Arthur Carlson ran a boarding house in Ontario. Holger's parents met there. Holger had a brother Håkan and a sister Elizabeth or Bette [Mallaghan]. Holger married Elizabeth (Bach) in 1944. Holger died January 27, 2001.

Martha A. Zachman

"We were down in the steerage when we first got on the ship. I went and squawked, 'We don't want to sleep in that part of the ship. It's dirty. Look at all those filthy people.'"

I was born Martha Alice Sunabacka-Forsman in Finland. Then I was Lillquist, then Zachman. That's the last, I haven't made another name. My mother died in 1907. I was two. My father moved to America in 1909. We children were left with aunts and uncles. My father sent for the three of us in December 1920. Walde our stepbrother was 18, I was 15, and Hildur was 13.

We were down in the steerage when we first got on the ship. I went and squawked. "We don't want to sleep in that part of the ship. It's dirty. Look at all those filthy people. I'm not going to sit around in front of these people." A minister and his wife helped us. They'd been home visiting, and they helped us, so we didn't have to stay there — we were in there one night, and that was enough for me. I told that lady, "I'll stay up in the lounge, sit up and sleep, I'm not going to sleep down there." The food wasn't like the farm food, nice fresh milk and everything. My sister would look at it, and say, "Aaah, do we have to eat that" — in Swedish. So I told her, you can't talk that broad Swedish. Everybody started to laugh like heck.

We had to stay in New York, because somebody had contracted scarlet fever. The ship had to be three weeks quarantined. And we didn't like that. Right through Christmas. It was fun, though. The orchestra was quarantined too. And they gave us little gifts. And then my dad start worrying. So they sent a telegram so he knew what was going on.

Well, I saw a lot of countryside. I saw snow. I said to Hildur, "Oh, they got snow in America." And then what we thought was so funny, seeing cows grazing amongst the snow, and grass tufts sticking up here and there, and the cows out. I didn't think that was very nice. I'd put them in the barn, feed them in there. That's what we did. All I thought of was to go back home.

We landed in Tacoma, where dad and step-mother lived. Dad came and got us from the station. Dad had been over there for the weeks before, and waited, and waited, and we didn't show up. Soon as my dad come walking, he looked like a big shot. Nice new over-coat, and a velvet collar in the back of his coat. And that hat like they wore at the time, the hard tops. I looked at him and I said to him, "Gee, is that our dad?" He had been in America more than ten years.

My father was a tailor, right at home. He sat on that big table he had down in the shop, doing hand work on the clothes that he was sewing for somebody. So, I said, "Gee, is that the way you do it? Tailoring? Sit on a big table and cross your knees?" He said, "Yeah, when I do hand work. I'm going to teach you to do hand work for me." So, I said, "Well, I already know that." I did, too. They wouldn't let us kids sit around idle. They always had fancy work to do for us. I even weaved. I made lots of rugs.

We stayed in Tacoma all winter. I learned English from the school there. The only thing I wasn't too smart in was the arithmetic. It was different from what I was used to. And I said, "I don't care if I learn a thing. I knew my stuff from Finland. I might go back there." Then she had me do it on the blackboard to show the kids how we did it in Finland. One kid says, "Teacher, can we do it like that here?"

That summer, I went to visit my brother, Ed Forsman, and his wife Helen in Seattle. Ed and his family came in 1910. I think there was Eddie and Vivian, and Lillian was on the way. They lived in a cute little house on 70th and 32nd. They had me sleeping on the davenport that opens up, and one of the kids slept with me. Vivian slept in the bedroom with them in her baby crib. The house was a little cramped after they started getting the kids.

I went to citizenship school, to night school up on Broadway. I went to Ballard, too, later on. It was in a basement of a church here on Loyal Heights, close to their house. I was studying English. And Ed said, "You've gone to more schools that anybody else we know."

I took my papers in 1940. The judge said, "Would you take up arms against Finland if they got involved in the war?" I nodded yes, just, yes. He just said I'm good, and I got my papers. No trouble. It was a hard time trying to get papers then, when I took them.

I was married to Gus Lillquist. I'll tell you how I met him. I was staying with Helen and Ed Forsman. And Koll and Wicks had a grocery store on 28th and 70th, right down below where they lived. [See Long p. 355] And the Johnsons lived next door there. And I went by there, and he said, "What are you going to do, Martha?" I said, "Helen is sending me to the store for some groceries."

So, I went in the store and Gus was clerking in there. He was off work, so he was helping Koll. He had just come down from Alaska. He'd been cooking in that logging camp. And, here comes Mrs. Johnson in. It was Saturday, and she says to Gus, "Gus, Martha wants you to take her to a show tonight."

I never said such a thing. So, I got the groceries for Helen and ran out. I told her and she said, "You'd better be ready. You'd better get your better clothes, and a sweater or a jacket."

Lo, and behold, at seven o'clock Ed was home then already, and Gus comes up and says to Ed, "Do you mind if I take your sister, Martha, to a show tonight?" I ran into the closet. I didn't want to go. He said, "Yes, she can go to a show. You can take her." "I don't want to go," I hollered.

We were married in '23. We stayed in Mount Vernon with his cousin for probably, six, seven months. Then after we lived in Ballard. We rented a little house close to 8th and 70th. We lived next door to Michaelson's in a little three-room house. Then the Bergs on the side. They were Norwegian. I liked the people there. I knew the Bardahls already from when we went to school. She was taking that citizenship, and I've known her ever since. And when we moved to 11th and 77th, they were on the corner. She had gotten married, and Lillian was just a little girl. She had Lillian, and I had Gus then, already. He was just two, I think. He used to run over there and want to play with Lillian. Lillian was three, I think or four.

We went all over. Sometimes we went to the Zoo or Green Lake. Bardahl used to drive. We had a lot of fun together. We used to walk down to Golden Gardens, her and I, take the kids and take a basket with food. And stay down there all day. Take a swim. We used to build sand castles. That beach used to be full because that was the only thing we could do at that time.

Martha Sunabacka-Forsman was born June 16, 1905 in Terjärv, Finland. Her mother died of TB in 1907 leaving five children: Edward (1893), Alfons (1897), Maurits (1898-1916), Martha (1905) and Hildur (1907). Her father immigrated to America (1909), sent for Edward and Alfons in 1910, and Martha and Hildur and stepbrother Walde in 1920. Martha came to Ballard in 1922. She married Gus Lillquist in 1923, and had one child, Lloyd. They divorced and she married Fred Zachman in 1940. Fred has a son, Jon Zachman. Martha died in 2004.

Greta Jensen Petersen

It is not often that one can profile three generations of women from their direct comments in individual oral history interviews. But interviews by Nordic Heritage Museum volunteers with Greta Petersen, Greta Petersen Larsen, and Lori Larsen have provided that opportunity. All three women of Danish ancestry shared an interest in acting, though only one -- Lori Larsen -- pursued that profession. Each played the lead in a play "A Sunday in Amager," at age 36. And all three proudly acknowledged their Danish heritage and worked to maintain ethnic customs from aebleskiver to mandelgave, the rice pudding with an almond prize, and occasionally a Christmas tree lit with real candles, though it could be scary. As actor Lori Larsen sometimes told friends: 'Danish is my religion.' Herewith their individual recollections and stories.- Gordon Strand

I was married in 1924, so that would be 68 years ago. I was born in Denmark, a small town by name of Give in March 8,1900. We had railroad, we have two churches, and of course two bakeries, a grocery store, it was supposed to be co-op. I went to school there and I got confirmed. After I got confirmed, of course, we get to working when we are in Scandinavia. We were eight children, I was number five. As soon as we were confirmed or as soon as we were old enough, then we had to get out and work and earn our own keep, make our own bread. So, so did I. I worked first as kind of a nursemaid for a little boy, then I worked for a man, and then I got to work for a doctor, Dr. Sweet. I kept on keeping in touch with him until he died. I'm still writing to get with his daughter, for all these years.

Well, the last job I had in Denmark was at a big sanitarium. I was in the linen department. I was there nearly four years, then I thought, no. It was such a good job and I hated to leave. But if I stay here, I thought, I'll be an old maid, and I didn't want to be an old maid. So, I said, I better try to get another job or go someplace else.

I went home to my mother in Give, and stayed. I hadn't been home for four years and I'm going home to stay a little while, until I get a job. While I was there, a young man who left for America when he was eighteen was home with his family. He knew my parents and he visited us. He was going back to Seattle, and he says to me, "Greta, don't you want to go to Seattle with us?"

I was twenty-two. He was in his thirties. He had his wife and two kids. His name was Jens Lauritsen He had his younger sister who was going to go with him. "That would be nice for Martha, if you would go along." So I said, "Gee, I'd sure like to." Then one day he sends a letter, "Greta, do you want to go or not to America? You come into Copenhagen and get you a sailing order." And I did and in ten days I was on my way to America.

We took the *Harry Olaf*, Scandinavian-American Line, we sailed over the Atlantic. Of course I had a terrific time, dancing every night. I was never seasick. All the others in the party were seasick, but that seven-year old boy, he was not. He followed me all the time, I could never get rid of that boy. There was one that said, "What did you want to go to Seattle for — out in that out-country? Why don't you stop in Chicago, we'll see you get a good job in no time."

"Oh no," I said. "I'm going to go with the man that brought me because he's going to take care of me. He promised my parents he's going to take care of me and I'm going with him."

Oh, I tell you, that was a lot of fun, I sure had the time of my life. We were under way for ten or eleven days, something like that. At that time is what it took to sail over. So we had to sleep again some hours, and he knew a man in Hoboken. That's where the ship laid in. He knew a fellow that had a restaurant and with it a hotel, kind of like. That's where we were going to stop overnight. We did, and then there were some guys that dropped by. He said, "You've got to go out and see the town tonight. We'll take you." There were several other girls from Denmark, you see, four or five girls. So they took us out to see New York that night we were there.

So then we got up to the Waldorf Astoria Hotel. He said, "Now when we go in this way, and we come out over there so you see the lobby, but now don't act like you haven't seen anything before. And we did, and we had fun. We came back to the ship at twelve. We were all sleeping in one room, there were three or four bunk beds, As soon as we put on the lights, we saw bugs running over the pillow. Well, we undressed anyway. We said, "Well leave the lights on because that keeps them away, the light." But then there's one girl, Sonja. She didn't want to take off her clothes, no, no nothing, she was not going to take off her clothes. She was the only one who took something with her. We got on the train, and here she got the bugs with her. We laughed.

Then we had to stop over in Chicago. We went out on the street and looked around and come in again, and we waited there. Then we were on our way to Seattle with the train. That was four days I think. When we came to Montana, we thought, my goodness, is that America? We saw all this barren land and sand. Then finally we came to Idaho, and Washington and we saw some woods. That was in 1922.

So when we came to Seattle, somebody came down to the train for us, and got us up to the Danish building, Washington Hall. That was where we were going to stay at night after work. That was the center for immigrants coming in. That was a boarding house and I worked there because I couldn't talk English, you see. So I worked there for eight or nine months, I think it was, then Jens Lauritsen, the fellow I came over with, he said, "I think you better get out, so you can learn to talk English." Everybody was talking Danish down there, so I didn't learn anything there.

I got out to Laurelhurst, to a family by the name Richmond. They were nice to me but of course there was another girl, but I was the cook. I could cook and I did quite well when one time we're having a ham, she showed me to soak it but I thought she said scorch. So sometimes there could happen some little misunderstandings. I was just there one summer, then I wanted to get out so I could go to night school up on Broadway.

I wanted to learn to talk English, and I wanted to learn to write it and read it, and all that stuff. So I came in and I got to work for the Norwegian Consul Einar Beyer. He was the consul. This was in 1923. So, Einar Beyer he was in Alaska all the time. He had his business in Alaska, fishing, canning or whatever it was. So he had a big hairy dog, that's what I had to take care of. But he did come home once in a while, and then I had to make the Norwegian dishes, and stuff. He was a nice man, very nice man. I could just call up to the grocery store and they delivered everything. That's what they did in those days. So I took care of this here big hairy dog, but then I was there for – I don't know how long I was there.

Anyway, then I got engaged. When I saw him the first night I came to Seattle, we came into the kitchen, but of course we looked terrible. We'd been sitting in that train for all these days and we were dirty, our hair was just like wire because we'd opened the window and the smoke from the train came right in on us. Oh, we looked terrible. God help us with those who just came from Denmark. We were three, we had to lay in one bed, a double bed. Martha was tall, she had to have a chair out. We laughed. Mrs. Fredrickson had to come up, "You have to be quiet because those men here have to go to work the next day, and you can't make noise." We had such fun and a good time.

I got out to Richmonds; to learn English, and I was there for that summer. But I came into Einar Beyer in November then, and was soon going to night school, but then Beyer come home and he had to have company for dinner, and that had to be home cooking, and the school started at two o'clock so I couldn't go to school anyway. But anyway, I said to him, "I got married".

His name was John Petersen. He worked for the bakery, He was from Denmark. He had to get a job right away, so that's what he did when he got married. But then he wanted to do something else, so him and Bert Nielson decided we're going to have a creamery store in Ballard. We had butter, eggs, cheese, and we sold lots of cottage cheese. [It was on] Market Street, in this building that was just finished. We started there November first, 1925.

There were two of them, then he felt he wanted to split. Bert Nielson kept this here, and we started on Greenwood Avenue with this store here, in 1931. We had that [store] a little over fifteen years.

And this here Norwegian place they had downtown. Well, anyway, every Saturday when there was a lady by name of "Mrs. Shea" and she fixed up everything to make smorgasbord, you know, sandwiches for all these here Norwegians with their dances every Saturday, so he took her down there with all the stuff.

Editor's Note: Harmony Hall was owned by Nordlandslaget — my mother, Caroline Rolie and Mrs. Shea had the intermission concession, and I would sometimes go there, rather than stay home alone. I was in my early teens. Lynn Moen]

Then of course, under the war, we had the food stamps and this and that. When that was over with, then John said, "I think we can sell the store and we're going to take a trip to Denmark." So in 1946, we drove over across America, the two of us,

I was in many plays, played in San Francisco. We played once in Tacoma. But we played up in Vancouver and we couldn't both go. We had our store, one had to be willing to take care of the store, and so my husband went there when we played up there and I was not in it. But we sure did - acting and singing, *ja*. I was singing to all the Silver Weddings, and all the Golden Weddings and all the parties they had for years.

I had my own party at the Nordic Heritage Museum [for my 90th birthday], I paid for every bit of it myself. Nobody had a party for me. Oh, my kids helped me. My son came — he was the postmaster and he boosts that kind of stuff. There was 149 eating, and then there was some who were serving and stuff. I think altogether 155, that's all we could have. Marianne she said, "That's all we can have, a roomful.

My daughter didn't sing much, but she took drama in University and she was playing down in Santa Barbara. Then she gets married and then you know . . . but my granddaughter [Lori Larsen], she's a professional. She's a professional actress, the one that was in Norway playing.

Well, in 1936 when I was in a play, [set] on an island next to Copenhagen where is now the airport, I played the main part and my daughter played it in 1961, twenty-five years later, and my granddaughter in 1986, twenty-five years later. Now I have a great-granddaughter who was also in the play here in '86 when she was just small, and she's going to play it in 2011. I think that was really one of the highlights of my career, that could go from one to the other, twenty-five years between.

[I lived for 52 years in our house —] I still have the house, 7101 Greenwood Avenue. My granddaughter is living there right now. I like it here [at Norse Home] but I'm worried a little about my house, but I go over often. Of course my flower beds and things isn't like the way I used to have things like that. You can't expect it.

I don't regret any of it, and I have been so fortunate, I've never been sick. I've had my knee fixed all right, but I wasn't sick, just had a little repair, had the whole business put in. They can do wonderful things now.

[Two of my sisters also live here.] I'm the oldest one. My sister is 89, she just had a birthday, and my other sister is 84. She has her husband there. She has a compartment like we have.

Greta Jensen Petersen was born in 1900 in Give, Jylland, Denmark. She immigrated to the United States at the age of twenty-two and married her husband, John Petersen, two years later. They had two children, Greta Larsen and Erik Petersen. Greta performed in musicals and plays presented by the Danish Dramatic Club, "Harmonien" and ran a popular Scandinavian Delicatessen on Greenwood Avenue in Seattle. Greta was a past president of the Danish Sisterhood, Lodge 40, a member and contributor to the Nordic Heritage Museum and the Northwest Danish Foundation. She was also an enthusiastic member of the Seattle Happy Danish Singers. Greta died in 1996.

Greta Petersen Larsen

"My mother and I walked on the stage [at Washington Hall] and I gave a little history of the play (En Søndag paa Amager- A Sunday at Amager) and how my mother had done it before, and I had done it 25 years after that, and now Lori was going to be doing it and so forth. And even my granddaughter was on the stage with us and we said, "And then Lori's niece is going to be doing it next." The audience loved it."

My father was John Hugo Petersen, my mother was Greta, Magrette. When they got their citizenship papers, very often new immigrants simplified their names — so she became Greta instead of Magrette. Her name was Jensen originally, she became Petersen when she married my father. My parents started out and it was quite a struggle because there was very little work. It was sort of during the Depression. But my father apprenticed as a *mejeriet* from Denmark, which means a mechanic or a person who worked in a dairy. He had a good job so they made it.

During the Depression era, my father tried all kinds of things, he had a restaurant, distributed gum machines all over the city. Eventually, my father settled into the dairy business. He became a cheese maker He opened a store in Ballard, in the late '20s. The major part of the store was a big churn, a churn that made butter. People came from all over to get this freshly churned butter, and especially the buttermilk.

My mother and he were great collaborators and they established a business on Greenwood Avenue where my mother did a lot of Scandinavian delicacies for the business. It became the 72nd Street Dairy and Delicatessen. My mother made *rullepolse*, and *leverposteja* and *sulte* and once a week she made codfish cakes. People came from all over the city to partake or buy my mother's goodies.

They were very successful in this rather specialized business but it was very hard work. My mother worked very hard, they worked seven days a week . After about ten or twelve years my mother and father decided, and they had done very well, they sold the business.

They went off to Denmark for three months and enjoyed life ,for the first time in their life.

In the meantime my brother and I grew up. We went to Lincoln High School, Grandview College in Des Moines, Iowa which was a Danish immigrant church college and then we both went to the University of Washington. My brother graduated. I was short a year because I decided to get married instead. I married a man who was the son of a Danish immigrant family as well. My father and mother were very pleased. Except my father said when I said I would like to marry this man, he said, "Yes, but he doesn't have a job." My husband's name was Otto Nyholm Larsen. We married on September 5th 1947 and we were married for 60 years before his death.

Prior to our marriage we had been at the university together. I was in the theater, in the drama department. I embarked on my new career as a nest builder, wife ,chief cook and and bottle washer, and all of those things. I dropped all of my ambitions . . . well, I changed in midstream and became a wife, a mother, a homemaker. In those days it was sort of what was quite common.

I was very fortunate, my husband was very successful in the academic. He had a Fulbright to Denmark for a year, and we took our family. We traveled all over the world. We had our Danish background in common, so we spoke Danish to our children. We sent our children to Denmark. We went to Denmark frequently. We had an extension of our Danish heritage that was reinforced and enjoyed by all of us. I think that was quite a plus.

My mother was known as the songbird of the Danish community. When she came to this country in 1922 she came directly from to Seattle from Denmark. My father, when he immigrated a couple years before that, came to the United States in 1920. My father was really the great actor in our family. He was very well known in his community. He was not a national figure, but he was a local actor in northern Svinninge, V. Holbaek. He did many of the major roles in the Danish Dramatic Society. He was just about in every play they ever did. But my mother, her major reputation, I think was for her singing.

When she came to this country my father was living at Washington Hall which was this sort of gathering place for the immigrants during the '30s and the '40s especially, '50s and even up into the '60s. In addition to the lodging, you know the halls where they could rent space for parties and conventions or whatever, they had a boarding house.

And they had enough room for maybe 15 or 20 residents. Well, that is where my mother came, and she worked in the Washington Hall when she first came. My father was living there . I think half of the marriages that ever took place or did take place in those days started at Washington Hall. Built by the Danish Brotherhood it was the place for the Danes to meet and for their celebrations and for their lodges.

We spent a lot of time there-my brother and I and children of my age—because our parents were there. In fact, I had my wedding reception at Washington Hall. And the Christmas parties and weddings. Washington Hall played a big role in our lives. It was a wonderful place. We loved it.

My mother participated in an epic play at Washington Hall. It was *Sunday on Amager*. Amager is an island. It's just a little plot of land. It has a bridge coming in, so it's hardly thought of as an island, but it is an island. And very early in the 1800s, Luise Heiberg wrote A play. She was a prominent actress. She wrote this play called *Søndag paa Amager*." And it was *Sunday on Amager*. And so the Danes, the Harmonien, produced that play. I don't know if it was their first play. 1911 was the first production. And 25 years later, my mother played the major part in the play.

Then when they had their 50th anniversary, I had just come back from Denmark with my family. So my Danish was pretty good, and so the head of the Danish the Harmonien, said, " I think , why don't we do *Søndag paa Amager* for our 50th anniversary? And Greta, you have to play Lisbeth. I said, " I do? What do you mean? Well it's a musical.

I could sing, but I didn't think of myself as a singer. I was coerced, I think—but anyway I did, and we did it in Danish. So I did this play in 1961.My mother had played the part and then I played the part. 1986 was the anniversary of Harmonin and our *Søndag paa Amager.*

Well, my daughter, Lori Larsen is and actress and in the theater, And she was asked to take it on. And she did . And she was very reluctant, because she didn't think she was quite , you know had enough background. But she was interested in it because of the family history of it. She did a lot of research and had to make it work theatrically, which was quite a feat , I think.

It was quite a project for her but she did it . She, having been in the theater in Seattle for quite a few years , She was able to bring together a very nice cast of professional actors.

And pulled it off . It was at Washington Hall, which was quite an event. I think we had about six performances. So I went on and we — my mother and I walked on the stage and I said, gave a little history of

28 - Greta Petersen Larsen

the play and how my mother and I had done it 50 years before, and I had done it 25 years after that and now Lori was going to be doing it and so forth. And even my granddaughter was on the stage with us, and we said, "And then Lori's niece is going to be doing it next." The audience loved it.

But the space, the Washington Hall, will be available for the production if it ever comes up. So we'll keep our fingers crossed on that one. That would be, what, 100 years? Yeah, 100 years.

My daughter as you know is an actress, and she sort of, carried on the family banner in the family. I've gained a lot of satisfaction from her. That's sort of, what would you call it, there's a way of reliving what you might have done through your child.

My parents were very practical. Not very flamboyant, but interesting, hardworking , serious people but they knew how to have fun. They knew how to enjoy life. I think it's kind of hard to get a good balance in life, but somehow they managed to do an awful lot in their lives. I think they were quite successful. I think I had a good model. Otto and I lived a good and fun and balanced life.

Greta Petersen Larsen was born in Seattle on September 25, 1925 to John Hugo Petersen and Greta Petersen. She studied at Grandview College in Des Moines, Iowa and at the University of Washington. For three generations she and her family have been cultural leaders within Seattle's vibrant Danish community. Their contributions to music and theater continue to enhance and enliven Seattle's cultural diversity. Greta was married to Otto Nyholm Larsen and had three sons, Paul, Chris and John, and one daughter, Lori.

Lori Larsen

"My father was. . . like **My Big Fat Greek Wedding**. *He was that way about being Danish. He used to distribute a little blurb. I don't know where he found it, proving that George Washington was Danish. He was related to Gorm 'the Old,' and he took the whole chronology back so that the United States is actually a kingdom of Denmark. He had a whole spiel."*

Even though Denmark's a small country, I had a relative, or a grandparent from each of the islands, and two from Jutland, because it's the biggest island. So, all my life I have been deeply imbedded in the Danish culture, due to the fact that my parents were children of Danish immigrants. We had a lot of the customs and a lot of the beautiful qualities that come from Denmark, in our lives here in Seattle, where I grew up."

My life took a very interesting turn in 1959 when I was nine. My father had a Fulbright Scholarship to study in Denmark. There were four of us children — one was just six months old and another one was two. I was nine and my older brother was eleven. The whole family traipsed off to Denmark and lived there for a year. I went to public school and I learned to speak Danish. We got to be real Danes. I remember going down to Copenhagen on the train with my brother, and buying Christmas presents in a little shop. We were speaking Danish to them. They couldn't believe we were from America. Nobody knew where Seattle was. We had a great year. It was like the most enchanting fairy tale year of my life.

Aside from having grandparents who all came from Denmark, I had this experience of the place itself. I saw where my grandmother, Greta Petersen, was born. That house is still in the family, in Give, Jutland. I went back when I was 20. I went to a pig farm, up in northern Jutland, with 300 pigs. That was such an amazing experience. One of my best friends in grade school, her house was 500 years old... I had these kind of fairy- tale experiences. I've always loved Hans Christian Andersen fairy tales.

I was so happy I had that year in Denmark, because when I came home in 1960, my paternal grandmother was 70, and my maternal grandmother was 60. They both lived well into their 90s, so I had many years where I could speak Danish with them. That was a great pleasure to them, and singing Danish songs with them. Enjoying where they came from. That was a great blessing in our family, that we had that integration, through the different generations.

I guess it culminated in the production of *En Søndag paa Amager* (*A Sunday at Amager*), when the Danish immigrants first came to Seattle and built Washington Hall in 1908. In 1911, they put on their first play.

One of my grandmother Greta Petersen's best friends, Elfrieda Petersen, was a great light in the early pioneer Danish community in Seattle. She formed this group called Harmonien in 1911. She played Lisbet, this leading lady. It was their premiere production for Harmonien. Twenty-five years pass, and, of course in Denmark, 25 years is a huge thing. When people ask me, "What religion did you grow up being in?" I'd say, "Well, I was Danish." They're good at dinner parties, and 25-year celebrations are part of their liturgy.

Twenty-five years later, in 1936, my grandmother, Greta Petersen, has come to Seattle, and is a songbird in the Danish community, sings at all sorts of events. Her husband, John Hugo Petersen, is kind of a ham bone. I'm an actor and so I believe that's where I got my acting prowess — from my grandfather, John Petersen.

He was a well-known actor back in Denmark. When he came to the United States he had a delicatessen in Ballard and then on Phinney Ridge, across from Ken's Market now.

They're putting on all sorts of plays in the 1930s at Washington Hall, in which both my grandmother and grandfather star. My grandmother does the 25th anniversary production of *En Søndag paa Amager* that her best friend, Elfrieda Petersen, had done 25 years earlier. So that was really great. There's even a little tiny film clip of it somewhere.

Twenty-five years after that was 1961, I'm an 11 year old girl. . . There's a whole new influx of Danes coming into Seattle around the late 1950s or early 1960s — a little mini wave — and they are all staying at Washington Hall.

At the 50th anniversary of the Harmonien a lot of the old folks are still around smoking cigars and eating cheese sandwiches downstairs. They had this Washington Hall and my mom, [also named Greta] put on this play. She was a budding actress when she was a young woman and acted for a few years before she married and had children and gave it up.

Lori Larsen - 31

As her big comeback she did *En Søndag paa Amager.* We'd just returned from our year in Denmark and our Danish was up to snuff and she did the whole play in Danish. I could understand the whole thing and was utterly enchanted by it.

A Sunday at Amager is a beautiful, beautiful love story about a young girl who lives with her father and sister, who's 20 years older. She was like an accident and in the process of her being born, the mother died and so the older sister is like a mother to her. She's a wild, little spitfire. Lisbet is her name and she lives in Amager. They were Dutch farmers in the 19th century at Amager, now where the airport is just outside Copenhagen. The playwright was Johanne Luise Heiberg, who was the leading actress of her day. She was revered by Hans Christian Andersen and Søren Kierkegaard. She was the leading light of the Golden Age of Danish culture. Her husband wrote vaudevilles, she starred in them, and they were very successful.

To make herself feel better between her performances, she would take long walks out to Amager. She would see these beautiful costumed Dutch immigrant farmers and their beautiful clothes and their beautiful vegetables and their very tidy little homes. She was enchanted.

A story started to go around in her head and she decided that she wanted to try to write a vaudeville herself. So she did it all in secret because she didn't want to upset her husband too much. He knew about it but he agreed to let her do it if she would do it anonymously. The good old days, right? So she agreed and she had these little melodies in her head. Then she went to see a very famous composer. This is 1848.

She knew that revolution was coming. The whole of Europe was engulfed in a revolution. She knew there was change and she knew that these little pockets of people who had their national costume were going to die out. She wanted to preserve the innocence and beauty of it. So she wrote this play, and it was a complete inspiration about this girl who is in love with a sailor who lives in Dragør, which is part of Amager Island down by the sea. She and the sailor come to a dance, and all sorts of shenanigans go on. They have a little love story and it all ends well. That's the plot in a nutshell. Suitors that are comical suitors and so on..

Then 1986 comes along and it's the 75th anniversary of the play, and I'm 36 years old. My mother was 36 when she did it. My grandmother was 36 when she did. Johanna Luise Heiberg was 36 when she did it. So there was this kind of wonderful connection. We were playing young girls but it was kind of our last stand to try to play a young girl. Because after that it's a little bit too tricky, but you can get away with it at the end of your blooming. Loveliness, you know?

So we did this play, and I fell in love with the director and had a son with him ultimately. Yeah, the prelude to the play included my mother and my grandmother. They came out and told their stories.

We said in 2011, we'll pass it on to my niece who was also going to be 36 in 2011. But she was pregnant and she wasn't an actress. We didn't do the 100th anniversary event, but my aspiration is that I tell the story about Johanna Louise Heiberg and how she came to write this. She wrote it, and then it was produced. It was the talk of the town because nobody knew who wrote it. Everyone had their suspicions. It became a huge mega hit. It ran forever, and she couldn't tell anyone.

She held it secret until she was old and wrote about it in her diaries. That's how we know. It's such a wonderful story. I've been working on a piece which tells that story as opposed to doing the play over again, doing excerpts from it.

It's my hope that I can give a gift to close the chapter on that whole generational experience and also, just to continue to share Danish culture which has such charm. People in Denmark even today know these songs... They're in the DNA of Denmark.

It's just part of the scenery now. The story of how it came about is so beautiful. The critics didn't like it. They thought it was too sentimental. But Johanna Luise Heiberg said when something is sincere and comes from the heart, people respond, even if the critics are saying what they will, people respond. I think that's true. It's been true in my experience, too, as actor.

My father's mother came when she was three. She was ultimately part of a family of 15. They came to Omaha, Nebraska. Her father was a dairy man who got into some kind of trouble in Denmark and happened to bring his whole brood over to America. So the rumor goes, but we don't really know. He was a tall fellow, a robust maker of children with 15, where the last two were identical twins.

My father's father, Lars Christian Larsen has his immigration papers on display in the Danish Room at the Nordic Heritage Museum.. He came the earliest by 1911. He was born about 1882. Right around the turn of the century, he came to Tyler, Minnesota, where my father was born. Both my father's parents went to Grandview College in Omaha, Nebraska, and that's how they met and then they went up to Minnesota where my grandfather, Lars Christian was a Lutheran minister. He had been a cabinet maker in Denmark. He was apprenticed as a cabinet maker. He was a Lutheran minister and ran an orphanage in Tyler,

Minnesota but then, they moved to Junction City, Oregon and that's where they raised their six children.

Times were changing and he couldn't do the services in Danish anymore. Junction City was a Danish community but everyone speaking more and more English, and his English was always a little bit dicey. So he came to Seattle and went back to cabinet making. He made all the beautiful cabinets in our old house and the beauty salon where I went.

My mother's father, John Petersen, came I think in about 1917 or 1918. He was living at Washington Hall. When my grandmother, Greta Jensen, came on the train in 1922 from Ellis Island all the way to Seattle, she came to Washington Hall because that's what the young Danes did then.

All the boys from the Hall were out on the front porch to see what the new crop was bringing in. Quite a few of them had an eye on my beautiful little grandmother. John Hugo Petersen won out, and they were married and started their family. It all happened down in Washington Hall.

There was a lot of pairing up naturally. They were young and they were in a [new] country and they were learning how to get through.

I think Greta had a sense of adventure. She was living in a small town in Give, and there wasn't a lot of opportunity. An opportunity came along and she had the courage to seize it. It was like that. I went to Give when I was 20. I had a boyfriend at that point and he was doing this acting program. I was going to wait for him to get done, and we were going to travel around Europe. It was 1970. I went to Give for six weeks. I was in Give, staying at the house with relatives, and it was very nice.

I was 20 and I was young. I was with old people, and I was really restless. I would wander around through the fields. I got a taste of what that restlessness that comes from, "There's something out there for me and this isn't it." I think that's what it was for her.

She was talented, too. She could sing. She had more chance to express herself here, and had a wonderful life filled with many, many friends, of all ages. She was quite a lady.

John Petersen understood her leanings. I'm sure that's why I ended up doing it [*En Sondag paa Amager*], because I always thought it was part of my family. Show business is kind of a family business, in a way. It's such an odd life, that you have to have a little taste of it somewhere in there, or it takes too much courage to try to do it. There was a lot of support for me to do it [the play]and have this kind of life.

I wasn't encouraged at all [to go into acting]. I just started doing it and had success in it from junior high and high school. I just tried it and made a strong impression. I went to Roosevelt [High School] and they had a wonderful drama teacher there named Norma Wills, who got a lot of people interested in the theater. There was this guy, Duncan Ross, who had come to town from England and I went to a lecture. He was forming this acting training program at the University of Washington and I thought wow, that's for me because I'd had so much fun doing this in high school. I auditioned and I got in at the second year of it. It was, at the time, called the Experimental Acting Training Program. It's now an MFA program and is quite well known around the country.

[Acting] is tough at times, there's a lot of rejection, but you don't focus on that. You get over it after a while. It's just part of it.

You get into a thing of complaining. You have to watch it, because it's hard. It is hard. You only have a job for eight weeks and then you're back at zero. This goes on for years and years. It's wearing.

[I grew up with] æbleskiver, big time. Now, I have an aebleskiver [traditional Danish pancakes] party every Christmas Day. All my friends come, and we have bacon and aebleskiver. Pounds and pounds of bacon.. candles at dinner. To me, it's more of a philosophy of conviviality and generosity and opening your hearts to strangers, the whole living well, living with some sort of grace that I really sense from the Danish culture.

So we have a lot of fun being Danish. In fact, sometimes when Danes come, they see us in Seattle, being way more Danish than they are. They're more a cosmopolitan culture, not so into the little fairytale customs like we are, but it gives us some ground that gives us delight.

[My grandparents maintained close ties with relatives back in Denmark.] They went back many times. In fact, my beautiful [maternal] grandmother went back when she was 96, with my parents... She went around and saw everybody she knew. She wasn't feeling well, a few hours later she died. Very close to where she was born. She was still having a beer and a cheese sandwich, and carrying on. She was a little weak, but she never was sick. My mother said there was some really, really ancient people, probably not as old as her but old ones who, lying in the bed, just lit up when they saw her. It was kind of a goodwill tour, she was such a dear. She just expired. It was a really extraordinary passing, one to emulate, I think.

Lori Larsen was born in Seattle in 1950 to Greta Petersen Larsen and Otto N. Larsen. She studied acting at the University of Washington with Duncan Ross and Arne Zaslove, graduating with a BFA in 1972. Her first acting job was at age 19 at Seattle's ACT Theatres. She has also appeared in productions at the Seattle Repertory Theatre, and the Intiman Theatre, where she received her Actor's Equity union card in 1976. Together with a group of actors, she formed The Empty Space, an acting company, in the 1970s. In the 1990s, Larsen directed six operas for Speight Jenkins, Seattle Opera director. Additionally she has appeared in plays in Oregon, California, New York, Delaware; Madison, Wisconsin, and Atlanta, Georgia. She has taught acting at Cornish College of the Arts. Larsen resides in Seattle. Lori has one son, Drew Rowny.

Dagney Kristina Stevenson

"It's terrible not to be able to talk or understand. I didn't understand a word of English."

The only place I lived before I came to the United States is that little place in Dalarna, close to Bonäs or Mora. We lived on a farm and I was milking a cow before I was nine years old. We helped with the farming, dug potatoes and everything. We were really crowded in our house. We had two rooms and my grandmother was staying with us. We had just a grade school there, six grades. My sister Margit went to high school and got into nurse training when she came here. I couldn't because I only went to grade school.

I was 14 and a half when some people left home in Bonäs. They had come home from America two years earlier but they were going back. I guess my mother thought that would be an ideal time to send me. My mother had eight children, and my grandmother had eight children, and they all came to the United States. My mother was here two years and she just loved America, but she was engaged to my dad and I guess she felt bound to marry him, so she went back. I think she had a baby every other year. My dad liked it much better in Sweden where he could work on the farm, and he did a lot of business too, which he couldn't do here.

All my mom's and my dad's siblings were here, too. So when she asked me if I wanted to go to America with these people, I thought it would be interesting. So we took a boat from Norway. It was terribly windy and I was sick the whole time. It was terrible.

We landed at Ellis Island and the officials there wouldn't let me go with those people. I was stuck at Ellis Island for a whole week. Didn't have anybody to talk to. I didn't know a word of English and nobody there was Swedish. They had to get word from my aunt that she would send me to school until I was 16. It took a week. They didn't telephone then. It's terrible not to be able to talk or understand. I didn't understand a word of English. They had high bunk beds, for us to sleep in — We got three blankets; one for the bed, one for the pillow, and one to put on. I always got the highest bunk. They showed movies there, too. You know, my parents were very religious, and seeing a movie was wrong. But I saw two movies in that week.

And then they told me I could stay in America. It didn't matter too much to me whether I got in or not — I'd get my trip home, you know. But my aunt said I'd be welcome there, and so they took me to the train. I was going to Minneapolis, and when we got to St. Paul, they had all those train cars that said Minneapolis, so I thought this must be it. So I got off. Luckily, it wasn't far from Minneapolis, so they could take the streetcar and meet me in St. Paul.

My relatives in Seattle sent me money for a train ticket, and asked me to come here. So on my 16th birthday I took the train to Seattle. I went to Ravenna school and I graduated from there. I think it took two years. It was kind of fun and I enjoyed it. I also did housework; I was a maid. It was hard work but I didn't mind. I had to get up early, work and do my homework, and come home after school and work. I stayed in the home where I was working. I got room and board and about $10 a month. I was so broke.

When I got to be 18, 19, I got tired of going to school, and I quit. I didn't have time for any fun at all. I just stayed home and worked. I did go to church on Sundays most of the time. This was almost 80 years ago. And then I started going to dances, and to my parents that was a sin, too. But I did go. I met my husband, David Stevenson, at a dance at Norway Hall. He was from Sweden, too. He came over around 1924 or '25. He spoke English when I met him.

We bought a house in Ballard, on 13th Avenue Northwest. We paid $1300 for that house in the midst of the Depression. It was a good house. We fixed it a lot.

Dave made a little money, but he didn't work that much at the time. We tried to save, too. I saved a notebook. I made a schedule of what we paid for groceries. I looked over that once and I just couldn't believe it. You know, eggs, I think, a loaf of bread — a dime. I think he made $25 a week or something like that. But we skimped. Every penny counted.

David was a glass blower at a place where they made asthma medicine, Stansbury Chemical. And I worked at a caterers, that served meals in the Highlands and all over. We were in charge of the tables — they had to serve swanky. And we washed the dishes afterwards, and cleaned up and everything. I think we started with 50 cents an hour, then I got up to 75 cents or a dollar an hour, by the time I quit. But I didn't make much. This must have been in the '50s. But I kind of enjoyed that kind of work. I like to move around. I don't like a sitting job. When I did that catering, it was late at night. Sometimes we worked eight to ten hours.

38 - Dagney Kristina Stevenson

We usually brought out a little of the Swedish traditions at Christmas time. We even had a few Swedish Christmas songs. I fixed *lutfisk* when my husband was living. I enjoyed having it once, at Christmas time. What most people have against it is it smells so awful. I didn't mind it. We sort of looked forward to it at Christmas when we were little. It wasn't Christmas without it.

We used to go across the Sound on Sundays to Virginia, you know where that is? Very pretty. It's across the bay from Poulsbo. We had friends there that had a cabin and we went there quite a bit. The boats stopped at all those little places on the Sound. It was the most beautiful ride on a sunshiny day. It really was a nice ride. One ferry left from Ballard at that time. That's why we could take it. It certainly wasn't very expensive and you could get to all those places. It was wonderful. [The Dogfish Bay Baptist Church was there on a little peninsula. The Seattle First Baptist congregation used to have picnics and church meetings over there.]

My oldest sister came over, too. She was a little older than I, but I was the first one to come. None of my brothers came to the United States. It was better in Sweden by that time. They got jobs and then cars came into existence, so they could get places.

I did go back and visit my family. My sister Margit here had gotten word that my mother died, and she never told me — she was afraid I wouldn't go. So, I didn't know that my mother died until I got home. And that was the hardest thing I've ever gone through, because I really, really longed to see my mother.

I know it was hard on her to send me here, because I was a pretty good worker, a good help. And I wanted to tell her "Thank you, for sending me to America." I never regretted coming to United States. I was grateful. I wanted to tell my mother.

Dagney Petersson was born 15 Sep 1907 in Dalarna, Sweden. She came to the U.S. in 1922, to Ballard in 1934. She met David Stevenson at Norway Hall and they were married in 1931. They had two daughters; Betty (1932), now Utter, and Marilyn (1936), now Karr. David died in 1985 and Dagney died in 2003.

Olaf Kvamme

"[On the train across Canada] my mother made, a sort of a hammock out of a blanket or a shawl and tied [it] to the baggage racks and so I swung across Canada. And the other thing my mother always complained about was my dad's sister, older sister, and his next youngest brother. The older sister was to come along to help her and take care of her, but she was seasick the whole trip, and so my mother had her also to take care of."

We're from what you would call in Norway a *gård*, a series of homes, seven homes, in a little valley, Kvamme, right near Bergen. Ytre Arna was the nearest town – at that time it was in the County of Haus – and now it's part of the Bergen city limits, but it's still fairly rural in its appearance.

My parents [Johannes Olsen Kvamme and Eli Alvhilda Rivenes], lived across the road from each other. In fact, as a five-year-old, my mother's family temporarily lived with my father's family and eventually bought some property from my father's family and built a home right across the road so that those two families were very close. Some of the older children in that family have more in common with the kids across the road than with their younger siblings because there were twelve kids

Infant Olaf with parents

in each family so you've got twenty-four aunts and uncles there, and that can generate an awful lot of cousins.

His [my dad's] older brother had the same name, Johannes – two brothers with the exact first name. So, that's a little unusual. …one was *Lille Johannes*, Little Johannes, and the other one was *Store Johannes*, Big John.

I was born in June, June 21, 1923, and we arrived here (U.S.) in mid-August, just a little – maybe August 15th, 20th, in that area. So, I was two months, two and a half months old.

It was really for economic opportunity. You see, with that many boys in the family and one farm, and the process of turning the farm over to your one son, or to your family, just didn't work. And so that meant trying to get other kinds of work and it wasn't -- the economic opportunities were very, very slight, of course, at that time in Norway.

What happened is that it [the farm] went to the youngest. …all of the other boys were here in the United States. They had all emigrated by the time it was ready to turn over. …each successive boy was asked if he wanted to come back and take over the farm, and there was no from the first one, no from my father, and then the third – Ole was the third – and he was asked, and he said, "Well, maybe. I'll think about it." And then his mother wrote back. She says, "Well, if you do that, I don't know what's going to happen to Harald." He had stayed home and had done the farm all these years. And so, Ole said, "Well, okay. Let Harald have the farm."

We took the Canadian train directly across Canada and down to Seattle where we were met by a relative [Bert Paulsen], who had been here since around 1905, and he met them at the rail station, at the Union Station now, in Seattle and drove down to Tacoma, and they remained there the rest of their lives.

My dad tells a story about coming to Quebec. There was a time to wait for the train, so he wanted to get a chance to get cleaned up, and a haircut, and he went into this barbershop to get a haircut, and, of course, he didn't know a word of English, didn't know what the fellow was saying. And so, the barber said, "Well, would you like a shave?" And he didn't know what he had said, and my dad just nodded his head and so he had a shave. And the barber said, "Would you like a shampoo?" So he nodded his head, and he had a shampoo, and then, finally, "Do you want a manicure?" And he said, "yeah," nodded his head – and he said, "What a wonderful place. You come in for a haircut and just look what they do for you."

[On the train across Canada] my mother made, a sort of a hammock out of a blanket or a shawl and tied [it] to the baggage racks and so I swung across Canada. And the other thing my mother always complained about was my dad's sister, older sister, and his next youngest brother. The older sister was to come along to help her and take care of her, but she was seasick the whole trip, and so my mother had her also to take care of.

I'm not certain why they came here. My dad's brothers and, in fact, my mother's brothers, most of them had a stop, a very brief stop, in Wisconsin, where there was another uncle and worked on the farm, some as short a period of time as four or five months before they came out, others for maybe a year.

Olaf Kvamme -41

The one [Oscar] that stayed four or five months determined that he might as well be back in Norway if he was going to have to work that hard. So, he called his aunt who was out here and asked, "Is anything going on out here?" and she said, "Oh, sure. Come out and you'll have a job." And that was a Friday, and on Monday he was on the train. He began as a sweeper in a mill and eventually he became a very, very skilled cabinetmaker.

Editor's Note: "In 1941 the United States entered World War II after Japan's attack on Pearl Harbor, Hawaii. Without evidence, key U.S. leaders claimed that all people of Japanese ancestry on the West Coast of the U.S. posed a risk to national security. Justifying it as a "military necessity," the government forced U.S. citizens and their immigrant elders to leave their homes and live in camps under armed guard."

From Densho.org "The Causes of the Incarceration"

I was out of high school, but they had the early graduation [for] those that left in, probably in March or April of 1942.

And they initially were sent to the Puyallup fairgrounds — Camp Harmony they called it. And I, at least I would say three times, and maybe more, went down to Camp Harmony to visit with classmates. And there was a barbed wire enclosure – they'd go and get the person – and the one that I visited with probably most often, although not the only one, [was] Yohei Sagami. He was killed. He was in the 448th regimental combat team. And it was interesting, in the Garden of Remembrance, down at Benaroya Hall, I went through that and I noticed that Yohei's name wasn't on there and I got that corrected. So – because I'm active, you know, in an organization of Japanese language army veterans, all – mostly all Nisei. See, I'm the only Caucasian that shows up, you know, most of the time. So, through that group I've had some documentation. They knew Yohei.

The Bainbridge Island Japanese were the first to go, and then I guess it was a matter of weeks before our friends were gone.

But it's interesting that there's this whole identification with Japan that as a kid from school and then in the Army and working for them and going back and visiting the owners of the farm where I worked most of the time after they had [left]. It's been a sort of a – there's a sort of a Japanese interest.

They were there [Camp Harmony] for quite a while. I think they must have been there, certainly until the fall.

And then most of them went to Idaho, Minidoka, most of the ones that

I knew, unless they were a kind of a recalcitrant type. You know, a few of what they called the "no-no boys."

Fife High School Class of 1942

It meant that "I'm not going to play this game with you. I'm not going to – I'm not going to be subservient. I'm a U.S. citizen." And the no-no boys didn't go – wouldn't volunteer for the Army and there was, in the Japanese community, there was a long time a sort of division between the no-no boys and the – "I'll do whatever you want me to do."

The [Japanese-American] farmer I worked with, they got their farm back and were successful farmers. A Filipino family took charge of that, and they weren't as effective farmers as the Sakaharas were. Many of the [farms] were run down when people came back, and, of course, they didn't all come back. Some had left camp, and I don't know what the circumstances were about how you left camp. You couldn't go back to the West Coast, but many places, you know, people lost their property. Taxes weren't paid and stuff of that kind.

In terms of the church issue, it's interesting in that I didn't become a citizen until I was in the Army. Typically, when your parents take out their citizenship papers, the children become citizens if your parents do that before you're 18. Well, my parents did not become citizens until after I was 18, and there was a provision of having to swear allegiance. And there's a provision in the Bible – there was a fairly strong, at some point back in the late 1800s, or 1900s, maybe, where that was an issue, and so my dad would not swear allegiance. And he eventually became a citizen because the wording then was changed where you could have an alternative. You promised or you pledged, or you did something that wasn't attributable to swearing allegiance, because you swear allegiance to only one God, and so that was the occasion of becoming a citizen.

In the Army I can remember the big Army truck coming out in the field up – down there in Camp Roberts down south, between Los Angeles and San Francisco, and somebody telling me to get in the back of the

Olaf Kvamme -43

truck and then driving down to San Luis Obispo, herding a few of us into a courtroom and said, "Put up your arm and swear allegiance" – "yes," and down, and back in the truck, and we were now citizens.

The church was the whole, everything, your acquaintances, that is my parents' acquaintances, their social gathering, all of that revolved around the church. There was no involvement with the Sons of Norway or any of the outside kinds of organizations. There was church Sunday morning, there was church Sunday evening, or, for a long while, there was church Sunday afternoon and Sunday evening, and during the week.

The Japanese-Americans would go in the U.S. Army, would go to the language school. Some were proficient, some weren't, but if they weren't, they went to school, and then they had a lot of instruction in military terminology, identifying what kind of a tank it is and what kind of an airplane it is and what kind of a gun it is and that sort of thing. Even if they were proficient, they — well, they probably didn't know those things, and that was in Minnesota. And then the white guys, like myself, who had no identification with this, went to school. I was 12 months at the University of Chicago, eight months at the University of Michigan, in the Army. Then went and joined them in Minnesota. We then became the officers, they were the team. So, you had the white officer, and the people who knew something, in terms of language, were the Japanese- Americans.

I happened to be in the very, very last class at Michigan, so we really didn't finish. Well, anyway, the war ended in August [1945] and my class wasn't finished, but essentially, things ended in terms of going to school. And so, I had the choice of becoming commissioned as a second lieutenant or going home, and I chose to get commissioned and go to Japan, which was a great idea.

Olaf Johannes Kvamme was born on June 21, 1923, near Bergen, Norway and immigrated to the United States with his parents when he was 2½ months old. The family settled in the Hilltop area of Tacoma and later moved to Fife where the young Olaf, working in the fields for Japanese-American farmers and befriending their children, began a lifelong fascination with Japanese culture. Olaf served with the United States Army of Occupation in World War II and rose to the rank of lieutenant colonel. Olaf received a degree from Pacific Lutheran University and started teaching in Kapowsin, Washington. He later moved to Seattle, taught in the public schools and retired in 1987 as an Assistant Superintendent of Schools. In his retirement Olaf has been active in many Nordic-American organizations and served as President of the Nordic Heritage Museum Board of Trustees from 1990 to 1995.

Paul O. Nielsen

"In 1976 we got a notice that Queen Margrethe II of Denmark will be in Seattle on a certain date and would have three and a half hours available if you would like to put on a party. We worked on it for three months...with the chief of the U.S. Secret Service, I went over the rules

Paul O. Nielsen with Ruth Andersen

again and again... We traveled from the airport through the city to the hotel upstairs, downstairs, from this place to that place. Every place they looked at every door and everything. Who could be hiding? What could happen? I had a private reception arranged. The Queen was led into the banquet room at the Olympic Hotel...Two hours later she left and it was back to the airport to say our goodbyes. A couple of people who were involved in the event said: 'Thank God nothing happened, she's gone.' "

When I was nine days old in 1902, I nearly died. In olden times, bedrooms were not heated. So there I was in an ice-cold house with ice on the window. They put in a kerosene stove to make me warm. But the stove started to smoke. When they finally came in and found me they thought I was dead. They frantically sent for the doctor who lived across the street. He said, 'Well there's a little bit of life left in him, but if you want to get him into heaven send for the priest.' "

The priest said I would not last and requested some hot water to baptize me. My parents did not have hot water. " Well get me cold water, anything, " the priest said. They got the cold water, the priest said his little speech, and sprinkled cold water all over me. Of course that woke me up. So I feel that was a second birth for me. My mother told that story a hundred times.

My parents started out very poor. My father came from three generations of country musicians playing for dances and drinking out and having a very good time. When my mother came along she said my father needed a profession. So he learned to be a wooden shoemaker and was quite successful. They later tried operating a country inn, then my father operated a country bus route until he became ill. My parents had decided that of their four children, I was the smartest one and they sent me to private school for four years.

When my father died, I was in my teens. My mother had relatives who had immigrated to America including some who were Mormon missionaries. One of those relatives, a college administrator, invited me to attend his college for two years. It took me four years to save enough money for the trip in 1924. I bought passage on the *Oscar II*, one of four American ships, and left my mother and siblings behind in Denmark to go to Pittsburg, Kansas. I completed the two-year course in a year, but could not bear the Kansas heat.

Those were the days before air conditioning. I lost 40 pounds in one year suffering from the heat. So I looked for a cooler climate and chose Seattle where I found work at a dairy. Milk was milk. Here was an ordinary dairy, they made butter, cheese and had eggs. So they hired me. After three years I returned to Denmark to visit family, as promised, but came back to Seattle and spent three months in an Alaskan cannery, which I would never do again. Then came a big event in my life – meeting a girl. Her name was LaVerne Gardner, and she urged me to return to school "because I want a house, I want a family and I want you to be somebody."

I took my wife's advice, studied and passed the Washington test to become a certified public accountant in 1933. In 1938 I became one of the founders of a CPA partnership, Moss Adams & Co. They started in Seattle, then expanded to Tacoma, Portland and Eugene, followed by offices in Idaho and California. At one point the business was the sixth largest accounting firm in the country. So it was a wonderful career. The business made me a rich man, and I could go home to Denmark as a rich uncle.

I would advise people to get an education. Mine was never organized, it was hit and miss. I was always going to school; going to night school for 50 years or more. I don't know if I would advise getting credits. My gain was direction. I should have known that I could have enrolled in a university for credit and a certificate. But what would I do with it? I also was an advocate of eating and living sensibly, and not smoking. My father had promised me a thousand kroner if I did not smoke at age 21, but he died before I reached that age. But I told my girls the same thing and they collected.

In the early 1950s, I got a call from the then Danish consul who said: "I am told to nominate five or six people as possible successors for me. If

I put you on the list, will you serve?"

I was confounded and said, "Well yes, I would. I'm overwhelmed. I would do the job." But it appeared that I was not the first choice. I was not a shipping man, I was not a tradesman. I was not the kind of man they wanted. The field was narrowed to one man who was chosen, but died before the appointment occurred. The others apparently were less suited to the job than I was.

Then the consul general asked me: "Tell me, if you were appointed can you afford it? You will be expected to do much entertaining and pick up the tab." I said, "Yes" and was appointed. I told my wife and she said "Oh, so what." I explained that it would change our lives a little bit. "We'll have to do some entertainment." She responded that she loved to entertain. And LaVerne was a perfect hostess.

I found the pace as consul very busy. Every time I was invited I was supposed to be there. It was a little too much sometimes, but the big one was the World's Fair [Century 21] in 1962. Denmark decided to participate. The consul general came from San Francisco, started living up here half the time. He had one million kroner to spend and he was determined to spend it. He had one big party after another. I remember one party at the Olympic Hotel where the Swedish people had held a party previously and they had such beautiful flowers, decorations everywhere. The manager of the hotel had told them to leave the flowers – they could use them. They were too nice to throw out.

So the consul general and I go over to the ballroom just for assurance. Blue and yellow flowers? The colors of the Swedish flag. "Where do they come from?" the Danish consul general asked. "The Swedes left them with their compliments," the hotel manager said. "Oh my God – get them out," the consul general said. And that was just one of the minor incidents.

Paul O. Nielsen was born January 11, 1902, in Nakskov, Denmark, died in Seattle on November 26, 1997. He immigrated to the United States in 1924. In 1936 he married LaVerne Gardner, who died in 1990. They had two daughters, Lynne Marachario and Jody Canady. He served as the Danish Consul in the Seattle area from 1953 to 1978. He received the Knight's Cross of the Order of Dannebrog from the Danish king in 1962, and was advanced to Knight First Class in 1969. In 1978, the Danish queen appointed him Commander of the Order of Dannebrog, a rare distinction for an American citizen. Paul died in 1997.

Odd Bjarne Andvik

*"He would take me to the car barns and
I got to see all the streetcars in or out of
the barn. Then I'd stand with my fingers
on the edge of the windowsill at the front
while he drove the streetcar."*

My dad, Berger Martin Andvik, came to
this country at about age 14 and settled
with his older brother, in North Dakota. He
then went to Minneapolis and began driving
streetcars there. One day he wanted to see
how fast these streetcars could go. So he
exceeded the speed limit heading back to the car barns one day and was
discharged as a result. He moved out to Seattle and got a job driving
streetcars. Here he met and married Ellen Tjelle who was of Norwegian
descent. They had two children, Arnold and Sylvia.

Dad heard that his oldest sister in Norway was going to sell the family
farm. Dad decided he'd like to buy the family farm, so he returned to
Norway with his family and bought the farm.

His brother-in-law had had the post office business at the farm, but
when he moved down to his store, he took the post office business
with him, and a community fishing net which was part of the farm's
equipment. Dad lost the post office and the community fishing net, both
with income potential.

While living in Norway, Ellen contracted TB and passed away.
Oftentimes Dad went to the pastor's farm with other men to do volunteer
work there. My mother, Olufina Duesund, worked for the pastor as a
domestic. One day the pastor said to her, "Fina, that's the man for you."
My mother married my dad June 30, 1922 and nine months later I was
born. I was a year old when Dad decided this farming was too tough.
He sold the farm and moved back to Seattle.

When the family moved from Norway to Seattle, they began to attend
the First Norwegian Lutheran Church on Boren and Virginia. After a few
months Dad bought a house out on Phinney Ridge, at 6513 Greenwood
Avenue. Dad bought the house in 1924 for $3,000. We grew up there.
Dad sold the house in 1954 when he retired.

Dad was a streetcar driver and conductor. Some of the streetcars had
secondary conductors, but later one man handled both jobs. Before I

started school, Dad would sometimes say, "If you'll take a nap today, I'll let you go along with me on my tripper this afternoon." A tripper was a single round trip during the rush hour. Dad worked a split shift. He'd go for a couple trips during the morning rush, come home, have a nap, then go back for a tripper in the evening rush hour.

He would take me to the car barns and I got to see all the streetcars in or out of the barn. Then I'd stand with my fingers on the edge of the windowsill at the front while he drove the streetcar. On the Fauntleroy route we'd go down a road called End-O-Line. The barns were in the Denny Regrade area, somewhere near Broad Street substation. There were streetcar lines on 15th Avenue and 24th Avenue Northwest, and I think as far west as 28th Avenue. They cut Eighth Avenue Northwest through the backyards of homes in 1927 or '28, maybe a few years later. The city limits at that time was 85th Street. One streetcar ran across 85th Street from Golden Gardens east to Greenwood, and perhaps further east.

In those hard times we ate lots of salt herring. We'd come home from school hungry as could be, and mother would have herring for dinner. I often got a herring bone stuck in my throat. I never looked forward to a herring meal. We'd have a keg of salt herring almost every year. A full keg of salt herring lasted a long time.

Dad had a lot of fisherman friends who provided us with salmon, halibut and other fish, and we enjoyed that. Dad was not so great on *lutefisk*. Years later I found *lutefisk* to be very delicious. We also had a lot of meat-and-potato meals, pot roast, meatballs. Leg of lamb was very popular with our family. Mother and Dad had a vegetable garden, with peas, carrots, onions, radishes and lettuce.

One favorite Norwegian meal was *raspeboller* also called *kumle* or *raspekake*. It was made of ground-up potatoes and flour wadded into a ball with a piece of ham in the center, then cooked in ham water. When it was all done you also had a nice soup that it had been cooked in. We'd dip the *boller* in hot bacon grease for a real flavor.

Odd Bjarne Andvik was born May 31, 1923 in Duesund, Norway to Olufina and Berger Martin Andvik. He came to Seattle in 1924 with his parents. He graduated from Ballard High (1940). After WW II service, he got a B.S. in Civil Engineering. He worked 5 years for Seattle City Light, 29 years for U.S. West, retired in 1985. He and his first wife Marion had three children. She died in 1993. In 1994 he married Elaine and moved to Camano Island.

Olufina Duesund Andvik

*"When he told me how he wanted to go
back to America, I said, 'Okay. I suppose
I can make it like others have done.'
I wasn't too excited about it."*

I was born in 1892 on a very little farm not
too far from the city of Bergen. Norway is
very mountainous country, and the farms are
very, very small. We try to live very simple,
and the food we have in those days wasn't like it is here. And so we
lived day by day.

It was no such a thing as a schoolhouse; our schooling was in the
homes of the people. I went to school eight years, that's all. And then
when I got big enough, I had to go out and work as a hired girl, to
neighbors and farmers and this thing and that thing.

In those days they took the cows to the mountain for the summer. We
hired girls, we went to the mountains with the cows and we'd milk the
cow and took it back to the cabins and make the butter. The people from
the farm came up, often with food for us girls and to pick up the cream
and butter to sell.

Oh, that was a long way, you know, to get the cows and sheeps (sic)
across from Duesund to the other side where the mountains were. They
had to take them in a boat. The boats were big enough for three oars on
each side. We then walked the cows to the mountain. There never was
an accident. Everything went well.

We milked the cows every morning, and in the evening we went out
to find the cows to milk them again. They had bells on, and we girls
knew the difference between the neighbor cows and ours because of
the difference in the bells. We took the sheeps to the mountains, too. It
wasn't much trouble with the sheeps. They went wild up there. In the
fall they went to the mountain and got hold of the sheeps and got them
home.

Knitting and crocheting was my hobby, because in Norway in those
days we had to make our own clothes. Stockings and the underwears
and everything was knitted. They had no money to buy anything. A
neighbor lady got us girls together and helped us to learn these things.

Oh, we had breakfast and a noon meal and a supper, but every-thing
was so simple in those days. Mostly we had sheep meat. We couldn't

eat the butter, for instance. We had to sell that and get a little money because there wasn't many things to get money from in those days at home, very little money. We always live simple, all my life we have been used to little things. My father was very satisfied. He worked hard and we got along, and that's the way of it.

I met my husband when he was home from America, and he worked on a farm. And the pastor who I worked for, lived on a little farm, and the neighbors came there off and on to help on his little farm. And my husband came to help on the pastor's farm, and that's how I met him. After that a friendship developed, and so we got married. I was never anxious to get married. And this pastor I worked for, he married us. Pastor Berg was his name.

I came to this country in 1924. This fellow that I married was a widower with two children. He had worked on the streetcars here in Seattle for many years, and he liked to take a trip home and thought he was going to take over his folks' farm. So he lived there for a few years on the farm, and he found out that was too hard to make a living. And so he liked to go back to this country. When he told me how he wanted to go back to America, I said, "Okay. I suppose I can make it like others have done." I wasn't too excited about it.

The ship came to Bergen. And we went from there over to this country. It took us eight days. And then I had three children to take care of, the two stepchildren and Bjarne, my oldest, who was born in Norway. He was a year old when we came and the two stepchildren were also small. We were on the ship for eight days with three kids, and another week from New York to Seattle on the train.

Everything in Seattle was new, and it was a little hard to get used to it, but I made it. By and by, I got acquainted with the church people. I attended Norwegian Lutheran Church and I got acquainted with some of those people. After a little while my husband got his job back at the streetcar company. The first World War had been on and those fellows who had been in the war were in front of him. We bought a house on 65th and Greenwood after he got settled in his job.

We lived very simple, and we never had much money. The Norwegian people got along with very meager things in those days.

I didn't have much problem with the language. Bjarne, my son, was home, and the two stepchildren went to school. Bjarne learned the language much sooner than I did. I never went to school in this country to learn the language. I took it all by and by. I always liked to read. So I read quite a bit and learned something by that. I'm surprised at myself

Olufina Duesund Andvik - 51

sometimes when I think how I was able to read the English. Now I read the New Testament and the church paper. I can't read too long because I just see with one eye and I get tired.

One of my grandsons — his mother went in a hospital for something. And he came — he was just a little guy, maybe four years old, came and he asked me, "Where is Mommy?" "Oh, she's in the HOOS-pital," I said to him. "Bestemor," he said — in Norway "Bestemor" is "grandma" — "Don't say HOOS-pital. Say hospital." And he has been in language work ever since.

Olufina was born September 8, 1891 in Duesund, Norway. Her mother was a widow with two children when she married her father. Her mother died after giving birth to a brother, a sister and Olufina. Her father remarried and seven half-siblings were added to the family. Olufina married Berger Martin Andvik June 30, 1922 and came with him to Seattle in 1925. Berger was a widower with two young children, Arnold and Sylvia. She and Berger had three sons: Bjarne, Martin, and Orville. Olufina died May 14, 2001, at age 109 years, 8 months.

Sissel H. Peterson

*"I've been in the Norwegian Ladies
Chorus for 20 years, and that's been
the big thing in my life."*

I happen to have a long full name: Sissel
Hedvig Bergitta Almaas Peterson. We
came from Haugesund, Norway in 1925.
My father left Norway in 1924 and the
next year my mother and we three children
followed. Olaf was almost nine, Elsie was
five and I was only three and a half. My
mother had some English in high school, so
she could understand a little English. My father was a brick mason, and
there wasn't very much work in Norway at that time. His three aunts in
Tacoma loaned him money for his passage.

When we lived in Tacoma we used to drive to Seattle, and go to
Volunteer Park, or Woodland Park or the Locks. My dad was always
dressed up in a suit and a tie, and the ladies with a hat. We stayed in
Tacoma for two years. We came to Ballard probably in 1926.

We rented a house on 23rd, just above 70th Northwest. Lots of
Scandinavians lived in the area. The Heggem [see p. 259 Signe Heggem
Davis] family lived across the street and we became good friends with
them. As we got older, we went to Webster School. My mother was
involved in PTA and the Mother's Chorus there, they don't have that
now. Lots of immigrants went to school there. I had to interpret for one
girl who came from Norway, May Gorud. She didn't speak English.

My mother did a lot of volunteer work, but, she never worked outside
the home. She was a seamstress by trade in Norway before she got
married. Gradually she got involved in all kinds of activities with her
friend, Mrs. Frodesen. [see Steiner p. 61] This was when we were in
grade school at Webster. My dad went to work every day.

He and my mother joined a Norwegian mixed chorus. And they'd go
to practice once a week in the evening. My mother joined the Daughters
of Norway and Dad joined the Sons of Norway. They met on the same
night. They were in a mixed choir here in Ballard directed by Rudolph
Møller. We grew up with lots of music.

My mother said in Norway they were sort of class-conscious. In a
store, the more important people were waited on first. She didn't like

that. Here in Ballard, first come, first served, and people were more down-to-earth and friendly. She was happy here.

My father had to take his car to work because he had to bring his tools. Most people were starting to get cars then. They weren't very fancy cars. We went way down to old Norway Hall, up on Boren. My mother and dad had their Silver Anniversary there. The building is still there, but they sold it when they built the one down off Elliott Ave — Norway Center they called it. That was sold to the Mountaineers, and they built this new one here in Ballard [57th & 24th].

Most housewives in Norway are immaculate, everything just perfect, but my mother wasn't one of those, so my sister and I ended up helping her a lot, to tidy up and that sort of thing. So many Norwegians just wear themselves out cleaning house. Except if we were going to have guests, we just worked and worked and worked to get everything all cleaned up.

During the Depression, we moved out of Ballard for a few years because we were evicted from our house. We couldn't pay the rent because there was no more construction work for my dad. We lived out in Alderwood Manor on a little three-acre farm. We pooled all our school savings to pay for the move. Puget Mill Company, who owned the farm, let my dad work off the payments of five or ten dollars a month, and he dug ditches — did anything he could to pay off the rent. Our friends in town came out and brought us food all the time. My sister and I picked berries and cherries and that sort of thing. We got a little bit of spending money with that. So we managed. And we liked it out there. As soon as things got better, we moved right back to Ballard.

One day we came home from school in Ballard and there was this big surprise. My mother had bought an old piano. And we were kind of disappointed, we thought it was going to be something special. We all learned how to play. My mother taught us little folk songs from Norway and they've been with me forever. Singing has always been a big thing in our family. We'd sit around the piano, somebody would play and we'd sing and sing.

And she taught us a song and at every program she put on at the Daughters or Sons, my sister and I had to get up and sing a certain song. We sang the same song year after year when we were little. It's about a fox that heard a little lamb bleating. He ended up wanting to help the little lamb find his way home. And the lamb said, "Oh, no, no, no, no, you'll just pick me apart and eat me." A gruesome song.

Mother sang all the time at home. We'd hear her singing when we came home from school. One time my sister's girlfriend came home with her and she asked, "Who's that singing?" And Elsie said, "That's my mother. Doesn't your mother sing?" And her girlfriend said, "No, she never sings" And we had thought that was just normal.

We were all musical. My brother bought an old accordion when we lived out in Alderwood. And he taught himself to play it. Then he taught me to play. Now he has two daughters, and they both play the accordion. And they perform quite often in nursing homes. I played last night at our banquet for the Ladies Chorus. Now my daughter, at 48 years old, has taken up the accordion. We're an accordion playing family. My brother is 83 years old, and he still plays all the time. And I still play. It's very popular in Norway. My mother had four or five brothers and they all played the accordion. And her dad played, so music has been a big, big thing in our lives.

Birthdays are big in our family. We'd go to the house of the one having the birthday. This didn't seem quite right, but that's what we did. I think they do that in Norway. Whoever has a birthday, everybody comes to their house. They usually bring bouquets of flowers. It's kind of an open house, but it's a big thing, especially like a 60th birthday, 50th birthday, 70th birthday.

Confirmation was very important. When you're confirmed, you're becoming an adult. Confirmation with the Lutherans is very important. It's a big day. And they have usually a family gathering after the confirmation ceremony at the church. And then they have a big family gathering or with friends. In Norway, usually they would get a piece of silver as a gift, which is very nice.

I've been in the Norwegian Ladies Chorus for 20 years, and that's been the big thing in my life. I really enjoy that group. We sang in Norway three years ago for the city of Trondheim's 1,000th birthday. And for the unveiling of Leif Erikson's statute. And then we traveled with the Male Chorus to Sweden and Helsinki, Finland, and to Estonia. It was quite a nice trip.

I met my husband during the war. He was in the Coast Guard, guarding the Ballard Locks. His father was born in Sweden, and he's a little bit Danish. He was born in Minnesota. We got married at Ballard First Lutheran Church 55 years ago.

When we had our golden wedding, we had a *kransekake*, with Norwegian, Danish and Swedish flags on it. It was at Our Redeemer's Lutheran Church. The Norwegian Ladies Chorus sang and my niece played the accordion. We had a very nice party.

I worked as a secretary until our two children were born. Then I was a stay-at-home mom. When my husband quit work because of a disability, I went to work again and retired when I was 62. Then we did a lot of traveling — all over, eight times to Norway.

Up at our church on Wednesdays, we have what they call Everybody Place. They were teaching the class in Hardanger embroidery. And so I took that up. I made my own apron for my Hardanger costume. You do a lot of embroidery and then you cut, pull the threads and do some more embroidery. It's kind of hard to explain, but it takes mostly patience and time. My mother did it. She did a lot of handwork.

I've never had any feeling of not being comfortable. I've always liked it here. Leaving our home in Norway — that was the bad part. But because my mother was so contented here, we never had any bad feelings at all. We were very happy here, being with my mother and father all the time. They were very down to earth, nice people. We just had a good family life.

Sissel Almaas was born March 31, 1922 in Haugesund, Norway. Her father, a brickmason immigrated to Tacoma in 1924. Her mother came in 1925 with the three children: Olaf, almost 9, Elsie 5 and Sissel 3. The family moved to Seattle in 1926. Sissel married Axel Peterson in 1945. Their children: Nancy (1952) and Norman (1955).

Harald and Ethel Kristjanson Sigmar

"We not only served this emerging Calvary Lutheran Church ... But, also, it became a real spiritual and cultural center for Icelandic events."

ETHEL: Harald was a student at the Seminary in 1942, when he was asked to come to Calvary Lutheran Church to do a survey, to decide whether Calvary could survive or not. Then he did a lot of services, and the people became very enthusiastic. We were there for about three months, then the committee in Seattle asked Harald to serve the church.

We moved to Ballard in 1943. Wally was born in 1946. Kristine, in 1948, and Karen in 1950. She was about eight months old when we moved back to Gimli, Manitoba, Canada. The children were very active preschoolers and I felt very busy, just taking care of them.

We did not have a car for four years. We walked, and we walked, and we walked. Harald did all his visitation of parishioners on foot. We shopped in Ballard and we walked. I remember having one little baby lying in a baby buggy, and another one sitting on the edge, walking down to Ballard to get my groceries. I shopped at this little corner store — they were very personable people, and they allowed us to have a charge account. And if we didn't quite have all the money to pay it with, they'd carry it over to the next month. It was almost like being in a country store or a very small town. Howard Almquist was the proprietor. [See Almquist p. 212]

HARALD: The first year we were there, we couldn't find a place that we could afford ourselves, so we lived in the basement of the church — they helped to clean up a room right next to the kitchen. And so we lived in that room in the basement of the church. We used the women's bathroom as our bathroom.

I have precious memories from those days as I look back at some of the old Icelandic people here. They were very supporting and were closer to the old country than we were. They carried on a lot of the Icelandic traditions, like the baking, like the familiar *vinarterta.*

Harald and Ethel Sigmar - 57

HARALD: We both attended Vestri meetings, the literary society. They were conducted once a month, all in the Icelandic language. At that time, they had a paper. It wasn't published, but as part of the monthly meetings, Jon Magnusson, the editor, would read the entire paper.

At that time I conducted Icelandic evening services once a month and English services in the morning. We always observed the Icelandic festivals as well as the English, like Easter and Christmas. It was a bilingual church. I was trying to draw people from the community, and did. It became a church not only for Icelanders — there just weren't enough Icelandic people to sustain the congregation — but we maintained a very strong Icelandic tradition through the evening services.

ETHEL: Around the time that we moved there, there was an influx of Icelandic people from the Midwest, who were coming to the West Coast to work in the war industry. And, of course, a lot of them ended up in Ballard. And there was another group, the Icelanders who had been there from very early days. Like the Palmason family [see Palmason, p. 400] and like Jon and Gudrun Magnusson and Kolbein Thordarson.

HARALD: When we were there for the summer in 1942, a lot of people from the Icelandic community in North Dakota were moving into Seattle. One time there were 40 members of my dad's parish in North Dakota who joined [Calvary] church. And when I knew people were moving, I would try to help them find a place to rent. That's one of the reasons so many people began to come to Ballard, rather than other parts of the city, because there was already an Icelandic community there.

The background of the whole thing was that, long before either a Lutheran or a Unitarian church was established, all of the Icelanders that were interested at all in any kind of church formed a group called Hallgrim's Congregation. They had no building. To begin with they met in the old Icelandic Hall. And then, when they organized and bought the building on 23rd Northwest and West 70th, they decided to become part of the Icelandic Lutheran Organization. At that time, those not comfortable being associated with the Lutheran Church, because they were, or leaned toward being Unitarians, formed a special separate group, and they built a church on 77th and about 25th, which is now part of the Northminster Presbyterian Church.

When I arrived there in 1942, there was no Unitarian Icelandic congregation. Therefore, I made an effort to relate to all of the Icelanders, regardless of whether they had been members of the Unitarian Church, or no church. Just if they were Icelandic, I would serve them, as well as members of the Calvary Church.

We used a lot of talent from people that were not members of the church, just because they were Icelandic. So it became again a center for Icelandic activities, including *Vestri*, as well as being a Calvary Lutheran Church. So, for many years, it was both known as Hallgrim's Congregation, and the church itself as Calvary Lutheran Church. We both felt very comfortable working with Icelanders, regardless of their persuasion. We not only served this emerging Calvary Lutheran Church, which gradually brought in other people. But, also, it became a real spiritual and cultural center for Icelandic events. We always continued having Icelandic Christmas services, and a lot of special events.

I taught Icelandic at the University of Washington for awhile. There was an influx of students who had the G.I. Bill of Rights. And I was among the several graduate students who were assistant teachers of English. I got to know the head of the Scandinavian department, and he asked if I would be willing to teach Icelandic if anyone wanted to learn it. I was very limited in my knowledge of Icelandic, even though I had studied it at the University of North Dakota when I was a young man, but I agreed to take it over, and I did. There were quite a large number who wanted to learn to read some Icelandic and I was glad to do it, even though I felt very limited in my speaking abilities especially. I did that for about four years. I never had any classes bigger than about seven or eight. I think I learned as much as the students, because I had to work hard at it.

We had left Ballard the first time to go back to Canada, where I served the church in New Iceland. We lived in Gimli. Following that, we spent a couple of years at the University in Iceland. We took our four children with us there, and we lived there for two years. I had a great experience. I was teaching at the University, in the Theology Department, and had a very significant time.

By that time, when we moved back, the Icelandic Synod was amalgamating into other groups, so I took a call to a church in Vancouver, and from there, to Tacoma, and from there to Yakima. And finally, in 1977, we moved back to Ballard when I was called as pastor of Our Redeemer's Lutheran Church. We were there for ten years in that capacity. During that time, we became a little bit involved with some of the Icelandic club activities. And Ethel became very involved in the beginnings of the Nordic Museum. She was on the Board for some time. We grew very active in both Icelandic and in Scandinavian activities in Ballard. And we remained in Ballard for five years after I retired from my ministry, and moved from Ballard to Mt. Vernon.

ETHEL: Wally got his degree from Western. He worked at Skagit College here for 22 years. He developed cancer in 1982, and after treatment, two years later, he went to the University of Texas and got his Ph.D. in college administration. He came back here and worked here for awhile, then he became president of Peninsula College, where he was when he died. Jean and his two boys survive him. Then Kristin got her master's degree and taught Home Ec. and English, both here and in California. She married and has two daughters. Our third daughter Karen is in Bellevue. She got her master's in reading specialties. All of our children are people people. They learned how to like and work with people. And then, we have little Emily, who is in a group home. She's our retarded daughter. She's in a group home in Richmond Beach. Out of all our children, I think that she has the greatest sense of self esteem. She thinks that she's the greatest thing that ever came into our family. So, we're very happy about that. She's a happy, happy person.

Harald Sigmar was born in an Icelandic community in Saskatchewan. Sigmar was his grandfather's given name and was taken as a last name by his father and his eight brothers. Kristbjorg Ethel Kristjanson was born April 14, 1916 in Saskatchewan. All four of her grandparents were from Iceland. They were married in 1940 and came to Ballard in 1943. Their children: Wally (1943-1999), Kristin (1948), Karen (1950), Thora (1953) and Emily (1960). Harald served as minister at Calvary Lutheran Church 1943-1951 and at Our Redeemer's Lutheran Church 1977-1987. Ethel died in 2011.

Anne Marie Frodesen Steiner

*"My mother was born liberated. I could
never understand the fuss about 'women's
lib' because my mother was always active
and involved."*

My father was Frode Frodesen. He was born in at Drammen in southeast Norway. My father's father was a sea captain of sailing vessels. We have a painting of his last sailing vessel, the *Helga.* He wanted his oldest son to follow in his footsteps, but my father got so seasick that my grandfather said, "No, Frode, you better get some other kind of work. You're not cut out for the sea." My mother was Inga Homlebæk, born May 13, 1888, in Hokksund, a country area not far from Drammen.

Frode immigrated about 1906 when he was 23, and Inga immigrated in 1909 — she was about 20. Frode traveled with his friend, Axel Borgerson, by way of Canada. They were interested in building, especially masonry. One of the biggest jobs they had was in San Francisco after the earthquake. Then Frode came to Seattle. Inga immigrated with a friend. She got a job on Mercer Island caring for the children in the Stewart family.

In 1915 they each decided to go back to visit their families. They met for the first time on the boat going back to Norway. My mother always said, "When Frode saw me climbing the gangplank with the sun shining on my auburn hair, it was love at first sight." He said, "Well, I liked her, but I had to get to know her."

They saw each other while they were visiting their families in Norway and came back to the United States on the same boat, apparently a real shipboard romance. Inga and Frode were married at the Stewart home on Mercer Island October 16, 1915 by Pastor Hans Stub of the Immanuel Lutheran Church in Seattle. There was no bridge to Mercer Island from Seattle at that time, and the lake was very turbulent that day. Pastor and Mrs. Stub told me they thought they would never get there because the boat was tossing so much. But they did get there, and Pastor Stub married my parents. Inga attended Immanuel Lutheran, and sang in the choir there.

The next year, my brother, Olav Haakon Frode "Fred" Frodesen, was born in Bend, Oregon, where my dad had work. Two years later they had another boy who died shortly after birth. He was buried in the Children's Garden at Lakeview Cemetery near Volunteer Park.

Frode and Inga, with little Olav, returned to Norway in October 1919. They were living with Frode's parents in Mjøndalen when I was born on a cold winter day, January 26, 1920. The snow was so high it covered windows. My dad and grandfather had to burrow their way out to get the horse and carriage to fetch the midwife. The family moved to Drammen, where John Martin was born a year and a half later. We lived there until I was almost seven.

Both my parents had become U.S. citizens, so Johnny and I were U.S. citizens born on Norwegian soil. Frode felt America offered him more opportunity, so they returned to Seattle in 1926. We moved to Sunset Hill, and my father borrowed $2,000 to start a business. He worked up and down the coast, building brick churches and schools. He built St. John's Catholic Church on 80th and 1st Avenue Northwest, a beautiful church with a steeple you can see from far away. That was his first job after returning from Norway. In 1930 he built the addition to Webster School, now the Nordic Heritage Museum, which included the auditorium and gymnasium, where "The Dream of America" is now. Later he and my brothers were involved in much construction at the University of Washington and at Washington State University at Pullman.

He was a mason contractor. General contractors hired him to do the masonry. My brother Fred also became a mason contractor, and my brother Johnny became a general contractor. Later they all worked together out of an office between Fremont and Ballard on 44th Avenue. It was F. Frodesen Masonry and Farwest Construction, Johnny's company.

My mother was born liberated. I could never understand the fuss about women's lib because my mother was always active and involved. She had a beautiful voice, and sang on the Lundquist Lilly Hour, a Scandinavian program. Lundquist Lilly was a clothing store. I'd come home from school and turn on the radio and hear my mother singing. She was also very involved with the Norwegian Hospital Association and a driving force in getting the Norse Home built. Ed Mahlum, the architect, said, "Your mother would get things done when no one else would. When the men wanted to give up, she said, 'No, we won't give up.'" She got FHA funding for Norse Home, the first retirement home to receive that.

The Norwegian Hospital was at 36th or 37th and Fremont Avenue. The Norwegian Hospital Association was founded in 1913, but the dream of a Norse Home came later. The Hospital Association was the first to work for the Norse Home. My mother is known as the Mother of Norse Home. Her portrait is there in the dining room. Abraham Kvalheim is known as the Father of the Norse Home, so their portraits are side by side. My father was vice-president of the board when the Norse Home was built. Peter Wick was the builder.

My mother organized the first 19 guilds of Norse Home. She had a severe stroke in 1957, the year Norse Home opened. She lost her speech and was paralyzed on her right side. So her friends, led by Haldis Jules, organized the Inga Frodesen Guild in her honor in 1960. It is still going strong. I'm president of it right now — for the second time after 35 years.

The guild hasn't really changed over the years. We have lunches and other events and raise money through different projects to help Norse Home. The garden club is building a beautiful garden in front of the home. We're paying for two benches and a table for inside the gazebo. It will have a plaque "Inga Frodesen Guild" on it.

The Norse Home has a great location on Phinney Ridge with a view of mountains and water. It's right across from Woodland Park where residents can enjoy themselves. Norse Home is situated right where the Ferris wheel was. I remember riding that Ferris wheel and looking down over Ballard.

It was established as a retirement home for Norwegians and has a nursing center for those who become ill. They can live out their years at Norse Home. Many people there now are not Norwegian. It is one of the finest retirement homes in the Pacific Northwest.

The Norwegian Hospital Association also is still going strong. I am a past-president of that, as was my mother. Through the years we've had many luncheons and helped support the nursing center of Norse Home.

My mother was more or less the heart of the Norwegian-American community in her prime, the mid '30s, until 1957. She was a wonderful speaker and the way she loved Norway just went to everyone's heart. She often spoke to large groups of people and inspired everyone with her passionate love for Norway.

She was chairman of the 17th of May celebrations when they were in the Civic Auditorium, now the Opera House. She was president of the Daughters of Norway and Grand Lodge president. And for *Nordmanns-Forbundet* [Norsemen's Federation]. She founded the Pacific Northwest Chapter in November 1948.

After Norway was occupied by the Germans, my mother showed movies she had taken in 1937 and '38, when she led two tours from the Pacific Northwest to Norway. She had 50 people on each tour. She was the first to lead large tours across the Atlantic on the Norwegian America Line, crossing the United States by train. Many on the tours had never been back to Norway since they left. They called her Mother Norway of the Pacific Northwest, [*Norges Mor på stillehavskysten*] and she took care of every one as though she were their mother.

For organizing a trip she received two free tickets on the ship. She took me along in 1937 and I stayed a year. And she took my cousin, Erik Schlutz, in 1938. She received one free ticket for each 25 persons. Unfortunately, when she arrived in Norway in 1937, her mother had hardening of the arteries and didn't recognize her own daughter.

My mother could not believe the German invasion could have happened. But she had some wonderful movies from her tours. So she showed these films at Norway Hall and other places, and raised money for Norwegian relief. That was one of the reasons that she received the St. Olav Medal. She would give marvelous speeches from the heart. My father would sometimes say, "Inga, you don't have your facts correct all the time." And she said she didn't worry about that too much. My father had to have everything exactly right. But my mother said, "Well, I get the point across, that's the main thing. And everybody liked it."

In 1957 my parents took a trip to Norway. But in November after they returned, she had a massive cerebral hemorrhage and was bedridden, paralyzed on her right side and lost her speech. But she kept that wonderful smile, never looking as though she were feeling sorry for herself. She spent three years at home, bedridden, and then two and a half years at Norse Home, where she passed away in 1963. And my father lived his last few months at Norse Home, and passed away in 1966. People came to see my mother and even though she couldn't speak, they were inspired by her radiant smile and the way she greeted them with her eyes. They said that instead of their comforting her, she comforted them. I don't see how she could have that optimistic disposition for five and a half years, but she did.

She was a person no one forgets. When I visit Norse Home now, some elderly people, way up in years, are sitting in the entrance. And they see me and they say, "Inga Frodesen's daughter! Oh, she was such a wonderful lady."

After I graduated from Webster, James Monroe and Ballard High School, I went to the University of Washington, graduating in 1942. Then I worked in California for a while. In the spring of '43 I joined the U.S. Women's Auxiliary Army Corp (WAAC) and was chosen to go overseas in the OSS branch of the Women's Army Corp (WAC) partly because I could speak Norwegian. The OSS — Office of Strategic Services — was the precursor of the CIA. We called ourselves the cloak and dagger girls.

I married Dan Murphy on VJ Day, the day the war ended, in London. We had six children: Rose Marie, Larry, Peter, Margaret Anne, Danny and Patrick Murphy. We were married at St. George's Hanover Square, in the Mayfair section of London, where I lived. We had to get our license at Westminster Abbey. He was an American soldier from New York. When we returned to the United States we settled down in Seattle. The children, born in Seattle, all went to Webster, James Monroe and Ballard High School. And they all live in or near Seattle.

Dan Murphy and I were divorced; he passed away just a few years ago. And in 1967 I married Jim Steiner, who had two sons, Steven and Dennis. Steven was married. Dennis was in high school and he moved in with us. So then we had a lot of teenagers. Jim married me with my six children — he was very brave. Two of them were away from home. Jim was very supportive of my Norwegian involvement. Dan Murphy was not; he would tell the children they were all Irish. Jim was of German descent. He said, "I've lost my heritage, but I want to help you with your heritage and support you."

After the war I received the *Frihedsmedalje* from King Christian X of Denmark in 1946. Working in the OSS, and I was very much involved in the Danish section as well as the Norwegian. That was from 1943 to 1945.

Later on, because of my work here in the Norwegian community in addition to serving Norway in the war, I received a St. Olav's Medal from King Olav in 1978. My mother received the St. Olav Medal from King Haakon, Olav's father in 1957, and my father later received the St. Olav Medal from King Olav.

I had two audiences with King Olav in the palace in Oslo. He was so approachable and had a big grin on his face when I saw him. Of course, you never turn your back on the king, you walk backwards when you leave. He was very easy to talk to. While I was there the second time, he had a telephone call and he said, "*Unnskyld meg*", "excuse me", '*jeg må ta telefonen for Sonja ringer.*" "I have to take a telephone because Sonja is calling." Sonja was his daughter-in-law, and he said "She and the children just returned from a vacation, and I have to see how they are doing."

Inga and Frode Frodesen

Anne Marie Frodesen was born January 26, 1920 in Mjøndalen, Norway to Inga (Homlebæk) and Frode Frodesen. Her brothers: Olav Haakon Frode "Fred" (1916), John Martin (1921). Anne Marie served in the OSS (precursor of the CIA) during WW II (1943-1945). She and Dan Murphy were married (1945). Their children: Rose Marie (1946), Larry (1947), Peter (1949), Margaret Anne (1951), Danny (1953) and Patrick (1957). She and Dan were divorced. Anne Marie and Jim Steiner were married in 1967. He had two sons, Steven and Dennis. Jim died in 1982. Like her parents, Anne Marie has been and is an activist in the Norwegian community and in Ballard.

Anne Jensen Ringstad

"When I was 12, my father died . . . Now I wonder what a lot of courage it took for [my mother] to make herself go for both of us. She had the responsibility of this stubborn 12-year-old. It had to be very hard."

My father left Norway because the farm was small, it went to the oldest son, and he was not the oldest son. Other people from Målsnes had already come to Seattle. He became a fisherman like everybody else. He had come earlier, worked in the lumber industry, and became a citizen. He returned to Norway and married my mother. I was born in Tromsø in 1925. When I was about six months old, he and my mother decided it was too hard to travel with a new baby, so he returned alone, and a year later, my mother and I came. It was really stupidity. Now she had a 16-month-old running all over.

We came over on the *Stavangerfjord* and landed at Ellis Island. Traveler's Aid got us on a train to Chicago and in Chicago another Traveler's Aid got us on the right train to Seattle. That was it — no more help. She couldn't speak English and I was running all over the train. The only word she knew was "coffee". In the dining room, she looked at other people's plates, then pointed to what she wanted. Then I ate, and what I didn't eat, she ate.

My mother was in her 40s before I was born. What a challenge it must have been for her at that age with not a word of English. She learned it, but never got rid of her *Nordlands* accent. I quickly became an American. My mother had to learn English because I wouldn't speak Norwegian back to her. I went to school and she participated in school as much as she could, mostly kitchen work and preparing food and that sort of thing, because it was difficult for her to communicate. But she coped because she had to.

We lived on Phinney Ridge, close to Woodland Park, but almost all our friends lived in Ballard. That's where we did our shopping. My dad was a fisherman, so he was at Fishermen's Dock. He fished for halibut so he was away from home for several months, spring and summer. Norwegian immigrants are not used to taking vacations. He was home in the winter when the weather wasn't really conducive to going around a lot, but we had a lot of company, other Norwegian immigrants. Many of these family friends were single men. There were families, too, of course, but many times the men would sit and talk to my father. They would sing *Ja, vi elsker* [the Norwegian national anthem] a lot. That was very moving for them. They had other Norwegian songs too. I learned Norwegian songs very early.

My mother told me the reason she picked our house was because the living room went across the whole front. The first thing she looked for was a place to put the Christmas tree where you could walk around it. One of my very favorite memories is going around the Christmas tree and singing Chistmas songs.

We always went to church for Christmas, most of the time to Ballard First Lutheran Church, to the English and also the Norwegian service. But we belonged to Phinney Ridge Lutheran, then on 70th and Phinney. But when there were any big Norwegian goings on, they were at Ballard First Lutheran.

My earliest memory of Ballard, in the late '20s, was two open vegetable markets on Market Street. They sold vegetables right on the sidewalk. That impressed me. At that time you had to take what was in season from the truck farms, because there wasn't such a thing as delivery from any place else. The city limits were at 85th, and north of there were many little truck farms. People who lived in town went out past 85th and had vegetable gardens. At Greenwood and 85th were little shacks where people kept tools and everything.

My cousin worked at the Melrose Dairy, near Market Street on Leary Way in their little ice cream shop. I still can remember the malted milks — in the big steel containers. They had electric mixers that could mix big, thick malts. They were good. That was before I went to work, but I had my dad there to pay for my ice cream. It was a nickel for a great big cone. I think malts were 10 or 15 cents.

We saw all kinds of movies. Saturdays they'd have special shows for children. The children got in for, I think it was a nickel. And there'd be a serial with a cowboy on his horse just going over the cliff. Then it ended, and you'd have to come back the next week to see what happened. Cliffhangers. But you'd come back on Saturday, and nothing tragic happened. But all week you worried about that.

When I was 12, my father died on a fishing boat. He was only 57 and my mother was 52. It must have been a terrible thing. It was still depression times and there was no Social Security. Now I wonder what a lot of courage it took for her to make herself go for both of us. She had the responsibility of this stubborn 12-year-old. It had to have been very hard. She got a job cleaning houses. Then, before I got out of high school, I got a job at the telephone company and worked part-time until I was out of school, in 1943 and then full time. Then I was able to pay a lot of the bills and to do a lot to help.

My first job was for Nordlandslaget at Harmony Hall, a large ballroom where they held dances. I was in junior high school, about 13 years old, and one of the men there asked me if I would like a job checking coats. So I did. It was downtown, on Eighth Avenue. It was large enough for dances; Norway Hall at that time wasn't big enough. My girlfriend and I worked in the checkroom, but every once in a while we'd sneak out and dance. It was wonderful. There was lots of accordion music and violins, the old Scandinavian music. I worked every Friday and Saturday night at Harmony Hall. I think I got five dollars, a tremendous amount of money.

Then I had a job in Ballard at Woolworth's Ten Cent Store. The wage was $13 a week, but of course, I was going to school, so I didn't work the whole week. I came after school to work for a few hours. I was marking prices and filling shelves — doing stock work.

We had an icebox on the back porch until I was in high school. I had saved money I earned and I bought a refrigerator for our kitchen and my mother bought a stove. It was a big thrill to get an electric stove and get rid of that icebox. The ice truck came once or twice a week, delivering blocks of ice. Down in Ballard there was an icehouse and an ice skating rink. The kids would watch for the ice truck, and as soon as the ice man took the block of ice with his tongs, put it on his back, went up to the house, the kids would run to the truck to get little slivers of ice. He always managed to leave several and we thought we were really getting away with something. It took me a long time to figure he was doing it on purpose.

And we went ice skating. I had this friend — a fisherman who was single and never had a family. I was the closest thing to a family that he ever had, and he spoiled me. One Christmas he bought my best friend and me black ice skates. We just were so excited, and we'd go down to Ballard and skate. You know, this was a big thing. We had the boots and the whole thing. Oh, yeah, that was a big deal.

I remember just like it was yesterday. I was getting ready for school one morning, and the radio was on in the kitchen. The announcement came over that Norway had been invaded. [April 9, 1940] I couldn't remember Norway, but my mother was devastated. Everyone she knew was there — all the relatives here were my father's. During the war my mother got a couple of letters. How excited she was to get mail from Norway. Her mother had died just weeks before the war, but the rest of her family were there. After the war we packed box after box of clothes and things to send to Norway. We always tried to put in a can of coffee and some sugar.

I went to Norway in 1980 and met cousins I had known only through letters and pictures. They told me how excited they were every time those packages came. It was just like Christmas. Forty years later they were still talking about how excited they were to get clothes and things. In 1943, I was aware of the war and my friends going off to the service. We had ration coupons for shoes, for tires, for gasoline, for sugar. We had meat coupons and we could only buy certain things only on certain days. But we got through it. A lot of people planted victory gardens in their yard. I was working, and I'd rather buy my stuff at the market. I wasn't ready to be a gardener.

Richard and I were married in 1949. We lived close to Loyal Heights School. There was a Safeway the corner of 24th and 80th and a couple bakeries, Larsen's Bakery, it was Engstrom's then, and Loyal Heights Bakery, a drugstore and other little shops. We got our meat at Loyal Heights Grocery across from Safeway. And there were gas stations, an ice cream store and a hamburger shop.

Well, it's fun to remember. Sometimes things just come back to you when you talk about them. I enjoyed it. Thank you.

Anne Jensen was born in Tromsø, Norway, February 22, 1925 to John and Martha (Olausen) Jensen. The family came to Seattle, Phinney Ridge, in 1927. She married Richard Ringstad, a Boeing mechanic, in 1949. They had six children: Carolyn (1950), Glenn (1951), Rick (1953), Larry (1954), Joan (1955), and Barbara (1959). Richard died on August 9, 1989.

Olaf I. Rockness

"They'd forbid us to talk Norwegian at home. They said, 'You talk English, so we can learn.'"

I was nine when I came here. I brought two suitcases with me. That's it. Those were hard times in Norway. Dad was a fisherman. He fished, but didn't make any money. It doesn't make a difference how much you work if you don't make any money.

We were Nordlandings. We come from Kvæfjord, just inside of Harstad, in the northern part of Norway. My uncle came to meet us at the train depot in Seattle. We had several relatives here. My dad's sister lived in Ballard and his brother in West Seattle. We stayed with my dad's sister till we got located.

My dad came over here to fish. He started fishing on his brother's boat, *Unimak*. He bought the boat later from his brother and he had that boat till his dying day.

It was terrible for me at first. I was a kid and I couldn't speak a word of English. I was teased to death — you know how kids are. I started in the second grade at Webster. My teacher was Swedish. We were out in the portable. My folks didn't want us to speak Norwegian in our home, because the only way they could learn English was from listening to my sister and I. They'd forbid us to talk Norwegian at home. They said, "You talk English, so we can learn." And that's what happened, they did learn. They spoke with an accent. No question about where they came from.

For my part, I don't think it was too difficult to get used to being here. It was just a short few years when I first came, that I couldn't speak English. But, you know, a young person picks it up real fast. It was a lot worse for my dad. He spoke only Norwegian — very little English — because when he was out fishing, everybody spoke Norwegian, for his benefit, I suppose. They were all Norwegians, maybe a Swede here and there.

We were just a short time at Webster, then we moved to 67th and 9th. And then, I went to Whittier, to James Monroe and then Ballard. After I graduated, I started going to Alaska. I started out as assistant engineer on a cannery tender and I've been in the engine room ever since. I had a knack for machinery, and that's what I wanted to be.

I stayed with that for a considerable length of time. Then I worked in shops. I worked with lift trucks quite a bit — got started with that during the war. I worked for private companies, not the government. I still wanted to get back on boats again. So I started fishing, working on draggers, mainly.

I worked on other people's boats. I couldn't put out a down payment on a free beer, much less my own boat. Worked all summer on the boats, fishing. In the winter I got shore jobs, because there isn't much fishing in the winter.

In my later life I worked for the University of Washington. I retired from there. I was on a boat all the time. It started with the idea they were going to use it for class work and they'd take students out on Puget Sound. And it ended up we got chartered. I'd been there maybe less than a year when the Halibut Commission wanted to charter the boat for the summer. The University didn't have that much money, so they were glad to charter it out. The only money we had to work with was what we got as charter pay. They couldn't afford to keep us otherwise. So we went from one agency to another, the Halibut Commission, California Fish and Game, Oregon Fish and Game, Alaska Fish and Game. They came down, wanted to charter the boat, then we had to go up, pick up their crew and go out on whatever they wanted us to do.

Olaf Rockness was born August 28, 1918 in Kvæfjord, in Northern Norway. When he was nine his family immigrated to Ballard. He married Elsie Mabel (Solberg) in 1950. They have three daughters: Judith (1951), Anita (1954) and Lisa (1963). Olaf died in 2005.

Edmund Sture Waldemar Olsson

"It seems like I spoke Swedish all the time when I was young, when I first got here, 'cause that's what they spoke at home."

I was born in Piteå, in Norrland, Sweden October 6th, 1923. We didn't live there, but my mother and father were traveling to relatives. Our home was in Husum, near Örnsköldsvik, where my grandmother lived. Most of my mother and dad's families were in that small area. The northern part of Sweden had a lot of snow. My mother always told me that I skied before I walked.

My mother and her oldest sister came here in 1914, sponsored by their aunt and uncle in Tacoma. My mother was only nine, so she went to school. Aunt Hildur was 17 so she went to work as a nanny for the Pantages, a well-known theater family in Seattle and Tacoma.

My mother went back to Sweden and later she and my dad got married. He had come to Detroit earlier with four of his brothers. We went to live in Wyandotte, a Detroit suburb. My mother got sick and in 1928 I came to Seattle to live with my aunt and uncle who later adopted me. My mother eventually recovered. At some time there was a divorce and in the '50s she came to stay with her sister.

I started kindergarten at Cascade school. We moved to Ballard and I went to Adams School, from first through sixth grade. I went to James Monroe Junior High, then Seward School, and after two years at Broadway High, we moved back to Ballard and I went to Ballard High. I delivered *The Shopping News* and the *Seattle Star* and I worked as a pin boy at the Ballard Bowling Alley on Ballard Avenue. It had six lanes, but there were only two of us pin boys. We always said we were glad only elderly women were bowling. I think for every line somebody bowled, we got paid a nickel. The cost to bowl was about 15 cents. I graduated from Ballard in 1942 and enlisted in the service.

My aunt, Hildur Oakson, had the Nordic Bakery & Delicatessen at 2205 Market Street. She started it in 1928 and later moved it to 56th and 24th next to Gerke's Music Store. She ran the bakery until about 1938. Then she went to help her husband, Evert, at the Ballard Tavern in the 5400 block on 22nd and later on Ballard Avenue. Later he sold it to

Olsen Furniture Company for storage, and then he opened a new tavern right by the Locks, which he called Lockhaven.

During this time my mother Mimi moved back here. She had remarried, and she and her husband, Emil Strasser, started Mimi's Coffee Shop near 20th and Market. At one time my mother, my aunt and my stepfather, opened a place down on 17th and Ballard Avenue, called O.K.'s Café. That was before Mimi's Coffee Shop.

I called my aunt "Ma" to distinguish between her and my mother, whom I called "Mother." So it was Ma and Pa and Mother and Dad. It seems like I spoke Swedish all the time when I was young, when I first got here, 'cause that's what they spoke at home. And I hadn't been gone from Sweden that long. And we talked Swedish with the neighbors. Many customers were either Swedish or Norwegian at both the bakery and the tavern. Seemed like every fisherman was a Norwegian or a Swede and they all had that accent.

I don't think anybody could make Swedish meatballs like my Ma did. We had potatoes and hardtack and Swedish pancakes and good old Mother's Oats. I don't know how to explain a complete Swedish dinner because it was always meat and potatoes. That was the basics, with some type of vegetable, parsnips and rutabagas. Often a bunch of friends would meet at one house or another. And there would be the smorgasbord type of thing.

We belonged to the Vasa order of the Swedish Club. The Swedish Club itself was on Eighth and Olive in downtown Seattle. And then Vasa Hall was opened in Ballard for meetings and dances. There also was a young people's group.

After I got back from the service in October 1945, I worked with my pa as a bartender in his tavern. I met my wife while working there. Her dad was superintendent of a Standard Oil plant on the waterfront at Pier 32. He suggested I try for a job with Standard Oil's Richmond Beach plant. I went out there about twice a day until the boss got tired of seeing me and put me to work in 1947.

Edmund Sture Waldemar Olsson was born October 6, 1923 in Pitea, Sweden. His mother had returned to Sweden from Tacoma where she lived in 1914. She married there and the family immigrated to a suburb of Detroit. Ed was later adopted by his uncle Evert and his aunt in Seattle. He attended Adams, James Monroe, Seward, Broadway schools, graduating from Ballard in 1942. His mother married Emil Strasser and ran several coffee shops in town. Ed married Jan Halbert in 1946. They have two daughters: Kriss (1948) and Gayle (1952).

Karin Gorud Scovill

"Our goal in the Daughters of Norway is to keep the heritage and culture alive."

I was born as Aase Karin Gorud. Aase was a difficult name going to school so I used my middle name of Karin and when I got my derivative citizenship, I changed my name legally to Karin Aase Gorud. My parents, my brothers, my sister and I immigrated to the United States in July 1928. We came directly to Seattle, sponsored by my aunt and uncle, Inga and Frode Frodesen. In the summer of '36, my folks bought the home they lived in for the rest of their days, at 929 Northwest 64th. We stayed close to our relatives, the Frodesens and Leif and Louise Schultz and did a lot of things together.

In my new neighborhood I found a friend, Ruth Andreen. She and I would walk to Green Lake to swim. It was quite a walk from 64th and 9th — up over the hill and down again. Her father worked three blocks from Green Lake at the water department. Sometimes when we went swimming, we'd get a ride home with him.

We'd take a bus to go shopping downtown where the stores were. We didn't have shopping malls. Everything was downtown. Of course, we always got dressed up to go to town. The whole thing, a dress, white gloves, even a hat. Going to town was a big thing.

In the early years Mother didn't speak English. She'd talk to us in Norwegian and we came back at her in our English. Mother and my dad would converse in Norwegian because it was easier for her. My father had gone to college in Norway to become a road surveyor and learned English there. Mother's education was in a home economics school, preparing her for marriage. But Mother was a very determined lady, and she took evening classes in English. My mother got her citizenship papers in the early '40s — she had a good command of the language by that time. My father got his papers in 1936. Mother didn't get derivative papers through her husband. She went through the schooling to learn what potential citizens must know. She would quiz us and we couldn't answer some of the questions she could answer. This was a very proud thing she did, getting her citizenship papers.

We still make the traditional cookies for Christmas. The tradition is to have at least seven kinds of cookies for Christmas, the special Norwegian cookies. My dad helped Mother with the *fattigmann*. One would cut out, and one would deep fry. Mother made a lot of them because they lasted for months.

In the Norwegian tradition, we celebrate and open gifts on Christmas Eve. For dinner we always had spare ribs, potatoes and *surkål* — a sort of a sweet and sour cabbage with caraway. We'd start with a little dish of rice porridge. A peeled almond was put in one of the dishes and whoever got the almond was the *jule nisse,* the Christmas elf, and passed out the packages that evening. And we'd always leave a little bowl of porridge or cookies for the *nisse* that evening so he would treat you well. Also, we'd hurry through our Christmas Eve so we could go visit cousins, because we'd have gifts for them. Christmas morning was more a family thing. We went to church and then visited friends. I kept that tradition going in the family. We no longer do the Christmas Eve visiting like we did. Our families have enlarged, so traditions change. Usually we can keep the Christmas Eve tradition going because other cultures celebrate more on Christmas Day.

Before 1950, Daughters of Norway meetings were in Norwegian. My mother joined a couple of years after they came from Norway and my father joined the Sons of Norway. The Frodesens, were already members. There they could get together with other Norwegians, an important social part of our lives. The Sons and Daughters met in the same location on the same evenings. Twice a month they'd have their individual meetings, then get together for their social time afterwards. They would usually have a dance, with maybe a three-piece group for the music. Children too young to be left home alone, came along and played games in one of the back rooms. During the dance we could mingle with the grown-ups. They danced all the old folk dances.

I joined the Daughters when I was 15. For initiation we marched around to the different stations for instruction and sang certain songs — a lot of ritual they don't use any more. The membership was larger than now, something like 300 members, but maybe only 50 or so, would come to meetings; more for dances or social events. Food was always an important factor, usually little open-faced sandwiches and traditional cookies, like *krumkake* and spritz.

Our goal in the Daughters of Norway is to keep the heritage and culture alive for the second and third generations. They want to learn the culture and how to make these cookies or the old traditional dishes, such as *rømmegrøt* with its heavy cream. Unless people will teach it, and others will learn, it'll be gone. I've got a big but interesting job ahead of me now. I've taken on the job of [Grand Lodge] president. This is our means of keeping all our 19 lodges together. We have a newspaper with information in it. It's another means of learning what's happened to these people who came, and the things still important to them.

Aase Karin Gorud was born in Hokksund, Norway Decenber 13, 1926. She, her parents, Kaspara (Homlebæk) and Anders Hansen Gorud, brothers John Helge (1921) and Steinar Egil (1924) and sister May Tyra (1922) immigrated to Ballard in July of 1928. Her youngest brother, Roy William (1934) was born here. Karin graduated from Ballard High 1944. Karin and (John) Milton Scovill, Jr. were married (1948). They have two daughters: Lynn (1953) and Anita (1959). Milt died March 17, 1990.

Herbjørg Sørtun Pedersen

"He said, 'You know, with seven girls, what do you think is going to happen to them in this little valley? They would have many more opportunities in the United States.' And she said, 'Okay, Martin, whatever you say.' That was my mother. She said that quite often."

My father's name was Martin Sørtun, and my mother's was Olianne Ramsdal. They married when my mother was almost 28 and my father was 24. We lived high in the valley in Eikefjord in Sunnfjord. Our farm was called Sørtun, and that was our name. The house was about 250 years old when we left there. We were a large family and our life on the farm was not easy, but my mother insisted that we always had time to play, even though we had chores to do, like turning the hay or maybe making waffles. We had at least five meals a day in the summer, often six. We would have an evening meal as late as nine o'clock during harvest. It was still light at 11 o'clock at night, so they took advantage of that.

We had sheep and cows that were taken up to the mountains to pasture in the summer. We often walked up with tanks on our backs, milked the cows and brought the milk down. We took turns doing it. When we were young, we often went with my mother. We always had a hired man and sometimes a hired woman, too, because there was lots of work to do. They would often go with us. When we got a little older, we went by ourselves, but we always went by twos, since one couldn't carry a full tank. We sang all the way up and down, and the cows would hear us and come. They liked to see us coming. Even the sheep would come and talk to us when we were milking.

My father came to America alone in 1925. He made up his mind before he went back home that he wanted to take his family to America. He came home and prepared us all for leaving. It took about a year. My mother was very reluctant. She didn't really want to leave her family. He said, "You know, with seven girls, what do you think is going to happen to them in this little valley? They would have many more opportunities in the United States." And she said, "Okay, Martin, whatever you say." That was my mother. She said that quite often.

Bergen was our first stop along the way. We stopped with my aunt who had a rather large house. My mother loved this aunt, because she was very kind. She took us all into her house and made my mother go to bed the minute we got there, because she could tell my mother wasn't feeling well.

We were leaving late in the afternoon the next day, but the next morning, at nine o'clock, we were on our way to town. My aunt insisted we couldn't go all the way to America without a hat. She bought caps for the boys. We girls got hats that were all alike. They were light blue and we thought they were very pretty.

We left Bergen on the *Stavangerfjord*, landed in Halifax, Canada, and from there we took the train to Seattle. We were very hungry on the train trip because we had not had much of an appetite on the boat because most of us were seasick. When the train stopped my father would run and get apples and a loaf of bread and a jar of jam or something. We thought it was the most delicious food we had tasted in a long time. We loved the apples.

From Seattle we went to Kent where my father had already arranged for a place for us to live. Before he went back to Norway, he had gotten a promise from a farmer who was about to sell his farm to let my father buy it. My father and mother lived there until they died many years later.

We came in 1929. The Depression was already very much a fact at the time. My father's relatives were concerned about us coming because they felt this was such a difficult time.

I learned English unbelievably fast. My father's cousin brought me about 20 comic books and told me, "Just read them and look at the picture, and figure it out. And every time you have a chance to talk to someone who knows, ask them." I could read those comic books very early, before I could speak English. "Li'l Abner" was one, and the man that flew around from tree to tree? "Tarzan." I used to laugh at "Tarzan." I had never seen comic books before I came to America.

We had probably been here about a half a year when I went to work for some people we knew from Norway. They had a boarding-house on Fairview Avenue and had 12 boarders. The woman had a baby, so she had to have help, so I became the nanny. The boarders were all Norwegian; they worked in the woods mostly. They would often be gone during the week and come back on weekends. Quite a few of them had breakfast — they had to shift for themselves for lunch — then they came home to dinner. I was there for about a year or a little more. Then I went home to Kent for awhile. Then I got another job in Seattle for Herbert

Carroll, of Carroll Jewelers, in his home. His wife was bedridden and very ill.

I met Einar Pedersen on Snoqualmie Pass skiing. The very next Saturday night, we met at a dance at the Swedish Club. That was the beginning of our romantic life. We got married in 1937 and rented a house on lower Sunset Hill. Our first two children were born there. We have four children: Susan, then Einar Jr., Mark and Ingrid. When they were small, my life was dedicated to caring for them. Einar was a fisherman, often gone for months at a time, then home maybe three days and gone again for three weeks. When our son was born, Einar was out fishing. Ballard Oil sent a ship-to-shore radio message to all the boats out there to tell Einar he had a son.

Einar was very aggressive and hard-working. He had an intuitive sense about fishing and he worked hard. We never had money because we saved enough to buy another boat from time to time. We had several boats when he died that my family are still using. He went from halibut fishing to trawling on the Sound; and tuna fishing and shark fishing in California and the Oregon coast. He was involved with several fishery organizations. He served for six years on the U.S. Government's American Fishery Advisory Committee, and I went with him to meetings at San Diego, to Boston, to Galveston, Texas, Washington, D.C. and Key West, Florida.

I had two sisters who lived in Ballard. All three of us married fishermen so we lived the same kind of life. And they had children at the same time. My sisters and I had a wonderful relationship with our children and with each other. While our husbands were gone, we relied on each other to watch the children, if we had to be away.

After Einar passed away in 1989, we continued on. We still have his boats and it's doing very well even today. My grandson is running the *Mark I*, which he bought. And Einar Jr. is managing the rest of our boats, especially on our mother ship. The mother ship is a boat where the fish are processed. Then we have catcher boats, that catch the fish for the mother ship. There are several owners in the mother ship. And they also have catcher boats. The boats actually bought the mother ship.

I've had a very interesting life. Looking back on it, I think I've had a very rich life. My husband taught me one thing. "If you want to do something, just try and do it and not worry about if it will work out." If you want to do something, you are ready to do it, was his philosophy.

Herbjørg Sørtun was born in 1915 at Eikefjord in Sunnfjord, Norway, to Martin Sørtun and Olianne Ramsdal. Martin had gone to America and returned for his family. The family immigrated in 1929 to Kent. The children were: Klara, twins Herbjørg and Hulda, Magnhild, Tordis, Kjellaug, Aslaug, Einar, Henrik, Solveig, and in the U.S., Alfred and Sonia. Herbjørg and Einar Pedersen were married in 1937. Their four children: Susan (1938), Einar Jr. (1939), Mark (1942-1982) and Ingrid (1946-2000). Einar died in 1989. Herbjørg died in 2008.

John G. Hendricks

*"Boy, if I'm going to work that hard,
I'm going to do it for myself."*

I lived in Norway, in a part of Sykkylven
called Aurdal, a short ferry ride from
Ålesund. I was about a month under ten
years old when we left for America. We
came into Seattle December 19th, 1930. We
stayed overnight in Ballard with my mother's
cousin, and then caught the ferry, over to the
south end of Kitsap County, where my father
had purchased 25 acres of land. It was my
mother and five kids; four boys and my younger sister. I was number
four. Before he got married, my father spent 1913 and 1914 fishing
halibut out of Seattle and in Alaska. He came over again in 1923. He
lost a commercial fishing boat in Norway in a storm. It left him heavily
in debt, so he came to this country to make it up. It took him seven years
to get enough money to bring us, the five kids and my mother, over.
We were poor farmers back in Norway, and we came to a sad situation
coming this way. Remember, 1929 or 1930 was not the best of times.

My father bought the tickets in this country and made all the
arrangements. He had gone through the naturalization process in
Ketchikan, Alaska and we children became citizens by his naturalization.
My mother had to take out her own. His name was Oscar Hendrick
Raftseth. He added an "s" to his middle name, and dropped the Raftseth
because he said everyone kept asking him, "How do you spell Raftseth?"

We came over on the *Stavangerfjord*, fairly new in 1928. The trip
took us eight days, and we more-or-less had the free run of the ship, as
long as we didn't get into the first class section. We didn't have any
problem at Ellis Island but I do remember it was cold. It was eight
degrees Fahrenheit — way colder than we ever got in Norway. It was
a raw cold that just went right through you. At Ellis Island we got on a
ferry to New York and to Grand Central Station. Then on a train to St.
Paul, where my mother had sisters and a brother. My mother got to see
her siblings who left Norway between 1901 and 1909. She was the last
of nine kids, and the last one to leave Norway. After two weeks there,
we continued to Seattle. My dad picked us up at the station and drove us
to Ballard where we spent a couple of days visiting my mother's cousin.

Olalla, in Kitsap County was our home. My father had bought 25 acres of land there, and a couple of cows, so we were in good shape.

When I first moved [to Ballard], I was fishing on the schooner *Celtic* with my brother. I went to California, came back and went to Alaska in the spring, 1945. After June, 1945, I came back to Seattle and worked for Northwest Ship Repair, on Westlake Avenue doing electrical work. Then I worked different yards up 'til about '46, when I worked for Puget Sound Bridge & Dredging, a shipyard and dredging company. They built the first floating bridge across Lake Washington.

I worked there as an electrician. In 1950, they built a new dredge for their dredging division and I was electrical foreman on the construction. At that time it was the biggest dredge in the world. And Horace McCurdy, president of Puget Sound Bridge & Dredging, came to me and said, "John, this is so big, you've got to go up to Alaska and show them how the electrical system works." So I thought, "Well, a couple of weeks won't hurt me. I'll go up to Alaska." A couple of weeks stretched into four months before I could break in a crew to get it in operation.

While I was up there, he said, "Broke all records of dredges up and down the coast," because in four months of operation in Wrangell Narrows out of Petersburg, we had less than an hour and twenty minutes of breakdown due to electrical problems. And most dredges, if you get by with eight hours a week, why, that's fine. In other words, if you don't break down, it's making money for the company. So I was proud of being the first chief electrician on board the boat. And then they needed a superintendent of ship repair, and I spent three years at that.

I said, "Boy, if I'm going to work that hard, I'm going to do it for myself." I quit and I came to Ballard.

I went to work for Lunde Electric here in Ballard, and I worked for them for some time. It was the same situation. I was putting in lots of hours. I says, "I'm working harder than I should for somebody else," so in 1961 I started Hendricks Electric, and we're still in business. We were located at 5109 Shilshole Avenue, which was Sagstad Marina at the time, and that's where I had a shop for ten years. In 1971 I moved to Fishermen's Terminal. We're still in there.

We work with anything that's electrical on boats. Automatic pilots, for instance. If a customer's boat breaks down anywhere in Alaska — if the generator quits working, they're out of business, and we fly up and fix it. That's what we're in business for. We don't just work on fishing boats. I've also done work on some pleasure boats. I went out to work on one pleasure boat, and the guy would drive up in a limousine. He'd be driving — his chauffeur was sitting in the back seat. He says, "Well, I know my company says I'm supposed to have a chauffeur, but I like to drive." He says, "John, I want to install this myself, and I want you to tell me what I'm doing wrong." That was his hobby, to do his own work. He was also involved in the Boy Scout movement. He was the national president, Norton Clapp.

We built all the panels for the remote pump stations on the Alyeska Pipeline. They got unmanned pump stations every so many miles. And somebody bid on building all them, and they needed their switch panels that had to meet the specifications. Do you know there wasn't a company anywhere near that built panels like they needed? Only one type of circuit breaker passed the inspection, and only two places in Seattle had Heineman circuit breakers: Boeing and Hendricks Electric. So we built all the remote panels, and that was a nice little contract. We finished them as quick as possible and every night I'd go out to the airport and ship them. The customer's air freight bill ran $20-30 thousand dollars a month. All the fittings had to be water-tight, they were steel, they couldn't leak, they had to be air-tested, and they were all threaded pipe. If you took a panel out from one place, you could put it in another, and it would fit exactly. In other words, they were identical, and that's not easy to do. But we did it. We built panels for lots of pipelines all over. My oldest son's son-in-law, in the service during Desert Storm went out on the pipeline. There he saw panels built by Hendricks Electric.

John Hendricks was born February 27, 1921 in Aurdal, near Ålesund, Norway. He immigrated with his mother, three brothers and a sister in 1930. His father came over in 1923. The family settled in Kitsap County. As a young man he came to Ballard to work as an electrician at shipyards and dredging companies. He started Hendricks Electric company in 1961. He married Doris Carlson in 1943. They have three children, Jeanne (1945), Stanley (1947) and Paul (1954). Both boys carry on the family business.

Greta Haagensen Roseberg

"To this day we have never had a Christmas without lutefisk. My children have always said they would not come home for Christmas if I did not have lutefisk."

My father, Wilhelm Hågensen, first came to the USA in 1924 and to Ballard first to go fishing seasonally. He fished out of California and Alaska, but his primary home was in Ballard with members of his family. He was engaged for ten years to my mother, Margit Kristiansen, and he came home every other year or so. He made more money coming here, and that was the purpose. In 1934, on a trip home, he married Margit; in 1935 I was born; in 1936 my brother Roald was born; and in 1937, we all came to the U.S. All four of us were born in Flakstad, Lofoten, Norway.

We came in October, 1937, to the home of my father's sister and her family, Fredrikke and Halfdan Nilsen in Ballard. [see Vatn p. 463 and Nilsen p. 380] My father, and many other fishermen, often lived in their home between fishing seasons. We then rented a house in Ballard and then in 1940, moved to California to follow the fish. In 1941 my father passed away in Monterey, California.

We returned to Ballard and lived close to my Aunt Fredrikke. Three fishermen, my mother's cousins, helped her with the down payment on a house at 2641 Northwest 63rd, right across the street from Adams Grade School and the Ballard Playfield. My mother got a job in the kitchen at Frederick & Nelson. After a couple years, she got domestic work through other Norwegian friends in some lovely homes in Madison Park, Capitol Hill, and in Ballard.

My mother cooked a lot of Norwegian foods to make extra money. We had an electric stove in the kitchen, but we also had a wood-burning stove. She made *lefse* on top of that wood-burning stove. She stacked the dry lefse on a shelf in the long narrow pantry, which included the sink and the ice cooler. She might get calls to sell it dry, by the round piece, or she might be asked to dampen and butter up a given number of a dozen. People would buy them for parties at home or lodge meetings. We children had to help her make that *lefse*. I felt it was very arduous. We stirred it with large wooden spoons and big heavy crocks between our knees. Mama also made *rullepølse* and pickled pigs feet for some Norwegian stores.

A man came by weekly, selling chickens. His name was Pasquale. There also was a bread man, a milkman and an egg man. Everyone was encouraged to have a victory garden during the war years. I don't think there was too much we were missing in our garden. We had a cellar door on the outside of the house leading to a dirt cellar with a slanted door [that you could slide down]. It opened up and out from the middle. That's where our fruits and vegetables and a lot of Mother's canning were stored.

The garage roof was fairly flat and it had apple trees on each side. We loved to lie down on that shed and pick an apple and chew on that apple, throw it away and pick another one. We would tell stories and look down at the playfield. It was a good life.

It was an arduous job to wash clothes. Our wringer washing machine was in the bathroom. Outside we would have a couple big tubs ready with boiling water; one with starch, another with blueing. The white clothes needed the blueing to make them even whiter. And ironing, oh, dear Gussy, there was a lot of ironing.

Every Saturday night we took our baths before going to chuch on Sunday. We didn't have central heating so in winter we bathed in big galvanized tubs in the kitchen. After we were through with our baths, we'd lay on our tummies on the floor and get a fruit treat or maybe a dish of Jell-O. We'd "watch" our tall old radio, while we listened to the radio programs. Baby Snooks was my favorite.

I'm reminded of a couple brief incidents that were very strong in childhood. One was when you had a childhood illness [chicken pox, measles, mumps, scarlet fever, diphtheria], you had to notify the health department. And they quarantined you. They came and slapped a sticker on your door, and no one could come in. And supposedly no one in the household could go out until that illness was over and the health department declared it so.

When Marcus Ness's fishing boat went off for the season, the wives and children, including us, would gather on the boat just before the boats went out. The wives would cook a big meal in the boat's galley, and we'd ride on the boat through the Locks, then get off at the end and walk home. You can't get on and off ships in the Locks now.

My brother and I would often go down to the docks to get jobs filling the shuttles needed to mend nets. We also made a little money by climbing over and under the fence up at the Olympic Golf Course.

We'd find golf balls and sell them. And in the winter we'd sled there. And I baby-sat. At age ten I helped a new mother in the neighborhood, with ironing, doing housework and taking care of the baby. I really felt burdened at that job.

There seemed to be a neighborhood grocery store on every other corner. The store on our block was owned by the Zimmerer family. Many of the neighbors came in, and if no one came when the bell rang, they would open up the till themselves. I did that. When I was older, about 10 to 12 years old, I sometimes helped him in the store, and I would write things down in the book. Mr. Zimmerer played the violin, and he gave me violin lessons. I helped him stock shelves — that was my payment for lessons, since my mother couldn't afford them. It was a thrilling, growing time for me, playing the violin.

But there came a restlessness about that violin when my friends decided to join the band in high school. The violin didn't fit. I got a summer job at Swanson's Nursery and earned money to buy a saxophone. I joined the Ballard High School Marching Band. I also played violin in the orchestra.

For me the best of downtown Ballard was Gerke's Music Store. Gerke's was on the west side of 24th, between 55th and 56th. Every music store had a resident piano player who would play any sheet music so you could decide if you wanted to buy it. Of course, it was just as much fun going just to listen. I spent hours there.

When I was young, the old Norway Hall was down on Boren Avenue at about Virginia. And then when Norway Center was built, we children were expected to be ready to get up on stage with a song to share for Christmas or other celebrations down there. And that evolved into the new Leif Erikson Hall down on 57th and 24th.

I remember Ballard Beach fondly. Ballard Beach was south of Golden Gardens. On the hillside there were a lot of cottages that don't exist any more. I often picked berries there with my mother and she would make jam. Ballard Beach was where we went to play in the water. There were pilings there where ferries had once landed.

Sometimes my mother would rent a rowboat at Ray's Boathouse. I don't remember that we ever tried fishing, but she liked rowing. She grew up with a rowboat outside her family home. There were no roads there when she was young.

We were 16 and 15 when Mama died. My brother then lived with the Marcus Ness family, a cousin of my mother and I lived with my Aunt Elly and her husband, Sam Bakke.

I had never had any hope of going to college, so I took a lot of business courses at Ballard High School so I could work while going to school and immediately upon graduation. When my mother died in my junior year at Ballard and the house was sold, I realized there would be some money for college. I went to Pacific Lutheran College and graduated from the University of Washington. I had a wonderful profession as a Dental Hygienist. I worked part-time in Ballard for Dr. Bleakney, and my second-cousin, Dr. Leif Gregerson. Then I worked 32 years in other long-time jobs.

I met Lee at Pacific Lutheran College. When I was at the U and ready to graduate in dental hygiene, I met him again, and we were married within a few months. So I was Mrs. Roseberg on my diploma, which was six years after I graduated from high school.

We moved to 9125 Cyrus Avenue, next door to my mother's cousin Marcus Ness. We now live at 9119 Cyrus. It's a quiet place with friendly neighbors, just off Golden Gardens Drive. We all have a little view of the Sound. To this day we have never had a Christmas without lutefisk. My children have always said they would not come home for Christmas if I did not have lutefisk. Trina and Tim love lutefisk, but my husband will not eat it, and yet his father, who was Swedish, loved lutefisk.

Greta Hågensen was born in Flakstad in Lofoten, Norway, September 27, 1935 to Margit (Kristiansen) and Wilhelm Hågensen. The following year her brother Roald (1936-1968) was born. The family came to Ballard in 1937. Wilhelm died (1941) and Margit died (1952). Greta attended Pacific Lutheran College and trained to be a dental hygienist at the University of Washington. She married Leland "Lee" Roseberg on March 23, 1958. They have two children, Trina (1959) and Tim (1962).

Randi Anderssen Ruud

"We were packed on that ship — absolutely packed. When we got into American waters, we were told that a German submarine followed us all the way across. There would have been panic on board ship had the passengers known that."

I was born in 1913 in Johannesburg, South Africa. My mother came from Oslo and my father, an engineer, came from Hamar, both from Norway. He had been down south at the turn of the century, just about this time a hundred years ago. Then he went back to Norway, then immigrated to the United States, about 1905 or 1906. He met my mother in Brooklyn. Her father, a sea captain, worked for the Texaco Company and was gone much of the time, but never to Norway. So my grandmother, my mother and two uncles immigrated to Brooklyn to keep the family together. My parents went to Norway and got married in Oslo. Soon after my brother was born my father decided South Africa was the best spot for making a living. He went on ahead and got a job and sent for my mother and brother. I was the second child. My sister, born after me, still lives in South Africa.

We talked a little Norwegian at home, and we went to an English speaking school, but there are also schools that are Afrikaans. It was compulsory that we learned Afrikaans. So, when we were maybe eight years old, we started with Afrikaans. By the time we were through high school, we were really proficient in Afrikaans, just as good as English. And yes, we held on to our Norwegian.

In 1937 there was an ad in our daily paper in Johannesburg. A mother and a daughter from Nairobi who had driven down for a vacation, were on their way back to Nairobi and they wanted two passengers. So, then Olav [Ruud] and I — we weren't married then — decided to go. It was a marvelous experience, but a long way — 3,000 miles. We drove on the Great North Road, which was no road, across the mountain and in grass.

We experienced some rain and got stuck in black soil. Before you know it several hundred blacks were there to help you get out. They were not used to seeing white people, but they were so helpful. Old women picked up rocks, some of them so heavy they put them on their head and held them there, and brought them to the car to get the car out of the mud.

The trip took six weeks. We camped out every night. We saw a lot of game. When we got to Nairobi, Olav went on. He took one of the Nile boats up to Cairo, then crossed the Mediterranean and went through Europe up to Norway. That was at the time Hitler was occupying the southern part of Europe.

I worked in Nairobi for a year and a half. My aim was to get to Norway one day — Nairobi was half-way there. It was wonderful, going on safaris and driving on the African plains and just sitting and watching the animals walking by. When I had saved enough money, I took the train to Mombassa, and then a British passenger ship through the Suez Canal and on to England and then to Oslo. Olav was in Oslo. I stayed with relatives — it was a big highlight for me to finally meet my Norwegian relatives. We went to America from Norway in 1939.

We were packed on that ship — absolutely packed. When we got into American waters, we were told that a German submarine followed us all the way across. There would have been panic on board ship had the passengers known that. We came right into New York. I didn't have to go to Ellis Island. I had no problems when I disembarked, perhaps because I had a British passport. I had relatives right in New York City and Olav was already there. He could talk English, and that was a big help, and, of course, English was my mother tongue.

We drove to Seattle from the East Coast with another couple. Olav and I were married in Seattle at Immanuel Lutheran Church.

When we came here in 1940, August Werner was directing the Norwegian Male Chorus and his wife Gertrude was directing the Norwegian Ladies Chorus. I got into the Ladies Chorus then. After his wife died, August directed the Ladies Chorus as well.

I've been with the Daughters of Norway from 1940, the Valkyrien Lodge, and I became a member of Leif Erikson Lodge of the Sons of Norway after Olav passed away, 30 years ago. I still attend the meetings every month and I still sing in the Norwegian Ladies Chorus.

Randi Anderssen was born January 9, 1913, in Johannesberg, South Africa. In 1940 she came to Seattle and she and Olav Ruud married. He was also an immigrant from Norway to South Africa. They have a son Olav, a daughter Karen and three grandchildren. She was widowed in 1972. Randi died on December 18, 2005.

COMING TO AMERICA:
AFTER WORLD WAR II

Immigration to the United States

1940-1945	241,708
1946-1960	3,379,556
1961-1980	7,720,849
1981-2010	26,837.537
TOTAL	38,179,660

United States: Foreign-Born Population

Place of Birth	1960	1970	1980	1990	2000
Denmark	85,060	61,410	42,732	34,999	36,241
Finland	67,624	45,499	29,172	22,313	20,540
Iceland	2,780	2,895	4,156	5,071	6,678
Norway	152,698	97,243	63,316	42,240	37,594
Sweden	214,491	127,070	77,157	53,676	53,246
Total	522,653	334,117	216,533	158,299	154,299

Source: American Community Survey, U.S. Census

Gudmundor Egill Jacobsen

"I love my country but you can never forget about where you're from. Never!"

My name is Gudmundur Egill Jacobsen, and I'm an immigrant from Iceland — came to the United States in 1945 when I was ten years old. I grew up in Iceland as Gudmundur Egill Oddsson. My father was Oddur so I became Oddson. My mother and father were divorced when I was about a year and a half old. I lived with my grandparents, Dr. Gudmund Gudfinsson and Margret Laurusdottir and my two aunts, sisters of my dad. My fondest days were probably going to a family farm on the south coast of Iceland.

My mother, Agla Brinhildur Jacobsen, decided to go to the United States and bring me with her. She had a sister married to an American in Seattle. We had to wait till the war was over to leave Iceland. German subs surrounded Iceland. We were not invaded, but Iceland was a very strategic place.

We left Iceland on October 14, 1945 on the *Span Splice,* a newly-commissioned freighter on its maiden voyage, It was also the captain's first crossing. We fourteen passengers shared a room in the lower part of the ship next to the engine room. It was a noisy journey.

I remember part of the journey so well. We met with a vicious hurricane with waves up to 50 feet high. The storm was coming from west to east and we were heading into it. We were tossed around and wound up on the north coast of Scotland. During the storm, water found its way into every area of the ship. The captain ordered every-body to quarters up on top, in case we had to evacuate. I wasn't afraid, but they were afraid I might be washed overboard, so they just strapped me in the bunk and that's how I went through the storm. My mother was frantic, but the captain very graciously calmed her.

Many days later the hurricane subsided, and the *Span Splice* arrived in New York, November 26th. The trip that was to take ten days had taken 43 days. I woke up one morning at dawn to silence. I heard no engines. From the porthole next to my bunk I saw buildings — a skyline of these incredible buildings. I thought it was a dream. The adrenaline started building up inside me. I jumped out of my bunk and ran upstairs.

Everybody else was still asleep. The ship had stopped out in the harbor. I saw these very large buildings in the distance. I turned around and I discovered another incredible sight, a large statue of a lady holding a torch. I had heard about this Statue of Liberty in school. I realized I was now in America.

Getting off the ship was an anticlimax. I knew no English but my mother could speak English. She had worked for the consulate in Reykjavik, but in spite of that, there was an error on her passport. They detained her for three days. Our relatives in New York were there to greet us, and they took me to their home while my mom was detained on Ellis Island until they got their records squared away.

We took the train to Seattle and we stayed a short time, with her sister, Tove Walters on Beacon Hill. I started school. For many years I had a hard time with the English language. They told my mother and Aunt Tove to stop talking Icelandic to me at home.

The teacher's desk was at one side of the blackboard and my desk, another just like the teacher's, was next to it, so I faced the other kids. I started in the first grade when I was ten and I was the biggest kid by far in that class. I kind of felt like Hugo, the big duck, because I was a big kid but I couldn't speak English. I got along with the kids and they were good to me, but we couldn't understand each other. It was a difficult time. And I couldn't speak Icelandic when I got home. They were speaking English.

Then we moved to Ballard. We rented an apartment on 70th and Earl with Sig Johnson and his wonderful mother, Sigurlaug Johnson. Mrs. Johnson got me off to school and when I came back from school, made sure I was okay. My mother took a bus early in the morning to her job at the telephone company. Sig was a lot older than me, but he became my friend.

My wife and I finally returned to Iceland in 1997. It was wonderful and inspiring. We met cousins, nephews and nieces and my half-brother and half-sister. We'll be back every year from now on, God willing. I love my country, but you can never forget about where you're from. Never!

Gudmundur Egill (Oddsson) Jacobsen was born Oct 8, 1935 to Brinhildur and Oddur Gudfinnur Gudmundsson in Iceland. In 1945 he and his mother immigrated to America. He married Sarah "Sally" Marshall in 1959. They have a son Eric and three granddaughters, Megan, Sarah & Emily.

Margarethe (Grethe) Cammermeyer

"When I was younger, and these folks were staying with us while they were waiting to escape from the Nazis in Norway, every time the telephone rang, or somebody rang on the door, the guests who were with us would take their plates and leave, so that there would be no indication that they had been sitting at the table. So, I started doing the same thing. Whenever somebody rang on the telephone, I'd take my plate and I would go into another room, so there'd be no indication that there were other people at the dinner table. My parents never corrected me on that until after the war."

I was born in Oslo, Norway, March 24, 1942. It was during the Nazi occupation of Norway. I lived with my parents in an apartment on the second floor in Camilla Colletsvei, which supposedly was catty-corner from Gestapo headquarters. My parents were working with the Norwegian underground, sheltering those at risk for being arrested by the Nazis. They had to flee Norway to Sweden or England because if found and arrested they would be interrogated, tortured, killed or sent to a concentration camp either in Norway or Germany.

My parents were sheltering those that were at risk for being picked up by the Nazis, so I was raised under the threat of being found out and killed. My mother, Margrethe Grimsgård Cammermeyer, used to say as I grew older that she was really pretty tough when they knew that the Nazis were going to be coming to our home until they knocked on the door the first time. That was intimidating and a reality shock of how dangerous it was to live under the Nazi reign.

We had a Polish refugee who had escaped from the concentration camp in Norway. He lived with us for several

Grethe and her mother during the war.

weeks until he could safely be taken out of the country. He would go out on our balcony, and sing Polish national songs whenever my mother would walk to the grocery store across the street. She would hear him from the street, and come charging back to get him to get off the balcony. Hearing these stories was exciting and frightening but generated pride at my parents' participation with the resistance forces.

Grethe and brother celebrating Norway's freedom in 1945.

My father was Johan Widding Cammermeyer, better known as Dr. Jan Cammermeyer MD. He was a neuropathologist. After the war, he was the first Norwegian to get a Rockefeller Fellowship, and went to Boston where he, and we, lived for nine months, and then went back to Norway.

When we came to Boston, we lived with this very prominent neurologist, Dr. Ray Adams MD, and his family, in their gorgeous home. Ray Adams was considered the father of modern neurology. We were with this very fine family. Whenever the doorbell or phone would ring I would take my plate and leave, because that's what I had been permitted to do during the war. It took several months for me to break that habit.

And then we went back to Norway I started school and went through the second grade. Then my father was invited to immigrate to the United States to work at the Armed Forces Institute of Pathology in Washington, D.C., for a number of years. Ultimately he transferred to the National Institutes of Health in Bethesda, Maryland, where he had his own neuropathology laboratory.

I was nearly nine when we came to the United States, not speaking English. Mathematics was the only subject I could do in school, and eventually when I learned to speak English I caught up with my classmates.

When you move to a new country and community you want to become part of that community. But my parents thought it very important we maintain both languages to retain our heritage so whenever we came home from school we would switch over to speak Norwegian. I got a little sloppy as a teenager and felt it was too much effort to switch languages so I only spoke English. Finally when I was a senior in high school I realized that if I didn't speak it [Norwegian] I was going to lose it and became quite avid about using my mother tongue.

I have four sons, and all of them were raised with Norwegian as their first, mother language. I spoke Norwegian to them from the day that they were born. My aunt, Aagot Grimsgaard, lived with us for a number of years and we all spoke Norwegian together which reinforced it for the kids.

Even today it is very unusual to speak English to my children, because it's been so automatic, that it's always been Norwegian. You could call it indoctrination.

In Washington, D.C., there were a lot of immigrants and lots of diplomats and we knew the Norwegian ambassador and his family and Bernt Balchen who flew over the North Pole. I didn't feel awkward until I went from elementary school to junior high and asked: "When is recess?" I did not know that in junior high you did not have recess. Everybody laughed at me and I didn't ask another question in school until I was a senior in college. That's how embarrassed I was by my own ignorance and I didn't want to be laughed at. But other than that I don't recall being ostracized in any way, or bullied because of being a foreigner.

In the early 1950s, when we came to America, it was a time when there was assimilation. So you didn't maintain your native language usually. You became an American, rather than being like a Norwegian-American, which is different from, probably the past 20 years, where all of a sudden you take your ethnic background, and tie it in with being American. So Norwegian-American is OK now, rather than to say you're just an American.

We [my parents and I] never talked about why they stood up against the Nazis, though looking back it was the right thing to stand up to defend your homeland. There was no question about that, both in their minds and in mine. You stood up for your country and did what needed to be done. It was the most natural thing in the world. It was just part of being Norwegians.

There was another story that my mother used to tell and that I have written in my own book, called "Serving in Silence." I was a baby used as a decoy where she would push a baby carriage around through town and just stroll along. Then we'd go into an alleyway and some people would jump out of the doorways. They would hand me to my mother while they would take the guns out from underneath my mattress. Then my mother would take me and we'd be on our way. She made it seem as though it was the most natural thing in the world. That's what every good Norwegian did. But it was never explicit.

I had always wanted to be a doctor and that was just part of my belief that's what I should do. Except that was not common in those days. Women's roles were as a teacher, wife, secretary or nurse. I ended up finding out about the undergrad nurse program where the Army would pay for two years of college, in turn you give back three years. Joining the Army Student Nurse program meant training to become a nurse. It fit in with having been part of the World War II experience as an infant, and being able serve where nurses should be taking care of the American service members.

I joined the Army student nurse program and went on active duty when women could not be married and be in the military. That policy changed. And while I was serving in Germany I met my husband-to-be and we dated for a year and then were married.

This was in the midst of the build-up for Vietnam and my husband got orders for Fort Lee, Virginia, and then to Vietnam. I was also transferred back to Fort Lee, Virginia, and asked to be sent to Vietnam if my husband were to go. He got orders for Vietnam; then I got orders. His were canceled and mine were not. So I was in Vietnam from February 1967 until May 1968 and my husband from May 1967 to May 1968.

I was forced to leave the military in 1968 when we started our family. Then in 1971-72 when the policy changed and women were allowed to have dependents and serve in the military, I rejoined but went into the Army Reserve. Now I was a part-time soldier, a mother, and I went back to graduate school to get my master's degree in neuroscience nursing. I also worked full-time in the Veterans Administration medical system taking care of soldiers. It was the whole package — send them to war, fix them up, take care of them afterwards.

Then my husband and I ended up divorcing. I left the area for a few years. The kids remained in the Seattle area with him. Then I came back and earned my PhD in nursing at the University of Washington. In the military I transferred from the Army Reserves and became the state chief nurse of the Washington National Guard.

I had — over an eight or ten years period — an epiphany. That epiphany was that perhaps there was a reason why I got divorced, and why my marriage always seemed a little off, and that I always felt different. I had related this to being Norwegian and an immigrant in America. That's enough to make anybody feel different. As time went on, I realized that I was a lesbian. It took a while for that to come to my consciousness. And it happened because I met "this woman" and couldn't quite put it all together for a while. The kids loved her and so did I.

There was going to be a clash between the military and my personal life. But I really believed that the military was going to take care of its own and that I'd already served for 25 years. I was decorated in Vietnam. I had a stellar military career and was finishing up my doctorate, so I wasn't exactly a dunce.

I had proved that I was a good nurse and a good leader, as a chief nurse of the National Guard. But I wanted to be a general. I applied for a top secret clearance and to be truthful said: "I am a lesbian."

Six months later, the military said that they were going to start discharge proceedings against me, based on my statement. I did not want to leave the military. Now it was my turn to stand up and challenge the military policy which prohibited homosexuals from serving in the military.

I decided that I was going to fight that discharge, because it seemed unfair and the policy was wrong. By this time, I had also learned that there were other gays and lesbians in the military, and many others who had experienced the same treatment and discharge. I got a legal team together, and after the military discharged me, I filed suit in federal court. Twenty-five months after my discharge, the court ruled that my discharge was unconstitutional and that I should be immediately reinstated.

There was a lot of notoriety around my case at the time, because people now began to question: "What's wrong with somebody who is homosexual and who's already served, and how dangerous could this grandmother be to serving in the military?"

There is a book and movie, "Serving in Silence," which describes in the events leading up to my discharge and lawsuit. Glenn Close played me, Colonel Cammermeyer. Barbra Streisand was one of the producers of the film. Curiously, after the final repeal of "Don't Ask Don't Tell" [the policy banning homosexuals from service in the United States military] the Norwegian newspaper, *Aftenposten*, printed a long article entitled: "Hun Forandret USA" April 21, 2012. It gave me credit for changing the USA. Obviously that gives me much too much credit, but it is nice to be recognized as a Norwegian taking on the American government and winning for social justice.

Margarethe (Grethe) Cammermeyer is a retired colonel from the United States Army Nurse Corps. Cammermeyer earned a nursing degree from the University of Maryland and a master's and doctorate from the University of Washington. She served in Vietnam and Germany and in numerous stateside posts. She retired from the National Guard in 1997. She is the mother of four sons, Matt, David, Andy and Tom Hawken. Andy died in 2007 in a snowmobile accident. On July 23, 2007, Cammermeyer and Diane Divelbess registered as domestic partners in Washington state. They reside in Langley, Washington.

Preben and Ruth Eva Hoegh-Christensen

"We were determined to take care of ourselves."

PREBEN: In 1940 I was an assistant dance teacher. Going up to a tournament my partner was sick. So I asked Ruth to substitute for her. She said I was crazy — she was just a beginner. But we went to the contest and we won it and we have been dancing ever since and that's now 60 years ago. We got married in 1942 during the German occupation. My aunt and uncle visited Denmark in 1947 after the war.

RUTH: His uncle promised to help him. Preben had wanted to be a doctor in his young days, but his father could not afford his education. So when he was in Denmark, Uncle had said, "You come over and I will teach you to be a physical therapist," which he was for the Ballard Hospital at that time.

PREBEN: We had the Russian army sitting on a Danish island [Bornholm]. They were there 18 months after the peace treaty was signed after the last World War. So I said to Ruth, "Let's go to the United States." We didn't speak English at all, but we just took a chance on it. We packed up, bought a ticket to a ship, the only cabin left. It was next to the captain and quite expensive, $706. We had used so much money on the shipping, we couldn't go on the railroad — we got tickets for the Greyhound bus.

RUTH: When we left Denmark, we had quite a bit of formal clothes — Preben had a tuxedo and I had all these long dresses I had used when we danced together in competition. The captain saw us dance up there in the ballroom and he asked us if we would dance for him at his captain's dinner. That was some experience.

PREBEN: So we came into New York and we sat at the Greyhound Bus Station till one o'clock at midnight. We hadn't had anything to eat all day, so we bought a whole handful of bananas. And there in the bus station we sat peeling and eating bananas like two monkeys.

RUTH: Uncle and Aunt lived down in Ballard in a little green house right across from Ray's Boathouse. The lot went all the way down to the railroad tracks. There was a rockery with a little bridge over it to the kitchen where we went in. We thought maybe we would have a meal now — they had just been eating. But they didn't offer us anything. Later on we had a cup of coffee. So that was the beginning of our first day in United States with his relatives from Denmark. I went to bed, crying.

We came to Ballard in November, and Aunt had been sick so I took care of the house and did the cooking. We walked to Ballard, got 25 cent from Uncle to buy a loaf of bread up at Van de Kamp — it was 18 cents at that time. On Saturdays, Preben and I cleaned his whole clinic. And it was loaded with venetian blinds. He had four rooms and I said to myself, whenever I get a place here in the United States, I was never going to have venetian blinds. I didn't like that work. I washed every blind off with a rag. And washed all the clothes and hand-ironed all the linen he used in the clinic.

When the train came by, the train man blew his whistle. Then he leaned out the window and waved and we waved back to him. That was our entertainment there. When Aunt got better, we visited some of their friends in Ballard on Saturday. Uncle took the car and drove us around. Nobody was home, so he went to the door, put a slip on the table that we had been there.

PREBEN: There was an open-door policy in Ballard at that time. There were no closed doors. It was interesting. Yes.

RUTH: After we had been here for a while, Uncle said to Preben, "What in the hell did you come to United States for? You can't even speak English and you don't even have a trade." So I said, "Well, I've been a bookbinder for four years in Denmark. If I can get a job, I'll be happy to help out again and we can start a new life here." Uncle said he would try to see if he could help Preben get a job. He knew a landscaping gardener. And he did. And Preben did get a job with that landscaping gardener, but not before January.

We were looking forward to go to this Christmas party. I ironed one of my good dresses, to wear that night. Aunt told me, "You're not going wear that. People don't dress up like that." So that was a big letdown. We were looking forward to dressing up for a nice evening out. We ended up sitting on the balcony, just looking at people downstairs in the Danish Hall, down on 14th Avenue.

PREBEN: I got to start with this landscaping gardener. The first week

Preben and Ruth Eva Hoegh-Christensen - 101

I only had ten cents to meet him at different places. I didn't have any lunch the first week. I didn't want to ask him for money. But I made it. I never had had a shovel in my hand, but I made up my mind I was going to continue with that.

After the first month, Uncle said, "You're moving tomorrow. My son is coming home with his new wife." He took us around and finally we found a nice place in Ballard on top of the house and there was a stairway outside and they charged $69. We had to share the bathroom with other people in the same building. When we first moved out of their house, they didn't give us any blankets or pillows.

RUTH: So we slept with our winter coats on the couch. I couldn't make a hot meal because I had no kettles, but we asked Preben's uncle and aunt to come over tomorrow, Easter Sunday, and have a sandwich. They came and Preben said I was crazy to do that. But I said, "Preben, I don't want any hard feelings with your family, because we don't know anybody else. And we have to get along." And I felt good we could do that.

After we had stayed one year there in Ballard, some friends found us a place on Capitol Hill. So we moved on Capitol Hill.

We were determined to take care of ourselves.

Preben Hoegh-Christensen was born December 8, 1918, Ruth Eva (Lieberg Andersen) was born March 21, 1920, both in Denmark. They were married August 2, 1942. They immigrated to Ballard in 1947. Preben worked in a government office in Denmark, and first got into landscape gardening in this country. He worked at Frederick & Nelson's Department Store in receiving and price-marking from 1950 until he retired in 1982. He got a Bachelor's degree in Business Administration from the University of Washington in 1954 — his Danish Master's degree was not recognized in this country. Ruth was a book-binder and she practiced her craft here in Seattle as well. Preben and Ruth have been active supporters of the Danish Brotherhood & Sisterhood, the Seattle Symphony, the Bellevue Philharmonic, the Vienna Ball, Overlake Hospital and the Nordic Heritage Museum.

Rita Vermala-Koski

"So my mother made a call at Christmas-time--I believe I was probably about five years old--and she wanted to speak with her daughter. I came on the phone. I didn't understand a word she was saying. She didn't understand a word I was saying, and she was crying her heart out on the other end. I was just shrugging my shoulders, and my foster parents couldn't do anything because they didn't speak a word of Finnish. So that was traumatic for her, and a few months later she said she wants her daughter back in Finland."

I'm an only child. My parents, Aino and Sergei Vermala, met on a cruise to Estonia when they were young. My dad was born in Russia. My mother was born in Finland.

I lived a rather charmed, wonderful childhood, maybe because I was an only child. Life was good according to pictures, anyway, and stories that I heard in my younger years. My first real recollection of any kind of things being out of the normal was one fall mid afternoon when I heard

sirens. My father was home. He had not had to report for army duty yet.

Mom and Dad were home, and the alarms sounded. My father ordered my mom and myself out of the house. We lived in a high-rise apartment building onto a grassy cliff that was covered in fall leaves. I heard some airplanes I thought, overhead, and I heard some popping noises. At that time I didn't know what popcorn was, but now I realize that it sounded like popping popcorn.

My father pushed me down to the ground very hard and flew right on top of me and covered my body with his body. He didn't have time to say anything to me certainly. I'm sure he probably told my mom to get down on the ground, too. What the popping noise was and what I viewed from underneath being under my dad were the leaves just jumping all over and around us, the fall leaves.

What I later found out was that they were Russian bombers making their first attacks on Helsinki. They had machine-gunners at the back of their bombers, and the machine-gunners were trying to do as much damage as they could. Now the interesting thing is why did we go outside? Why would you be told to go outside if there's an attack alarm? In those days for some reason, that was the rule.

Well, I had a chip on my shoulder, you can imagine, for quite a while against my dad. It wasn't funny to be shoved down when you're just a little girl. But those memories soon faded, and my dad joined the army.

My mother was very active in the home-front women. The order of the day again was that everybody who had gold rings would put them in for collection. They got a little iron band in exchange for this support to fund and to outfit the Finnish Army. That was a part of it. Anybody who had reasonable linen sheets, pillowcases, whatever, they were torn into strips for bandages for the Red Cross and for the Army Corps of medics to use on the home front.

There was sacrifice and duties for youngsters and children as well. Our chore was to collect, for example, dandelion roots. They were then dried and then made into chicory, which was like a pretend coffee for the forces. We also collected raspberry bush leaves, which again were dried, and they were made into a kind of a tea. So there was something for everybody to do during those years.

After a while my mother felt that it really was unsafe for me to be in Finland. Mom and Dad had made arrangements. My father was in the hotel business, so he had colleagues in Stockholm. Arrangements were made for me to be transported to Stockholm to stay with a family that we knew.

So I went the first time, I believe it was 1940 or maybe 1941, on a ship from Åbo to Stockholm, was met by my Swedish family, and became a part of their family very quickly. I learned to speak perfect Swedish very quickly and totally forgot Finnish.

So my mother made a call at Christmastime — I believe I was probably about five years old — and she wanted to speak with her daughter. I came on the phone. I didn't understand a word she was saying. She didn't understand a word I was saying, and she was crying her heart out on the other end. I was just shrugging my shoulders, and my foster parents couldn't do anything because they didn't speak a word of Finnish. So that was traumatic for her, and a few months later she said she wants her daughter back in Finland.

Things had calmed down anyway, so I was shipped back to Finland. Of course, it didn't take me more than a few weeks to relearn my Finnish, and I never did forget my Swedish, thank goodness. Soon after I came back from that first trip, things started heating up again. The alarm sirens were going off almost every day. The orders were to go into the bomb cellars, and there was one time that we spent six nights in the bomb cellar without being able to come up at all.

We forged a lot of great friendships. Obviously, the families pretty much knew each other living in the apartment complexes, but we forged stronger friendships and a lot of innovative ways to entertain the children. A lot of these bomb shelters were also cellars, so people would have their supply of potatoes there. We learned to carve faces on potatoes and make puppets out of them and do all kinds of goofy stuff.

As soon as that longest stay in the bomb shelter was cleared, Mom decided that if it's going to be like this, Rita might as well go back to Stockholm. So this time I was put on a bomber plane. Yeah, it was a bomber, but all the guts were taken out. There were about eighty or ninety of us children that were all strapped down on the floor of the bomber. We flew over to Sweden the second time.

I think the reason we were flown was that it was not safe anymore to have ships traveling between Finland and Sweden, especially passenger ships, because the waters were mined. There was a lot of war activity going on. So back I went to the family then. The second time I was enrolled in a school in Stockholm, Sofia Folkskola.

I went there for a full year, had an incredibly wonderful teacher, learned a lot of incredibly wonderful things about growing, making, and an appreciation for life. We grew our own wheat on a windowsill. We dried it. We chafed it, separated the kernels. We ground it between two rocks and made bread out of the flour that we made. It was just wonderful for a city girl to see how it really happens. It's great.

I stayed there for a year that time, and then came back home and went for the next two years of school in Helsinki. Then the war ended.

My father came back from the war. He went back into the hotel business. Now, he was born in Saint Petersburg, Russia, and he escaped during the Revolution in 1917 to Finland with his grandmother and his aunt, who had a condominium in Helsinki. He was five years old.

Dad was then brought up by these two wonderful ladies and went on to be a great school boy and a wonderful attribute to the community. He was a water polo player and went with the Finnish water polo team to Berlin in the 1936 Olympics. He was on the governing board of the orphan boys' home or shelter in Helsinki. He was very active, a very positive, very wonderful, fun, kind guy, but his past caught up with him.

After the war, the war crimes tribunals started, and people were being brought in to answer for war crimes against the Russian people. It was an agreement between the Finnish government and the Russian government that this could take place. So we had a knock one evening at our home, and Dad answered. He was asked to step outside, and we didn't see him for a day or two after that.

Records indicated that he was born in Russia, was a Russian citizen, and had fought in the Finnish Army against the Russians throughout the war. In other words it was a Russian fighting against the Russians, so therefore he would be charged with war crimes against Russia.

He came back from that. I don't remember very much, but things started happening that I later on realized were some sort of preparations being made, which I didn't pay much attention to. I was going to school, playing outside, having a good time, going to Girl Guides, and whatever.

Then probably about a month or so after that first knock on the door came a second knock on the door. This time Dad was interrogated for about two days, and he got home from there, too. That time I remember he came home and he was very pale.

He and Mom went in the kitchen, closed the doors, and had some sort of a pow wow. It wasn't too long after that that we simply escaped from Finland to Sweden, long story short, because Dad would have been arrested and sent, I don't know, to Siberia or whatever.

So there we were in Sweden. Dad was a Russian citizen. No passports to go anywhere, but he had his army papers to show that he'd been in the Finnish Army. Mom and I were issued Finnish passports, so we were basically free to go wherever there would be immigration availabilities, through the intervention of the president's wife, Alli Paasikivi. Paasikivi was president of Finland at the time. Alli Paasikivi and my grandmother had gone to the same girls' school in Helsinki. So through her intervention, [I] have no idea what all was done, but lo and behold after about three months my father was issued a Finnish passport by the Finnish embassy in Stockholm. Off we went by ship from Gothenburg to New York. We were given a forty-eight-hour transit to go through the United States, that was the longest we could stay in the States, and to Canada.

So that in a nutshell is what happened in the war years. They were memorable. I was shielded from a lot of the agony obviously. I was shielded from the lack of food, the lack of clothing. My mother always made sure that I had something to eat, several versions of oatmeal porridge if nothing else.

Rita Vermala was born in Helsinki, Finland in 1936, immigrated to Montreal, Canada, with her parents in 1947, then to Chicago, Illinois in 1963 and moved to Seattle in 1981. Mother of three and grandmother of five, Rita now lives in retirement with husband Alvar Koski in Mukilteo, Washington. In 1968 Rita found work at a local travel agency in the Chicago area and began a career that continued for some 40 years. In Seattle Rita was offered the opportunity to buy the agency she was managing and that deal worked out well for all concerned. Rita has been president of Finlandia Foundation Seattle Chapter, Nordic Heritage Festival and Finnish-American Chamber of Commerce of the Northwest. She was on the board of trustees for both the Nordic Heritage Museum Foundation and Finlandia Foundation National; served on the Finnish Lutheran Church Council and was an officer for SSK/Finnish School of Seattle and Lloyd W. Nordstrom Guild of the Seattle Children's Hospital - serving as treasurer for both organizations; volunteering at community events as well as raising funds for Seattle Children's Hospital. Rita chaired Northern Lights Auktions for NHM and served as vice-president for the National FinnFest USA in 1989, a five-day festival, held on the University of Washington campus. In 2002 Rita Vermala-Koski received Knight, Order of the Lion of Finland medal awarded by the President of the Republic of Finland, Tarja Halonen, in recognition of civilian merit in support of Finnish culture in the USA.

Norman Westerberg

"I was very proud to have a little Army certificate [so I could] move on my little bicycle in the city when there were air raids. If they didn't have telephone contact with headquarters downtown I was going to go there by bicycle."

The name Westerberg comes from Sweden, southeast of Stockholm in the archipelago. My great-grandfather was a sea pilot. And his father, too. About eight Westerbergs have worked as pilots and head sea pilots at that station. It was quite a life. When they saw a ship coming, they jumped into a small sailboat. They had to get first to the ship to get the job.

But my grandfather moved to Finland in 1894, when my father was two years old, and founded a wine store. He did very well. It was the biggest, best-known wine store in Helsinki on Alexander Street. And then came prohibition and he lost everything. Finland, like the United States, had prohibition for about 10 years in the 1920s.

My mother, Hellin, was born in Loviisa, a small city about a hundred kilometers east of Helsinki and very Swedish-speaking. Her grandfather, Johannes Carlson, was known as Skipper Muufa. Muufa is mother's father and he had four girls. And together the girls had about 30 children. He was a fiddler and, also, he was a farmer who had his own home, but on somebody else's property. He had to work some days for the owner. He was a fiddler at weddings and things like that. And he composed a folk song called *Skipper Mufa's Wedding March*. My mother used to sing that. My younger brother Sven, who played violin, wrote down the music for the Loviisa fiddlers. I have a tape of one of their presentations of that song on the Finnish radio and this tape has been used at all of our three children's weddings.

So when somebody asks me, "What are your roots?" I feel strongly about the Swedish, Finnish, farmers and fishermen. My grandfather Lennart was a fish peddler, and my grandma used to sell fish in Loviisa. He took, in the winter, every week, two horse loads or sleds with frozen fish to the St. Petersburg Market. Finland was part of Russia.

From Loviisa to St. Petersburg. A lot of Finns lived there. At that time there were two Finland-related congregations in St. Petersburg, one Finnish and one Swedish-Finn. And they each had about 20,000 members. St. Petersburg was really very important for Finland at that time, before hell started breaking loose.

My father was born in 1892. About 1925 he emigrated to work in America. He ended up in Detroit where he had connections with good Swedish friends that were involved in this Swedish-American ship line. He was an agent for that but he basically worked on an automobile assembly line. My mother arrived two years earlier. She was born in January 1900. So she was about 23 years old when she went over with four other girls in their twenties from Loviisa, all heading to Vancouver Canada where the husband of one of the girls had gone and said, "Now you can come. Take your friends with you." They all went to Vancouver except my mother who met a Finnish girl on the ship that they really liked and those two stayed in Toronto. She ended up in Windsor working as a maid and a cook for a very wealthy family. She learned English there very well.

Windsor was just a short ferry ride from Detroit. She and my father, Sven Eric, met at a Finnish club in Detroit and married. I was born on February 10, 1928. In January 1930, my mother and I took a Swedish-American line back to Finland and my father followed a few months later.

We landed in Helsingfors (Helsinki in Finnish), and I spent my first several years there. My father had an interesting job because of his languages. For several years he worked for Hotel Kamp, an illustrious hotel known all over Scandinavia.

And then when I started school, my father thought that it was a good idea for me to learn German. But I only did kindergarten and first grade because my father got a job in Turku. That's where I feel my hometown is.

Some years before, in 1916-1917, my father had worked at a Finnish trading company in St. Petersburg, Russia. Finland became independent on the sixth of December 1917. There were still a lot of Russian soldiers in Finland and, of course there were many, many people, especially factory workers, that sympathized with the idea of being associated with Russia and getting the socialist movement to power in Finland. They realized - we don't want to be a part of Russia. But they also didn't want to take all the orders from the factory owners and people like that. But the farmers in the North said we don't want to have anything to do with that. So they arose and organized and were called the Whites. The others were Reds, so there was really a civil war, and that was terrible. There were tens of thousands killed. My father and a couple of his working friends skied from St. Petersburg. There was a skirmish between the White and the Red. Then he was sent to be trained for about three weeks, and then to the final battles in April 1918. He participated in those as an officer on the side of the White Army.

Years later, in 1939, things started to happen. We knew that Russia and Germany had made a non-aggression treaty. But we didn't know that there was a secret paragraph that said that Russia would take care of the Baltic countries and Finland. And Germany would take care of Denmark and Norway. Pretty soon after that, Germany and Russia both had beaten Poland and threatened the small Baltic countries and Finland. They demanded use of air and ship ports, but soon had occupied the Baltic. Finland said, "No." And then, of course, on the thirtieth of November, 1939 they attacked Finland.

And they were thoroughly beaten by Finns in the Winter War. My father was running around there, as a 50-year-old officer. It was hard on him. I'm lucky to have some of his hand-written reports about his experience. Already, three months before the invasion by Russia, he had been called in for maneuvers.

His battalion was sent down to the Loviisa area during the beginning of the war and on New Year's Eve, they were sitting up on trucks, open flatbeds, in minus 40 degrees, going to the front. He had diabetes and was overweight. And on the first or second day of the battle, he pretty much collapsed. The doctor said, "You're not going to run around here. We're going to send you back."

Later, during the Continuation War, which was from 1941 to 1945, he was way north in northern Finland, commander of a prison for Russian POWs. I have a picture, hand-done with pencil, by a Russian colonel who was the highest officer there. My father spoke enough Russian so that often in the evening my father invited the colonel to his room and they put the fire burning and told stories.

After the war he was very sick all the time. He died in 1949, 56 years old.

I was a soldier boy. There were 70,000 of us. Some of us were more organized and paraded and had exercises. I did that a little bit. In 1941 at the age of twelve, I worked for several weeks as a messenger for an anti-aircraft Unit in Turku (Åbo in Swedish). I was very proud to have a little Army certificate [so I could] move on my little bicycle in the city when there were air raids. If they didn't have telephone contact with headquarters downtown I was going to go there by bicycle.

I was going to school in Turku since 1932. The war started and schools closed. All the children were sent out of the city. I and my two younger brothers were sent to a known family about five miles south of the city. Turku was bombed heavily. Most of the housing was wood, ideal for the Russian bombs which were usually just fire bombs. The bombers used to come right over us. We were up there looking at them. They had their bases in Estonia. It only took them ten minutes to fly over Helsinki.

The Soldier Boy:
Turku, Finland 1942

We were there a little bit over a month or so when the opportunity to go to Sweden came. Sweden actually invited us and the Finnish women decided that it's OK to go. I turned eleven that day and my brother was a year and a half younger, so he was nine, and then we had a four-year-old little brother, Finn. So the three of us went with hundreds of other kids with our name tags by train.

We travelled from Turku north to Tornio. There we walked over the bridge to the Swedish city of Haparanda. And so we were put on a train south to Stockholm. It took three days to go up there and then back down to Stockholm. This was in February 1940. And there we were given assignments of where to go, where we were to be shipped, maybe got some new clothing if needed, and food, and things like that. Me and my brother Sven, the nine-year-old, were sent close to the border. There was a family that had seven children. They were elderly, and the youngest child was my age and was home, so that's why they took me and my brother, but they didn't want the four-year-old. But he ended up with a very nice young couple in Stockholm. We were there only a couple of months because the war ended about a month after we came there. By then there were no ships or anything to get home, so we were there until early May, when we went back. Then there was about a year and a half before the war started again.

There were seventy thousand children that were sent to Sweden during the war. Most of them were very small, two- or three-year-olds. They spent maybe four or five years and they really didn't want to come home to parents who didn't understand Swedish, and had very poor conditions.

In 1947, after the war, there still was harassment, because of the Russian influence, although Finland was independent. The government, for the first time, had a big Communist party as dominant. A lot of people, if they could, moved to Sweden. My father was very sick, and pretty much stayed in Finland in health centers, and things like that. But my mother and my two younger brothers moved to Sweden. My mother came back when she was retired and settled in her birth city of Loviisa.

And so, in 1947 I graduated from high school. I was the only one in Finland. My father traveled to both places. So I took the entrance exam to chemical engineering at Åbo Academy Swedish University. And then I said, I can't do that with a family the way it is. I went to Sweden for one year. I learned that being born in the United States I should have the right to citizenship. And my mother had a birth certificate so it took me about a month to get a U.S. passport.

*Norman and Benita's
1950 wedding photo*

I first had a wild idea that they're going to draft me anyway, so why don't I at least enter the U.S. Army in Germany? But they didn't want me because I didn't speak any English. So, I stayed in Sweden for a year but then I realized I'm not getting anywhere here so I went back to study. In high school I already knew Benita, now my wife. That summer after we graduated we were pretty close. But then I said bye-bye and during the next year we had no contact. But then when I decided to go back she had studied one year at Åbo Academy. We married in 1950.

When I graduated, we talked about why don't we go [to the United States] for a couple of years? "I have a passport, you know, why don't we do it?"

So when I graduated in 1953 we decided to start plans. I applied for a visa for Benita and it took forever. I found out later that it was the [Sen. Joseph] McCarthy thing: That's a Finn, so a Finn must be a Communist. Even if she was married to a U.S. citizen, they would not give one to her.

In February 1954, almost on my 25th birthday, I flew all the way alone. At the entry in New York City I had to fill out a piece of paper to send to the Army Selective Service. About three weeks later, I was working for an old friend of my parents from Detroit. By early June I was in the Army. Benita was in Finland and I was in South Carolina and then the people I had stayed with contacted a senator friend. It didn't take long and Benita got her visa. We spent about three months together. She got pregnant and I was ordered to transfer to Germany. She was a Finnish citizen. The Army would not pay for her coming and joining me. So she stayed alone in Massachusetts, rented a room for $7 a week.

That was in 1954. I landed in Germany two days before Christmas Eve and was sent to a unit called military intelligence. And in June 1955, our first born, Danny, was born at the military hospital in Massachusetts. A week before Danny was born Benita was sworn in as a U.S. citizen. It was a special law: If your husband was in the Army abroad you could get citizenship quickly. In September 1955 they joined me in Munich.

When we went back to the U.S. we went to the same place she had lived, Gardner, Massachusetts. Lots of Finnish-Americans there, Finchburg next door. But then, I took a job in Ohio so we moved to Cleveland for two years. They wanted me to take the professional engineering exam. There were fifteen-hundred taking it and six hundred passed and I had the highest score.

[But] we decided to go back to Finland in 1958 and I joined this company, Ekono Consulting Engineering, that was the oldest engineering company in Finland, started in 1911. We were in Helsinki where daughter Christine was born 1960. Then we were sent to Oak Ridge, Tennessee for a year, for me to study nuclear power safety. Son Kenneth was born there.

In 1965 I became manager for international affairs. We started increased exporting. I got the job to open an office in Seattle. So in 1967, all five of us came to Seattle and really liked it. And then, after two years, I was called back. I was mostly involved in foreign affairs and taking care of high VIPs from other countries. In 1971 I was promoted to Senior Vice President for Ekono. It involved much travel world-wide, and I eventually learned that we could just as well have our home in Seattle. So in 1979 we made a final move from Helsinki to Bellevue. I worked at Ekono, Inc. in Bellevue. It had grown fine since I left it in 1969. I served a few years as its President. But I soon noted that I had competing interests, wonderful opportunities to be involved in activities in the Finnish and Nordic communities. I retired from Ekono in late 1986. For some time I worked for myself under the name ENW International.

As to the Finnish Expatriate Parliament (FEP) we have many organizations that have approved the bylaws and things for the parliament and [may] send a representative to the session that's held at two or three year intervals. A total of about 250 or so from the whole world come to Helsinki for maybe two or three days of meetings and submit initiatives about youth matters, senior matters, and what have you. So it's fun, a big thing. And at the first session in 1998 when they elected vice-speakers, I was elected vice-speaker for this U.S. area. The work is ongoing.

Eric Norman Westerberg was born in Detroit in 1929, but grew up in Finland. He earned master's degrees in chemical and nuclear engineering and worked worldwide as a consultant to the forest products and nuclear industries. He and his wife Benita, with their three children, moved to Seattle permanently in 1980. Norman has held leadership roles in more than twenty Finnish/Nordic organizations, including FinnFest USA, the Advisory Board of the University of Washington Scandinavian Department, the Nordic Heritage Museum and the Swedish Finn Historical Society. He was founder/President of the Finnish American Chamber of Commerce in 1981 and served as Washington State Honorary Consul of Finland from 1985 to 2000 and vice-speaker of the Finnish Expatriate Parliament. Norman is a Knight Commander of the Finnish Order of the Lion.

*Norman Westerberg with Tarja Halonen,
the President of Finland, at FinnFest USA 2004 in Florida.*

Stig B. Andersen

"When World War II and the occupation [of Denmark] ended, it was not like the world just suddenly turned beautiful. There were a lot of serious problems in all the previously occupied countries, economy, industry and what have you -- everything had been torn apart. The political situation had become oppressive with the Russian forces now occupying all of Eastern Europe and also occupying the Danish island of Bornholm for almost a year after the surrender of the German forces. So we were looking at moving out of Europe."

Ruth & Stig Andersen

My father had a sister, who in the early 1930s had moved to Santa Monica, California. She provided the guarantee to the United States government in order that we could be accepted as immigrants, given "green cards" and not become a burden to the public. We left Denmark on December 31, 1948, and arrived in Hoboken, New Jersey, on the eleventh of January 1949 with, officially, fifty dollars per person in our pockets.

My family consisting of my parents, Inger and Finn Andersen, and my brother Ib and me made our way across the country in a car we bought with dollars from the black market in Denmark. We travelled the southern route to avoid winter snows, but California was colder than anywhere else when we arrived. I was amazed to see all these kerosene pots under the orange plants trying to keep them warm. It was not what I had expected.

In Santa Monica we stayed with my father's sister and her daughter. I went to school at Santa Monica High School and was classified as a junior, the same level as I had left in Denmark. After six weeks my father changed jobs and moved to Santa Barbara, then he got a better job in Fresno, so we moved there. I transferred to Fresno High School and, having figured out how far along students were and where I could place myself, I was able to talk them into making me a senior. The level of what I had been taught in the gymnasium in Denmark was considerably higher than the level in the American high schools at that time.

After high school graduation, I got my first job in America: cleaning toilets in a waffle shop. After a few weeks I was promoted to dishwasher. Then I got a job as elevator operator in a third-class hotel with about six floors and an old-fashioned cage elevator where you had to really adjust the brake when you came in for a landing so you could come out even.

My father was a master cabinet maker and furniture designer who had had his own factory in Denmark, where he had designed and made furniture primarily for a large Danish bank and police stations throughout the country. In the U.S., in the beginning, he worked mainly as a draftsman. Towards the end of August, however, my father became ill and for the sake of family security, it was decided to move back to Denmark. In order to do so, we needed funds for the tickets. My father had brought his two prize pieces of furniture along from Denmark, and he gave those to a Danish family against $500 each, and the promise that we could have them back any time we wanted. The pieces were a standing clock that he designed and made in 1929, and for which he received a silver medal and a stipend to study in Paris. The other, a sideboard, was his masterpiece, the examination piece that qualified him as a master cabinetmaker. It also received a silver medal. Years later I was able to recover those items. I kept the clock and my son, Peter, inherited the sideboard.

Back in Denmark, I applied for admission at the university on the basis of my American high school diploma, but was told: "No way." So I went back to my old gymnasium – a year behind my regular classmates – but fit right in where I left the year before.

My father's medical problem had improved and in late September 1950 the family returned to America aboard the steamship, *Bolivia*. We could only be out of the U.S. for one year or else our visas would expire, but we returned just inside the deadline. We then went by Greyhound bus to Grand Rapids, Michigan, where my father started looking for a job and got hired by Baker Furniture in Holland, Michigan. We rented a little loft some place, a couple of rooms, and I started looking for a college to continue my education. I felt very fortunate to find Hope College in town and be admitted, even though the semester had started six weeks earlier.

To finance my tuition at Hope College, I worked at a variety of jobs including in a souvenir manufacturing woodshop and retail store where I learned how to carve and decorate "klompen" – Dutch wooden shoes.

I was accepted to the University of Michigan Medical School in Ann Arbor and started my medical studies. That took just about every minute of 24 hours of the day and was a lot of hard, demanding work. I could not work during the school year, but I did get a job during vacation and summer breaks at Spring Lake Country Club, near Grand Haven, where I was a bartender. That was a very neat job. It was a pleasant, small country club with many very friendly members. I got a chance to play golf, gratis, in the mornings before the course officially opened, except that I didn't really know how to play. But it was great to be out walking on the pretty green fairways.

During the fourth year of medical school, I was accepted to become an extern for three months at the local hospital in Charlotte Amalie, St. Thomas, in the Virgin Islands. With my Danish background it became a particularly interesting three months because the island had belonged to Denmark until 1917. Some of the old natives had actually been educated in Denmark and spoke Danish. Although I had a hard time suddenly transferring to Danish, it worked out all right and I had many wonderful experiences, getting accepted as a local rather than a tourist and I got in on seeing a lot of stuff that one would not get a chance to see or experience as a tourist.

To relieve my chronic economic crunch I had applied for and been accepted into the U.S. Army medical student program, which amounted to getting a commission as second lieutenant in the Medical Service Corps and being placed on active duty with station at the medical school. In return, after I finished school I then had to 'pay back' year for year with true military service. I had no problem with paying back a year or two or three, for I was pretty desperate for money and it was helpful to have the kind of income the Army provided.

With my improved economic liquidity, I started dating a young woman, Ruth Metzger, who was behind the cash register in the Old German, a very nice local restaurant. It showed up that she was the daughter of the proprietor, sister of the head waitress and sister of the main bartender. It was an old family restaurant and, in fact, her mother was in the kitchen supervising. They all worked there. We became engaged and decided to get married. Our honeymoon was the seven days trip to Portland, Oregon, where I had an internship waiting at Emanuel Hospital.

During our stay in Portland, we got to enjoy the Pacific Northwest more and more, and I started looking for a nearby university to further my education and to take a residency in obstetrics and gynecology. One of my professors from Ann Arbor had recommended I consider the University of Washington where the residency was served at Harborview Hospital – before the present University Hospital was built. I applied and was accepted. After finishing the three-year residency at Harborview,

I was transferred to the U.S. Army Hospital at Fort Lawton, where I became chief of the obstetrics/gynecology unit. Subsequently, I went on to serve the military elsewhere in the United States, eventually returning to live and practice in the Pacific Northwest in 1967.

Stig B. Andersen was born September 13, 1931, in Frederiksberg, Denmark. He married Ruth Metzger June 20, 1957. They had two children, daughter, Kirsten Andersen and son, Peter Andersen. Stig graduated from Fresno High School, Fresno, California, 1949 and from Hope College in Holland, Michigan in 1953, with majors in chemistry and biology. He completed medical school at Ann Arbor, Michigan in 1957; general internship, Emanuel Hospital 1958. His residency in obstetrics and gynecology was at the University of Washington 1961. He served in U.S. Army Medical Corps and retired from private medical practice in Bellevue in November 1998. Stig is one of the five incorporators for the founding of the Nordic Heritage Museum and he also served as a vice-president and president of the Museum's board.

Berit K. Sjong

"[When I immigrated] it was a whole lot different in Seattle Public Schools than what it is today. Now they have special classes and special things for kids who don't speak the English language. But they didn't have anything special when I came here. They had one of the kids go out to the hall with me and look at these little books and say 'door' with a picture of a door and so on with cat and dog."

My name is Berit Sjong formerly Ingebrigtsen. I was born in Aalesund, Norway in 1936. When I was two years old we moved to Lillestrom, a small city near Oslo. Our house was very close to the airport, not a good place to be when the war with Germany started in 1940.

My parents and I moved to a rural community. We had a nice house up on the hillside overlooking Nittedal and Lillestrom. The Germans bombed Lillestrom – particularly the airport. Later it was the Allies that bombed the airport because the Germans were using it. Often at night we could see the flashes as the bombs hit. We lived there until the war ended in 1945. I started the first grade there.

The Germans often came to our home in Nittedal looking for my dad, Anton B. Ingebrigtsen. He had been an officer in the Norwegian Army and was therefore a target. It was usually the Gestapo that came looking for him but my dad would go into hiding in the hills. I was always very scared and cried. Once however, they came when he was home. They were going to arrest him. The Gestapo in charge had a little girl back in Germany so I started sobbing, "Please don't take my dad." He felt bad. He said, "Ok we are leaving." They left. I really remember that day well.

My dad had gone to school at the Military Academy in Oslo at the same time as King Olav V. During the war, he was active with the Norwegian Resistance, but I didn't know that. While in Nittedal, his job was being in charge of the Ration Card office. He had a big office and was able to help a lot of people with undocumented extra food.

I remember that we took lots of trips. For instance, he borrowed trucks and Mamma and I went along to places like Toten where they had potato farms. They would fill the truck with potatoes and then put lots of other stuff over it. The Germans had lots of checkpoints where we were stopped and checked. It seemed less suspicious because Mamma and I were along (not that I knew that at the time). Pappa would give the potatoes to people who had less ration cards. Even though you could buy the ration cards on the black market, many people didn't have the money. Pappa helped a lot of people.

Mamma and I used to take trips on the train. We'd go into Oslo and go shopping and to restaurants. It was very nice, but there were a lot of air raids. We could pretty well count on at least one while we were there. When that happened it was a matter of finding a restaurant, a hotel or someplace where they had shelters; basements actually.

The Germans were extending the railroad up in northern Norway. My Dad was a civil engineer so he was one of the people picked to go and work there. It was for many months at a time so Mamma and I got to go and live there for six or seven months. The place where we lived was a very small town named Hemnesberget.

We kept our other home so that we had a place to come home to when the railroad was done. We made friends with a nice German named Kato. He missed his family and came to visit often and he brought me chocolate. The German soldiers didn't have a choice; they were told what to do and where to go. The Gestapo was a whole different breed. Our friend Kato was later sent to the Russian front.

The war was bad and I am glad I wasn't an adult at the time. As a child, I was pretty well shielded from much of it except when the Germans came around. This was when I became very nervous.

The day the war was over, Mamma, Pappa and I went into Oslo. We wore red, a color not allowed during the war and we had flags. I am still a "flag person."

The reason we came to America was that my grandparents were here. They had gone to America in the early part of the century. They lived in West Seattle. After the war, they came back to Norway and talked my parents into coming over. After the war Norway didn't have a lot so they decided we should go. In 1947, we came on the first *Queen Mary* from England and stayed with them for a short time. Then we moved to Ballard. We had absolutely no regrets about coming to America.

It was a whole lot different in Seattle Public Schools than what it is today. Now they have special classes and special things for kids who don't speak the English language. They didn't have anything special when I came here. They had one of the kids go out to the hall with me and look at these little books and say "door" with a picture of a door and so on with cat and dog. I knew three English words at the time: "Yes," "no" and "chewing gum"... My Dad probably would have liked to have gone back but didn't because Mamma and I didn't want to go. He just didn't feel like he fit in here. Back in Norway he had really good jobs. Here the language barrier made it hard for him.

I graduated from the University of Washington. Later John Sjong and I met each other at the Saturday night Norway Center dancing. At the time, Norway Center had a big dance every Saturday night and everybody was there. We married in 1967.

Berit Karin Ingebrigtsen was born March 20, 1936 in Ålesund, Norway. At age 11 she immigrated to the USA with her parents Anton and Hjørdis Ingebrigtsen. She graduated from the University of Washington with a bachelor's degree in marketing/business in 1958. She married John Sjong on February 4, 1967. They have three daughters, Tina Lapham, Lisa Wilson and Vicky Jaquish, and seven grandchildren. Berit has co-chaired for the Northern Lights Auktion for the Nordic Heritage Museum numerous times and is a longtime board member.

John K. Sjong

"After I got out of the (U.S.) Army, I got together with Sam Hjelle, also from Sykkylven. He had just come home from a crab season in Alaska. I jokingly said, 'Well, if you have an opening let me know and I'll go up with you.' A short time later he called ... I flew to Kodiak for the spring season. I think we got 9 cents a pound for the crab. When I left, I had $3,500 in my pocket and that was more money than I had ever seen before."

My parents came from Sunnmøre, Norway. My dad was a Navy officer. I was born in Horten in 1936 and we lived there until 1939. When Dad went on a voyage up north my mother decided to move back to Sykkylven and that's where I grew up. My dad died in World War II when his ship got torpedoed.

Skotet, a mountain farm, had been in my mother's family going back several hundred years. It's not far from Geirangerfjord, a deep cut in the Seven sisters mountain range. During summers and holidays we went back to the farm and I pitched in to help my grandparents. At the time we moved there from Horten, my grandparents lived there with my youngest uncle, John. We had chickens and pigs, a half dozen cows, maybe twenty goats and fifteen or so sheep. There was no electricity, running water or refrigeration. My family used oil lamps for light and burned wood for heat. We were pretty self sufficient. I enjoyed milking the cows and goats with my aunt Kari and my grandmother when I was small.

I spent a lot my time driving something or other while I was a teenager. When I was twelve or thirteen, I drove a horse and sled one winter, hauling chair frames through the snow from one side of town to the other. I was sixteen when I went to work in the furniture factory. However I could see how easy it might be to get stuck there. I decided right then to quit.

When I was about 22, I came to the United States. A friend of mine, Jarle Stromme, had two uncles in Seattle and one day he said, "I'm going to immigrate to the United States. Why don't you come along?"

I wrote to my aunt in Oregon. She guaranteed for me and I got my visa. The weekend before I left in January 1960, Jarle got married. He never made it to the United States.

I came to North Bend, Oregon. My first job was on a green chain in a lumber mill. I lasted there for four days. I said, "To heck with this. I got to find something better."

I got in my $75 car and drove north, stopped in Tacoma, met some friends from Sykkylven and ended up staying there for about six months. Then I moved to Seattle.

I got a job here in a machine shop, got an apartment and thought I was doing pretty well when I got a letter from Uncle Sam: "Your friends and neighbors have elected you to serve in the United States Army." I had served 16 months in the Norwegian Army. If I had served 18 months in Norway, I would not have had to register for the draft in the United States.

So, after I'd been in this country for about ten months, I found myself drafted into the Army. I became a maintenance machinist for a helicopter company.

After training in Virginia we loaded everything on an aircraft carrier – helicopters and all – and went through the Panama Canal and up to Anchorage, Alaska.

At that time, I didn't know much English, but I guess I learned pretty fast. And the time in the service was good for me because they teased me a lot, so I thought about everything I was going to say before I said it.

Soon after I got out of the Army, I got together with Sam Hjelle, also from Sykkylven. He had just come home to Seattle from a crab season in Alaska. I jokingly said, "Well, if you have an opening, let me know and I'll go with you."

A short time later Sam called me. He said: "I've got a job for you up in Kodiak on a boat, but you have to leave tomorrow."

I was going to be the engineer on the *Robert M.*, an old cannery tender. They didn't have anything rigged up, no crab pots or anything. So we got the steel and the web and I welded up every pot and the rest of the crew sewed the web on and cut the line and so forth. I was there for the spring season 'til sometime in April. I think we got 9 cents a pound for the crab. At the end of that season I had $3,500 in my pocket, and that was more money than I had seen anywhere. I had never fished before but I had sailed on a ship as an oiler. I had worked around engines all my life. I was a machinist by trade and I thought it all fit together.

When I got back to Seattle I went looking for another job and got on the *Victory*, based out of Sitka. We would be tendering salmon for the summer and then go fishing. I stayed on that boat 'til Christmas. In those days, you didn't quit. You could change boats at Christmas or in the summer, but not in-between. Nobody quit in the middle of things like they seem to be doing now.

In the spring of 1965, I took my citizenship test, which I knew I'd have to do if I wanted to get my skipper's license. It was then that I officially changed my first name from the Norwegian "Jan" to the American "John." In English "Jan" sounded like a girl's name. Although if I had to do it over again today, I wouldn't change my name.

In the fall Sam got the opportunity to buy into a boat. So he left the one that he was skipper on. The engineer, Pete Myhre, also from Sykkyleven, took over as skipper and I got on the boat after Christmas as engineer.

We were fishing out of Akutan near Dutch Harbor. So I was there for that spring season and then, when we got back to Seattle, Sam had some crew changes and I got on as the engineer on the boat he had bought into, the *Viking*. Usually, two or three people owned a boat like that. Torleif Pedersen and Harald Hansen were Sam's partners.

Sam wanted to go home for Christmas, so he offered me the chance to take over as skipper for a month or so. And then I got three friends to come up as crew members and that was my start, I guess. That was in 1966.

Each crew member got 10 percent of the crew share. And the skipper got an extra 5 percent on top of that. So that was 45 percent to the crew and 55 percent to the boat owner. Since then that has changed quite a bit. But the price for fish has gone up tremendously, you know. We were fishing for 9 or 10 cents a pound then.

The king crab fishery started in the 1950s. The early 1960s was when it started to make some money. By that time the fishermen had learned most of the tricks, how to build the pots, how to catch the crab and so forth.

In 1968, Harald Hansen, Sam Hjelle and I had Marine Construction and Design (Marco) build our first boat, the *Olympic*. It was 94-feet long and could carry more crab and more fuel than any other vessel at that time. The fleet had been mainly wooden boats, sardine boats and so forth in the 75 to 82-foot range. The Olympic was built for crab — house forward and a big deck — and was tanked, of course, to hold the fish. But we had to go ashore to deliver our catch.

The second boat we built, about two or three years later, was made by Martinolich Shipyard in Tacoma. Konrad Uri and I built that one.

Each of the boats was part of a different company. I was running the *Olympic*, and Konrad was running the *Rainier*. We also got into a little shrimp boat with another partner, John Boggs. Then it just multiplied from there.

By 1973 or so we were using a lot of pots. So, we decided well, heck, let's build them ourselves. So we started a pot-building factory. There was a lot of demand. For three years running there, we were producing about 14,000 pots a year.

Then, of course, there were new boats being built all along. Marco was pumping them out a new boat once a month. It was an exciting time.

The *Olympic* cost $322,000. But at the time we signed the contract for that boat the catch price was 10 cents a pound. Six months later, when the boat was on the fishing grounds, the price was 35 cents a pound. I paid for that boat in a year and a half.

And then we built some more boats. Tom Bender had a shipyard in Mobile, Alabama, and his boats were a little cheaper. I had four boats built there.

In 1975 we bought the *Deep Sea*, an old boat that had been processing crab in the 1960s, so that we could process our crab. At the time, there were two groups. You had the processors and you had the fishermen. We were the first group that got in between. We got kicked out by the fishermen and we weren't accepted by the processors. So we were sort of floating out there in the middle.

We — John Boggs, Konrad Uri and I — formed a company, Trans Pacific Seafood Inc. And we also controlled some boats, so we had enough production.

We anchored the *Deep Sea* in Akutan and were processing the crab there. At this time there were several new processors coming on line, and increased capacity on the old ones. Therefore freight had become a problem.

Western Pioneer, which was a freight company, had more business than it could handle, The same with Sea Land container service out of Dutch Harbor. However Sea Land said if we could get the containers to Kodiak, they had lots of capacity from there to Seattle.

We leased a supply ship from Foss Tug and Barge Company that we could put six containers on.

We picked the containers up in Kodiak. Then we drove out to Akutan and loaded them full of crab and then back to Kodiak. They lifted off the full containers, we got empty ones back and hightailed it back to Akutan. We kept that system going two, three years.

John Sjong -125

We produced the crab in sections, as it was called, packing the legs and shoulders in wire baskets, brine-freezing them and then put them in cartons. We designed the cartons to fit in the containers and got about 35,000 pounds in a 35-foot container. It's amazing how many mistakes we made. I would say that we made money in spite of ourselves because it was such a growing industry. Prices went up and markets expanded. Thinking back on it we were in the right place at the right time.

Jan Kaspar Sjong was born to Ragna Olivia Skottet Sjong and Severin Elias Sjong in Horten, Norway, on December 3, 1936. He served sixteen months in the Norwegian Army, and immigrated to the United States in January 1960. In November 1960, he was drafted into the United States Army. On February 4, 1967, John and Berit Karin Ingebrigtsen, a native of Aalesund, were married. They have three daughters, Tina Lapham, Lisa Wilson and Vicky Jaquish and seven grandchildren. John has owned or partially owned 28 fishing vessels. In 2011 he wrote and published "The Goat Farmer," a family history for his daughters and his grandchildren. The title comes from a nickname that Sjong's friends used to tease him. John is a board member of the Norwegian American Foundation, which promotes contributions of Norwegian Americans and strengthens ties between the two countries. He has also served on boards for Key Bank and the Nordic Heritage Museum, and is a member of Ballard Rotary.

Bertil Lundh

"So I walked back on Greenwood Avenue, while it was snowing, and a big Lincoln stopped and the driver said, 'Would you like to have a ride downtown?' I said, 'That would be just fine.' He says, 'Go in the back.' So I get in the back and I told the guy sitting there, 'Thank you very much for taking me downtown.' He says, 'Where are you from?' I said, 'Sweden.' 'Well,' he said, 'Here's another Swede, Senator Magnuson.'"

I was born May 1, 1927, in Landskrona, Sweden, and I had a wonderful upbringing. In my second grade I wrote a little essay saying that by the time I became 23, I will be in the United States and on the West Coast. And that's exactly what happened.

But before that happened, I was in the Air Force in Sweden from 1946 to '48. And I knew that I was going to the U.S. one way or the other. I found out that my grandmother had a brother who emigrated in 1892 when he was only 12 years of age and he went to sea. And, sorry enough, we never heard from the guy until 1947. My grandmother wrote letters to the Salvation Army in New York, and they finally found him in Castle Rock, Washington. So, it took close to 50 years for him to write a note that he was still alive. And the only thing he said in that card was, "Everything is fine with me, I hope it's fine with you," to my grandmother and that was the end of it.

But I got the address anyhow and I never told anybody and I wrote him a letter. In those days it took about 30 days to get a letter from Sweden to the U.S. or vice versa. So I got a letter back and he said, "You want to come to the U.S.," but, he says, "I can't help you because I have no money and I couldn't take care of you." But he said, "I've got a relation, a young girl who is a lawyer and she might."

So he talked to her and I got a letter from her and she said, yeah, she would underwrite, which was quite a lot to do in those days because (it meant) you were responsible for everything, including financial (support) and hospitalization.

I came over the 8th of December, 1949, to Boston. I came to Seattle about the 2nd of January of 1950 and as a good immigrant, the first thing you did in those days, you had to register with the U.S. Government and the U.S. military service, which I did.

Getting a [construction] job then was pretty tough because of snowy weather. But I found a contractor who lived two blocks away from the Seattle Golf Club. I walked there from downtown. And I got there about 9:30 in the morning. So you can imagine how many hours I walked. Unfortunately, he had just left.

So I walked back on Greenwood Avenue, while it was snowing, and a big Lincoln stopped and the driver said, "Would you like to have a ride downtown?"

I said, "That would be just fine." He says, "Go in the back."

So I get in the back and I told the guy sitting there, "Thank you very much for taking me downtown."

He says, "Where are you from?"

I said, "Sweden."

"Well," he said, "here's another Swede, Senator Magnuson."

So they drove me downtown and, I can tell you, I became a very good friend of U.S. Senator Warren Magnuson. Two days later I walked back to see this fellow by the Seattle Golf Club and finally met him. And he said, "Yeah, I'm building a building at the University of Washington, but we are down because of the weather."

"Well," I said, "Is there anything I can do? Like, can I clean up the building . . . or anything?"

He said, "If you're willing to do that, that would be fine."

So I cleaned that building up. It took me about ten days to do it. And The job gave me enough money to eat, anyhow.

There's one other thing about coming to Seattle. I took the train up from Castle Rock and as I was leaving the King Street Station, I happened to run into a guy I knew in Kalmar, Sweden. And I said, "I have no place to stay, you know," and he said, "Well I haven't got anything, I've just got a tiny room. But, I know a lady close to the University of Washington who has a big house and she takes in some students."

So he drove me out there. I didn't have any money, but everything works out, you know. So I talk to her and it's, "Yeah, you can move in." And, she said, "I'd like to have some money." And I said, "What about if I gave you my U.S. [immigration] card?"

"That'd be fine," she said. I gave her the card and I stayed about two months. Got the card back and paid her off. So that was kind of

128 - Bertil Lundh

interesting how everything just fall in place, you know?

After that job at the UW, the weather got a little bit better. I started out as a carpenter and worked for a couple of pretty good companies.

And then, in middle of May, 1950, the U.S. government wants me to come in to the military. I was in the first draft for the Korean War in Seattle.

I went down, I think it was down on First Avenue, you had to go in and register and everything. And because it was the first draft, Senator Magnuson was there and he was the guy that interviewed me and signed me up for the service.

Then, in a short time, I moved into the Swedish Club and one of the fellows that lived there was a superintendent up in Alaska.

So he said, "I know you haven't got any money, so why don't you take a job up in Alaska with me, in the fishing industry, Peninsula Packers?"

I said, "Fine." So I went to Alaska and worked up there for a month during the fishing season. While I was up there, there was a guy came in on a short, little airplane, about a two-seater, and got to our big ship. And he asked my friend, "Who's this guy?"

My friend said, "He's Swedish." The guy said, "For Christ's sake, can't we hire anybody but Swedes on this Goddamned boat?"

So anyhow, it was a pretty good job, paid a lot of money. After one month's working I earned six thousand dollars and in 1950 that was a lot of money. You could even buy a house in Magnolia for that kind of money.

So I got back in Seattle [and] I went to Frederick & Nelson [department store] and ran into Senator Magnuson. And he asked what I was doing and so forth and said, "Well, look, here are two tickets for you to go to the Chamber of Commerce dinner tonight. Have you got a friend?"

I said, "Yeah," I said, "I find one."

So I got two tickets from him and went to this elaborate affair. So we get in, sit down, and I was lucky enough to sit right across from Senator Magnuson. And his friend next [to him] was the guy that owned the fishing company that I was working for and who got off the airplane and said, "Can't we hire anything but Swedes in this damn boat?"

I mean everything just kind of falls in place.

So they start serving dinner and in those days, remember, they had those big crab cocktails, you know, that you had before the salad. So I ate mine and my friend ate his. Senator Magnuson and the other guy says,

"Here's one more." And we ate theirs and then the salad came in, we ate the salad and then Maggie and the other guy said, "Here's the salad."

So, basically, we each ate two meals.

Then I went in the service and I spent four months in the U.S. and 20 months overseas, four months in Japan and 16 months in Korea. And I have to say, that was probably the worst thing I've ever been into. Not only the war itself, I mean how many people get killed, it was just incredible in 1950 and 1951, but the weather. I had never seen anything like it. Twice as cold as in Sweden, but the worst thing for me was summertime, 120 degrees with the full uniform and helmet and everything on.

Anyhow, I got back to Seattle and, again, I met a friend at the same doggone King Street Station. He was a young lawyer and we had joined a place called the Soldier Club, Alaska Club, and they served dinner and had dancing every night. He said, "Where are you going tonight?" And I said, "Well, I'm just coming back from San Francisco and the war."

And he said, "Well, good, I'll drive you wherever you want to go."

So, we went to this place for dinner and there was this whole group of people there from one of the offices in Seattle. There were two ladies left at that party. So, naturally, they moved over to our table. One girl was from Copenhagen and the other one she was just moved up here from Oregon. And, after about four years, she became my wife. We are still married. So it really takes luck. Everything just falls in, you know.

And then in 1958 I went into construction and had my own company. And I had a wonderful time. We retired that company in '92. Now I got to give something away. I'd already been president for ten years of the Nordic Heritage Museum. So I start learning [about] a lot of non-profit organizations [to decide] which one I was going to carry on with. In the meantime I was president of the Swedish Club.

I finally joined the Northwest Kidney Center in 2000. I was president of the Northwest Kidney Foundation for three years and I'm still in the foundation and out raising money every day. So I've had a pretty good life.

So I've always been lucky. But, you see, luck, you create that yourself.

Bertil and Jarene Lundh

Bertil O. Lundh was born May 1, 1927, in Landskrona, Sweden and immigrated to the United States on December 8, 1949. Drafted into the U.S. Army in September 1950, he served in Korea and Japan. Bert was a founding member of the Swedish Royal Roundtable and the Nordic Heritage Museum, where he served as president from 1985 to 1995. As a member of the Associated General Contractors of Seattle from 1958 to1994, Bert served on the steering committee for Century 21, the Seattle World's Fair in 1962, and built the Swedish Pavilion. He established the Porcelain Gallery in 1973. He also has been active in the Swedish Club, Vasa Order of America, Swedish Business Association, Rotary Club, College Club, Millionair Charity Club Inc., Magnolia Chamber of Commerce, Norse Home and Swedish Council of America, the Northwest Kidney Foundation, the Moyer Foundation. Additionally Bert chaired festivities for the visit of the Swedish King and Queen during Scandinavia Today in 1983. In 2000 he was fundraising chairman for the Viking Exhibit for the Smithsonian. In 2002 he was awarded the Royal Order of the Polar Star, Commander first class, by King Carl XVI Gustaf. The award is conferred on foreign nationals to recognize service to Sweden and cultural promotion. Bert and the former Jarene Fair were married in 1954. They have two sons, Michael, who died in May 2012, and Steven (Susan); daughter-in-law, Kathy, and four grandchildren.

Halvor Olimb Ryan

"Ballard is a unique place and I didn't think of living any place else. . . . It's hard to pinpoint why, but you can see people here, you see friends here."

I left Norway because I never did enjoy farming. I was the oldest, so I was what they called *odelsgutt* [heir to the farm]. But I had absolutely no interest in farming. It's a smaller farm in Hadeland, with 8 to 10 milking cows, three or four horses, sheep and pigs and the like. Forest or *skog* was a big part of the farm.

During the Occupation I was part of a small unit outside of Oslo called the *hjemmesterkene* [home forces]. What they did was mostly in the background, but they had quite a bit to do with the *sleps* [drops] — supplies dropped for the underground people. I was pretty young, only 17, so they didn't let me get into the big acts. In 1945, when the war was over, we came down to Hønefoss. Some British troops were dropped in immediately after the *frigjøring* [liberation]. The first day I was in Hønefoss I was shot through my leg by friendly fire, by the Brits. I didn't get to take part in any celebrations — there was a lot of fun at that time. I'd never been in a Catholic hospital before, and I heard this big sermon in Latin and I saw ladies wearing white hats, like nuns wear. I woke up and thought, "I'm in heaven. I'm dead." I pinched my arms. Anyway, that was the end of the war.

In November, 1945, Norway sent brigades to Germany to help in the occupation. I spent eight months in Germany attached to the British occupation forces. I spoke a little bit of English at that time so I was in *sambandet,* the communications group.

I came home and started to get interested in the United States. I decided to immigrate at the same time as a couple of friends. We left January 8, 1949, and arrived in New York January 18, 1949. I went to North Dakota and spent the winter there with my great-uncle who had guaranteed for me. In 1950 I got on the train and came to Seattle. I wound up here in Seattle with $18 in my pocket.

I got off the train and I found this cheap little hotel on Pike Street for $2.50 a night. I stayed there four or five months. The first thing I had to do was find a job. I saw a sign by the old Frederick & Nelson downtown where there was a huge parking area. I walked in and asked the general manager for a job. He looked at me and told me to come back. I said, "I can't come back. I need a job. I don't have any money. I want a job now." And he said, "Who in the hell do you think you are anyway." Then he said, "Come to work tomorrow." I had a job. I didn't know how much I would be making, and I'd never parked a car in my life. That was my introduction to the Seattle job market.

I connected with people through Norway Center. They had dances there every Saturday night, so it was a good place to meet people. I got a job at Langlie's Sports Store, across from the Washington Athletic Club, on 6th and Union. It was Governor Langlie's brother's store. I worked for him for six or seven years and became quite involved in the skiing part of the business. I bought all his skiing equipment for him.

And I was at Seattle U when I worked at Langlie's — I got a skiing scholarship there. That's a Catholic school, but with a name like Ryan, I could get in there immediately. They needed some skiers on the Nordic team. I skied two years for Seattle U.

I also became involved with a guy named John Thorsteinsen from Norway, who had been on the Olympic team. We developed a new ski, the first classic ski to be developed. We went to Norway and I spent six months at Madshus Skifabrikk in Lillehammer developing a ski called Mambo. We had a lot of people skiing on it, but we couldn't get financing. Nobody believed in the plastic ski at that time.

I taught skiing on the weekends at Steven's Pass for six or seven years, also midweek, because I was working in sporting goods, and that drew a lot of the customers.

Myrtle, my wife, and I met in Sun Valley, both of us on skiing vacations. She was born and raised in Ballard. We lived on Capitol Hill for a few months. Myrtle was working as a school nurse. We bought a house in Ballard in 1958. We were expecting a child and we wanted to be near where Myrtle grew up, in Loyal Heights. We first lived over on 3rd Avenue, near Carkeek Park.

I was involved in the Commercial Club, and I was president of the Kiwanis Club, and of the Chamber of Commerce here. I got involved in the travel business in 1956 or '57. American Express asked me to escort some groups to Alaska in the summer. Then West Tours, now called Holland American West Tours, hired me full time. In 1963 we started our own business, Northland Tours. Our first office was on Greenwood. As we grew, we moved to Northgate and then downtown. We became part-owner, with *Bergenske dampskips-selskap* [Bergen Steamship Company], of a ship called the *Meteor,* and brought it over to go to Alaska. We were the second steamship company to go into Alaska.

Then a tragic thing happened. On the *Meteor's* first Alaska trip, in 1971, the ship caught fire outside of Vancouver B.C., on its way back, and 31 crewmen died. Our whole program was based around the ship. We lost all of our business overnight. We were almost broke, bankrupt, but we made it through that. Then we invested in a dry cleaning business, Crown Cleaners up on Crown Hill, which we owned for about three years.

In 1973 we went back into the travel business by starting Royal World Travel Service. I reached mainly towards the big tour market and we were very successful. At the same time we were one of SAS's top producers for many years. We sold the business to a Norwegian, Arne Thogersen, in 1987. I worked with him for three years after we sold and Myrtle worked for about a year.

Ballard is a unique place and I didn't think of living any place else. You've got to be close to Ballard. It's hard to pinpoint why, but you can see people here, you see friends here.

Halvor Olimb Ryan was born July 8, 1925 in Hadeland, Norway. He immigrated to the U.S., arriving in New York on January 18, 1949. After a short time in North Dakota and Minnesota, he came to Seattle in 1950. He met his wife Myrtle (Monson) at Sun Valley. They were married August 9, 1958 and started their travel business in l963. Their children are Tina Ann (1959), Erik (1962), Ingrid (1965) and Paal (1966).

Solveig Torvik

"So it was a topsy-turvy kind of world. You were not safe if your lights were on. That's what we were told. For me wartime was the norm. Children that grow up in wartime countries, that's all they know. It's sobering to think about. I was quite distressed the day the war ended because I didn't know what this [peace] was."

I was born in 1939 in Oslo and I spent the war years near Ålesund. The Nazis arrived in Norway on my first birthday and they left when I was six years old. So I have some very intense war memories from about the time I was four to age five and into six. So there were about two and a half, three years of the child's view of this war. Much of that is set down in my book about my family, *Nikolai's Fortune*. But I can talk a little bit about what we experienced. The matter of food was uppermost in our minds. I always say that cod saved our lives because we had codfish seven days a week. It was boiled because we had no butter. We had no oil. So my mother dropped it in a pot of boiling water and that's what we ate. If we had potatoes we felt very happy. If we had carrots we were very, very happy. If we had cabbage, that was terrific.

This was basically our wartime diet and I think it was a pretty healthy one given what other people suffered.

We had very little milk. That became hard to come by. We lived outside of Ålesund in a little hamlet called Hatlehol. It took about maybe 30 minutes to get to Ålesund by bus. There was no gasoline, so the bus ran on those wood chip things that they put in the back of the boilers, and this was a big old red bus that rolled once a day back and forth.

This was how we had to go to find whatever food was going to be available to us in the city. There came a time when there was no flour and so bread almost

Solveig, age three, in Ålesund during WWII.

disappeared. So my mother and I would stand in long lines, waiting at various bakeries to see if we were the lucky ones who could get a loaf of bread to take home. One time we finally got a bread loaf. When we got home my mother cut it up very carefully and gave me a sandwich. She had a little bit of greasy margarine to put on it. We ate it and something stuck. It was like a kernel, supposedly like wheat in this bread. But I picked it up and I unrolled it. It turned out it was brown paper that had been put into the bread for filler.

Trying to find fish was always a big deal and we had a number of adventures when we were trying to obtain herring on the sly or mackerel, the things that the fishermen would try to bring into the fjords without

Solveig, age six, shortly before the end of the war.

the Nazi troops knowing anything about it. When the codfish came in you really couldn't hide those. I remember as a child standing on the docks when the boats came in from Borgundfjord. They were loaded with cod. They'd come into the docks and we never got our hands on those fish because they were requisitioned. They went to feed the troops.

We had ration cards as you did in the United States – red ones and green ones and they were supposed to be for sugar or flour, various things. Often the cards were useless. I have intense and painful memories of shoes because there weren't any. Finally, they were made out of fish skins. They had this kind of a fish-skin look on the outside. They were made of fish skin and cardboard, with a little bit of leather soles that had been re-soled from something else.

My mother was a seamstress and also a very resourceful woman. All of these difficulties of life became a real challenge for her. She was a real fighter, so the more hurdles anyone put in her way and the more hurdles the Nazis put in her way the more determined she was to find some way around them. We lived out in the country so she developed suppliers and did black market work. I was always quite a well-dressed child because she would take old clothes, cut them down, and have what fabric was left to make something wearable and looked very nice. A few people would come to her with their old clothes to have them made into something more for their children and this is how she made what money she had. My father was in the Merchant Marine and he had money coming in but there was very little of anything. And you talk about old values. Norwegians that I knew who responded to this adversity that had fallen on them weren't complaining so much. They were trying to find ways to survive and to do it without getting into trouble.

My father had a brother who lived in a little place called Syvde, which was a day's boat ride away from Ålesund. There was food to be had from the farmers here. My mother and I went there with empty suitcases. And my mother went in there and sewed for those people, and then made all kinds of food on the sly. And eventually we came back on the boat with these very heavy suitcases – past the police on the dock. It was very obvious to anyone who was really looking that this woman was dragging these suitcases along the ground. But she brazenly walked by. So it was this kind of thing that went on constantly in my early life that I remember - food and getting clothes on our bodies. That was what life was about.

We saw the periphery of the war in Ålesund. I say periphery because we were not a battleground at that point. But I do remember seeing Ålesund bombed. It was in the summer. We were standing outside of our little cottage, a hundred-year-old red cottage with grass on the roof. There was a little hill next to the cottage where kids would play. We stood there and we heard the noise of the bombers and didn't understand what was happening until we began to see the flames come out from the buildings. All of our family was living in Ålesund so we spent a very worrisome night before we could get on the bus and go to town to see if they had been hit. Everyone in our neighborhood was saying, "Did that fall in such and such neighborhood, was it where grandmother lived, was it where aunt so-and-so lived?" It was frightening.

That is the only time we saw bombing. There was one time as a child when there was some activity out in the fjord outside our house in the night. Two ships were engaged and one of them sank. And there was an explosion. You could see fireworks and we didn't know who had sunk whom. We didn't know if it was the British or who it was. And that was the odd thing about it — we were always having to pull down our blinds at night, not to hide from the Germans but to hide from the British.

So it was a topsy-turvy kind of world. We were not safe if lights were on. That's what we were told. For me wartime was the norm. Children that grow up in wartime countries, that's all they know. It's sobering to think about. I was quite distressed the day the war ended because I didn't know what this [peace] was.

Solveig Torvik - 137

After the war Norway tried to get back to normal as quickly as possible but it was a long time before any consumer goods appeared in the stores. There was great scarcity even up to the time that we left in 1949. Things like knives, and fabric and thread – all of the things we take for granted - simply weren't available. My mother would spend a lot of time picking at these old clothes and saving the thread because you didn't throw that away. You couldn't buy it anymore. This terrific sense of frugality was forced on them by the war. But I also think that as a generation they were already frugal. So it probably wasn't that much of a leap for them as it would be for us today.

My mother had a brother Alfred Nymo who lived in north Norway in the valley called Signaldal. He was decorated by General Dwight D. Eisenhower for his work in the Resistance, and had also been decorated by Finnish forces for helping the Finns. He was very active in the Resistance for the three months that it lasted. He tells a gripping story about his encounters with the German troops [after they had killed his friends]. He was the most kind and generous and just wonderful man. When he told me about the way he fired upon and killed people, and how he was just enraged. He said he could hear the Germans crying and screaming. And he said, "We laughed." "War turns you into a beast, That's what happens.

There were wartime things that were sort of everyday experiences – walking along the street in Ålesund in winter dark, and you hear, "Svarte Maria kommer [Is Black Maria coming]?" and it's the police wagon coming with the siren on, and there's that siren sound that I always associate with the Nazis coming to someone's house and dragging people out while you're standing there.

In the last winter of the war I was trapped in the house because the Germans seemed to be withdrawing out of Ålesund and moving past where we were. By then they had lost their control, their discipline, somewhat. They were shooting randomly around the houses. And they were shooting pieces off our chimney. My mother had refused to let me go outside and play.

Finally, I just had a temper tantrum. This was probably about the third day inside and I was going outside no matter what. So, she just threw up her hands and said, "Go." And out I went. I was going to go skiing. There wasn't a living soul anywhere and I had these huge long hand-me-down skis that were handmade. And off I went. I was going to go around this little bend that was maybe two blocks from our house, because, supposedly, that was where the Germans were camped. Well,

I came around the corner on my skis and I see them, all camped there in this field and they are all in their white camouflage snow suits.

I'm sort of thunderstruck and watching and suddenly I see that one of these men is on his skis and is coming toward me. I am terrified instantly and I turn myself around on my skis and start taking off. I look over my shoulder and he is coming like this. I am moving like I'm in molasses. In those years in Norway in the winter, there was a lot of snow. So I'm kind of up to my armpits in this snow trying to get away from this soldier coming behind me. And I am terrified, so finally I just kicked off my skis and grabbed them up and ran into the house. And I threw down my skis and yell at my mother, "Shut the door, the German is coming!"

He was gaining on me and it was clear he was coming after me. So I got in the house. I dived into the living room under the table. It had a green tablecloth over it. There is banging on the door and in comes the German soldier. My mother, I'm sure, must have been quite terrified. She had no idea if I'd done something or what this man wanted. So he comes in, standing in the hallway, and I could see, because the door is open into the dining room. All I could see are the tops of his boots. They have this conversation in kind of halting Norwegian. My mother raised rabbits because that was one way she could feed us, and they had discovered her rabbits down by the neighbor's barn. So the soldier came to obtain the rabbits for his men. He came to tell her that he was requisitioning them and the two of them walked down there. I watched out the window as they were gesturing about what to do about the rabbits.

Mother came back and I asked her what was happening. And she said "They have nothing to eat." So there went the rabbits.

My family in the north had more intimate interactions with the Germans because they had occupied Uncle Alfred's house where his foster parents were living. He had fled with his family, to Sweden. Then he came back and remained in Norway to fight. My father had the misfortune of being in port on April 9 so he ended up sailing for the Fuhrer. His brother had the good fortune to be at sea on that day and he sailed for the Allies on the Shetland runs.

My father was up near Murmansk and as he told the story, it was a completely Norwegian crew on the German ship. He and the Norwegians hear this airplane and they realize it's the British and they had this instinctive reaction and started to wave. Suddenly everyone is waving and the man next to him drops dead from a bullet through his brain. And my father realizes, "This not where I want to be." He and two or three other men go overboard. They swam to shore and they were the only three that got out of there. They lived in a cave for two or three days. My father had taken shrapnel in his leg, so he tore apart some of his clothes and tied them up into a tourniquet and kept his leg. The Germans sent people to look for them. And we got a telegram from the German command saying that the ship was sunk and all hands were presumably lost. That's what we knew, that he was gone. But in fact he had been taken behind enemy lines by the Germans to a hospital. They kept him there for about six weeks until he was able to make his way home.

So one November day there is a knock on the door and there stands my father, a mere shadow of his former self. And I thought my mother was just going to faint — the blood just sort of drained from her face.

My mother was very resourceful and she was really the person that provided for the family, which was a large one. She drew on these characteristics but also on things that she had been taught. This is what you do: You work hard and procure what you can. So those were the values that my mother and father brought to the United States when we came here in 1949. We came to Idaho because my mother had converted to Mormonism as had my grandmother. My father did not convert but he was quite willing to come because there was that whole second wave of emigrants who left Norway after the war.

We came to Idaho because that was where our sponsor lived, a Mormon missionary my mother had known back in Norway before the war. My parents' idea was that we would go to Blackfoot, Idaho, and stay there and learn the language, get on our feet and then look around and see where we might want to live, Seattle or somewhere where there was a larger Norwegian community. They never did it. They got there and they would stay for seventeen years. When they retired they decided they wanted to go back to Norway.

My mother was forty-two years old when she came here and my father was fifty. Had they been younger I think they would have stayed. But they had a huge family in Norway and they saw that Norway was becoming livable for them. So they went back to Ålesund. After my father died, my mother re-married and moved to Hamar, where she died and is buried.

I think that their lives in Idaho were quite interesting because when we came we were the only immigrants in a town of about 8,000 people. The Mormon church had been very kind and prepared a place for us to live, furnished it and had a job for my father, who spoke almost no English.

My parents had an apartment in this hospital where they worked because my dad was supposed to be on call all the time. When I was in high school they decided they would rent out their home and live in the hospital. There was only one bedroom in their apartment. The hospital administrator said to me, "Well, we haven't opened the second floor yet so you just go up and pick out whatever room you want to be in and you can be there." So I picked the room that was right over the emergency entrance so I could see all the excitement that happened on Friday and Saturday nights when emergency vehicles were coming in.

My high school peers thought this was wonderful because I had a sink you could turn on with your leg and I could go down the hallway and watch the doctors operate. This is how I lived for about a year. Before I finished high school my parents had moved to another situation and I had about three months left before I was to graduate. I had a couple of after-school jobs. So my boss at one of these jobs, who happened to be a portrait photographer, she said, "Well, you can come and live with us and finish up (school)." This meant living in the mortuary because her husband ran the mortuary. So I would come home in the afternoon to change clothes and there would usually be someone lying there nicely laid out in the parlor. I'd ask, "Well, who's that?" and go out the door on to my next job. It was an unusual upbringing, I would say.

So, I think, life as an immigrant in Idaho was very fortunate. The church was very supportive. And it worked out well for my parents. But they were homesick for Norway and the family, and they realized that with their Social Security from the time they worked here and with what they could get in Norway, they would be far better off financially living in Norway than retiring in the United States. So that's what happened to them. My parents left for Norway when I was twenty-six years old. By then I had become a teacher and had really settled my life here.

I graduated from Brigham Young University with a degree in music and education. I taught school for eight years – mostly high school, some junior high, in Idaho, American Samoa and Utah. And I really enjoyed teaching. It was a good time. But, of course, then I became a journalist and the rest is history.

I think the thing that I like about journalism, that I've always liked about it, is that every day that you step into the newsroom you have no idea what your day is going to be like. You always know that you are going to learn something that day. I think that is what keeps a lot of us going back to it, even though the pay is lousy and the working conditions are awful. And right now is not a happy time for journalism in this country. But it was a good career move for me and I enjoyed it.

Solveig Torvik was born in Norway in 1939 and immigrated to Idaho with her parents, Magna and Ingvald Torvik, in 1949. She retired after a distinguished journalism career as a reporter and editor that included winning a Knight Fellowship at Stanford University. She worked at United Press International, the *San Jose Mercury* and the *San Francisco Chronicle* and at the *Seattle Post-Intelligencer* for thirty years. She was the *P-I*'s first Washington, D.C., correspondent and, for her last fifteen years, was an editorial page writer and associate editor. Solveig is the author of a novel, *Nikolai's Fortune*, and *The World's Best Place: Norway and the Norwegians*. She lives in Winthrop, Washington.

Henning C. Boe

"If you enjoy what you do, it doesn't matter if you had to work long. That's how I feel about it. I had the newspaper 32 years. I was 75 years old and I felt I had done enough."

I was born in Oslo, but my father died when I was two years old. So my mother moved back to her home place, Tvedestrand, a little town in the southern part of Norway, with 1,000 population. That was a nice place for kids to grow up — everything you need in summer and winter for entertainment.

I was educated as a printer. The war was over and I had a good job in Hamar. I took a year's leave of absence and went to Decorah, Iowa to work for a Norwegian newspaper there. Before I returned to Norway, I was offered a job at the Norwegian newspaper in Minneapolis. So [for a few months] I had been back to Norway with a new car. The gasoline price was so sky high I couldn't handle it. I decided to go back to America. When I came back to Minneapolis just before Christmas, I got a call from Ole Ejde in Seattle. He owned the newspaper, the *Washington Posten,* and he [offered me a job]. The newspaper in Minneapolis was going on strike. I didn't like to go on the picket line, so I left there and came to Seattle in 1954.

After a couple of years, I had a column in the newspaper, "The Way I See It," about Norwegians in Seattle and also in Norway. Ole Ejde said he was getting old, and he thought because people liked my articles in the newspaper that I should take over the paper a year later.

I went to the University of Washington School of Journalism for a year in the evening to qualify a little more. I took over the newspaper, and there was hardly enough to live on. So my wife and I started a travel agency. After half a year or so, she took that over.

Because I felt Ballard was the Scandinavian center, we moved the newspaper from downtown to out here in Ballard, to 2040 Northwest Market and we had an entrance at the street level.

I bought some other papers — the one I worked for in Minneapolis and the one up in Vancouver B.C., and so after a while we had the biggest Norwegian-American newspaper circulation in America.

Henning C. Boe - 143

We did fine and kept working. For the hundred-year anniversary [in 1990], I put out a hundred-page edition. Then we decided it was time to retire. Nobody had had it for that many years, but I had fun doing it. If you enjoy what you do, it doesn't matter if you had to work long. That's how I feel about it. I had the newspaper 32 years. I was 75 years old and I felt I had done enough.

I've been involved in all the Scandinavian organizations. When you have a newspaper, you report what's going on in the Scandinavian community. I was involved in Ballard Chamber of Commerce, the Rotary Club, the 17th of May Committee, 17th of May Parade, started the *Bergen Clubben* and I was in charge of an organization called Seattle-Bergen Sister City Association, so I've been very busy.

There had been a 17th of May Parade many, many years ago, but in later years it was celebrated downtown in a big meeting hall. One day Mrs. Lafferty, of Lafferty's Pharmacy, came over and said, "Henning, we should do something about it." She had the idea and I started calling various Scandinavian organizations, got positive responses, and called a meeting for the presidents to all come together.

Actually, what made me [volunteer] for the 17th of May Committee was because the year I came here, there was one parade from Seattle Center up to Norway Center, with a truck with a loud-speaker and five or six ladies in their Norwegian *bunad,* or costume. This was about the size of it. I remembered the parades in Oslo, with the kids and all, and I felt we could do something more. And the organizations responded to it, one after the other. Jim Vatn came in a couple of years later. [See Vatn p. 463] He was associated with the Seattle Seafair and Commodores, and they were about to become a big event. One of the Bowman brothers was announcing on the speakers and making jokes about the fact that he was a Swede running the Norwegian parade. Everybody had a good time with that.

I was involved in Leif Erikson Lodge, the old place and the new place also. The whole building was built by volunteers. Arne Olsen got people coming from contractors and all fields of construction. When they came to work, I took pictures of them for the newspaper. So people in other trades wanted to be involved too — everybody likes a little publicity. I think that helped to a certain degree.

The Chamber of Commerce wanted to mention that we did have some problem making Ballard a Norwegian community or village. We worked on that and even went to Leavenworth to look at the German community there. We thought we could do the same thing in Ballard. We tried it, but the biggest difficulty was that most of the buildings in the center were owned by people who don't even live in Seattle. They didn't respond favorably to spending money to make the front faces Scandinavian-looking. So the thing died.

I was involved in naming Bergen Place. Some people wanted to call it Nordic Place to involve all the Scandinavians. Then I wrote that King Olav of Norway was coming here and would dedicate the place. I presented my case to the Seattle Parks Board and they went for Bergen. My wife's first cousin, Emma Vatn, [see Vatn p. 463] was very unhappy about it — she wanted it to be Nordic Place.

The biggest event during King Olav's visit was his appearance at Blake Island. I was in charge and was the only one allowed down at the pier to greet him when he came ashore. Security people were all over. I was almost scared myself with all of these people — do they think they're going to kill us here or something.

I received the St. Olav Medal many years ago. I was in charge of the Norsemen's Federation at the time. They had a 25th Anniversary with a big party down in the Olympic Hotel. I didn't know anything about it. The ambassador was here, and I was supposed to say the table grace. Instead, it turned out that the ambassador came with a medal and put it on me. That was for my work with the newspaper and for what I had to done to expand it and my other work in the community.

I came to Seattle single. I went to a group called Fremad Society at Denny Park Lutheran Church — their Easter party was mentioned in the paper. I met a lot of Norwegians there who had also come over from Norway after the war. One of the ladies playing and singing in the chorus was a neat little girl — I could tell a lady. My beautiful maroon Buick was outside the door. I invited her to come along to another party afterward, and she did. She was not only nice-looking but was also very intelligent. Within three or four months, I proposed to her. We were married in the fall of the same year. Her name was Ragnhild Wulff-Nilsen, and she was from Lofoten. She had lots of family here. When I took over the paper, she had just been offered a position at University Hospital; she is a registered nurse. She gave that up to take care of the newspaper. [See Nilsen p. 380]

After we got the travel agency going, I went back to see my mother every year at Christmas as long as she lived. We celebrated here on Christmas Eve, flew to Norway on Christmas Day and stayed for five days, then I flew back to get the paper out the next week. And every August, when the paper stopped for one month, I went to Norway and visited my correspondents in the official news outfits. So I had good connections that way and got all the news from Norway.

In the office on Market street we had the travel agency in front, a little divider, then the newspaper composing department, an office for me and an office for the typing girls in back. When we shifted to offset printing, we were the second paper in Seattle to do that. *Queen Anne News* was first. We took classes to learn the new trade. Eventually all the papers went offset, but we were among the first.

It's a problem when you have been working and you get to be 75 years old, you have to stop sometime. I didn't like it but I had to. Now I help out with the 17th of May Committee a little bit, that's all. I was an officer in the Sons of Norway for two years. I'm trying to cut it out. I think they should find somebody a little younger than 85.

Henning Boe was born April 27, 1915 in Norway. He came to the U.S. first in 1951 and to Ballard in 1954. He married Ragnhild Wulff-Nilsen in 1954. They have two daughters, Nina and Ellen Gene, and four grandchildren. Henning Boe died in 2010.

Leif Eie

"We had no indoor plumbing until 1945. We did have a two-hole outhouse with a small hole for little rumps. . . My grandmother taught me how to card wool. Father used this yarn to make clothing. He had located and bought a large knitting machine, which he installed on a wall in one of the upstairs bedrooms, and at night he would knit socks and other wool clothing for us children to keep us warm during winter when we would be out skiing or playing ice hockey on the frozen lake. . . Father made hockey sticks from branches that had a little bend at the end and looked like a rough hockey stick. . . Father made a sled for us to ride the many hills in the area. . . He also made skis for us, homemade that looked like they came from a sports shop. We put newspapers between our undershirts and sweaters on really cold days to ski. When our shoe soles wore out, my father would go to the tannery for leather and get some horsehair thread and pitch to make new waterproof soles."

On April 9, 1940, we went to school like any other day, but when we got there we were told that the Germans had invaded Norway. We were somewhat bewildered and didn't know what would happen to us all. War was about killing people and that didn't sound good. We were told to go home to our families and we would be advised when we should come back to school. Germans had landed in Oslo and later we were told that German soldiers were on their way to Flekkefjord and we were told to evacuate to a safe place. Where is a safe place? I didn't know where we might hide from the Germans so we wouldn't get shot and killed. It was a day when we usually put money in the school bank and we didn't get to do any banking transaction that day. I had one krone in my pocket that my great uncle Ole had given me and I told my friends that maybe my father could use the money to buy ammunition.

Early the next morning we gathered all the food we had and brought some extra clothing. Father rowed us to the cabin, which sat on a small hill overlooking the lake. We had some distant relatives in the area about a half hour walk from the cabin. Early that evening I walked to our relatives at Stordrange to see if they could spare some milk. They said we could come and stay with them since they had a big farm house and a barn. After awhile the German soldiers settled in Flekkefjord and it became somewhat quiet. We returned home and continued our life as best we could, but with uncertainty.

The Peoples House [a community center] was located right next door to our home. In May the Germans took over the house and a few soldiers moved in. There must have been twenty to thirty soldiers. There was cold running water, a small outhouse and a wood burning stove. We had no major problems with the soldiers except one officer came to our kitchen almost every morning for hot water for shaving. Rather than turn their blankets over to the Germans, many Norwegian families elected to burn them. Originally the Germans promised cash for all blankets taken. Then the Germans designated all blankets received as rags and offered to pay rag prices for them. No cash was paid whatsoever. During one period the Germans took privately owned skis and ski boots, and as if dissolving the Boy Scout organization was not enough, the Germans ordered the Scouts to turn in their uniforms and all other scout equipment.

Sometimes we would cut a raw potato into slices and put them on the oven in the living room and wait until they got warmed up, then we would eat them and they tasted a little like today's French fries. The supply of milk never satisfied our needs and we always seemed to be out of milk. As things got more difficult Mother would insist that we take a spoonful of cod liver oil every night before we went to bed to keep us healthy. I have never had any cod liver oil since the war ended; the same is true for oatmeal. Oatmeal was made with water since we didn't have milk most of the time and it was very sticky. I think it would have worked very well as wallpaper paste.

I visited the [family] farm quite often and sometimes I would spend a few days during school vacation working on the farm, planting potatoes. First we had to cut last year's potatoes into eye sections and then plant them. There was a certain way they had to be planted but first the earth had to be prepared and long shallow ditches had to be dug. In the fall I would help dig the potatoes. Raking hay was another annual job and the hay had to be hung on wires for a few days to dry. Then the hay was bundled up and carried to the farm.

Drangeid had one of the largest leather tanneries in Scandinavia and a lumber processing factory where they made small wooden barrels. Most of the barrels were shipped to Iceland where they would be filled with Icelandic herring and shipped back to the European Market. Lunch was the main meal of the day in many homes and many workers lived close to these factories so they could walk home for lunch and my father sometimes managed to get a short nap before going back to work.

Årnes Tannery sponsored a marching band and I joined when I was 16 years old [after World War II]. We rehearsed every week and when the 17th of May came around we were ready to march and play in the parade in Flekkefjord.

Leif with actress Shirley Jones.

The band leader, Fritjof Jensen, asked me what we should do for midsummer night, the longest day of the year. It is daylight for almost 24 hours a day. We talked about bringing the band out on the water, and Father assisted in getting a large barge which could easily hold the band. The barge was decorated with large birch branches and Norwegian flags and we were towed by a small tug boat from Drangeid to just southwest of the city. We drifted between Flekkefjord and Gronnes playing music. Somebody had donated an old boat that was loaded with sawdust and some gasoline and oil had been poured over it. When it started to get somewhat dark, the sawdust was lit and created a beautiful midsummer's night fire.

I continued to play guitar and accordion and I met two brothers, Finn and Odd, in Årnes Brass Band. One played accordion and the other guitar. I suggested that we start a trio to play dance music. The brothers suggested we call it "Eie's Trio," but their last name was Stromland and that sounded more musical so I suggested we call it "Stromslands' Trio" and that's what we called ourselves. Since we had two guitar players, I learned how to play the 3/4 bass, and we now had a good rhythm to back up the accordion.

A couple of months after the war ended we were told that there would be a small airplane coming to Flekkefjord from Kristiansand that would give sightseeing tours for a small fee. The tour took only a few minutes. It took two people at a time. I bought a ticket, took the trip and got hooked on flying. Maybe I could become an Air Force pilot sometime in the future.

Klubben Humor was an amateur variety club in town which was founded in 1938. During World War II the club was closed, and after the war it started up again and produced entertainment for the local people and was very popular. I signed up as a member and participated in a show in April 1947 called "Come Along." The local critics were very complimentary regarding my performances, as a comedian and singer, and the experience I had at *Klubben Humor* helped me later when I became a professional entertainer with Jens Book-Jenssen, the director of Oslo's famous Chat Noir Theatre — Book-Jenssen liked to be called "Book'n" and was known as the Bing Crosby of Norway. I also got a job as a touring actor in Norsk Folkescene.

I told Mother and Father that I planned to visit the USA and that if I liked it there I might stay, at least for awhile. . . I said goodbye to my Mother, Father and siblings. I packed my suitcase and left home for the railroad station for the return trip to Oslo.

Joe Granquist, my sponsor [for the USA], had seen an ad in *Aftenposten* that the Norwegian-American Line needed English-speaking people because the ship was going on a cruise with American tourists for a 56-day tour to the Mediterranean and Caribbean. And it helped that I was a musician and could entertain passengers. On January 1, 1952, I was hired onto the crew of the NAL's *Oslofjord*. When I finally arrived in the USA in April 1952, it seemed odd that only yellow automobiles were at the pier. "Are all American automobiles yellow?" I asked someone. "No, those are taxicabs," I was told. Bloomingdale's department store offered me a job. But I decided to visit the nearby Scandinavian Airlines office instead and went to work there as a weight-and-balance agent.

I knew I wanted to stay in the USA, so I joined the Army and became an American citizen on June 14, 1954, while serving with occupation forces in Stuttgart, Germany. While in the Army I was proud to be awarded the American Spirit Honor Medal for leadership best expressing the American spirit, honor, initiative, loyalty and high example to comrades in arms.

When a soldier was discharged from the military he was entitled to get back the old job he had before going into the service. I reported back to SAS and it was like being reunited with family. Somebody had taken over the load control job I had when I left to join the Army, so I worked the arrivals and departures where I came in contact with many people. One time we had the two princesses from Norway, Princess Astrid and Princess Ragnhild, and I was assigned to handle their departure and escort them on board. Dag Hammarskjöld, Jussi Bjorling, Sonja Henie and Thor Heyerdahl were other people I met.

Under the CAB [the Civil Aeronautics Board; later the Federal Aviation Administration] regulations in that time no hot food could be served in economy class on airlines. Scandinavia is known for its open-faced sandwiches and that's what we served: The most fancy

sandwiches anyone could imagine. Other international airlines complained to the authorities that we had put too much lobster or ham and cheese on the sandwiches so the bread was not showing. It looked more like a gourmet dinner plate than a sandwich. This was written up in TIME magazine and it created the "sandwich war." SAS got a lot of positive publicity. We did make a small change to the sandwiches: we left a small part of the corner of the bread showing. After this change we could still serve the same fancy sandwiches.

Leif Eie with Washington Governor Dan Evans, 1964

SAS became very popular during that time.

By February 17, 1957, SAS had promoted me to sales representative. I felt proud having gone from grocery deliveries and working in country stores in Flekkefjord to SAS sales agent in Manhattan. I often was asked to sing and play guitar and combined performances with appearances in lodges, churches and before travel agents. Also I had worked with a ventriloquist in Norway and I created "SAS Captain Sandy," a puppet, for those events. It was an exciting time of my life.

On January 1, 1964, I took over as the new district sales manager for the Pacific Northwest, including Montana, Wyoming, Oregon Washington state, Alaska, Idaho and Saskatchewan, Alberta, British Columbia, Yukon and the Northwest Territory in Canada . . . On July 15, 1966, I received a teletype from Washington, D.C., that read: "Permit granting SAS traffic rights at Seattle, signed, sealed and delivered at 1500 hours." Time to roll up the sleeves and go to work. September 2, 1966, was the first scheduled departure from Seattle for the nonstop Polar route to Copenhagen. The first SAS plane landing at Seattle-Tacoma Airport arrived from Copenhagen at 5:20 pm. It had 82 passengers destined for Seattle. In addition we had 1,500 pounds of fashion clothing from Uppsala Kappfabrik, Sweden.

In the late 1970s, after a visit to Seattle by King Olav V, representatives of various Scandinavian organizations thought a joint museum could be an excellent cultural facility. But nobody wanted to take the responsibility to fill in the application to take over the old Webster School [for the museum's site]. After the last meeting my good friend, Svein Gilje, and I walked together to the parking lot. I said to Svein: "If you will take the job as the president of the museum for the first year, I will take the responsibility to fill in the application and sign the papers on behalf of the Scandinavian community." And that's what happened. Somebody had to step forward and get the museum going. However, Svein stayed on as president for five years. It took some time to agree on a name and it was finally decided to call it The Nordic Heritage Museum. The museum opened its doors in 1980, dedicated to collecting, preserving and presenting the Nordic heritage.

Leif Eie was born July 12, 1929, in Drangeid, north of Flekkefjord, Norway, the fourth child of six boys and two girls. Served eleven months in the Norwegian Air Force. He immigrated to the United States in January 1952, and served two years in the American Army. He worked for Scandinavian Airlines Systems for 39 years retiring in 1991. Leif and Patricia MacKean were married June 21, 1957. Daughter, Lisa Eie, and son, Christian Eie. Pat and Leif resided in Bothell, WA., for many years; now live in Tucson, Arizona. Marianne Forssblad recognized Leif as instrumental in the founding of the Nordic Heritage Museum. In appreciation, the museum began the "Leif Eie Oral History Project" in 1991. Leif was knighted by both King Olav V of Norway and King Carl XVI Gustaf of Sweden. He was instrumental in founding sister cities, including Seattle-Bergen, Tacoma-Ålesund and Seattle-Reykjavik. He founded the Norwegian American Chamber of Commerce and the Swedish American Chamber of Commerce chapters, and in 1988 was chosen The International Norwegian of the Year. He also helped found Ski for Light of North America, a cross-country skiing program for visually impaired and mobility impaired adults. While in the Northwest he served as a regent for Pacific Lutheran University and as Royal Norwegian Vice Consul.

Martin D. Metzon

Ruth and Martin Metzon

"In the [resistance] group that I belonged to, two of the people involved were arrested that morning [September 30, 1943]. So I was ordered underground. I had to go into hiding. It was fantastically organized by the Danish underground. Each afternoon I went to work if the Germans didn't come at 5 o'clock in the morning. That's the time they would arrest you. The story, after the war was over, was that the Danish said: 'Now if the bell rings at 5 o'clock in the morning, we know it's the milkman.' Each night I had a different place to stay. In the morning when it was light, you went out of there. Before they [the residents] had a chance to see you. Nobody could testify against each other."

My father's family had lived in Denmark for 300 years; my mother's family came from Northern Germany, which also was partially Danish at some time. My father was born in Randers, Jutland, which was always Danish. I think my grandfather was in the business of tobacco import and at one point he moved to Germany, when my father was four years old. But that must have been in 1892 and subsequent to that the family moved back to Denmark, but my father stayed in Hamburg. I was born in Hamburg, however as a Danish citizen.

When I was about eleven years old we moved to Copenhagen. I didn't speak Danish. My father was the only one who spoke Danish at that time. There was a German school there where you were able to casually learn Danish. I think we [my brother and I] stayed there in that school - I don't know - for one or two years. And then we moved to a Danish school. And the interesting thing is I had a teacher there at that school who later on was one of the top Gestapo guys in Copenhagen. And he even tortured some of his former students.

My father had several representations [clients] in Copenhagen. Later he bought a very large and prominent tobacco and wine shop in the center of Copenhagen. My mother worked in the store too.

There really were two different groups of Jews in Denmark in those years. There were the ones who were the so-called old Danish families like ours. And then there were all the new immigrants of basically Russian Jews who came in around 1900, 1905. They were the immigrants who came during the Czar period in Russia and the war with Japan, where they tried to get out of serving in the Russian Army.

Quite a few German Jews came to Denmark when Hitler came to power in Germany [1933-1940]. Everything went on as usual between the ninth of April 1940, the day of the German occupation, and the twenty-ninth of August 1943.

On April ninth, it was about 5 o'clock in the morning. Those huge German airplanes - bombers - came over our house. They made a tremendous noise. But at that time, the Danish government already had capitulated. There were battles at the southern border between Germany and Jutland, and there were battles in Copenhagen at the port, where the Germans had sneaked in with some coal boats the night before. But instead of coal, they were filled with soldiers.

So I got dressed fast to see what was going on. I was nineteen and I took my bicycle. We lived very close to the harbor. I rode down there and everything already was closed up.

After the first few hours everything went down and the Germans at that time had promised that as long as nobody does anything, Denmark was going to be treated as a *Musterprotektorat* [a model protectorate]. We were going to be the showcase for the whole world - how you treat a little country if they are nice. So nothing really happened. The Danish government existed and King Christian X continued. The king was riding on his horse through the streets every morning without any protection. Life went on as usual until 1943.

Then the Danes started waking up and doing more and more sabotage against the Germans. Certainly there was censorship on the newspapers. They could not write what they wanted to. So the Danish underground movement started and I participated in that. They [the Germans] came rolling in with tanks and, so to speak, took over completely.

In the [resistance] group that I belonged to, two of the people involved were arrested that morning [September 30, 1943]. So I was ordered underground. I had to go into hiding. It was fantastically organized by the Danish underground. Each afternoon if the Germans didn't come at 5 o'clock in the morning I went to work. That's the time they would arrest you. The story, after the war was over, was that the Danish said: "Now if the bell rings at 5 o'clock in the morning, we know it's the milkman."

Each night I had a different place to stay. In the morning when it was light, you went out of there. Before they [the residents] had a chance to see you. Nobody could testify against each other.

154 - Martin D. Metzon

Before the Germans could get hold of the Danish ships, the Danish Navy sunk itself in the harbor at Copenhagen.

Certainly there was great concern about what happens to the synagogue. It was decided to have a youth corps that guarded the synagogue every night. We went before blackout and stayed there all night. The day before Rosh Hashanah, Rabbi Marcus Melchior told his congregation in Copenhagen that it was time to go into hiding. He had been tipped off by a German attaché that Nazis planned to begin the next day to arrest all 7,800 Danish Jews and ship them to concentration camps.

Denmark was an easy mark. It had adopted a policy of almost complete disarmament before the war and maintained an army of only about 20,000. We did not have a chance against the power of the Germans. The Danish government stepped down because they could not operate. The king did not abdicate, but he was, so to speak, a prisoner in his castle.

My father had heard the news, and he called me at the place where I worked - a book store. My parents had spent a couple of vacations on a little farm in North Sealand and we thought that was a good place to hide out for the time being. The Danes that were caught by the Germans were basically older people who could not move and the very orthodox who did not want to move because of the Holidays. And there were I suppose, some that didn't believe it was happening.

The farmer in Sealand went up the coast and established connections there with the Danish underground and arranged for us to get on a small fishing boat to get to Sweden.

In our case we had one scare on the way over. I couldn't stand to be under the decks. I was on top of the deck and a spark from the smokestack lit up some sacks which were soaked with oil. And the sparks caught on fire and you saw all the German boats lying far away with their big searchlights, and here we had this fire on board. We just took those things and threw them overboard as fast as we could. We were not discovered. [The journey took] an hour and a half, two hours, something like that. And then when we arrived in Sweden, the Swedish soldiers standing saying: "Welcome to Sweden." They had it all prepared with camps, the schools where they put you up.

You have to realize that the relationship between the Scandinavian countries has always been a very close relationship in international relations. From the day we arrived in Sweden, we had all the same rights as far as work permits are concerned, medical insurance and the same rations as the Swedes had.

Martin D. Metzon - 155

The Danish government in exile established an armed force in Sweden called Regiment Danforce. [In January 1945] I got into the engineering group outfit. We were stationed north of Stockholm, very, very cold area. It was so cold at some times that our machine guns wouldn't shoot because the oil froze. We were about five thousand. Quite a few Jews and quite a few non-Jews. The middle of April you could see where the war was going. On the fifth of May in the morning, we came over on the first shipment [to Denmark].

Most of my mother's family got out of Germany, partly to the United States, partly to Israel, partly to Australia. There was one of my mother's sisters who was married. They had three grown-up children. The two daughters got out, one to Israel, one to Australia. But the boy was somewhat retarded. The parents could have gotten out, but they did not want to leave the retarded child alone in Germany. So they were all deported to Theresienstadt concentration camp at the time. And we

*Martin and Ruth Metzon
with Victor Borge*

knew that. And my parents sent packages there and got receipts back that they had received it. At one point, I think that must have been somewhere in 1943, word came back that they had moved, but we didn't know where they had moved.

I got married in 1943. We had two children. My son was born in Sweden in 1944 during our time as refugees. And our daughter was born in 1946 in Denmark. I was in the book business. I started out as an apprentice in an import-export book business and that became my specialty over the years, basically importing books to Denmark from all over the world. We re-sold them to all book stores in Denmark.

After the war I had already been hired in Sweden by a large Danish publishing house that had a book store in Copenhagen.

In 1952 I got divorced. I always wanted to go out and see the world. I had two of my mother's sisters living in Seattle. And I thought it was a good place to start out and see what's going on. My daughter stayed with my former wife and my son came with me to America in 1953.

I think it was a seven-day voyage stopping in Halifax. We arrived in New York and my cousin and her husband were down at the pier to receive us. But when we arrived in New York, my son and I were not allowed to go ashore. We were then taken to Ellis Island for no actual reason that I was aware of. We couldn't talk to anyone, except that I could make one call to the Danish consul general to find out what my rights were. I figured that the laws were broken. I was used to freedom. Danish citizen, Danish passport. Legal American visa with all the health requirements and everything complied with. They didn't tell me anything except: "We're very sorry." I called the Danish consul general and he said: "Well there's not much we can do. That's an internal American affair. What we can do is we can ship you back to Denmark if that's what you want. That is the authority we have."

I told him I was not interested in that because that's not why I came over. We never found out what happened. We stayed at Ellis Island for three weeks in June 1953. Finally I got a hearing. I got a tremendous amount of questions about my Communist relationships which I didn't have. So the next day or two days later we were released on parole. We have to report once a week to somebody. There weren't any charges at any time. No documentation of anything. I still believe there was a mistake of some kind. I never found out.

But before I even had to go to my first parole meeting, the parole was revoked.

EDITOR'S NOTE: Some information for this entry was provided by the Special Collections Division at the University of Washington.

Martin D. Metzon was born October 15, 1920, in Hamburg, Germany, as a Danish citizen. He died January 7, 2011, in Seattle. In 1953, Martin married Ruth Lehmann Frankel, and became an American citizen in Seattle in 1957. Martin studied at the University of Washington and became a certified public accountant in 1959. He became a materiel controller in the Boeing Co. Plant 2, and later worked 20 years at Moss Adams & Co., a large CPA firm, with then Danish Consul Paul O. Nielsen. Martin served as both the Danish vice consul and consul, for a total more than 40 years. He was a charter member and past president of Temple Beth Am; active in B'nai B'rith. He also served on the board for the Nordic Heritage Museum, as president of the Danish Club of Seattle, and as secretary-treasurer of the Consular Corps of Seattle. He was knighted by the Queen of Denmark in 1988. Martin's wife Ruth, was born in Barsinghausen, Germany, escaped to England in 1939, and arrived in Seattle in 1944 to join other family members. She was a widow with a young daughter when she met Martin. She taught patternmaking and dress design at Edison Technical School, now Seattle Central Community College, and the YWCA. She died June 29, 2011. Their children are Jorgen Metzon (Clara), Kirsten Silberman (Birger), Sue Covey (Peter), and Jeanette Calderon (David).

A modern-day immigrant recalls arrival in the New World – Cinerama offered an instant view of America

by Svein Gilje
Seattle Times staff reporter

"When I wrote my parents about the schol-arship (education) that I would earn for time in the US Army — the Korean GI bill still was in effect — my father wrote back: 'Better check that information again, son. I have never heard of anyone earning four years in college for serving in the military.' Only in America."

A strange sight greeted me as I stepped ashore from the old-time immigrant ship.

Noise all around. A buzz of foreign words. Passengers being greeted by waiting relatives.

And there, at last, being hoisted onto the Manhattan pier was my huge trunk – the trademark of the immigrant – the kind that was labeled an "America trunk" back home in my native Norway – along with my skis and other paraphernalia.

That's how it was to arrive in the New World.

The year was 1954 and the arrival scenario was not much different from that of 30 to 50 years earlier, except immigrants arriving by ship were landing directly in Manhattan because Ellis Island had been closed.

"Taxi, sir? Taxi?"

Ah, I had been warned about the New York cabdrivers.

"Watch them," friends had advised. "They'll take you for a ride." Not this kid. No sirree. I wasn't going to be taken for a ride. Uh-uh. "Greyhound station," I announced, hoping my voice would sound as nonchalant as that of any seasoned traveler.

Out of the corner of my eye, I closely watched the street signs as they zipped past. After all, I carried only $125 with which to start my new life, some of it bought at a high price on the black market in Norway.

There was a severe imbalance in foreign trade to most European countries in those post-World War II years. Norway was no exception, and the government had imposed tight restrictions on how much "hard currency" dollars its citizens traveling abroad could buy.

158 - Svein Gilje

Next to my little treasury in the innermost pocket was a pre-purchased Greyhound ticket that would take me to Seattle.

While on the nine-day Atlantic crossing I had studied a street map of Manhattan, and memorized its major streets and landmarks. Now I watched to see if the cabbie's route would match my acquired knowledge.

It did and I was relieved.

Frankly, I don't know how I would have handled the situation if it had not matched. My high-school English was not such that I could hope to win an argument with a fast-talking cabdriver driving me uptown in Manhattan.

What a sight the cab was!

My "America trunk" was so large that the cabbie couldn't close the cab trunk. A suitcase, almost twice the size of today's comfortable three-suiter, was stashed against the trunk.

Inside the cab were my trusty ruck sack and assorted other bags. The long skis with bamboo poles were poking out of the rear side window.

"Just over from Norway, huh? Do a lot of skiing? Student? Immigrant?" His friendly chat never stopped. "You'll love New York. You must see it before heading out. Going where? Seattle, huh? Never been there. Nice place I hear . . . "

There, 41st Street. The bus depot.

It's been a long time since I thought of my first cab ride in this country as a young student. I have forgotten the exact fare. I remember the meter read just a few dollars, perhaps $3. I knew there would be an extra charge for my bulky luggage and had a fair idea about how much to tip him.

The cabbie helped unload and a redcap took over. I reached for my money in the inner pocket and handed the driver the smallest I had, a twenty.

"Thanks," he said. Then he was gone. "Hey! My change!"

But he had gone. The cab disappeared in the traffic down the block.

Lesson No. 1 for young immigrant-student: Carry change.

It seemed an expensive lesson, but it was not repeated as I traveled west to Chicago, Minneapolis, Montana and, finally, Seattle.

In New York, friends had introduced me to the first Cinerama production, the wonders of the huge screen on which an impressive introduction was given to the beauty of the U.S.

My Cinerama-introduction to this country was confirmed as I traveled west. Years of travels, backpacking, climbing and skiing since have convinced me further that I simply shifted base from one beautiful country to another equally beautiful.

And if I set out to find areas with likeness to my native country, I don 't have to go far – the "Norwegian fjord" of Hood Canal, the "Norwegian fishing village" of Poulsbo, the forests, mountains and valleys. They all harbor a striking resemblance to areas in Norway.

Not everything appeared like back home. But it was easy to adjust, even though the food was strange and habits were different.

The hustle never seemed to stop. Broadway was as crowded at 11 a.m. as 11 p.m. But even outside New York – which I quickly realized was not very "American" – habits were quite different from the more tranquil country I hailed from.

It was a society on the move and highly flexible. The informality, friendliness and hospitality helped ease the transition, and a couple of year's service in Uncle Sam's Army taught this newcomer much about the American way of life.

When I wrote my parents about the scholarship that I would earn for time in the Army – the Korean GI Bill was still in effect – my father wrote back: "Better check the information again, son. I have never heard of anyone earning four years of college for serving in the military."

Only in America.

Education initially had attracted me to this country. Europe still was rebuilding after the war and its universities did not have the capacity to handle the big post-war influx of students.

Thus, I became part of a new wave of immigrants. They no longer were leaving their native countries for economic reasons so much as for educational opportunities. The Norwegians, whose country had pulled itself out of poverty and into the wealth of industrial development, were no exception. They came searching for degrees in engineering, architecture, medicine and other fields.

I sought a degree in journalism, and at the University of Washington there was a large group of Norwegians and other Scandinavians in various departments.

A decade or so later, the nature of immigrants changed again. Starting in the late 1960s, immigrants from the industrialized countries came here already educated, often specialists in the new technology. Thus, when The Boeing Company built its 747 plant, it recruited a planeload of Norwegian computer specialists.

I had found it easy to adjust to my new environment. I came with a good working knowledge of the English language, having studied it for seven years in school. Back home I had practiced my English whenever possible, by listening to the American forces' network for soldiers in Europe, watching American movies – the original dialog was used and translation was done by adding Norwegian text on the screen – and buying western paperbacks for 7 kroner ($1) apiece.

When I boarded the immigrant ship in Norway, my parents had wondered, with good reason, if they ever would see me again. Norwegians have migrated to the United States by the thousands over the past 150 years, and frequently they never made it back home.

But the airplane changed much of that, and immigrants now make frequent trips to their native areas, some once a year, others less frequently.

The pioneers who came here a century ago did not have that luxury. Nor did they have the luxury of knowing the English language. Some largely were ignorant of what the U.S. was all about.

One story that circulated in Norway in the 1830s was that America consisted of a vast land with many large farms, all abandoned for some unexplained reason and just waiting for the immigrants to come and take over. Later, of course, the word was that the streets of American cities were paved with gold. Little did they know of the mud and the boardwalks.

By contrast, I walked onto a university campus which offered the key to open my horizon about this new society. And I entered a community in which the values of music, theater and visual arts readily are at hand.

I felt at home.

Originally published September 17, 1982 in The Seattle Times*; reprinted with permission; Copyright by* The Seattle Times

---

Svein Gilje was born April 17, 1934, in Stavanger, Norway; died November 13, 2009, in Seattle. He immigrated to the USA in 1954. He became a US citizen while serving with the American Army in Paris, France. He earned a bachelor's degree in communications, and a master's degree in public affairs at the University of Washington. Svein married fellow journalist, Shelby Collard, on August 2, 1958. Daughter, Kari S. Gilje; son, Kurt Nelson Gilje. He reported for *The Seattle Post-Intelligencer*, *The Bremerton Sun* and *The Seattle Times*. In 1975, he chaired the Norwegian American Sesquicentennial group locally and served as vice president nationally for the celebration of 150 years of Norwegian immigration to the USA. He was the founding president of the Nordic Heritage Museum. For his efforts to keep Norwegian culture alive here, Gilje received the Royal Norwegian Order of St. Olav, Knight First Class, from King Olav V, and later the Royal Norwegian Order of Merit, Commander, from King Harald V.

Kari Lihaug Knudsen

"I always envied my young friends, the boys, because they could go out to sea and sail and see the world. And now, when I was done in nursing, I decided I wanted to see the world just like my boy friends at home had."

I lived in a small town called Stavang on the very west coast of Norway, midway between Bergen and Ålesund. My father was a schoolteacher there, the only teacher. We had one schoolroom, and we went to school there through eighth grade.

Everybody in that little town of 200 people, besides the store keeper and the pastor, had a little farm and fished for a living. The farm wasn't big enough to live off of. But there was nothing for the young people to do. You could, of course, marry a fisherman, or leave to make a living. I always envied my young friends, the boys, because they could go out to sea and sail and see the world. And now, when I was done in nursing, I decided I wanted to see the world just like my boy friends at home had. So I went down to the American Embassy, downtown Oslo, and got an application and applied for a visa to go to the United States.

I left Oslo in November 1953, on the *Stavangerfjord.* I didn't know a soul in the United States or on the boat. My father came to Oslo to see me off. On the ship I met several hospital people, including a Danish nurse who was going to Philadelphia, where I was headed. I had gotten a job there through the Norwegian Nurses Association, and the American Nurses Association. I first wanted to work in New York, but they didn't need anybody in New York.

It was quite an event when we came to Manhattan. We were looking at the Statue of Liberty as we sailed in and thought this was exciting and wonderful, a big adventure. By that time we had been on the ship nine days, Reidun Rist, my roommate in the stateroom, and I became friends. We were told that when we came ashore we were to go and sit under a sign for our last name initial. We were supposed to sit there and wait for someone from the Nurses Association to meet us there and take us to the YWCA on Manhattan to stay the first night. Finally, after it was getting deserted there, a little lady came trotting down there. The next morning she took us to the Greyhound Station and saw that we got on the right bus. I went to Philadelphia.

I had always intended to go to Seattle where my aunt lived, and one of my reasons for stopping in Philadelphia was I felt I didn't have enough money to go clear across the country. When [the next] November came, my friend and I flew — the very first time we had ever been on a plane — from Philadelphia to Seattle with a stop in Chicago. It took a long time, and I think we paid $132, one way. That was a lot of money because in Philadelphia we made $190 a month. And out of that they took money for meal tickets. We came to SeaTac — it was just a little airport in '54 — and my cousin met us at the airport, and we were taken to Ballard where my aunt and uncle lived. We stayed with them for a few weeks, looking for a job and deciding what to do.

We went down to Ballard Hospital on Market Street. I'm sure they had a lot of Norwegian nurses already, and weren't dying to have more. My uncle had taken us down there; he was so disappointed. Then we tried Swedish, downtown, and there we were hired.

When I came to Seattle the summer of 1963, I came from New York. This was my second immigration to the United States. I immigrated with my husband and two children in 1961. We came to New York. But I had to leave my husband after two years because he just couldn't quit drinking. I finally saw the writing on the wall that he would never quit. So I took the kids under my arm, literally, I borrowed money from a friend, we took a plane and flew out here.

Then Harald started in first grade at West Woodland. Anne was just four and the twins, Ellen and Laurie, were four months. I got a lady to sleep at my house while I worked at Ballard Hospital. So I worked nights the first year. A friend of mine took me down there, and I went in and asked for a job. Miss Needham, the director of nursing there, hired me on the spot, and I worked there for ten straight years. That was my home away from home. I was really treated very nicely by the people who worked there. Ballard Hospital was a small place, and everybody knew everybody there. And I lived in three different houses before I was able to buy my own home. They were all three in Ballard, sort of in the same row, more or less. One on 6th Avenue Northwest, the next was on 65th and 14th Northwest. The third one was on 65th and Jones, not far from the Methodist Church.

Twice the owner of the house, my landlord, would say, "You got to buy the house or you have to move." So, finally, the third time I scraped together all the money we had. I even took the kids' money out of the bank. My two oldest, Harold and Anne, had a bank account because grandparents had given them money for Christmas and birthdays. And we bought that house on 20th Avenue Northwest.

Kari Lihaug Knudsen - 163

That was a big step up and forward for us. People at work were so friendly and helpful. I worked with Ethel Claus. She had six children, four boys, and she volunteered her high-school age boys to help me move. Whatever the kids and I couldn't move, like big furniture and the TV, her boys came and moved. And a day or two after we moved, my neighbor at 20th, Dorothy Bredal, came over with a big pan of pot roast for us because she saw I was struggling with the kids and we were moving in. I really felt welcome there in the street. There was only one house from my house to Salmon Bay Park so the kids could play in the park anytime they wanted to.

I had to have baby sitters in those days, but now it was much better. I could drive them to the baby sitter. I had learned to drive since I came to Seattle. And in 1967, I think it was, I got an old Chevy. And before that we had to walk to the baby sitter. But now I could drive them to the baby sitter in the morning before I went to work. And then they would walk from there with her daughter to school. And I would pick them up there in the afternoon. They didn't like going to the baby sitter. But I said, "Life is tough, you might as well know it." And there was no other way. We had to do it that way.

Pete [Knudsen] was a widower for ten years, and part of that time he was a steady guest at the Kaffe Stua at Leif Erikson Hall. He enjoyed the people, and he loved to tell stories about the olden days when he went fishing and things like that. The first time I got to know him was at the Norse Home Board. We were both serving on the Board for the Norse Home. He was in his late 70s then. In '92, when I retired, I said, "Now, can you use me in Kaffe Stua because I'd like to start working there if you have any place for me." I wanted to pay back some of the benefits I had harvested when I couldn't donate time. Of course, it wasn't very long before I found myself behind a counter making waffles and sandwiches and enjoying the companion-ship. Pete and I would talk there. And that's how he invited me out for dinner the first time. And that's how we started going out then and eventually got married [in 1995].

In the '30s Pete and his brother John worked for the Stimson Mill down in Ballard till they went fishing. And then Pete, later, started working for Doc Freeman, and bought the store from Doc Freeman, and that's where he spent most of his working years. He loved every minute of it and he missed it when he retired.

Pete also had a community spirit. He supported a lot of things — the scholarship in the Norwegian Commercial Club, when they were building Leif Erikson Hall, he donated money to that and he bought the piano for them. He was also a very practical man. And he bought chairs and tables for the Kaffe Stua, and a dishwasher and practical things that they needed in the Kaffe Stua, the Nordic Heritage Museum, and the Norse Home. I wish he was here, he could have really told you tall tales. Pete enjoyed the people, and he loved to tell stories about the olden days when he went fishing and things like that.

Kari Lihaug was born in Stavang, Norway November 30, 1926. She trained as a nurse. She immigrated in 1953, and came to Ballard in 1954. She returned to Norway, married Fischer, had two children, Anne and Harald, in Norway, moved to Long Island, New York, where the twins, Ellen and Laurie were born. She divorced Fischer and returned to Ballard. She worked at the Ballard Hospital ten years and retired in 1992. She married Pete Knudsen, a widower, in 1995. Pete worked for Doc Freeman. In 1951 he and Bob Braas bought the store. He retired in 1985. Pete died in December 1999, 88 years old.

Bergljot Ringset Roswick

"I don't dance very much anymore, but I teach them Norwegian songs and teach them how to dance. Keeping up the traditions, I think that's important."

Icame in 1954. It was after the war in Norway, and America sounded fantastic to us. I was finished with my education and I worked several years in Norway. I was a nurse. I took a leave of absence for a year and I'm still here.

My father had had three brothers and three sisters in Seattle. I took the train here and was met by family. We get together Christmas Eve. Last year there were 57 of us. I came the end of May. It was beautiful here. I fell in love with it.

I went to work at Swedish Hospital. I had to take an extra class, mostly in high school curriculum to see if I passed in my English. And then I got my registration as a nurse here. I stayed with Swedish for 33 years.

I started folk dancing when I was a kid at a country school. The teacher took an hour for lunch and walked to his own home. We had an organ at school, one of the boys could play it, so we took the desks away and danced for an hour. Somebody watched for the teacher, so all the desks got back in place.

I danced in Drammen when I was there, and when I came to Seattle, I went to Gordon Tracie's dance class, but he didn't dance song dances, and that was my favorite — the Norwegian song dances. So that's when we started *Leikarringen*. Mary Viken started it, but I was dancing there ever since they started. I danced with them for several years. I also taught. We've performed lots of different places. And, when he was here, we danced for Crown Prince Olav, who is now Norway's king.

We went to Vancouver, Canada almost once a year and danced with people up there and had a great time — and other places around here, too. We traveled a lot.

There are some fabulous little kids and families in *Leikarringen*. Right now, I think they are six, seven, eight years, are the oldest ones. I teach them Norwegian songs and dances. But I don't dance. My feet are not good anymore. And you need two good feet to dance.

I met my husband over here. He was born here of Norwegian descent. His parents came from Lofoten. We got married in 1961. Then he died in 1969. So it was a few good years. But we had a good time together. He went with me to Norway, once.

I don't dance very much anymore, but I teach them Norwegian songs and teach them how to dance. Keeping up the traditions, I think that's important.

Bergljot Ringset was born June 16, 1916 in Stranda in Sunnmøre, Norway. She was trained as a nurse in Norway, came to the U.S. in 1954. She worked at Swedish Hospital until her retirement in 1988. She married Arnold Roswick in 1961. He died in 1969. Bergljot died in 2008.

Susanna Martina Malinowski

"My father said, 'When the light goes to a certain point, we're going to run.' So when the light came and passed us, we went across, and then we laid down in the mud, and when it passed again, then my father said 'Run.'"

My father was a baker in Hungary. Before the revolution, he had his own bakery, but the Communists were going to come and take his business away, so my father sold everything. My father was educated. And he also went to Germany after the war and he helped the Americans in camps to translate. When the revolution broke out, he took the UN representative of Hungary to Austria. And, when there was actual fighting in Hungary, he wore a Red Cross band on his arm, and he helped remove the wounded. When the revolution was over, my father was going to represent Györ in the Parliament in Budapest. But the Russians came back one night, and a few days later his friend, who was a secret policeman, told my father, "You have to leave, because we're going to come and get you." My father decided we were going to leave.

When we went back to our house, we'd only been gone maybe five hours, the secret police had already ransacked the house. My father and I had to get bicycles to get my mother and two brothers.

We got a train from Györ and, instead of going all the way to the Austrian border, we got off and we hid in the cemetery. We had six other people with us. My father and my mother's cousin, a young man who was also in the Hungarian service, went to ask farmers which way to the border, because we'd never been in this very small town. My father came back, but the young man didn't come back. Later we found out he got caught by the Russians.

So we found a way to the border. And as we were close to the border, there were haystacks — and I'll never forget this — in the haystacks were children. Children were crying in the haystacks. It's something you never forget. Because the people, instead of taking their children with them across the border, thought that they were doing their children a favor by hiding them inside the haystack. A young boy came up to us, not more than 12, 13 years old, and my father said that he could come with us. His parents had been killed. He came with us. And then two other gentlemen also came with us.

We probably went about ten more minutes, and between the borders there were these wheat fields. We saw the tower. And we actually did what you see in the movies: My father said, "When the light goes to a certain point, we're going to run." So when the light came and passed us, we went across, and then we laid down in the mud, and when it passed again, then my father said "Run." We did the same thing until we crossed over. We didn't know if we were in Austria. We spent our first night in a barn in Austria, the very first week in November, 1956.

We left the week before Christmas in 1956 to come to America. We came on a U.S. Navy ship to New York, January 1st, 1957. We were a family of five, and it took a long time to find a sponsor for five people. We went first to Burien, because the Lake Burien Presbyterian Church sponsored us. We lived there for a year. We moved to Ballard in 1958.

The very first house that we lived in Ballard, was on 56th and 14th Northwest in an apartment house. We were very close to St. Alphonsus. I'm the only one who practiced the Catholic religion in our family. I used to go to St. Al's all the time. In those days you always had to have something on your head. Didn't matter if you were a little girl with no parents, you had to always be dressed right. The best part of church was after Mass, there would be donuts.

The nuns were very, very strict. They would tell you if you wore something that they didn't think was appropriate — I just came from Europe, so the way I was dressing was totally different. In Europe, the girls were wearing short dresses, above our knees and those hideous-looking tights. My hair, the way mine was done, wasn't the way that they had wanted it done.

Whenever I went to a new school, they would always introduce me and say that I'm a refugee. We were refugees and it was like instant celebrity. We used to spend a lot of time at the Carnegie Library, checking out books and reading. For us, that was a way to learn the language. So we mainly went to movies, to the library, to the drug store. And we used to go fishing down to the pier.

Being from the old country, wherever my brother and I went, we had to take our little brother. It was just understood. Green Lake was the place to go. There were a lot of other European children, Swedish and Norwegian, and Finnish. I think they grew up the way I did — the parents worked, and they [watched the younger children]. We'd fix our lunch to take to the Lake, and other children did the same.

Susanna Martina Malinowski - 169

In school there were other children from different countries, we would know each other just by the way we dressed — and by the time I went to junior high, I made sure that I wasn't dressing any different that anybody else, because kids can be very cruel.

When we were at school, we had one life, we'd go home, through the door, and the American way was gone, and for me, the Hungarian way — the language, the food, the upbringing, totally different.

When we lived in Ballard, my mother and father thought that they could raise chickens and we could sell eggs. Well, one of our neighbors turned us in, and my mother and father had to kill a hundred chickens. All the chicken and all the blood, because Europeans don't throw anything away. They would fry the blood with onions, and the heads of the chicken, they would cook in the soup.

My father made 75 cents an hour working as a baker at the Ducz Viennese Bakery. My mother worked at Langendorf Bakery and Hyde Chocolates. They also worked at night time. They were janitors. They'd come home from their regular eight-hour job, fix dinner, unless I fixed dinner, and then they would clean till three, four o'clock in the morning so I had to be home to take care of my brothers. We're talking 10, 12 years old. They cleaned at a car place in Ballard and at Fishermen's Terminal. Didn't make much money, but they cleaned a lot of buildings. My mother also did housekeeping in homes in Ballard. Very little money, but she did that.

My grandfather came to America in 1965, and he became friends with a gentleman who also was like him. He was speaking Hungarian, and the other gentleman was speaking either Norwegian or Finnish to him. They were communicating by sign language.

Zsuzsanna Marta (Susanna Martha) Dold was born in Györ, Hungary, February 17, 1948. Her mother Magdalena Pinter Dold was born there in 1927. Her father, Zoltan Gergely Dold born there in 1926. His father was from Prussia. Susannas's brothers: Zoltan Gergely (1949) and Ferenc (1954). The family emigrated in 1956. Susanna graduated from Ballard High June 10, 1966 and on June 17, 1966 married John Szigeti, a Hungarian. She and John divorced in 1980. She worked at Mako's Office Machines in Ballard. In 1987 she married Mike Malinowski, also Hungarian. Her children: Susanna (1968), John (1971), Stephanie (1989) and Christopher (1989).

Borje (Bud) Saxberg

"My charge in the summer was to take the rowboat and row to a big island and then walk through the island to come to the dairy to pick up the milk. Then walk back, and row back to the base island. I can still remember that I was just plain scared. I was alone in the rowboat, and then I was walking through the forest of this bigger island, when a big bull came through what looked like a weak spot. I had to go by him then jump across the fence then pick up the milk. Then walk back in the dark when the 'trees were talking' and the moon was shining. There was motion and I still had to find the way back to my island. That remained a real picture with me. As a result, I have never seen the need for using the water and boating as recreation, because there it was connected with food, and survival."

My father had grown up on a small farm north of the city [Helsinki]. He left home at nine or ten because he thought it was time to get going. He started as an apprentice for my uncle Edwin in Helsinki who had a funeral parlor. My mother came from the archipelago south of Dalsbruk. Her dad had a small island outside the town of Dalsbruk and made his living as a tax collector for the county. I spent my summers with my grandfather [Filip Granberg]. He saved up his most interesting tax collection cases until I arrived. Then we took off in the motorboat to go visiting. That went on for many years. He was a wonderful man.

My charge in the summer was to take the rowboat, and row to a big island, then walk through the island forest to reach the dairy to pick up the milk, then walk back, and row back to our island. I still remember that I was just plain scared. I was alone in the rowboat, then I was walking through the forest of this bigger island, with a big bull tethered at a heavy iron pole that didn't look that strong. I had to go by him, then jump across a fence and finally pick up the milk order. Then walk back in the dark when the "trees were talking" and the moon was shining. I still had to find the way back to my island. That has remained a real experience with me and I have never seen the need for using water and boating as a recreation, because there it was connected with food and survival.

My father and mother had an education that went through third grade. There was a certain degree of "practical pragmatism" that they practiced. I always thought that it was a special feature that my mother put both myself and my sister into a Finnish playschool. That meant I learned the Finnish language right from the beginning. It has stayed with me as a second language. For the Swedish-speaking, Finland's second ethnic group with their own language, it's very difficult to learn Finnish. You can't fake it if you were not born with it.

My mother self-educated herself, and as a result she was the one who kept the books, as my father eventually got into the transportation business. She kept the business on an "even keel." The sad fact was that as World War II came into being, my dad was called in to do armed forces duty from 1939 to 1945. The trucks were picked up by the government to support the war effort. We survived because the government paid a monthly charge for the trucks.

When my father came back he had actually lost the use of one arm, and the remedy that he got for that was sending me to the beer brewery to pick up a liter of the yeast that floated on top of the brewer vat. That's what he had, his cure. His arm came back into shape. Part of it is apparently that the B vitamin has a very strong impact on your nerve system. For fun, I once bought a bottle of beer yeast tablets. When I opened the bottle, with the smell I could bring back that memory.

During the first part of the war [Winter War]we were living with my grandfather out in the archipelago during one of the fiercest winters that has been seen.The Gulf of Finland was frozen and there were stories about the Russians actually able to walk across the Gulf of Finland. The Russian planes were known for picking out civilians who were walking. They were like little black dots against the white. I remember dressing in white sheets whenever it was a question of walking out on the ice.

During the second part of the war [Continuation War], I had started to work for the Finland Steamship Company as an errand boy so the family decision was to remain in Helsinki. I would have been ten or eleven years old. I remember walking the attic with an adult. We had a metal bucket and a shovel. The idea was that if incendiary bombs would fall into the attic, we'd pick them up and put them into this metal container. Somebody had figured that it might work. During the Second War, the adult was left out of my companionship. I was alone walking the attics of the apartment house. It was kind of scary. You heard the plane and you were wondering if there will be an incendiary bomb coming through. And one time, I was actually helping to put out the fire in one of the apartment houses. That's when I discovered the enormous weight of these water hoses from the fire department. I still have the memory of holding on to it, trying to direct the water towards the fire.

I came home one day and to my surprise my mother said we are sending my sister Berit to Sweden. I said, "How did you work that one out?" One of the things I collected were safety matchbook covers. My mother had gone into my collection and found the name of the president of the Association who lived in Sweden. She had written to him, telling him she had a daughter that needed to get to Sweden. By golly he had arranged it!

It was quite clear the war had taken a lot out of my father. He had been driving one of his own trucks and had once broken through the ice and dropped down into ice cold water. He came out of it, but lost the truck. He got to know an enormous number of people during his service years. But he did not have the strength to start up his business again. He went to work in an automobile repair shop and actually became a supervisor. But some of the "oomph" that he had early on when he started up his business, that was lost. But he never said anything.

Svenska Normallyceum was the prime place for developing budding Swedish-speaking teachers. For languages, we had German as our main foreign language. I actually had eight years of German through high school. Then I had another three years of German in the school of business. I was always interested in languages. I was disappointed I had not been able to incorporate French as an elective into my schedule. I did it by correspondence.

Then I found myself feeling that, given what had happened during World War II, English would probably rise as an important language. I found my mother very supportive so I did English as a private venture. My mother was willing to spring for a bit of tutorial. When I went to the Swedish School of Business (Svenska Handelshogskolan or Hanken) I chose in addition Spanish. I learned school Spanish and later I had the occasion to live in Mexico. I came out of there being more fluent in Spanish than anything else.

I had seen my dad and my mother, at work, maintaining a business enterprise, dealing with borrowed money, and at the same time creating a standard of living that enabled us to go to school. My sister was in a private school. Business was an avenue through which I was going to be career oriented. I had been back to Finland Steamship Company for probably ten summers, and each summer I gained increased responsibilities. The final summer there I was actually the manager of the treasury.

Borje (Bud) Saxberg - 173

I was also lucky to be one of the founders of the AIESEC [*Association Internationale des étudiantes en sciences, économiques et commerciales*] organization, which is an organization for students by students to establish internship exchange programs. Today it's across the world. That became available because I had the language capability. I had another opportunity to go to England where there was a conference of students of previously warring countries. We were located in Oxford and we lived in the Oxford colleges. When my scout came in the morning and opened the curtain and said, "Good morning, sir," he had tea ready for me. This is where I should have had all my school years!

As I came back home and I came towards the end of my period at the business school, the question of course was, "What was I going to do?" I had the opportunity to go to the first AIESEC conference in Paris. I never did go back to Finland. While I was in Paris, it was a convention for the first traineeship exchange. Then I thought I'll be a trainee myself in Paris that summer. I extended it from four weeks to three months and while I was there, there was word from Helsinki that I had received a fellowship to go to the United States for an MBA. I said, "OK, I'm going to go on from here."

I arrived in New York City on the *Queen Elizabeth.* I went to the Greyhound bus station and bought a bus ticket from New York City to Portland, Oregon. A bus, that's the way you travel. When I got out five days later I said, "This is a big country!"

I wrote to my mother first, "I'll be gone for another year." Then I said, "Another year." "Another year." Then I met my wife at the University of Illinois, so then it became more permanent. It took sixteen years before I was back, to say goodbye, with my oldest son in tow in 1966.

I came to Oregon State University to do an MBA degree, but it turned out that Oregon State didn't have a master's program in the School of Business and Technology. As a result I decided then to do an American undergraduate degree. I opted for forest technology because I thought I was going to go back to Finland, and Finland is a big forest product country.

I had come to get a master's degree but I didn't have it. Then somebody said, "There are ten wealthy Midwest universities, surely one of them can afford you." I got one positive answer, University of Illinois. The chairman of a new department wrote and said, "I have just been appointed chairman of a brand new department of management and you apparently are interested in management." "I'll assign it to you." And so I had a fellowship for a year and that of course then put me on the way to University of Illinois, Champaign-Urbana.

I met my wife at University of Illinois. She is originally from Norway and was actually in the process of changing her career path. She had graduated in architecture from Oslo and she was going into nutrition. It was a new field. She just never really thought that she would get hitched to me, somebody from a business school, somebody that was from Finland. So she was very hard to convince!

Then the time came that the decision needed to be made where we would establish our roots. We agreed that Norway wasn't right for me and Finland wasn't right for her. I had an offer from the University of Washington in Seattle and I also had an offer from a corporation. I had been on the West Coast and I had liked my stay so we agreed to give it a couple of years and see what it is like. That's how we ended up here in Seattle.

At the University of Washington, I had come with the thought that I would teach management. That had after all been really my strength. But I was a jack of all trades. I had taught in the management area. From Finland I had the financial accounting area. And then I had forest technology. So I went to my senior colleague who was the senior in the area, and said, "I really want to teach management in your area. But he said "You'll never be competent to do that. Just forget it." Now that was a bit harsh.

At the time there was a big to-do about the business schools. Are they really, truly academic, or are they, as some contend, vocational schools? Both the Carnegie Foundation and the Ford Foundation had worked out some hefty reports. They felt there was a need to change the whole culture and make them into academic establishments. I discovered that Ford had something called "post-doctoral fellowships." I applied for a post-doctoral fellowship to Cornell University, in sociology, social psychology and anthropology. I got it. The whole family moved to Ithaca, N.Y., for a year.

When I came back, I went to my colleague and said, "Well, I'm ready for management." I taught human relations, organization structure, organization behavior. I taught organization design. Now for the last 10 years I've been teaching strategic management and business policy.

When I started out at the business school, I was interested in the potential of consulting arrangements to gain practical experience. One of my colleagues had been lecturing at an executive development program in Switzerland where he met a representative of Rolls Royce Aerospace. He became their consultant on manufacturing. Then he was asked if he would he take on the scientific engineering area? My colleague Al Shriver came to me and asked, "Would you be interested in doing that because I'm not really available to work with that group?" For the next fifteen years, I was the senior management consultant to Rolls Royce Aerospace. That was a wonderful period, just a really first class organization. My dean was very open to my travels. Because to have University of Washington as a label that shows up in connection with Rolls Royce he regarded as valuable for our classroom work.

The university was a very a supportive base for our family, because all of our members have had degrees from the University of Washington except me. My wife, Margrethe, did undergraduate work at Illinois in nutrition and later completed an undergraduate degree at the University of Washington in French.

It was quite early, that I got the opportunity to be the associate dean for the Business School and its graduate programs. I made a contract with my dean that I'll do that for three years and then go back to faculty status. He really thought I would be caught and stay on. But then he put his administrative hooks in me anyway. A year later I was chairman of the Department of Management and Organization. Now it was my colleagues who had elected me to be the chair and then you can't really say no. So that took some four years, or five years, I can't remember. Then I was out of it, and then it was just another three years, I was chairman again!

I was elected as the business school representative to the Faculty Senate. Then I was elected the chairman of the Faculty Senate. I also had the opportunity to serve as the first chair in the position of ex-officio member of the Board of Regents.

It was a year of recession and budget pressure. It was probably about 1980. Bill Gerberding had just come in as a new president. He was very courteous. He invited me to sit in on the sessions he had with the deans who were talking about what they wanted to do with their particular school and program. What then was on the docket was this question of how do we manage the budget squeeze in 1981. The question came up about releasing tenured faculty. When you're dealing with tenured faculty that's pretty sensitive, but at the same time if it really comes right down to it you have got to have some way of getting your expenses down. I thought that there was merit in trying to get it done. I saw Bill Gerberding and told him that the Faculty Senate Executive Committee can see the need for developing a procedure for how it might be done. We did, and out of that, finally in 1981, we actually worked out a formal procedure for laying off a tenured faculty member. A very cautious procedure, but it was a procedure that could be activated if need be.

When I came into the chair of the department the second time around, I felt like there was a need to jack things up. We were not really recognized the way we had been. Remembering my own family origins and recognizing that new companies were just springing up like mushrooms in the Northwest, I said, "We need to start up a program in entrepreneurship and innovation."

Around a big bureaucracy it's very difficult to get resources to do anything new. But as chairman of the department, I could arrange some coursework on an experimental basis. I introduced courses in entrepreneurship and in management of technology, first at the undergraduate level, later at the graduate level.

I talked with our development officer and she said, "Well, I have somebody who has been wondering, where else could he put his money in relation to his interests? I think that he would be willing to put some money on your idea." He also turned out to be one of my former students, so Neal Dempsey became a very important initial supporter of my idea of a program in entrepreneurship and innovation. We went on and I collected money. I was tin-cupping downtown and I got support from the dean's office.

The budget administrator had a little money that she could allocate for my secretary. She found a room and my sponsors provided the equipment, and I had it all working. Then I set up a recognition process so that anybody who took enough entrepreneurship could get a certificate. This worked out really well. Then it was time to find new talent to manage the program. "How do we take care of the succession?" Fortunately, I had a colleague that I knew who would be just right. I managed to persuad him to take over the program directorship after me. He took it across the campus to include students from other schools and colleges at the University of Washington. It's our biggest program at the moment.

But in between I had another one of my former students who had joined with me at a Saturday seminar about how to start up a new business. I was raising the question, "How do we get the word out, because I have no money." And he said, "I can get a freebie from a TV station." He knew because he had been a professional in the TV field." "Thirty seconds." I said, "What can I do in 30 seconds?" And he said, "If you know what you want to say, you can say a lot."

That taught me a real lesson, that it's really a powerful way of reaching a population. And then he and I put our heads together and worked out the TV program on entrepreneurs and innovators for PEI - The Program in Entrepreneurship and Innovation. We decided to see if we could get from *The Seattle Times* the business writer for technology to be a member so that we would have access to the *Times* archives, and at the same time have him on board.

We started the TV program and it worked. Of course, it was outside all protocols of officialdom, and I was no director in any formal sense. Finally there was somebody on our business administration advisory council who one day observed, "Say Bud, you've got a certificate and you've got courses and you got programs and numbers, but we never approved any of it."I said, "That's right." "You better be ready to come to our meeting next week and tell us what you are doing and ask for approval. If you have a success, you will be forgiven." PEI was authorized officially. My former student, Neal Dempsey, gave $10 million to the university, $5 million to the Huskies and $5 million to the program in entrepreneurship.

My greatest personal honor was when the business school put on a 50th anniversary celebration for me and invited all of my colleagues, contacts, friends and alumni. There might have been a couple of hundred people, downtown at the Continental Club. So that was very nice. I completed another two years of service and then decided it was time to quit.

I did join early the Finnish Chamber of Commerce and then later on the Swedish Finn Historical Society. These were board assignments and then likewise the board of the Nordic Heritage Museum and then for a time also the board of the Swedish Cultural Center.

Saxberg family Christmas in Norway, 1993
From left: Bo, Siri, Sheila, Denise holding Tor,
Margrethe and Bror.

178 - Borje (Bud) Saxberg

I'm on the advisory board for the University House, Wallingford and Issaquah. It becomes more interesting when you yourself get grayer and need to consider what's available for the mature population. [I'm also on the Board of Directors for the School Employees Credit Union of Washington and the PEMCO Insurance Company.]

Bjørkeli, the family home of Margrethe Haug Saxberg in Norway

---

Borje O. Saxberg was born January 25, 1928 in Helsinki (Helsingfors) Finland, raised with younger sister Berit. He arrived in the U.S .to study at the Oregon State University. He completed his studies at The University of Illinois and earned a PhD in business. He served as a professor in the UW school of business and spent a year as a Ford Foundation fellow at Cornell University. At the U.W. he served as department chair and chair of the Faculty Senate. He taught undergraduate courses in strategic management and business policy. Borje met his wife, Margrethe Haug, at the University of Illinois and they have two sons, Bo and Bror. He and his wife have a farm in Norway where they spend part of their year.

Marianne Forssblad

"And I must say that, my God, the Museum was almost my fourth child which might sound ridiculous but I felt that it needed a lot of care. So I was willing to give it."

I was born in Gothenburg — or Göteborg as we call it in Swedish — and have a brother and sister and lived with my family there. My father was involved in the maritime business. He was the head of the Swedish Ship Owners Association so we traveled a lot. So we all got the travel bug as children and we liked to go places. Ever since I was about fifteen they sent me to various places in Europe - especially to England to learn the English language properly.

I went to school in Gothenburg in the regular school system. In those days it was different from what it is today. It was first four years elementary and then four or five years intermediate and then four years in what we called *gymnasium*. Then it was the same thing as the last two years of high school and two years of college.

I spent every summer abroad, especially then, in England and in France. Then my last year of gymnasium I was toying with the idea of what could I do. I had various ideas. One thing was that I wanted to go into the Foreign Service. I wanted to become an ambassador. So in order to[do] that I decided to spend one year in the United States and I applied to the Swedish American Foundation for a scholarship and I did get it. So I came to the United States in 1957 to go to college in Virginia, a four-year college for women. After my first year I realized I could get my BA in two years so I asked my parents if I could stay another year which I did. It was a lot of fun and I had all the time been taking political science and history because this I thought would be really good for my future diplomatic service.

But I met an American and we got married [in Lexington, Virginia] only two days after I graduated. Of course my idea of getting into the Foreign Service and studying law in Sweden at that time then disappeared because now I was a young married woman and had to go back to the United States after the summer with my husband.

But anyway we ended up in Texas. And I continued my studies

there and studied international law. But after he was finished with his studies, we decided to go to Sweden and stay for a year. We went there and stayed in Gothenburg where we met a very nice American family. And that family happened to be from Seattle. And that's how we ended up in Seattle afterwards. Because they told us in glowing terms about the wonders of Seattle and by that time I had totally dismissed Texas. I thought it was a horrible place. The heat, the heat and I didn't like Texas at all. And I didn't like the Midwest and the East Coast was out so by elimination we chose Seattle.

And we came here in, I think December, January 1964, and that's when I came for good to the United States. And then I had my first child here in Seattle and I later had another one. I associated a lot with the young Swedes that were here at that time because Boeing had been in Europe and had recruited – that was in the 1960s – and had recruited Swedish engineers that came here. And we formed a kind of circle of friends and did a lot of things. But I had no idea of working for a museum or doing anything like that. I did have thoughts of going back to the university. I had my BA and my Masters but thought of continuing.

Well as life goes on, things happen and I was divorced. I had started to study library science actually at the University of Washington and I got my Masters of Librarianship at the UW. And I was looking at what I could do - thinking of maybe being a law librarian or something similar since I had studied international law and some law courses. But then as it turned out I was recruited by the Scandinavian Department to teach and be a kind of TA and continue in that department instead. So I started my studies towards my masters in the PhD program.

In 1976 I had my daughter Eva. At that time I had become involved a little bit with the Scandinavian community. I had met Gordon Ekvall Tracie and he invited me to various events, dances and so on. And I was interested in 1976 when they had the bicentennial celebration in Seattle. So at that time I became interested in the story of the immigrants. Before that I had interest in other things and not necessarily about the immigration issue. I never even thought about it. I had been involved in what I called the newer immigrants, all those people that had come, doctors, researchers, etcetera. I think it was my time in the Scandinavian Department that opened my eyes for the influx of Scandinavians in Washington State.

Then while I was at the University of Washington I was recruited by the Seattle Art Museum to become a consultant on an exhibit that they had, the "Art of Norway." I became responsible for their education

Marianne Forssblad - 181

program and went around giving lectures in the Northwest and up in Alaska on Scandinavian art, especially Norway. That again increased my interest in the immigration issue because I put on a symposium and, we talked about immigration, and I was given the task of writing a little history of the Norwegians in the United States – a very short, four-page thing, to give them an overview why there were so many Scandinavians in this area especially Norwegians. And then when I got involved in the community naturally there was talk about building a museum. I was at that time teaching at the University of Washington and I was recruited by Svein Gilje who is really one of the founders of Nordic Heritage Museum. And he asked me to be involved in this. I remember he came to my office at the University of Washington and I was very enthusiastic and I came to some of the meetings.

Actually there had been talk about a museum many years before the Nordic Heritage Museum was started. The Norwegians already in the early early part of the 20th century had wanted a museum because they realized the richness of their heritage. But nothing happened.

So talks continued off and on and then during the United States' celebration of its foundation in 1976 we talked again. And at that time it was realized that not just the one nation should do it but the five Nordic nations should be involved. So that was already from the very start very adamantly stated. It must be a museum that covers the five Nordic countries.

Of course a lot of people were saying that Scandinavia means the five countries and in the beginning there were some that wanted to name it the Scandinavian Heritage Museum. But the Finns and the Icelanders were adamantly opposed to that. So a group from all five countries was convened and discussions took place. It was agreed it should be the Nordic Heritage Museum. It should be a museum that describes what the Nordic-Americans did in the Pacific Northwest. That was the main vision.

I saw then what's possible and I met Leif Eie who was very much [involved] with Svein Gilje and others. And very instrumental in getting the museum started. Leif Eie is the one who went around and looked at various buildings for the museum. And there were buildings all over the geography here. And finally they found this empty school and actually the person that heard about it was Randi Hansen, a sister of Elsa Ellefsen who for many years was our wonderful cook in the kitchen. She called Leif about the school that was empty [Webster Elementary]. By that time there was a Nordic Council that had been established with only the idea of founding a museum and they went to the school district and gave a bid. Actually it was Leif Eie, I think, who proceeded to meet with the school district. And I know that at that time Carl Helgren, Bert Lundh and Egon Molbak and others were very, very much involved.

As it turned out the Nordic Council, the Scandinavians, were the only ones interested in the building. It was a rundown building, very rundown building and I remember the first time I came there in early 1979 and I saw it. It was rather dismal. It was dark and, of course, the entrance was not where the entrance is today. It was at the front. We still have doors there and it says "Nordic Heritage Museum" in small letters above the door facing 67th Street. But we thought it had potential. But as we were the only ones that gave a bid we realized that the bid that had been given was too high. So we started to negotiate and ask that it be given for less money and since there were no takers it was agreed.

And if my memory is right I think that the first year we only paid $300 a month in rent to the school district. And of course then we also had the big huge parking lot and there was a playground on it too but not like the playground today. As I said the building was rundown, a lot of broken windows which, you know, is now a legend – how many there were. There must have been about ninety broken windows. In the auditorium there was not the floor that we have today. It was a dark brown linoleum floor directly, I think, on the cement. Very hard. The kitchen was not like it is today either because IKEA helped us remodel the kitchen. It was a very dismal kitchen. The whole building was more or less abandoned because the school district realized that they were not going to use it anymore and they also leased it to a theatre company that made a film in the building and they really trashed it.

When we finally took it over it needed a lot of tender care and all we could do was clean it up and replace the windows. We had a wonderful volunteer by the name of Paul Mathisen. A little man – he's no longer with us either – who was the volunteer janitor, volunteer maintenance man, volunteer all and took care of the boiler and seeing that everything was fine. And also we rented out the gymnasium which is now where the Dream of America is. And that had nice wooden floors and you could dance on it. So we rented that out to the Skandia Folkdancers and it was Gordon Tracie who really was the liaison there and ran it. And in the little office that is now the Post Office he had his office and we had musical instruments there. But you know the school was not safe from burglary in those days and there had been a break-in and they had stolen some of his equipment which he was very upset about. But it was an interesting period and everybody was very enthusiastic. A lot of hard work went into it, incredibly hard work.

Marianne Forssblad - 183

I spent the early days – that was in 1979 or even 1980 – between teaching at the University of Washington and driving to the museum to help with the first exhibit we were going to put on. And Svein Gilje, using his journalistic skills, was the one who did the PR for us and wrote all the news releases and told how we were establishing a museum.

But it was interesting to see because the Nordic colony was not exactly optimistic about it. I remember well when I went around and talked about it they said "You'll never manage. …you should rather go in with the Museum of History and Industry and do something with them." The Museum of History and Industry had had in 1975 an exhibit because of the Norwegian Sesquicentennial. They were celebrating the 1825 arrival of *Restauration* to New York. But in 1975 they had had an exhibit at MOHAI and gathered a lot of different objects and so on. And it really became quite obvious the importance of the Norwegian community and in a bigger sense the Scandinavian community. So it was really at that time that they started to think about this, having a museum and now it was coming to fruition.

So we started then collecting. We went around and we got a good start. It was rather eclectic of course because we really did not have very thorough guidelines. We were willing to take more or less everything because we were an upstart museum. We had enough to put together two rooms which I was very proud of. At that time then in 1980 I was then head of the exhibits and the exhibit committee. And we focused on what we called home life and had different objects and material documents of the Scandinavians such as textiles, house wares, wooden objects, decorative objects, in one room. And in the other room we had occupational objects such as boat building which of course was very prominent, and logging. Boatbuilding and logging, those were the two main exhibits we started and those are the two rooms that are now on the second floor called the Heritage Rooms. Those are the only two rooms we had available. The rest were just empty horrible classrooms with green walls and big huge dirty windows.

But we opened on April 12, 1980, because there had been a fundraiser for the museum. It had been at the Space Needle and Bert Lundh was one of the organizers of that and I know that Carl Helgren supplied the champagne. It was a very fancy Scandinavian menu that we had. It was up on the Space Needle that rotated and we were able to raise quite a bit of money. And the first year's budget was $28,000. I was hired and the reason I was hired was that we were able to … Svein Gilje and I wrote a grant, and [I was] put on as the Acting Director at that time in 1980.

I think that in the first year we were able to get about 218 members of the Museum and the person who was in charge of the membership – of course everything was done by hand, no computers or anything, maybe a typewriter – was Sirkka Wilson.

But when I was given the Directorship, of course, I had to give up my board membership. Then, of course, the rest is history. I was then Director from that time until my retirement on April 30 or May 1 in 2007. It was many difficult years to start with but very exciting years. It was like a little family that had no money. Because the budget was small and we were not always sure that we could pay salaries, my little salary, or the maintenance, running it. Because, after all, we were heated by oil. I think that was the largest bill, the oil bill.

So I remember .. it must have been within the first year, it must have been 1981 we were in dire straits and I decided that I would take a cut in my salary. I think I was under $500 a month and at the same time I taught at the University of Washington so that the Museum would survive. I taught in the morning at the UW and then I ran over to the Museum and I was there for the rest of the day. Also at that time we got a young intern from Portland State University – Janet Baisinger. And she started then a more direct policy of registering the acquisition of the objects, recording the objects. Because back in 1979 we had, what we call, a volunteer curator registrar, a young man who was [there] for a little while, who was quite cantankerous actually. And he and I did not get along too well. But he later quit and Janet took the position. Then Janet went back and got her Masters and after that we hired her as the first Curator of the Nordic Heritage Museum.

There were many funny incidents of course. You realize that we needed to entice the Nordic community to become involved and it was very hard to become involved and enthusiastic about a rundown, damp, dark, rather scary building. So there were many work parties where they were painting. We painted ourselves. I've been standing on many a scaffolding painting the then exhibit rooms. The configurations of the exhibit rooms are different now especially on the second floor in the temporary exhibit galleries. Those were not joined and we didn't have an elevator. They were just individual classrooms and each classroom had a closet where the kids were supposed to hang their clothes.

But we painted and some of the board members helped us paint and I remember one of our early board members, Carl Jarvie, who was also a good supporter of the Museum, coming to paint and he was really an accountant by trade so this is somewhat symptomatic of how we worked in the early days — really by pure labor and being obstinate. And then of course the board met and it only met six times a year. We had a few committees working but it was not at all streamlined and official and with the many committees and departments that exist today of course. Because we were just beginning to run – not even run, to walk – we were crawling first and then little by little we were able to walk.

I remember well in the early days when we had Scandinavia Today and that was a big, big undertaking. Seattle had been chosen by the American government in conjunction with American Scandinavian Foundation to be part of Scandinavia Today. In those days, many years ago, the United States government focused on different countries to show what the countries were like in today's world. And Scandinavia was chosen in 1983 I think it was. And Seattle was one of the cities, one of the many cities that were going to be part of Scandinavia Today. And we competed for some of the exhibitions. Of course [we were] very young and as I said had only two or three exhibit rooms but we cleaned up a couple of classrooms that now are the temporary art galleries and we were given an exhibit that dealt

Marching in the 17th of May Parade, 2006

with Greenland — "Greenland Today," fascinating exhibit. And at that time, Janet was working full-time and I was working full-time and then we had a part-time, two to three days, assistant who was very artistic too. Her name was Issa Parker. She worked with us and the three of us were supposed to mount this humungous exhibit but we had the architect who had designed it from Denmark with us, Søren Sass. He was really a very talented man and very friendly because he always went around with a little bottle of cognac in his back pocket. He took it to strengthen himself because he said, "I can't believe this. This is amazing." You know our museum. He was used to working in bigger museums, but it was really a challenging time but a fun time.

You have to realize that this was taking place on the second floor. No elevator and very heavy objects to bring up. Very heavy backdrops to bring up and stuffed animals like the sleigh dogs, big huge sleighs, big huge things. We had to get volunteers to carry everything up the stairs and into the rooms. And I remember I recruited some of the professors

186 - Marianne Forssblad

from the University of Washington to come and help me carry those things. We had it stored in what now is the beginning of the "Dream of America" because that wasn't an exhibit space yet. It was partly a playground for kids and was partly opened to the outside. There was a big half-brick wall with a netting towards 68th so it was very cold and very open space. But the kids used to go there and play when it was raining outside on their breaks. And this was where we first stored all these heavy objects and then brought them up the stairs which was very different from today. The configuration upstairs was different too. But anyway Søren managed to get it all under control and we helped him – Janet and I – and we had some other people too – volunteers to help him. And we opened. It was a beautiful, beautiful exhibit showing Greenland today with three-dimensional objects. Like I said sleigh dogs, sleighs and everything else.

And that was on display when the King and Queen of Sweden came to visit. They came to the United States. They had been invited and they did different things and, of course, the King went and met with the Swedish community. We had a variety of banquets for them and we even put on a fashion show. Actually I had decided I wanted to do a really fun fashion show in those days and we had it at the Westin Hotel I think it was. I gathered volunteers to help with the dressing people and even I at that time modeled something. So you can see it was really a hands-on operation but the King and Queen enjoyed it and of course the Queen was very, very gracious. When I look back at it, it's amusing because we were such a small museum and we had so little to show for it. The only thing we had upstairs – we had decided to use the room which is now – it used to be a gallery when it had been modernized, but in those days it was still a classroom but now it is part storage of the museum and part office space on the third floor. Anyway then it was just a classroom with the windows but we had installed a rosemaling exhibit up there. So we had our two heritage rooms, we had the Greenland exhibit at one end and upstairs we had the rosemaling exhibit. The King was not interested in going up there. He probably thought that we were really very small operation but the Queen very graciously wanted to go up and see it.

And then we gathered them in what we then made into the library on the mezzanine which is now also partly the Music Library and partly office. It was a classroom because we had classes there. Ed Egerdahl had started with us already then so it was just a classroom. And we gathered school children from Ballard who could meet with the King and Queen of Sweden and Olaf Kvamme was involved with that. Olaf Kvamme who later became a board member of the Museum. Olaf, of course, was working for the School District and there are many good photographs of Carl Gustaf and Queen Silvia and the children.

For many, many years it was just Janet and I and a person who helped with the office. It wasn't easy but we made strides and in 1985 we were contacted again by the Danes about an exhibit that they wanted to bring to the United States. It was the "Dream of America." It was a fascinating exhibit. It was the core of what we have in the Dream of America plus a little bit more in Denmark. The Board also asked me to travel over there to look at it. And in the meantime Andrew Price who has been a great supporter of the Museum had also been over there and gone to what is called Moesgaard, that's the Danish Museum outside Aarhus, and looked at it and thought this would be perfect for Seattle. It shows immigration and it's done in a very three-dimensional way. But I was over there and went through it and was very, very enthusiastic. And came back to the Board and said we must really try to get this one and I showed them the layout and plans. And they became enthusiastic and Bert Lundh was really the driving force here too in saying that we should yes really get this one.

Fashion show for 2004 exhibition,
"Duodu: Contemporary Norwegian Knit Fashion."
Marianne Forssblad (right) introducing models.

Bert was the second president after Svein Gilje. Svein Gilje was president for many years in the beginning and then the next president was Bert Lundh. So we decided to raise money and at that time Andrew Price had become so enthusiastic and he became my main helper in raising money and he went around and talked to people. We were able

188 - Marianne Forssblad

to accomplish incredibly much. I wrote grants. I wrote lots and lots of grants and we did raise the money and we also approached Jens Bruun of Scan Design because he was Danish. And he said he would sponsor the actual purchase of the "Dream of America." Because what it is — it was not a travelling exhibit. They wanted … they were going to just destroy it or send it to someplace who wanted it. And at that time we were ready for it. So Jens Bruun said he would pay for the core exhibit as it was brought over here. In those days I think the Danish Crown was 10 crowns to a dollar but by the time that we were able to get the exhibit and pay for it, it had gone down so it became quite a bit more expensive than we had thought. So anyway Jens Bruun helped us acquire it and he also loaned one of his carpenters from Scan Design, one of his workers. And

then Moesgaard Museum sent over the designer and somebody else, a man who worked with us for several months. Because we had to totally re-do the downstairs. We had to close in the open play court area where now is the beginning of the "Dream of America." We had to break through into the gym and make that available. And then we had to bring the huge exhibit over to Seattle. We got

Seattle City Councilmember Lois North celebrates the Council recognition of the "Dream of America" exhibit with Bert Lundh, Marianne Forssblad, and Trygve Jorgensen

Maersk, the Danish company, to sponsor it and they brought it over free of charge.

The opening ceremony was gigantic, wonderful. The choruses sang. I know the Norwegian Male and Women's Chorus sang. Alf Knudsen was directing them. We had many important politicians coming and there was a line out, a long, long line to go through the Museum. And at that time we got three young girls from Scandinavia to come over and help as guides. …And they were with us for three months. But it was an exciting time because this really put us on the map. It had taken us five or six years to get there but now we had the foundation so to speak of a permanent exhibit that was well done and we could build further on it.

And at that time I started to think "What do we need to do now?" We had two main galleries that little by little were improving. We had put in another gallery that showed women's work, etcetera, but we needed

Marianne Forssblad - 189

upgrade. We continued upgrading and I thought that we needed a ,hing exhibit and a logging exhibit. So there was lot of grant writing. , did the grant writing in those days. And I remember it cost me a lot of nervousness to be able to do that plus everything else. And it wasn't easy but we did get grants to mount the fishing exhibit and we were able to get someone to design it and we did the same thing with the logging exhibit. It was really thrilling to see those three exhibits come to fruition because they are so important in the history of the Nordics here, especially for the Norwegians and for Ballard. The fishing industry has such impact.

In 1980 I was approached by somebody from Sagstad Marina... they had an interesting big ship there that they thought the Museum should be interested in. I went and looked at it and I said yes it really is great but how can we do that? They said well it can stay here for awhile but soon we need to move it. And it's the Nordlands boat that now evidently has been renamed the *Nordic Spirit*. But anyway it is the Nordlands boat. It was used as a fishing boat in Norway in the early 1800s. I had an expert from Norway come and look at it. And also Ingrid Semmingsen, historian and authority on Norwegian immigration to the United States, saw it and she said "Yes indeed it has been used in Northern Norway as a fishing boat." But it was purchased by Volvo and Volvo used it as a gimmick and sailed up and down the Potomac – outside Washington, D.C., with it. And it had sails which said – it was typical striped sails, red and white Viking sails – and the shields had in runic letters Volvo, I think Volvo Penta or Volvo on it. What's interesting is it was a Norwegian fishing boat that Volvo had hired a well-know sculptor in Gothenburg to do the embellishment on it. So the head, the Viking head on the boat was sculpted by this sculptor and swirls on the side and the embellishments on the sides were all sculpted by him. It was embellished this way to look like a Viking boat. So Volvo took it around different places on the East Coast but eventually, of course, it ran out of news worthiness so a man who worked for Volvo lived in Seattle in those days and decided to bring it to Seattle. And pulled it all the way across United States to Seattle and stored it in the Sagstad Marina where we looked at it. And where we then got it. Then we were building the Dream of America so then we brought it outside and put it where it was outside on the west side. And eventually it was covered by our volunteers with scaffolding and awnings.

But there were challenges of course. There were challenges. One challenge was when we were planning the expansion – re-configuration – of space in the Museum and putting in the HVAC system and all the building that was happening. The Executive Committee met every week

190 - Marianne Forssblad

at 7:30 in Jan Kiaer's office on Denny. And that was a challenge for me to always to be there at 7:30 once a week and have my kids to school and Eva to her school, etcetera. So it did take a lot of special organization at home to be ready to do all of these things.

Yulefest started before the Museum was founded. It started in 1978 in order to raise money for the potential museum. And Elsa Elefsen's sister, Randi Hansen, was very much involved in that and Elsa also became involved. That was held in downtown Ballard in what now is the restaurant in the old Carnegie Library, the Carnegie Restaurant. On the top floor we had the Yulefest. And we were very lucky because Rosanne Royer, the wife of then Mayor Charles Royer, became interested in the Museum because she's ethnic herself, she's Croatian-Serbian. And she became very involved in starting the Ethnic Heritage Council and she felt that the Museum was an important aspect of ethnicity in Seattle. So she was promoting this sort of thing too. So in 1978, Yulefest started as a fundraiser and then when we got the Museum from the School District. Before we opened to the public, Yulefest was held in the auditorium of the Museum in 1979. Very few artisans and craftspeople were there but there were some musicians. It was kind of an almost forlorn group of people that was there I think because the building was not up to par yet.

Then our wonderful volunteers have helped with ideas, helped with every aspect of it. And it became very important for the volunteers to be involved. So they were the ones who suggested - let's get a *kaffestua* in the "Dream," let's get something else, etcetera. So it evolved over the years and became a good fundraiser.

In the beginning we did not have *glögg*. We just served beer and wine. And then we started discussing – it was suggested by a Swedish volunteer I'm sure – why don't we serve glögg as well. I felt that was a great idea but nobody was willing to make it. So I just said "Well I'll make it." And I started to make the glögg and since I made it then everyone relied on me to continue making it.

It's glögg that I like. And I do it by taste. I do not put *akvavit* in the glögg like sometimes one does in Sweden. But I only use burgundy and spices – the spices that give that kind of extra little touch to it. It has to be sweet enough but not too sweet because wine can be slightly sour if you buy the fairly inexpensive burgundy. So you have to taste it until it's just right and you have to get the proper spices in it like the cloves, the cardamom, the cinnamon sticks, etcetera. And I also use the tiny slices of oranges, the peel of oranges. And sometimes one can even put a little bit of ginger in it but not too much. Because ginger is so very, very strong so I usually don't do that. It has to have just the right taste and it must be served piping hot. It's very similar in a sense to mulled wine. It has the spices of Swedish glögg but not the akvavit. So there is no real secret. It just has to taste right. And it must be very hot when it is served.

As far as Tivoli was concerned it was the same thing there. Actually the person who really suggested it was Bert Lundh because we needed more fundraisers. He said "Why don't we have a summer festival?" So we started to talk about that and we decided "Yeah why don't we a summer festival?" Again it became my responsibility to realize and we decided to have an outside festival. In the beginning it was only one day and our crews – Monday crew and Thursday crew who were then functioning – talked about it and become involved in it. It was Trygve Jorgensen who ran the Thursday crew who devised and decided on the booths that were made for Tivoli. Booths that were then also in the beginning not having – I don't think they had awnings over them – the blue awnings over them. And that grew and again it was the volunteers who were the driving force seeing to it that it could expand by their willingness to work and their willingness to take on functions.

It wasn't exactly a [bed] of roses having the children and having the Museum. I know that it put a lot of demands on me. I tried to balance in a way family life with the Museum but I know that some of the family life aspect had to be sacrificed. And I know that my children had to give up a lot of things and I must say that I am very grateful to them because they were great kids and very understanding. But there were times when I was rushing home to prepare dinner for them and then putting dinner on the table and rushing back to the Museum for there was a meeting in the evening. That was when the children were still young enough that I was needed at home to do this. My daughter, Eva, was the youngest, only three when the Museum started – and she was in a nursery school, a small school that I had to pick her up afterwards. I brought her to the Museum very often and she loved actually being there and being with me. She was very shy in those days but she had her own little office. In the very beginning I had an office that now the office manager has and there was a little – that was where the principal had his office and he had a little opening into the other, next room which is now - I think there is a printing machine. There was a little opening with a lid that you could drop and I made that into my daughter's office when she was three and four.

So she could sit and draw pictures there and she could open the little lid and hand me the drawings she had made. And I also allowed her to roam the second and third floor. Because when we were only open very limited times – we were only open on Wednesdays and weekends but the work went on. From 1 to 4 on Wednesday or something similar. So I allowed her to bring her skate board and she skated on the second floor and she kept herself occupied that way.

But she was also very interested in the Museum with all its nooks and crannies. There were a few times when I couldn't find her and it made me terribly nervous because I always envisioned something happening to her, something going wrong in this place for her. When she was older, she took the bus and came to the Museum and I put her to answer the phone at the Museum. So she answered the phone at the phone desk and she did a really good job. Because all of us still then were answering phones because we did not have an answering machine in the very beginning.

I also put my youngest son to work in the "Dream of America." He did some of the installation and he also did the painting of the seascape behind the ship there and used his artistic talent. It's still there after twenty years. There's a backdrop which is painted. Otherwise it went okay because my kids were good and they understood that it was important for me to work. And I must say that, my God, the Museum was almost my fourth child which might sound ridiculous but I felt that it needed a lot of care. So I was willing to give it.

Marianne Forssblad, former Executive Director of the Nordic Heritage Museum, retired in 2007 after 27 years with the Museum. Prior to that she worked at the Seattle Art Museum and the University of Washington Scandinavian Department. Marianne came to the United States in 1957 as a young student at Hollins College in Virginia and received her B.A. degree in 1959. She continued studies at the University of Texas and at the University of Washington. Marianne has M.A. degrees in Political Science and Library Science. She received a M.A. degree in Scandinavian Language and Literature in 1976 and completed coursework to receive a Ph. C at the Department of Scandinavian Languages and Literature at the University of Washington. Marianne was honored by the nations of Denmark, Norway and Sweden for her contributions to Nordic-American relations. Marianne has three children: Anders, Lars Erik and Eva. She spends her summers in Laholm, Sweden and the rest of year in the Seattle area as well as in Palm Springs, California.

Hanna Aasvik Helmersen

"And then I started to put it all together, and it became this little book called **War and Innocence.** *"*

When my children were small, they would often ask my husband and me: "Tell about when you were little, tell about the war in Norway." The war in Norway was the Second World War. We spent many a Sunday morning all snuggled up in our bed telling stories from our war experience. As we shared these stories with our American friends, we were surprised to find that this was a virtually unknown part of World War II to them. To most Americans we had contact with, World War II was primarily the Pacific War, the bombing of Germany, the landing on the Normandy beaches, and the horror of the concentration camps. The Norwegian experience, if known at all, was just a footnote to history. But to those of us who experienced it first-hand, it was something entirely different. It marked us for life. And then I started to put it all together. It became this little book called *War and Innocence*. I wrote this book primarily for my children and grandchildren. I wanted to describe a childhood vastly different than theirs.

I wanted them to understand what privileged lives they had. I wanted them to know and feel what it was like, coming of age when horrible things took place. I was eight when the war started and thirteen when it was over. I wrote this book because I came to think that it was a story that ought to be told, and that was worth telling. Yes, this is the story of my childhood years, and of my family's life, but it is more than that. It is the story of every child, every family who lived through those years. I wanted to show how, under harsh circumstances, ordinary people could live both ordinary and extraordinary lives. The setting of the book is primarily Northern Norway, above the Arctic Circle. Into this remote region World War II literally arrived with a bang in the very early hours of April 9, 1940. Life was suddenly drastically changed. Whole communities were uprooooted and in flight. The sounds of war were everywhere. Panic gripped the population. Men, women, and children fled the cities and heavily populated areas in great haste, not really knowing where to go, but seeking safety in the countryside and smaller towns. We joined the rest of the community.

And so we became refugees. For 18 months we moved from place to place. Sometimes we were received with friendliness and compassion; other times with indifference, and at times also with a certain hostility. I felt that we had to excuse ourselves for even existing.

Although Norway was a neutral country, in the seven months between the allied declaration of war and the German invasion of Norway, 58 Norwegian ships were sunk and 392 sailors perished.

My home town, Narvik, had a large ice-free harbor all year around, and was the shipping port for high grade Swedish iron ore which Hitler needed for his growing war machine. Germany was the biggest buyer of iron ore before the war.

Two chapters in my book deal with the extensive Underground activities, the torture and executions which followed when these cells were discovered, the vast network of young and old who were involved.

One of the horrors of my childhood was the executions. On the telephone poles would be attached big posters with black borders. Inside were the names of those who were either condemned to die, or had already been shot. I cannot fully express the kind of fear and deep anxiety this caused. No one was really safe, for it sometimes took very small infractions to release the wrath of these foreigners who had swarmed over our land.

Still, young men and women risked their lives by fleeing the country. Some crossed the mountains on skis and foot, going east to Sweden. My sister did that. Others went west in small fishing boats across the stormy Atlantic to Great Britain. These men and women joined the Allied forces in all branches of the military. My father's two youngest brothers fled to England. They sailed all through the war. One was torpedoed and rescued twice. The other took part in the Normandy Landings. Almost every family had loved ones involved in Norway's freedom fight.

Nasjonal Samler (members of the Norwegian Nazi Party) infiltrated every part of the school system, from school boards and supervisory positions to councils of education, which decided what educational material was to be used. They controlled the teacher training colleges, and tried in every way to impose the new order. But they were never able to Nazify Norway. The schools and the churches provided the firm backbone to resist, and guided the parent organizations in how to protect the children from Nazi influence. It was a spiritual battle for Norway's soul which the Nazis could never win.

But still, this dark, ominous shadow continually hung over us. Although we tried to go on with our lives, and in some ways we had a happy childhood, we felt very strongly that we were not free, and this longing for the day of liberation was an ever-present theme. Every day we would say: "when the war is over, when the war is over." We never doubted that it would be, some day. And we never doubted that our side would be victorious.

One of the things we longed for most was to have enough to eat, for we did indeed starve a great deal of the time. I remember one late spring day. The winter store of potatoes was gone, there was no flour from which to make bread, no butter, no milk, no dairy products whatsoever. We had a barrel of salted herring in the cellar storage room. So mother asked us to go and see if we could find some wild burning nettles. She had heard that they were edible. We put on woolen mittens, and set out, and we did bring home a bucket of nettles. Mother cooked them, and that was our one meal for the day: salted herring and cooked burning nettles. I remember us laughing and joking about this, but it was really a stark reality. And I don't know how my mother managed to feed us, every day, and keep us alive. I think all children who experience war are marked. Rooms in our houses were requisitioned for the soldiers to live in. We were not allowed to go upstairs in our home, because that is where they lived. They were mostly very polite and considerate, and sometimes they would even bring something edible for us, such as an apple, or piece of bread, or perhaps a piece of sausage. We were Seventh Day Adventists, and on Fridays Mother would clean house and make ready for Sabbath. When the soldiers came home that night, they would remove theirs shoes before going upstairs, and one of them always said: "Morgen sabbath?"

Yes, mother answered: "Tomorrow is Sabbath."

And so the war and occupation dragged on, year by year. I hope I have given a taste of what life was like for us.

Hanna Aasvik grew up in Ankenes, Nordland, Norway. After *examen artium,* she went to Denmark for a four-year course in Physical Therapy. She has practiced her profession for 43 years in Denmark, Norway, Pakistan and the United States. In 1957 she immigrated to the United States to marry Hjaltar Helmersen, also from Northern Norway, whom she met some years earlier. They made their home in a suburb of Seattle. Hjaltar and Hanna have both been active in the Norwegian community in Seattle. Hjaltar died July 29, 2009. They have two sons and five grandchildren.

Per Kristian and Sandra Johnsen

"I was young enough so I learned English without an accent. A year later, I would probably have a very strong Norwegian accent. Earlier, I would have lost much of my Norwegian. So it was a very good time to acquire another language."

*Per and wife
Sandra Williams Johnsen*

I was born in Bodø, Norway Feb 3, 1944. My parents and I came by ship to New York on August 30, 1957. I had an older brother and sister who stayed in Norway. Our only contact in Seattle was Gerd-Lise, a family friend. She and her husband lived in Ballard on 69th and 28th. She was from Bodø, I think he was from Bergen. Within three or four days we found a tiny house in a back yard on 62nd between 22nd and 24th. I think the rent was $55 a month. We had no furniture and the house had only a bed and a sofa, maybe another single bed, and a stove and refrigerator. I had two years of English in school in Norway. My mother spoke a little English, and my father almost none.

I enrolled at James Monroe Junior High School. They expected me to take part in the regular program. Within a week or so I knew the routine fairly well and was doing fine. In one class two girls were from Norway. One was the daughter of a one-year exchange teacher at Ballard. The other one had come to Seattle when she was about ten years old. She was in two of my classes and was a good help. I sat behind her, so if I had questions, I could whisper them to her. I was young enough so I learned English without an accent. A year later, I would probably have a strong Norwegian accent. Earlier, I would have lost much of my Norwegian. So it was a very good time to acquire another language.

In some ways I found school easier than in Norway. There were more choices, more interesting classes I could take. The teachers I had were generally pretty good, friendly and helpful. Some teachers said some cruel things, but I remember those things were said in Norway, too, so it wasn't very different. By the end of the first semester in January, I had top grades because by then I was fluent. That was eighth grade. My ninth-grade language arts teacher at Ballard High didn't know I wasn't

American. I told her later. She had no idea I had been in the country less than a year.

My dad worked on the waterfront for two years after we came. His business was food processing and canning in Norway, he was manager of a cannery. He got a job at a fish house, Pier 31, hauling frozen fish in and out of freezers. It was not very healthy work, so he declared himself a carpenter, and he did that for a year and a half.

A Norwegian woman [Bjørg Hoel] had the Ballard Dairy and Delicatessen at 2203 Northwest Market Street. Mrs. Gordon had run the store for years in the past, but continued to supply the store with the things she made — Norwegian pressed meats like *rullepølse* [pressed rolled lamb], and things like that. So it became gradually more and more a Norwegian store. At the end of 1959, my dad bought it for $6,000. He was 41 years old. In his 20's, he had owned a fish market in Bodø. He opened the Ballard Dairy & Delicatessen January 1960. He expanded and made all kinds of Norwegian foods — codfish cakes, fish pudding, soups and pressed meats, smoked salmon and sausages. He also started importing more cheese, crackers and canned goods from all of Scandinavia, but primarily from Norway. The store was little. You could touch all the walls if you just turned around in its kitchen.

There were plenty of customers. The days just before Christmas, the store would be absolutely full of people, with a line 50 yards down the street. I was 16 when he bought the store. I worked there every day through college. When they took trips to Norway, I ran the store for them. In high school, I would go down and open the store, mop the floor, get the meat case ready and the food stacked and the shelves stocked, then go to school. And then, depending on what sports were involved, I'd usually work after school and all day Saturday.

We sold just standard stuff, primarily pressed meats, *sylte* and smoked salmon. And cured dried lamb, which is a leg of lamb cured and dried, so it's like jerky. We made hundreds of them. Eventually we had another space in the alley next to the Ballard Fish Market, with a much larger kitchen, so all the production took place there. And we had a big walk-in cooler. I would roll carts of food down the street to the little store where we'd sell it. We also had room to make *lefse* and some baked goods for Christmas. We hired a couple of women who baked for us during the winter. All of those things combined into an incredible amount of business at Christmas time.

The New Bagdad Meat Market, across the street, had a produce stand in front, partly open to the street, and a meat counter in the back. My dad bought the place and moved the store there in April, 1963 and then business was like Christmas time all year round, because it was a large food store with lots of production room. We made lots of sausages, fish cakes and all the meats. And we imported lots of cheese. My dad had United States import rights to all the popular Norwegian cheeses, Jarlsberg, for example. We imported just tons of cheese. That's where Olsen's Scandinavian Food Store is now.

Ole Bardahl was a regular customer in our store. He was a nice guy, very shy. He waited his turn and was fairly generous in what he bought. He'd buy large amounts, for example, $10 worth of smoked salmon. And he bought *lefse*, cheese and salmon, things like that. In 1958 the first Miss Bardahl was built, the hydroplane, the racing boat. So I became a hydroplane fanatic for three or four years, and followed the Miss Bardahl, faithfully. I knew every race, every speed, every size of every boat and who had driven it.

By 1970 I was done with graduate school and had my doctorate, and we were gone and I had a position at the University of Wisconsin in Green Bay. I was 26. It was pretty clear to my parents that I was not going to take over the store. One thing they valued was that I should go as far as I could in school. So I went straight through: undergraduate degree, then graduate school and right to work at a university, for 20 years.

My parents ran the store until 1972, when they sold it to Reidar and Ebba Olsen, who had worked for us for many years. He was a sausage maker and she worked in the store. They were from Svolvær in Lofoten. It's the coastal steamer's first stop north of Bodø.

We always spoke Norwegian at home, and it was also a business necessity. If you didn't speak Norwegian, you couldn't work in the store. And you had to be able to speak to anyone from Scandinavia, plus English. Customers might use any of those languages, and you needed to be able to switch without thinking and to add and tell prices and weigh things, everything in any language.

My parents had planned to come only for a year or two. After a couple years they realized there's no way could they get enough money to go back rich. They stayed for 15 years. They sold the business in '72. They moved back to Norway because there was no family here. My wife and I were in Wisconsin, my brother and sister and their other relatives were in Norway. There my dad, in his 50s, started a beauty bark business in Larvik. He ran it for about 17 years and retired at age 70.

Now I'm an education and training coordinator for Kitsap Transit.

Per Kristian Johnsen - 199

And I teach part-time at local colleges, as well. I met my Sandra in high school.

SANDRA: I had heard about this good looking Norwegian young man at our school, and got to meet him. We kind of hit it off, and the rest is history. I grew up in Ballard, with two sisters, Julianne and Melissa. We all went to Ballard High and we all played in the band. My dad was a musician, and played in dance bands [see Williams, p. 474]. I trained to be a teacher at the University of Washington. My first job was at Coe Elementary on Queen Anne. After four years of marriage, we moved to Wisconsin. I now teach physical education and health in Bremerton. I try to stay active and healthy and have a good time. My mother's mother was from Norway. She immigrated by herself in 1910. She was from a little farm by Mandal. Nine kids left, one after another, because the farm was so small. The parents never came.

PER: The old folks in Norway saw all of their kids leave, one after the other. The youngest one stayed 'til her mother died, then she left. We were in Norway in '68 and we went to the farm. Two cousins of Sandy's grandmother were living in the house, a brother and a sister. Sandy was the first relative ever to come back. Over two generations people had left and no one had ever been back since.

SANDRA: We lived in Norway twice, just for a year. Per had a research sabbatical two different times.

PER: So our kids had a chance to live in Norway.

Per Kristian Johnsen was born in Bodø February 3, 1944 to Einar and Clara Johnsen. He and his parents came to Ballard in 1957. After working in a fish processing plant and as a carpenter, his father bought what became the Ballard Dairy & Delicatessen (later Johnsen's) in 1959. The parents sold the store to Reidar and Ebba Olsen in 1972 and returned to Norway. Per and Sandra Williams were married in 1966. They have two daughters: Kristianna (1970) and Randi (1976).

Pirkko Borland

"I was born on June 10, 1944. The day before was the [beginning of the] major Russian attack on the Karelian Isthmus.

"For at least a couple of weeks after giving birth, my mother still had not heard anything from my father. So there was a question as to whether he had survived. He did. And he received leave for the first time in August.

"Since he was coming home, I was to be baptized that day. There were not too many cars in Finland at that time. And those cars had been taken to the war. So the old pastor from town, along with his wife, rode their bicycles about seven or eight miles for the baptism. But my father had not yet arrived because the train that had brought him from the front was delayed.

"Eventually he got to a place — I'd say 30 miles — 30 miles plus from home where an aunt of mine lived. He went there, got a bicycle and then pedaled. And the old pastor said, 'We're here for the baptism. We're not going to baptize the child until the child's father gets here.'"

In April 1942, because his two brothers had been killed, my father was left with the family farm while he was in the war. His mother was still alive but she had Parkinson's disease and was pretty much bedridden. All able-bodied men were at war. . . So the farm labor was being done by Russian war prisoners who were distributed to the Finnish farms to do the work.

In the fall of 1942, my parents got married and my mother quit the Wetterhoff textile school in Hameenlinna and moved in. She took on the farm that had Russian war prisoners doing the work and had all the old and feeble people in addition to people who were evacuated from the front or from the border area. There were two families for a fairly lengthy time, housed on the farm. And in the middle of all that she gave birth to me. So it wasn't an easy time for her by any means.

After the war we gave up a part of the farm to help settle the Karelians who were coming in. The housing shortage was very severe in Finland, because it was about one-eighth of the population that had to be settled in the rest of the country. Most farmers in Finland had to give up land to enable these people who had lost their homes to build new homes.

All my childhood I remember that towards the end of the day — or maybe just at the end of the week — on the Finnish radio you would hear how many mines had been cleared from Lapland.

When Finland was negotiating the peace treaty with the Russians, part of the deal was that the Germans had to leave in two weeks or so. So they scorched the earth as they retreated and put mines everywhere to keep Russians or others from pursuing them. So this mine clearing was going on for years and you always heard this report.

I used to love milking cows. I thought, "It's great work [because] you see what you're accomplishing. You see it coming out." There were many opportunities for hand milking as electricity wasn't 100 percent reliable on the farm, even after we got it. I was about five years old when we got electricity.

We [siblings and cousins] would help in the hay fields. . . But if it was raining then the kids would be excused and that's why I still like the sound of rain because we could go and we had these hiding places in the hay loft up above the barn. And we could hear the rain and we'd just lie there and read books.

My mother would often make ice cream. It would be frozen outside in the snow bank and you had to keep stirring the batter so that it wouldn't get so crystallized. In my early years there was no commercial ice cream available, so my cousins always were looking forward to my mother's ice cream.

After high school, I went to the University of Helsinki to study English and Latin with the idea of being a high school teacher. After two years my roommate, who also was an English major, and I decided to apply for scholarships in the United States. It was an extremely lengthy process. By the time we had gone through all the steps we had a thick stack of papers, and I think there was a statement from everybody who had ever known me or seen me walk by in the street. These applications were sent to New York from where they were distributed to various universities. And if there was a living group at that college who would accept that student as a guest — in other words provide room and board — then the university would waive the tuition fees. And that's how I ended up at the University of Washington.

I lived at the Chi Omega house that year [in 1964] and met my husband, Brad, that spring. But I of course was going back to Finland and he was in the Navy at the time. So we corresponded for a year and then he came to Finland the following summer. I was still at school so I kept on with my studies and he stayed in Helsinki for awhile and had a job there. Then that fall we ended up getting married and moved to Seattle in 1966.

It wasn't exactly in my life plan [marrying an American]. My family were not very keen on it obviously. But I think what was very helpful was the fact that my husband stayed in Finland for several months. So they had an opportunity to get to know him.

And I remember the first time they came to visit us in 1970. It was in June and we had a very unusual warm spell. We were on the Olympic Peninsula at La Push on the beach, watching the sunset and we had a little bonfire. My mother went swimming in the Pacific Ocean because she said: "I did not come this far not to swim in the Pacific." And we're all sort of sitting around by the fire, watching the sun go down, and my father said to my mother, "Now if we had really made a stink about this marriage a few years ago, we wouldn't be sitting here."

Pirkko Borland is a native of Finland. Pirkko Helena Hietala and John Bradford (Brad) Borland married on October 23, 1966 in her home in Joutsa, Finland. They have a son, John Kaleva Borland, married to Tonjia Archie Borland, and a granddaughter, Sohvi Eloise Borland. Pirkko received her B.A. in English and Latin from the University of Helsinki; her M.A. in Classics from the University of Washington, and is a certified public accountant. Pirkko retired from U S West Communications as Executive Director of financial accounting. In the early 1980s she was among those instrumental in saving the Finnish Lutheran Church at 8504 13th Ave. N.W., Seattle, from being taken over by another organization. She was president of the national FinnFest USA celebration held in 1999 in Seattle. She has served on the board of Cascade Natural Gas Corporation and many non-profit Boards including the Nordic Heritage Museum and the UW Scandinavian Department Advisory Board. In 2011 she was awarded the insignia of the Knight of the Order of the Lion of Finland by the President of Finland.

Hrefna Milner

"I miss Iceland. I miss the view sometimes. But I can also just kind of put that inside me. I feel where I need to be and then I don't need to have it in front of me."

Well my name is Hrefna Thorsteinsdottir and I married Milner so that's what I use here in the States. I am born in Reykjavik, Iceland on August 5, 1942, and lived there the first thirty years of my life. I moved here in 1973 or 1974 and have lived here in the Seattle area since.

My father Thorsteinn Hannesson was a merchant. He had a store in Sudurgata City in Reykjavik, where I was born. He sold and made lamps and lampshades for many, many years. We sometimes would help him on off-time from school, sewing lampshades and other things and it was really a good time.

My mother's name was Aldis Alexandersdottir. She was a homemaker like women were in those days and usually stayed in. She would love to go out to work but her husband didn't want her to, so she was home and made home for us and it was good time.

To a child, life was a vacation. I really loved growing up. You were free. You grew up really healthy and happy as a kid. The whole neighborhood would play together and do all kinds of games. In the evenings, especially in the spring, we would be allowed to be out until about nine o'clock, because it was light. It was light all night almost. So it was long, nice evenings that I have good memories from.

Being a little community like Reykjavik where we lived, you just followed the rest. You go through school, you do everything like you're supposed to be, and that's it. I swam through that like the rest of it. I went to grade school in that little community where we lived. Then when I went into high school, I went to an all-girls' school.

In this girls' school, there was a lot of sewing. They were sort of preparing us to be in a house, being ready to take on doing all that stuff.

While I was still in high school, in a summer time, I went to Sweden, because living on an island you need to go and see some other places. So I went just for a few weeks to Sweden. That was kind of the beginning, then.

After high school I started working in a hospital in Landspítali, which is the country hospital in Reykjavik. Then they opened a new hospital in Reykjavik, which was a city hospital. One of the doctors that I worked with asked me if I wanted to go over and be part of his team. But he needed me to go to Sweden and work there for a year and see how they did it. He was going to imitate it. So I did.

Then I came home and started working at the new hospital. That was in 1966, something like that. I worked there in the Department of Radiology until 1974 when I met my husband, John Milner. John had come for a visit to Iceland. We met and fell in love. A few years later I moved to the States.

He was half Icelandic, half Danish. His mother was Icelandic, his father had been a Dane. One of his sisters was ten years older than John. She got to know and fell in love with an American. They moved to Tacoma, Washington. A few years later, his mother and John and his sister pulled along after the first sister came, and moved here.

When John was about twenty-seven or something, his mom sent him to Iceland, and says, "You need to go to Iceland and find yourself a good girl." That's how I came into the picture.

We met at a dance in Iceland. His story is, he saw me and he says, "I'm going to marry this girl." I thought, "America? Nah." My image of the States was New York and lots of crime. Of course, this was in the early seventies.

He invited me to come to Seattle, and we spent some time. When I flew into New York, and then came over to Sea-Tac I couldn't believe it. There's lots of little houses. It's nice. I really fell in love with this place.

I probably would not have thrived if I had come to a different place of the United States. I would not have been able to live in many other places than this. Here it's very Scandinavian. It's very Nordic. It's allowing yourself to be yourself.

When I came here, I felt I started breathing. I drove down the freeway and looked at Mount Rainier and I said, "I love this place." I was shooting [putting down] roots. I could just feel that I was shooting roots. That's wonderful. But I still love my country. But I don't miss it to the point that I needed to be there. I really feel here. I feel that this is better for me.

When we lived in Edmonds I got to know a lot of Icelandic people you know, my age or families. They became my aunts and uncles and I would meet them at the functions. They were like a family at the family gathering.

Hrefna Milner -205

I was active in the Icelandic Club when I was younger and my children were small. I needed to do this for them. I needed to give them memories because I didn't have the family to do that. They needed the memories for their build up so I did the Christmas party for many years and it was fun, it was good.

Today, my children and their families always come to me on Christmas Eve. That is a tradition that I started, wanting to, needing to have Christmas Eve.

Now, there is twelve of us at the dinner table on Christmas Eve. My two sons-in-law, they have adhered to it. It took one of them a little time to get used to the food, but now he loves it. It's actually funny that last year, for twenty years that they have been coming, I said I was getting a little tired of that same meal. I wanted to change it and I did.

Our dinner was asparagus soup, leg of lamb - smoked leg of lamb - which is just cooked and served with white sauce and boiled potatoes and green peas. Afterwards, rice pudding with an almond. Then, like in many other cases, whoever gets the almond is going to win a little prize.

I changed it. No soup. I made the little cups, bread cups with meat, and beat [mashed] peas and white gravy and then I had New York steak and the rice pudding. This did not go with them. They just fell apart. I promised them I would not change this. I would go back and have it the same [old] way.

I have now started helping with the Christmas dance at the Icelandic clubs. Here, again, my daughters come with the kids and now the grandchildren. They are from five up to fourteen years old, so they are all there, even the fourteen-year-old. He comes still. It's important for me to go and help out also. Now it's time for the grandchildren to have memories.

Hrefna Milner was born in 1942 in Reykjavik, Iceland. She immigrated to the United States in the early 1970's and married John Milner. She has three children: Alexandra, Christine and Arthur. Hrefna continues to be an active member of the Icelandic Club in Seattle.

Liisa Jussila

"I would pull the blankets over and cover my ears. I was petrified. My mother told me that I begged and begged and begged. I had heard in the news that children were sent to Sweden."

When I talk to my younger sister, Sirkku, do you know that neither one of us remembers a single rainy day growing up? It was always sunshine. I don't remember much about Turku, but as soon as we moved to Naantali the days were always sunny.

We lived outside Naantali, called Maijamäki. It was a little old farm. We ran through the trees and we were on the ocean playing and swimming. On the other side was the old road. We ran across that and there were rocks and little ponds and we had free reign of everything there.

In the wintertime, we did a lot of skiing. Every day we waited until my father came home. Then cross-country skis went on, and that gave my mother time to cook while he took us into the woods. So we skied a lot. We skied to school, we skied back.

When the Winter War began, I vaguely think that I heard that the war was starting. One time, I was standing outside with my father, and there was some really strange fog or smoke over Naantali and we could see it. All of a sudden, a huge bomb came. My father and I were standing out in the yard. I was standing right next to him and we heard this noise and this huge shrapnel, with thick, jagged edges went right over my head.

I remember my parents becoming more and more tense. Then one day, a map of Finland appeared on the wall. Lots of people had that, I learned later on. They marked Russian troops with red little flags and Finnish troops and German, Swedes, all over. They [the flags] kept moving and I literally became almost hysterical. I was totally sick and worried. I was too young to understand what was going on but I understood that something bad was happening.

When I saw those flags, they were moving back and forth, and every night, ten o'clock, it's okay to see. The news came on and I remember that we were in bed always at that time, but our parents listened and I would pull the blankets over and cover my ears. I was petrified. My mother told me that I begged and begged and begged. I had heard in the news that children were sent to Sweden.

I put so much pressure on my parents that my mother then began to think, "My goodness, if something bad happens, we get hurt in the bombing or something, how would she feel?" And here we would have had the chance to go. So she finally made the decision.

Sirkku, Topi and I were put on a train in Turku. There were some Lottas that were looking after us. We were shot at several times. The Russians thought that there was ammunition or something going somewhere, so the planes would try to shoot us down. We had to run into the woods and sleep in the snow. Then the Lottas gathered us back and many times afterwards, I thought these poor women with masses of little kids, how could they even find us in the dark, in the snow? You couldn't have any lights on anywhere.

I distinctly remember the women telling us when you see Lapps and reindeer and you cross this big river, you will be in Sweden. We would hear Swedish and then you can relax. No more running and hiding in the snow. They won't shoot at us anymore.

We arrived in Uppsala. I remember standing there on some building, a train station or something, and there were lots of people picking up these children. We all had name tags.

My mother told my brother, because he was the oldest [twelve] "You look after these girls and it's your responsibility and you stick together." He took it very seriously because when this young minister and his wife came to pick up the two children that they had planned on, my brother would not let go of our hands. He held both. I stood right there and I guess somehow— I think it is my brother's beautiful, long eyelashes and big eyes that broke them. So they took all three of us.

We called him Father Nils, Nils Hedlund and she was Alice Hedlund. They seemed friendly to me, right off the bat. I wasn't afraid at all. I was just relieved that we were away from all the bombing. Being a child I did not understand there was anything wrong that they took us, all three, not two or one.

I recall that my brother and I went to school right away but I don't remember much of the school. However, after Father Nils was ordained, the Winter War ended, and we came back to Finland. Then this young couple invited us back for the summer.

By the end of the summer, the Second World War started. So, Father Nils and Alice wrote to my parents, "There's no way we're going to send these children back. Is it okay if we keep them until things settle down and the war is over?"

We then ended up spending a little more than a year the second time. Father Nils had this position in a countryside. He was the most loved person. After every single Sunday service, he would visit on his bicycle all the village - all folks that didn't make it to the church. So, you can imagine how he was with us.

For example, across from the farm they had this long beautiful driveway with castanea trees on both sides and we always had to keep it clean and rake it. Father Nils was always out there helping. He never had us do anything alone. He said, "You do this," and he showed us how and I still remember how we raked that. I was so proud because the lines were straight.

They had told us a million times that we were absolutely like angels, which is not true. Once, I snuck into Father Nils's big beautiful office. I knew where the cigars were. I was sent by my brother to see if I could snitch a cigar. I got this big beautiful cigar and we were so silly. There was a little ditch, a little ways away from the house and we went all in there, our friends. We'd pass the cigar back and forth. Well, Sirkku and I got so sick, we were sick for a week. Neither Alice nor Father Nils ever said a word. And they must have seen smoke coming up from the ditch. But they were absolutely marvelous. All I remember was fun. It was such a relief, maybe, to be away.

When we came back to Finland again, we went to Turku then to high school. From there, I went to nursing school. One day I got to talking to this woman I worked with in Turku. I was interested because she was an anesthetist, and she was telling me lots of things, and I realized that I needed to learn what she knows. She said, "Well, do you want to go the United States and go into anesthesia training. You don't have to stay if you don't like it." And here I am. I don't know how many years later.

I bought this ranch in Cle Elum. Naantali is home, and that's why I love Cle Elum. There is literally hillside that we used to slide down, very, very similar. There are lots of pine trees that are arranged around like the Finnish pines. I have found a little bit of Finland.

NOTE: The term "Lottas" came from Lotta Svard, a longtime Finnish auxiliary for women. During World War II, men whose jobs were taken over by "Lottas" were freed for military service. The Lottas worked in hospitals, at many other jobs, as well as at air-raid warning posts and other tasks in conjunction with the armed forces, and cared for children sent to Sweden.

Liisa Vasama Jussila (née Toivo) was born November 17, 1932, in Turku, Finland. Liisa was one of 70,000 children evacuated to Sweden during wartime in Finland. In England, during the 1950s, Lisa served as a nursing assistant to Queen Elizabeth's house surgeon, and later, in Turku as the assistant to the chief nurse of surgery at Turun yliopistollinen keskusairaala. Liisa immigrated to the United States and began training as an anesthesiologist. Now, she lives with her Finnish husband, Clyde, in their home in Cle Elum, Washington.

THE DESCENDANTS

Individuals claiming Nordic ancestry in the State of Washington:

Source: 2008-2010 American Community Survey U.S. Census

Danish	72,082
Finnish	48,499
Icelandic	6,800
Norwegian	389,982
Swedish	241,920
TOTAL	807,220
Born outside the U.S.	9,938
Entered U.S. before 1990	71%

Howard and Gladys Margaret Almquist

"And we told them because we did not smoke a cigarette, we could afford to take this trip."

HOWARD: We didn't have any Depression. We had the grocery store at 1918 West 65th, and it was pretty hard, but we got along fine. We delivered and in those days people liked to have their order delivered. The store was on the corner across the street from the Norwegian Fisherman's Church [Ballard First Lutheran]. A little barbershop and the YMCA branch were also in that building. Within a year we bought the building. We got married, and after a honeymoon in California, we took over the store in August of '35. We had it for 30 years.

GLADYS: I taught out at South Park, and I put on a big May festival program. They danced the maypole or they did races where every child in the school could have a part in that day. In the fall [the school administration] assigned me to Adams School because they needed a physical ed. teacher. Before the junior highs, we had an eighth grade, and we had city competition in baseball and soccer. I had physical ed. for the boys and the girls. I'd send the boys out and I'd go out and play with them. That's why we won. I played with them. And I tried to teach them to be good sports. I taught Physical Ed. and Health from the fifth grade up. I stayed home when I had kids of my own, but they called me and asked me if I could substitute. Howard had the grocery store, so I'd stop downtown and pick up anything he needed at the wholesale house, I'd work in the store while he delivered, and then I'd go home and cook.

The boys worked in the grocery store. We took a trip around the United States when they were nine and ten. And we told them because we did not smoke a cigarette, we could afford to take this trip. We got enough to take them on a trip around the whole United States.

HOWARD: Three months we took on this trip during school, from

March till the end of school. We went through 36 states, and they had to write back to their class every week.

GLADYS: We sent a letter every week. In the evening in the motel, they'd write what they had seen and done that day. My mistake was that I didn't ask those teachers to save those letters. They had their lessons and their music. I worked with them, taught.

HOWARD: Seven of us little stores advertised specials every week in the Ballard Tribune, and that helped our business.

GLADYS: What helped our business most was because you put the fresh vegetables out. You didn't leave the old stuff there.

HOWARD: Well, this man used to come every morning with fresh vegetables and people liked that, and it was reasonable.

GLADYS: The children kept me busy enough. I was on the play field by 7:30 in the morning, and never got out of there till 5:30. I stayed there with the kids, even roller-skated at night with them.

HOWARD: I only had my grocery store for 30 years. Then Bob Stewart at Ballard Oil Company called me down there one day in 1954. They sold oil, and the furnaces would get sooty. They weren't satisfied with the service available, and would I be interested. I didn't know much about it but I bought a special truck, so they were glad to train me. There isn't too much to learn about how to clean a furnace. The next year I had to get another truck, and now they have ten trucks. The boys worked at the furnace cleaning during the summer. and my daughter and her husband and our youngest son have it now.

GLADYS: We could have gone bigger at the store, but I said, "We've got to get something that the boys can go to college on." We didn't know they were going to get scholarships.

HOWARD: From Yale and Stanford and Harvard — they had five different colleges that contacted them and wanted them. They'd find out when they're good students, they both played the horns and they were athletic — that's what they want, one who's well rounded.

Gladys Helstrom was born March 18, 1908 in Minnesota. Her parents were from Sweden. The family moved to Washington in 1912. Gladys taught Physical Education and Health at South Park School 1925-1927, then at Adams from 1927 to 1935. Howard Almquist was born in Seattle, December 9, 1910. His father was from Sweden, his mother from Holland. Howard and Gladys were married in 1935. Their children: Howard Theodore "Ted" (1938), Jon Richard "Dick" (1940), Mary Jo (1943) and David Wayne (1950). Howard had Almquist Grocery from 1935. Howie's Furnace Cleaners and Innovac from 1954. David, Mary Jo and her husband Charles Mott, run it now. Gladys died in 2002. Howard died in Seattle on February 3, 2011.

Gladys Margaret Almquist - 213

Carl J. Anderson

"I'd say Ballard was a pretty good place. I bought a home here and we've been in this house for almost 60 years, with one wife and two sons, Norm and Craig."

My dad came to this country on a sailing ship around Cape Horn, and stopped in San Francisco. He took out his citizenship papers about 1885. He lived in California in the early part of 1900, and at one time owned a cigar store in San Francisco. He ended up in Seattle and worked for Schwabacher Company. He helped people get outfitted for the Alaska gold rush. He used to tell stories about that. He also went to Alaska but never looking for gold.

He lived in a boathouse on Salmon Bay renting boats. In those days men would take their girlfriends out on dates in little 17- or 18-foot round bottomed boats, beautiful boats. Sometimes a fellow would pull a boat up on the beach and forget to bring it back. My dad would go out and pick up the boats with a launch. Later he used that boat to take longshoremen out to work and back to Ballard, to ships laying out in the Sound near where the Locks are now.

I think the boathouse was built a little before 1900. It was quite large, built of logs and lumber. There were two stories; we used to store all the boats underneath and lived upstairs. It was 80 feet long by 40 feet wide, quite a building. It was moored at the foot of 20th.

The boats came by — sometimes they'd keep their speed down, but sometimes they got carried away when the ships raced each other. They'd put up such a wake it would break up the floats we had around that big boathouse. Then we'd have to go out and re-tie or sometimes even re-plank them. Sometimes the dishes and stuff would fall on the floor, but my mother got used to it.

I lived at the boathouse until I was 24, when I got married. I had two brothers, one about five years older than I, and the other almost two years younger than I. It was a worry for my mother with three boys on the boathouse. Both my brothers got to be good swimmers. I didn't like the water that much, so I didn't do much swimming. Once in a while I'd fall in and I'd see her looking out for us. Then they'd pull me back up again.

But we survived. We had a wood stove in the kitchen. Later on, when we got fancy, we got an oil burning stove in what we'd call the front room or living room. We'd get some diesel oil and dump in there, and that's how we stayed warm.

Underneath the boathouse it was 80 feet, all wooden planks and whatnot. We fished. We had trikes and what other kids had. And we had a bicycle at one time. We'd go to a sandlot nearby and we'd dig holes in the sand. In those days, once in a while, a door on a boxcar would fall off, so we'd put it over the hole and crawl in underneath. We had regular rooms down there. But we came home with a lot of the sand, so my mother didn't especially care about that.

One time we were playing down below Ballard Avenue. And here came that streetcar they called a Dinky and its front end went up Ballard Avenue and the back end went up 20th. The streetcar practically stood on end, then dropped down onto the street. There was glass all over the place. That was kind of interesting.

When they were putting the sewer line across from the foot of 20th over to Magnolia, a scow came in full of sand and gravel, mostly gravel. I was just a kid, about 12 years old. I looked up and saw the sand was slipping. I told my dad and he says, "We got to get out of here." He knew what happened when a scow tipped over.

Well, the scow did tip over. The tug backed out and blew its whistle three times; that's all the warning they had. When the scow tipped over it landed right on top of a little sound steamer and sunk it right away. And our boathouse took quite a beating. But a boat laying alongside another one next to us took the brunt of it. It was a serious accident, but nobody was killed.

The boathouse was quite a ways out of the main stream. When the Locks were built, the lock master gave my dad permission to leave it where it was. This boathouse sat on big logs on a fairly level grade. When the tide went out, it would set down and up again. My dad was in the towboat business there long before the Foss Company. He'd move logs for the mills and scows alongside the ship. He kept busy.

There were a lot of good times in Ballard. Some of the streets were heavy planks. Eventually they got paved. Salmon Bay Sand & Gravel Company furnished most of the cement for pavement. I remember when horses pulled the fire wagons, and the harness would drop down and the horses got hitched up and then they charged off.

The kids in Ballard used to roller skate in front of the old fire station, right off Market Street. They'd play roller hockey, and every time there was a fire, off went the goal-tending area. They'd all go for the sidewalks and wait for the horses to charge off.

In those days Ballard was full of mills, long before Seattle Cedar and Stimson Mills. Ballard was very busy. I think more logs, lumber and whatnot were shipped around Ballard than anywhere on the whole west coast, before Ballard took in the rest of Seattle. [Seattle annexed Ballard in 1907.] The streetcars ran back and forth over the Ballard Bridge and the Canal went pretty well up to Lake Union.

My dad had a tugboat built in 1912 at Fryberg's Shipyard on 24th. His was one of the first boats to go through the Canal to Lake Union and through Portage Bay into Lake Washington.

I went to Washington Irving School where the Ballard Hospital is now. Another building to the west or northwest had offices. My son Craig has a dental office down in that area. He's been practicing there for close to 20 years, and is well-known.

We all went to Ballard High School. I didn't take the college course. In those days not many kids went to college; they couldn't afford it. So I learned trades. I went to school for half a day and then I'd go down to work in the machine shop in sort of an apprenticeship. That worked out pretty good for me. It didn't have anything to do with the high school, but it was an opportunity to work. At one time I worked at the Seattle Cedar Mill for a little bit, another time I worked for an outfit that made oilskins. We'd smear oil all over these pants and hang them on a rack to dry. Finally I had to get out of that job because I broke out so badly from all that linseed oil. And then I became a machinist and at one time worked for Northwest Instrument. And I worked at machine shops.

We made halibut winches, anchor winches and some trolling girding. Some were made of brass, and others were cast iron.

I fished right around Ketchikan and above that not too far. And I fished down the coast and off of Vancouver Island. And I fished down here at Cape Flattery, and then down the Columbia River and Grays Harbor. And then I went 400 miles into Mexico, fishing for albacore tuna. I kind of liked that albacore fishing. We used to drag 10, 12 lines behind the boat, different lengths, with feathered lures with hooks. But pretty soon I got too old to fish. So then I went back and I did finish backup with a machine shop for a couple years in order to keep my pension from the Machinist Union. It's kind of hard to remember what happened, how it happened, everything. But to the best of my knowledge, that's my story.

I worked at Boeings for a little bit making 60 cents an hour. Then I went to work at the Navy yard and my pay went from 60 cents to $1.08 or $1.10 an hour. And I worked at the Torpedo Station in Keyport. I didn't like it there, so I went back to the Navy yard.

I was active in the Machinist Union. At one time Dave Beck, who ran the teamsters, tried to take over the machinists. But the machinists held and didn't go with Dave Beck. Dave Beck didn't like that very well.

I'd say Ballard was a pretty good place. I bought a home here and we've been in this house for almost 60 years, with one wife and two sons, Norm and Craig.

Carl Anderson was born May 6, 1916 in Ballard. His parents were both born in Norway. He had two brothers: Floyd (1911-1996) and Fred (1918-1959 — he drowned while fishing). Carl married Margaret Haines in 1941. They had two sons: Norman (1942) and Craig (1946). Carl died March 25, 2001.

Margaret Haines Anderson

"Ballard is our place."

My father was born in Skudeneshavn, on an island, Karmøy, close to Haugesund, in Norway. My mother was born on the other end of the island at Avaldsnes. They met in Seattle at a church, a common place for immigrants to meet. My father came over when he was about 17 to an uncle in Montana. He didn't like working on a ranch, so he drifted on to Seattle and fished. He had his own fishing boat for a long time. My mother came over at age 16 to her sisters in Iowa and for a long time worked there as a housemaid. Then she came Seattle to her brother. My mother and father met each other at church.

My first memories are of going to school, not being able to speak English, then forgetting the Norwegian. It didn't take long with all the children in our neighborhood. We lived right across the street from the school, and on the streetcar line. When the school bell rang, we ran out of our house. We came home for lunch every day. When I became an assistant in the school cafeteria, I was so excited because I could have American food for lunch. I didn't have to have more fish for lunch at home. And I learned about hot dogs. I asked my parents, "Oh, please, can we have a hot dog for dinner?" Well, of course, we could have a hot dog. But Norwegians always have potatoes for dinner. So our hot dog was wieners, potatoes, carrots — no mustard, no bun. Norwegians didn't know what mustard was, didn't know what ketchup was. But with such a rebellion on my sister's part and mine, the next time we had hot dogs, my father ate his potatoes and my sister and I had the bun and the mustard. Hot dogs, what a treat.

We didn't have radio or television. We kids would each get a potato from the bin, gather in an empty lot, build a fire and roast our own potatoes. No butter or sour cream or chives or cheese. We just loved it, the sociability of it and being with the kids and doing something different.

We had a chicken coop in the backyard. When my sister and I became a little older, my parents built a chicken yard in the empty lot next door. Then the chicken coop became our playhouse. We had a wonderful time in that playhouse. All the neighborhood kids would come in. It was probably the size of a bathroom or closet.

We were alone a lot, my mother and sister and I, because my father was a fisherman, and in those days they fished the whole year. He would come home for a couple of days and be gone for two or three weeks. When he was home it was just great because the whole house would be open. We had a coal and wood furnace. My mother wouldn't bother to keep the coal and wood in it to heat the whole house. So my mother, sister and I spent most of our evenings in wintertime in the kitchen in front of the wood range. Sometimes she would scrub potatoes, slice them real thin, clean off the stove real good and oil it. Then we had real, real potato chips for a treat.

I remember as soon as school was out my sister and I had to help with the spring cleaning. The rugs went out on the line, beaten, beaten. I still have that rug beater. And everything had to be cleaned because of the dirty oil and coal furnaces. We weren't allowed to go out and play until we had done our chores.

In the summer my mother canned peaches and pears. They always came wrapped in tissue papers. My mother was very thrifty, and that tissue paper was used in the bathroom. We never had to use a Sears Roebuck Catalog, fortunately, but we did use tissue paper. I hated that. I cheated most of the time.

My mother would preserve the extra eggs the chickens laid, by putting them in a crock of waterglass. If you've ever put your arm in to the bottom to get the last egg, you will never forget that experience. Waterglass is a thick gelatin-like substance [sodium silicate] that's used to preserve eggs. It has a consistency of maybe the plunger hand soap that we use these days. It had no aroma, but it was just a slimy feeling substance; great for Halloween.

I'm sure our winters were colder and lasted longer than now. We had a lot of snow on the ground for at least a week. Third Avenue Northwest was up a big hill above us, so the kids would block off the streets from car traffic. There wasn't much car traffic then, but we were careful. The neighborhood boys built big toboggans out of extra wood and bike wheels, and put metal on the runners. Although I had my own store-bought sled, it was a real honor to be invited on that toboggan and coast all the way from 3rd to 8th Northwest. When we went home we always had a nice hot cup of chocolate waiting for us.

We always took care of ourselves, we never had to accept charity. Once one of my father's fishermen friends came to the house and asked my father for some money for the light bill because he was going to lose

Margaret Haines Anderson - 219

his electricity. My father considered him kind of a spendthrift, so he went up in the attic, got a kerosene lamp and gave it to him. I don't think there was much friendship left after that.

My father half-soled our shoes during the Depression. I still have the machine he used. The half-soles were all right, but then rubber soles were invented, and they had to be glued on. After so many wearings they'd start to fall off and you'd go flip flop, flip flop with those horrible half-soles.

Oh, the fish. My father brought codfish home from Alaska. My mother would hang it on the line to dry so we could keep it for the winter. It was very embarrassing to bring one of my girlfriends home from school. We would go out in the backyard and she would say, "What's that stuff hanging on the line?" And I would have to tell her it was fish for our dinner next winter. She wasn't Norwegian so she didn't understand that part of our background.

My sister and I would trudge from 5th to the Carnegie Library on Market Street two or three times a week. We were allowed to check out only five books at a time. And we were avid readers and fast readers. We would go home with our five books carried under our arms. Read them. Two or three days, back to the library to read some more books. When the library closed and became an antique store, I still trudged up those steps and looked at the worn spots. I'm so glad that the library still stands there because it was a wonderful place for anybody who liked to read. Maybe that's why I am a volunteer librarian for the Leif Erikson Sons of Norway Lodge. I'm going into my 14th year. We have 3500 books in our little library, and I think I know every one. But we do get new books all the time, and I eliminate some of the older books. Reading is my passion.

When I graduated from high school it was still Depression times, so my folks sent me to Wilson's Business College where I got another education. My skills in bookkeeping and typing were increased, but I also had many little small-time jobs. Finally I became an employee of the Seattle First National Bank on Market Street in Ballard, next to the Pheasant and Wiggen Mortuary. I started as a file clerk, became a bookkeeper and then secretary. I ended up as head of the Savings Department. I always remember paydays with apprehension, because there were so many mills in Ballard at that time. The mill workers would come in Friday to cash their paychecks. And they were missing fingers, so many fingers.

Growing up we had wonderful weekends when my father was home because all the Scandinavian lodges would have their summer picnics at various parks in the area. They had dance halls with hardwood floors. Live music would start about four in the afternoon, then a break for your picnic lunch, and dancing again. I met my husband at one of those dances.

The best places to meet someone were at the public dances. All the Scandinavian lodges had picnic dances in the summer, and families would go. And with the live music, we would meet on the dance floor. After Carl and I started dating, we went to the Trianon every Saturday night. Sunday, after skiing, we'd come home, change clothes and go dance at the Swedish Club some more. Our dates were mostly dancing and going to the show, stopping for a hamburger afterwards. When we became engaged, we got serious about saving money so we skipped the hamburgers. We did go to dances and shows, so we were able to put a down payment on a brand new house.

I've only lived at two addresses. I lived in the house at 5808 5th Northwest for almost 22 years, got married, moved to a new home, 8054 20th Northwest. I've seen so many of my neighbors go. We are the oldest couple on the block now and have been here the longest. We used to know everybody by their first name, knew all their kids, knew when they were gone and where they were going. Now we know nothing. But I'm still here. Ballard is our place.

Margaret Haines was born June 24, 1919 in Ballard to Karen Kristine Nilsdatter Sliksvold and John Edward Haines, both from Norway. She had a sister, Shirley (1921). She married Carl Anderson (1941). They had two sons: Norman (1942) and Craig (1946). Carl died March 25, 2001. Margaret is the volunteer librarian at the Leif Erikson Lodge in Ballard.

Theodore Richard Beck

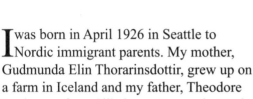
"My childhood at Madison Park was filled with adventures: building underground camps and tree houses, swimming, canoeing, roller skating, playing kick the can, catching bull frogs. Exciting, too, was a black bear caged in a neighbor's front yard."

Iwas born in April 1926 in Seattle to Nordic immigrant parents. My mother, Gudmunda Elin Thorarinsdottir, grew up on a farm in Iceland and my father, Theodore Beck, was from Silkeborg, Denmark. Mother died when I was two and my father and I then boarded with a family, the woman of which was an Icelandic friend of my mother from Winnipeg. When I was five and a half my father decided to take me to Denmark to live with his parents and unmarried sister in Silkeborg. On the steamship *Leviathan* from New York to Europe my father met a Danish woman and they were married in Copenhagen. We returned to Seattle in the summer of 1932.

We lived in the Madison Park area until I was eleven and I attended McGilvra School. We then moved to Beacon Hill and I attended Columbia School in Rainier Valley. I became fascinated with electricity and chemistry. Don, a school friend living six blocks away, and I made our first telephone connection between our houses using hair wire from an ignition coil from a Model-T Ford. One afternoon after school we wrapped friction tape around the heads of nails for insulation. The next afternoon we drove the nails into power poles and trees and strung the hair wire. We took a pair of headphones apart to make a transmitter/ receiver at each end. We were absolutely amazed that it worked. But then we each had to go to dinner and in the meantime the wind blew down our wire, so that ended that telephone system.

Then Don and I each got our bikes and roamed all around Seattle. One trip to the Sears outlet store below Beacon Hill to the west, we jointly bought a Chemicraft set for five dollars and I set up a lab in the basement of our house. We did numbers of experiments by the book but then I did a more original experiment. I stored a little alcohol burner in a jar with the lid on it to prevent evaporation. When I took the lid off and I put a match to it a flame would flicker around the edge. I scaled up the experiment and blew up a can of alcohol, which put me in the hospital for a year with seven skin graft operations. My father told me, "You lost a year of school in grade eight. You're going to have to go through high school in three years," which I did.

I attended Franklin High School. I was interested in math and science and not much else, but I did play bass clarinet in the band. I got A's in math, chemistry and physics and C's and D's in everything else. During my second two years I worked every Sunday in the cleanup crew at Puget Sound Sheet Metal Works. I graduated in 1944. In the summer of 1944 I worked with the roofing crew of Puget Sound Sheet Metal Works and earned enough for my first year at the University of Washington, majoring in chemical engineering. Tuition was then $35 per semester and I lived at home paying room and board. The next summer I worked as an electrician helper in a shipyard and the following year as helper at a steel fabricator. Two years I lived in Eagleson Hall YMCA, next to campus with a fellow chemical engineering student. In my senior year I was a teaching assistant for freshman inorganic chemistry.

I graduated in 1948, began graduate work, and moved into Cascade Hall on campus that was originally built for returning WW II veterans. The first year I graded papers for a senior chemical engineering class and then received research fellowships. My graduate research was in electrochemistry. In the summer of 1952 I received my Ph.D. in Chemical Engineering.

In my senior year I joined the Mountaineers, took the climbing course and participated in experience climbs and in skiing at the Mountaineers' Meany Lodge at Stampede Pass. I started folk dancing in the evenings there and then at the Mountaineers' monthly dances in Polish Hall on Capitol Hill and to the Scandia Folk Dance Club at Eagleson Hall started by Gordon Tracie. That's where I met Ruth Schaumberger. We were married in December 1951.

Interview trips to potential employers were made in the spring of 1952 and I accepted a job with DuPont near Wilmington Delaware. In September, Ruth and I drove across country visiting national parks on the way. We took a month for this trip of exploration and enjoyment of the out-of-doors. I joined the organic chemistry department at DuPont. My job was to improve the new process to make one of the intermediates for a new product, polyurethane foams. Ruth taught home economics at a junior high school. We joined the Wilmington Trail Club and participated in their trips, went to concerts and folk dancing in Philadelphia, the opera in New York, the sights in Washington D.C. In a two week vacation in August 1953 we car camped through New England.

Theodore Richard Beck - 223

In the fall of 1953 I was contacted by Kaiser Aluminum that I visited in Spokane in September 1952. I was offered a position in their research laboratory in the San Francisco Bay Area as Group Leader to run their new ten thousand ampere aluminum cell program. Of course I jumped at the opportunity and Ruth and I terminated our affairs in Wilmington and took two weeks to drive to California through the southwest deserts. The job was very rewarding and we made many friends at Kaiser. We joined the Sierra Club and participated in numbers of hikes. Ruth taught at a junior high school and then took courses at U of Cal, Berkeley.

But all good things come to an end. A financial crisis that hit Kaiser Aluminum in 1958 caused a reduction in force at our laboratory and shut down my project. I decided to leave. The summer of 1958 was the perfect time to do the seven-week car camping trip to Alaska that Ruth and I had planned since 1952. In 1959 I accepted a position at American Potash and Chemical in Henderson, Nevada as section head of research on electrochemical processes. We sold our house in Palo Alto and moved to a new tract house in Las Vegas. The desert was wonderful for explorations in fall, winter, spring but after two and a half years the company planned to consolidate our Henderson laboratory with the main laboratory in Los Angeles. That was unattractive with all those people and freeways, so it was time to go back to Seattle.

I joined the Boeing Aerospace Division and did R and D on batteries and fuel cells for the space program. After a couple of years, I joined the Boeing Scientific Research Laboratories. At the time Boeing planned to build the supersonic transport out of titanium, and there were numerous technical problems connected with it. I worked with Dr. Martin Blackburn, a metallurgist from England for six years and we became the leaders in the field of stress corrosion cracking of titanium. We attended numerous technical conferences in the U.S. and Europe. That was a marvelous time.

Boeing employment in the Seattle area dropped from over one hundred thousand to thirty-seven thousand in a matter of two years during the 1968 recession. The Boeing Scientific Research Laboratories was a casualty. I decided to leave Boeing and start my own company, Electrochemical Technology Corporation, first located on Leary Way, then on Dexter Avenue North in Seattle. Ruth and I worked together. She managed the office and I directed the engineers and technicians doing the contact research.

During our years back in Seattle I have been involved with numbers of organizations: chairman of the Puget Sound Section of the American Chemical Society, president of The Electrochemical Society (with worldwide membership), a board member of the Seattle Youth Symphony Orchestra, the Icelandic Club of Greater Seattle, the Nordic Heritage Museum, the North Cascades Conservation Council, and the advisory board of the University of Washington Scandinavian Department.

In March 1971 I received a phone message: The family in Iceland is trying to locate Mr. Beck. A sister of my mother had died. I was able to spend a weekend in Reykjavik a few weeks later on return from a scientific conference in Portugal. I learned from an uncle about my mother's family and genealogy back to the first settlers of Iceland. Since then I have been to Iceland twenty-four times, have met all living relatives, have explored the country and have visited ancestral farms.

When I closed my laboratory in1995 I donated my technical library of a thousand volumes to the University of Iceland. I'm currently working in collaboration with an Icelandic engineer who has a company that sells equipment to aluminum companies worldwide. My ideas have the potential to save about twenty percent in the capital costs of a new aluminum plant and about twenty percent in the operating costs. Further, it will produce oxygen rather than carbon dioxide and carbon fluoride greenhouse gases.

Ted Beck was born on April 11, 1926, in Seattle, Washington. His mother emigrated from Iceland to Canada and then to Seattle in 1920. His father emigrated from Denmark in 1921 to the United States. His parents married in 1925. Ted's mother died when he was two and his father remarried a Danish woman. Today Ted and his wife Ruth live in Seattle. They have two daughters, Randi and Maren. He was on the board of the Nordic Heritage Museum for a few years and is involved with the Icelandic room at the museum. He has published more than 80 technical and scientific papers and filed a dozen patents. He has been working on his autobiography for a number of years and continues to work on new technology to make aluminum.

Lisa Bergman and Olaf Kvamme

"In fact, Gordon, you introduced us and said 'This is the jewel in the tiara of the museum.' And I was so proud when you said that. Because you know, we weren't certain if this thing would take off, and it has, 15 years later." - Lisa Bergman, Artist Director, Mostly Nordic Concert Series

OLAF: I got involved with the museum by attending a banquet of some kind. I had my friend Mary Henry along and she sat next to Marianne Forssblad and announced to Marianne, "You ought to put that guy next to me on your board." And that was my introduction to the Museum. So, I was involved and on the board of the museum for a few years and then President of the board for a couple of terms and, since then, I've been interested in the museum and have been involved and stuck with it and have enjoyed every minute.

I was with the Seattle School District for a good many years and, the latter part of that, was involved with community activity, lobbying in Olympia and Washington, D.C., a little bit. This particular building we're in here today, Webster Elementary School, at one time, this was one of the schools I had administrative responsibility for, the schools in this northwest part of Seattle and the schools in the southeast part of Seattle.

LISA: I'm Lisa Bergman and it so happens that I barely missed meeting Olaf as a child, because I attended school in southwest Seattle. My father was a Swedish immigrant, my mother first generation Hungarian and they met in Stockholm during World War II. She called him her "male war bride." They came back to the States and I was born some five years later. They then moved to Seattle from Washington, D.C.

It so happens that I am a professional musician, a pianist. I graduated from the University of Washington, the State University of Stony Brook in New York and also the Juilliard School. I was on the faculty at the University of Washington for 10 years as the Opera Coach and the accompanying instructor, and I've run a number of music nonprofits in the region since then. And now I am the Executive Director of the Icicle Creek Music Center.

OLAF: I'm an immigrant also. I came as a two-month-old and I did not become a citizen of the United States during that whole period when, ordinarily, in most families, I would have become a citizen.

My father and mother refused to take out their citizenship papers. My dad would not swear allegiance, he would promise allegiance but he would not swear allegiance. There was a Biblical reference that he used to maintain his position. So, it wasn't until I was in the Army that I became a citizen.

I think it [Mostly Nordic Concert Series] grew out of the 1993 celebration of the 150th anniversary of Edvard Grieg's birthday. And that was a very, very big deal in Norway, and they spent a lot of money outside of the country supporting the celebrations. They had celebrations in Japan and in Seattle, we were grouped with Tacoma.

Tharald Borgir, who had been a head of the music department at Oregon State, had moved to Seattle and he was acquainted with the person in Norway who allocated the programs, Einar Soblu. I think that was in our favor, so that there were many, many events, musical events, here in Seattle.

The museum was very involved in that, many of the concerts were here, some at the University of Washington. Pacific Lutheran University was involved with its own series. They were topnotch groups. The Grieg Trio, the Norway String Quartet, the Norway Wind Quintet and also some things that weren't classical music.

But these people were supported by the Norwegian government to come over here and then we had, of course, some responsibilities. A very substantial conference here, in this room right here, on Grieg's music that was attended by people around the state.

But I remember Leif Eie who was on the committee. My role on the committee was a sort of liaison with the Chair of the Committee, Jean Gardner, the outgoing governor's wife at that time. So Leif said, "Now, what are you going to do? They've invested a lot of 'Grieg' in you, and you ought to do something about it."

So I contacted Lisa, and Lisa may say she contacted me. I'm not sure. But I feel better when I say I did. As I remember it, we met at the Kaffestua down at the Leif Erikson Hall, and talked about this.

The one thing I know is I really had some questions about how is this classical music going to go over with this crowd here? Lisa came up with the solution that just clinched it. "We will feed them. We will have a smorgasbord after the concert and that will bring them in." Certainly, she was correct.

Lisa Bergman and Olaf Kvamme - 227

LISA: I remember the very same thing, and that we had wonderful coffee and gjetost on rye bread at the Kaffestua, and I thought to myself, "Something tells me I'm going to enjoy this relationship with Olaf and the Museum." My husband and my parents and I were all members, original members, way back, 35 years ago, and really supported this place and all that it represents.

So, this was my chance, then, to give back to the cultural community of the Nordic countries in Seattle. So, I took it very seriously when Olaf came with the concept, but I had some misgivings, too. I, of course, wanted this to be an enormous success, and I was looking for gimmicks, let's say, to make sure that audiences would be attracted, particularly those who are not of Nordic descent.

There is, and was, a very active chamber music crowd in this town. So the question was, "What models really worked and still do?" The Seattle Chamber Music Society was just getting started at that time too. Their concerts were all held at the Lakeside School, a beautiful campus in the summer. You could buy a concert ticket and a box dinner, which you would enjoy out on the green and then go into the concert. You'd only have to park the car once.

I thought, "Aha, there it is. There it is'"

Then I got to thinking about what would appeal to local audiences, because at that time, we were thinking quite locally, and that [meant], of course, local musicians because, as one myself, I was getting a little fed up with a Seattle organization importing musicians from Chicago and Los Angeles and New York when we have, we were teeming with them and still are.

I was very careful to also preserve the integrity of each of the cultural presentations on each series, which, of course, had and still do five concerts representing Norway, Sweden, Denmark, Iceland, Finland, so that each concert was segregated from the other nationalities. I did this not out of some sort of mean spirit, but to make sure that we didn't wind up with one big conglomeration, because it's of interest to audiences to hear Swedish music on one concert and Norwegian music on the next.

So along with that cultural theme came the food so that, ideally, if there was a Swedish concert, the food would be mostly Swedish; the Icelandic would be mostly Icelandic.

So now looping back to how to grab that chamber music community that might not be so enthused about Nordic chamber music because, mostly, no one's ever heard it. My gimmick there was to call this series 'Mostly Nordic' patterned after the Seattle Symphony's ' Mostly

Mozart,' which you may remember.

Now, I had to be very careful because I never wanted to have a preponderance of the non-Nordic component, but I was also very careful that when it came to the 'Mostly' part, it would be mostly whatever the theme of the concert was, and that the other part was non-Nordic altogether. That way I never mixed, or tried not to, let's say, Danish and Finnish music. So if it was a Finnish program, it might include some Brahms and Chopin, for example.

So then came the big challenge. Once the committee was established, which, by the way, the original members were Olaf as Chair, Christine Ewing, Marianne Forssblad, the Museum Director at the time, Marianne Mitmoen, Karen Oleson and Marie Snow, and of course, myself, it was just a little band of people. We would meet in a corner of the auditorium, have coffee, and bat these ideas around.

So we had a slam dunk. We knew we had a series that could sell. Then came the ultimate challenge, which was to find the printed music for the musicians to play, because these scores are not commonly found in music stores.

So two things surfaced almost immediately and they saved the day. One was stumbling across this volume, "Nordic Instrumental Music for Colleges and Universities, " by Professor Mark Lammers, who received a grant from Gustavus Adolphus College to create this volume. And in it is contained information not only on the various composers, but the difficulty level of the compositions and how to find the music. So that then led me directly to the Ohio State University system at Columbus [where there] is a Nordic music archive for both sound recordings and printed scores. This was like stumbling into a treasure chest.

So I bought a plane ticket and flew to Columbus and made friends with Steven Long, the librarian there at the time. And I became a household word at the library. I was calling every week looking for this and for that. And they graciously allowed me to make photocopies of the various scores so that I could take them home in my big suitcase.

Then what happened quite naturally was getting in touch with all five of the Nordic Music Information Centers, which are state funded. All five of the Nordic countries have them. And there, with a quick phone call I could call and ask specifically, 'Do you have a work for flute and guitar?' 'No, but we have one for flute and trumpet.' And so it would go, and I would craft my series that way.

Now this became quite a challenge for an artistic director because not all of the music I programmed over the last 15 years is music that

I myself had heard because some of it is unrecorded. So that's when I had to rely on the expert opinions of various musical colleagues across the pond, who could tell me, 'Oh, well it's not a strong piece but if you really need something for piccolo, then go ahead.' So it became a very interesting fabric of communication between music professionals in the Nordic countries and my home here in Seattle.

[For the first season in 1994] I went by things that I personally had heard because it was just too risky for the first season to do otherwise. And I collected, as I mentioned, a number of recordings and I sat in the library in Columbus listening with the earphones and making notes.

So I was able to put together a series that I personally liked and I thought that the audiences would too. And I engaged a number of beloved and well-known musicians from the area: Carmen Pelton, Dean Williamson, Randolph Hokanson, many familiar names.

We paid our guest artists very, very little. It was really a gift of love on their part. And they were fascinated, too, with the unusual repertoire. And we had to be very fiscally careful because we weren't sure if this series was going to come out in the black, which of course, it did. And we learned too that providing beer and wine and so on as a part of the cultural experience didn't hurt.

OLAF: The wine, I'm not an expert on wine, but I think people were able to pay three to four dollars for a glass of wine that came in a bottle that was the in the $3.00 class. So I think we made a little money on the wine.

LISA: As a classically trained musician, I, like many, have been steeped in the tradition that classical music be performed in a sterile environment: no daylight, no outside sounds, no unrelated smells of any kind, just mostly darkness and silence.

So imagine the very first concert, I was in the back of the auditorium, which is right next to the kitchen, which is part of the charm of this whole thing … And no matter how they tried, the cooks back there made some noise and unavoidably, came the scents of meatballs and boiled potatoes and green salad and a little bit of caviar. And of course, none of this is objectionable. But I thought, 'Oh my God! You can't have cooking smells with the music!' And occasionally dropping a spoon and so on. So I was horrified at first, until people came to me later, and said, "You know, it adds to the enjoyment, to be listening to the music and smelling the scent of dinner, and realizing what other pleasures were in store for us." So in this case, it worked.

OLAF: My impression is that, for a good part of the audience, or of the people who are eating, that's a nice time to sit around, talk, they have people lingering here after the concert for an hour and a half, maybe two hours for some of them. It's sort of a down home, around the kitchen table event.

LISA: Oh yes, we make sure of that, and make sure they [the artists] mingle. It is a downhome sort of thing, with very much a touch of the highbrow.

I think we were relieved, because we didn't know if anyone would come [in the first season]. To our astonishment, I guess, and delight, we had fair sized crowds. The crowds have grown and grown.

OLAF: It's pretty near the maximum right now, we couldn't hold another 50/60 people.

LISA: The determiner of any kind of project is what the marketplace will bear. So I learned, through the years, on what would sell, and what wouldn't, or when audiences would be willing to take a chance, based on previous good experiences. So I have had carte blanche, but I've used a good deal of common sense to make sure I don't take advantage of any of our listeners. I remember one such misstep, was a particular program of Finnish flute music. Well, there isn't much, and most of it was written after 1960, and it was very avant-garde.

I knew it, and it was a little on the long side and so on, and I was pacing in the back hall, and sure enough, the concert was finally over, and I actually was tempted to go out the back door and just leave town. But I resisted the temptation, and people came to me and said, "Oh Lisa, that was interesting!" So I knew, of course, never to do that again. There was another [concert], with a pair from Iceland, an accordionist and a double bass player, and they played a program called "The Slide Show Secret," which I assumed was going to include a number of visual effects, that would save the day, in case the music wasn't popular.

Well, they, for some reason, didn't bring very many slides, they only had about five. So if you take five slides, and divide that into 90 minutes, you have to stare at the same slide for about 15 minutes each, and they were mostly like a wooden church tower, or some dried cod heads. [laughs] I think I will never live that concert down, but the interesting thing is, is that's the concert most people still talk about, not the ones that they really liked.

Actually, Elsa Elefsen was our first caterer, who was unbeatable, and we were crushed after four years or so of her wonderful cooking, she said, "I'm all pooped out! No more of this!" Then she retired. So then we went to Valdi Bjarnason who ran, you may recall, one of the few very

Lisa Bergman and Olaf Kvamme - 231

successful Nordic restaurants on Ballard Avenue, but he too moved on to other things.

We, for years, used the Scandinavian Specialties on 15th. Now we have the great fortune of Me and You Catering from Edmonds. Regardless of who took on the responsibility, it's always understood that each concert needed to have a certain flavor of that particular concert. So the audience has become quite educated, along the years, on what they might typically expect for the Finnish concert, which is that meat stew that's made out of three meats. We might have to do a little research on that. What would be a typical Norwegian dish?

OLAF: You could almost put herring on, and then that would count for anybody!

LISA: We've had a few disasters in that department along the way, I know for sure, the first thing the caterer asks is, "How long is the program?" I try to be very accurate, but I can't always be. So we've had some beautiful cod that turned into cod soup along the way, but no one ever complained, by six o'clock they were so hungry, and it smells so good that they enjoy it anyway.

What's really interesting is how the source of the artists has evolved through time. Remember first, one of my concepts was that we would use local musicians. To my great delight, our reputation has traveled across the ocean and now Nordic artists are contacting me for the chance to play here. And when that happens, that's a lucky day. Because then I can rely on their experience with the varied repertoire that they most often play in their home countries.

Then we discuss it. And then we add something that most likely something that's already in their repertoire that's non Nordic so they don't have to spend a lot of time working on a piece that they'll never play again.

And that's how the programs are formulated and it works beautifully.

Sometimes I get lucky with a tour. The Reykjavik Wind Quintet comes to mind. The Wooden Flutes from Denmark were fantastic. They played baroque block flutes. The Wegelius Chamber Strings, which was an academic project from Finland where Ana Wegelius came with some 30 musicians. It was quite a tour de force to produce that. The Habbestad Ensemble, which is a family of musicians all by the name Habbestad from Norway. The Norwegian Piano Duet which I think Gordon was one of your favorites. A dual piano team from Norway. One year we strayed and went into the folk idiom and invited the Karelian Folk Ensemble, which were these three guys wearing seal skins and their dread knots, and all these ancient instruments from the Finnish province of Karelia, which of course had been Russian for many years of its history. So these guys sort of were a unique blend of both.

I really need to mention the Greater Puget Sound Tuba Ensemble that graced our stage one year. They did a lot of their own research because there isn't a lot of music written in the Nordic countries for tuba. But they were so glad to be invited. They did all the work. And they proposed the program. And all I had to do was sign the rental check.

There was a wonderful story about finding the music. And it happened to be a living composer from Denmark. Ib Norholm was his name. And I had chosen to program one of his more famous works, but I couldn't find it anywhere in any of the sources that I had previously mentioned. I had no choice but to contact him directly. So I called him on the phone.

I said, "Ib, Lisa Bergman, Mostly Nordic, Seattle, Washington." I said, "I'm desperate to get the piece, it's the 'Serenade for Horn and Piano.'" I said, "Where am I going to find it? The concert is in three months. I've got to have it."

And he said, "Oh, you can't find it? I have to look." So he put the phone down, … And he came back five minutes later and here I am on an international call, and he said, "Sorry it took so long, but it was out in the garage." So, he faxed it. And it was enough for the musicians to play even though faxed music typically looks sort of funny. But it was enough. We managed.

I remember another concert where I had hired a violinist who played in the Seattle Symphony to perform. And the problem was that because of his concert schedule he could only stay for the first half of this concert. And I needed a violinist to play the second half of this concert too. So, his good buddy agreed to play who was coming from a performance of the Northwest Ballet.

Well, in theory, this was all going to work out just fine, because the one violinist would play, and put his coat on and leave, and just in time for the second violinist to arrive and take his coat off and play. Well, it didn't work that way because the Ballard Bridge went up.

So, violinist number one was out the door and violinist number two had yet to arrive. And of course the audience - I had already clued them in. They knew this was going to happen. So, they had really bought into the excitement of the moment. So, I kind of made do because we couldn't go on until he showed up.

Everybody else was here, the cellist and the pianist and so on. Until we heard this crash and bang and this pounding of feet and the violinist came on stage with his coat flapping, and threw the case down, whipped out the violin, and stuck it under his chin and said, "Play ball." And the audience rose to its feet and cheered like at a real baseball game.

I would venture the guess that at least one quarter of the works presented on this series in the last 15 years has been North American premieres. Much of the music is unusual certainly, even in the Nordic countries, but most particularly here. You won't find the Toivo Kuula piano trio on the Lincoln Center series. But this series is as far as I know, unique, which is a very strong word in North America, where all five nationalities are represented and consistently so for 15 loyal years.

Svend Rønning, Violinist; Kathryn Habedank, harpsichordist and Meg Brennard, cellist performing at Mostly Nordic concert June 3, 2012

Elfrida Andrée was a highly regarded, but unfortunately not during her time, woman composer from Sweden. And some researchers at Whitworth College in eastern Washington made the discovery, put the program together and brought it here to us, ... The music was quite romantic and the notion that Elfrida (Andrée) herself never lived long enough to understand that she would have an international reputation. That was quite a moment.

There was a concert [2003] where I didn't realize how fast a person could grow gray hair. But, the Monday before the Sunday, I got a call from Finland, it was a Finnish piano trio. And the violinist had suddenly taken ill and she had to be hospitalized. And the question was whether to cancel the concert or proceed. And she said "You really must proceed." She said: "I have a good friend from the San Francisco Conservatory who is one of the few people I know who could actually throw this together in a short amount of time." And I said "Oh my God, absolutely, whatever it takes. He must be a Finn." And she said, "No, he's from

China." And sure enough, he arrived a few days later. The other two musicians came from Finland. And they practiced night and day and they pulled it off. And it was a fantastic concert.

Mostly Nordic has been a favorite of critics from the get go because it's newsworthy. It's not the same old, same old. This is chamber music with a real zing. Because, as I mentioned, at least a quarter of it are North American premieres. And we've gotten such reviews as "Mostly Nordic and entirely successful." And I have to say, R.M. Campbell from the *Post-Intelligencer*, Melinda Bargreen from *The Seattle Times* and Philippa Kiraly freelancer to the Times and PI have all received us extremely well and we are grateful for it. Now, that's not to say that if there's something wobbly we don't hear about it. But that's the job of the critic.

From our annual questionnaires at the end of the last concert on the series where they are invited to fill out a series of questions on how did you hear about this, what did you like about it most, what did you not like about it most, how was the cooking, et cetera, et cetera. And boy, I have to kind of fasten my seatbelt, because people are quite frank and they do it anonymously, you see. So we learn a lot from those. You know, sometimes we read it and then say "Yes, so what?" We're going to go ahead. You have to have the courage of your artistic convictions after all.

The whole museum staff has embraced this. In fact, Gordon, I think you even said once, you introduced us and said "This is the jewel in the tiara of the museum." And I was so proud when you said that. Because you know, we weren't certain if this thing would take off, and it has, 15 years later.

Lisa Bergman is a professional musician, a pianist who graduated from the University of Washington, the State University of Stony Brook in New York and also the Juilliard School. She was on the faculty at the University of Washington for 10 years as the opera coach and the accompanying instructor. She has also run a number of music non-profits in the region and is the former Executive Director of the Icicle Creek Music Center.

Olaf Kvamme is a former Nordic Heritage Museum Board of Trustees member who served as the Board's president from 1990 to 1995. He retired from the Seattle School District in 1987 after 38 years of service including periods as a teacher, principal and central administrator. In 1996 he was awarded the St. Olav Medal by His Majesty King Harald of Norway.

Beatrice A. Björklund

"She said, 'I came to this country and found out I had to work just as hard as I did in Finland.'"

My husband's parents came from Finland, but they were Swedish speaking. Paul's mother said, "Well, my brother was already here, and he wrote and told me how wonderful it was here." I think that was about 1912. And he told her, "You come here, you don't even have to wash the clothes. When they get dirty, you just throw them away and buy new. And the apples, you'd lie under an apple tree and apples just fall to you." Well, she said, "I came to this country and found out I had to work just as hard as I did in Finland."

My parents both came from Sweden and they met in Seattle, and married here. His whole family came to this country, his parents and all 12 children. The children were all grown by then. They came because of the [poor] economy in the old country. My mother came to Seattle from Sweden in 1913. She had two brothers here — they had small farms up in Arlington.

We moved to Ballard about 1925. I went to Salmon Bay School, about a block and a half from our back door. I went to James Monroe the day it opened, a brand new school, and to Ballard High, where I graduated in 1936. I played the violin in the school orchestra all the way through school. Started out at Salmon Bay. We performed once at a PTA meeting. When I think back of what it must have sounded like, I'm surprised those mothers could keep a straight face while we played. When I was 12 years old, I also started playing in the orchestra in our church, the Swedish Tabernacle [now the First Covenant Church]. In those days we had two good sized orchestras at school, and we would audition, and hopefully, get into senior orchestra. I was in the senior orchestra in both junior high and senior high. There was an all-city orchestra and we auditioned for that, too.

I baby-sat for a family, the Kvalseths. They had just one child, a little boy named Elmer. They were from Norway. I remember walking with her and the baby carriage up to Sunset Hill Park one day, looking for her husband's fishing boat to come in. I never dreamt that I would live about two blocks from there about 50 years later.

I remember when the Ferris wheel at Woodland Park burned. We had moved at that time to 57th Street, near 20th. And could just look right up the hill and see the thing on fire. It was a spectacular sight. It was right across the street from Woodland Park on Phinney. There was a merry-go-round and a big Ferris wheel. That was probably about '34 or '35.

Paul and I had both played in the orchestra in our church so we knew each other there. His family lived in Everett until 1934, and then they moved to Seattle. He went to Chicago to the North Park University and Seminary. He finished seminary in 1943, and we came back here to get married that fall, then we lived in Chetek, Wisconsin, Chicago, St. Paul, Pittsburgh, Orlando, and back to Chicago before coming back in 1984 in retirement.

Beatrice Johnson was born in Seattle on January 20, 1918. Her mother Elizabeth Benson came to Seattle from Sweden in 1913. She had been trained as a nurse in Sweden, but worked as a domestic in Seattle before her marriage in 1916 to Nils Victor Johnson, a carpenter, who had immigrated from northern Sweden. The family moved to Ballard in 1925. Beatrice graduated from Ballard High in 1936. She married Paul Björklund, a minister, in 1943. After serving in many ministries, they retired to Seattle in 1984. Beatrice died in 2012.

John Boitano

"Man, we got along well. That's important in growing up — to get along with your neighbors and be able to get along without any problems"

My dad worked in Ballard as a garbage man. He collected garbage all around Ballard and dumped it in various empty lots in the lower part of Ballard where we lived. He was a farmer in the old country [Italy] and in San Francisco before he came to Seattle. We got a kick out of our situation in that we ate well because my dad was a garbage man.

He had two Belgian horses called Moody and Queeny. My dad took care of his own horses with hay and straw and oats and saltlick. His barn was down by where Ernst Hardware was. One time when one horse got away and he gave me a rock to hit *cavello* — that means horse. "When the *cavello* comes around, hit it." I was really scared to do that.

My mother could talk real good because she was born in America and she met with other women, but old Pa couldn't command the English language. I loved my mom and never talked back to her. I respected my dad. He had a hell of a time with English, but when he talked, you respected Pop — he was in charge of things.

My mother was the first one up in the morning. She built a fire and in winter we'd grab our clothes and run down to the kitchen to get warm and get dressed. She fed us oatmeal for breakfast. My mother was one great cook. We had pasta three times a week and on Sunday we had chicken cacciatore or ravioli. Once in a while she would cook for others, especially her ravioli and chicken cacciatore. Raising kids is a chore especially in a poor community. You had to make ends meet, and she was great about that.

My school was called Washington Irving Grade School, which had been the first Ballard High. Earlier it was Central High. Irving was a nice school with grades K to six. We had good teachers at Irving. Miss MacIntosh had all the Boitanos but she couldn't pronounce our name exactly. She called us Boitini, Boitono. But she was a good teacher. I went to James Monroe Junior High, then to Ballard.

Robert Fulton School was also in lower Ballard. We called it Peanut

College because the less-advanced kids went there. During World War II, Ole Bardahl bought it for $4,000, the school district tore it down for him, and he built a big plant there on 52nd and 14th.

Lower Ballard — from the locks to Fremont and from Market Street to the canal — where I grew up was kind of a melting pot of immigrants: Greeks, Italians, Swedes, Norwegians, a couple of Japanese families and two black families then. They came there to work in the mills or to fish. Fishing and cedar mills were the big industries. Seattle Cedar, was the largest cedar mill in the world at the time — it made shakes and siding — and at one time there were 23 mills. Now there aren't any. A lot of immigrants worked in the mills. The Greeks did cleanup, and the Swedes and Italians ran the long saws for cutting slabs off the logs. The logs came in on a boom. It was all hard work. I think they made about 50 cents an hour and that was considered pretty good pay.

Some of the shingle weavers had fingers cut off because they put their hands in too close, and lo and behold, they'd cut off some finger.

I heard a lot of whistles. At Seattle Cedar one group started work at 7:30, one at eight o'clock, and with that came whistles. At noon, a whistle for lunch, and then at 4:30, five o'clock another whistle. We had whistles from boats and trains going through Ballard. Even the streetcars had a whistle.

I was born across the street from where Ballard Hospital is today. I could see this cloud of workers come out of the mills, going home or going to their boarding houses during the week. Men who lived in a boarding house during the week would go home on the weekends to Snohomish and Everett and Issaquah.

When I was young I worked as a hod carrier for 22½ cents an hour. Then I went to the cannery near the ice plant and got 45 cents an hour. My dad told me, "Don't sit down when you're working. Don't sit down." We were blanching blackberries in a big vat. Five of us were working, pushing them in. The other four sat down. I pretended like I was turning a valve. The foreman came in and said, you four guys can get your time, Boitano will stay and keep working. That stuck with me, and I tell my sons that many times.

We used to stand on the platform to get hired, hired every day and laid off every day. Only three of us came back. We'd slice the strawberries in a slicer, add sugar, put them in 30-pound cans and put them in the freezer.

I got 45 cents an hour, then I went to the ice plant and got 75 cents an hour driving an ice wagon. This was in summer because I was going to school during the winter.

John Boitano - 239

My brothers all worked in the ice plant, They were ice pullers. The Bennetts who owned the icehouse hired a lot of Ballard kids. And a lot of Ballard kids worked in the cannery.

Ice was made in big tubes. The ice pullers would pull a tube over, fill it with water add a de-icer to purify the ice cake and then freeze them. They dipped the tubes in hot water so the ice would slide out; then stored them in the icehouse. We ice drivers, would score the ice in 25, 50 and 100 pound cakes and put them on our truck and deliver it to homes, to taverns, grocery stores and bakeries.

The homes would have a sign in their window, 25, for a 25 pound cake of ice, 50 for 50 pounds. Turning the 25 sign upside-down meant 75 pounds and turning 50 over meant 100 pounds. And we were tough. My brother was one of the toughest guys in the place. He could lift a 400-pound cake up on edge to put them in the truck. We went to what were called doghouses [small houses to store ice for sale], out where they didn't have home delivery. I loved the ice wagon. Best job I ever had. I got 75 cents an hour, that was top pay.

After my dad retired from the garbage company he and my brother had a fuel yard, and sometimes I went along to work in the woods, cutting wood, getting slab wood. We had a big buzz saw, and one Sunday my dad cut his elbow on it. My mother said, "You'll never work on Sunday again." And we did what she said.

Ballard High School was a great school — the teachers took you as you were. They took us guys that weren't so smart and brought us along. Good teaching. And at Ballard, yes, I wore cords and shoes and T-shirts and sweaters like the other kids. I worked and wore mostly hand-me-downs.

At the cannery one summer I told the boss, "I got to go to school and turn out for football. I want to thank you for letting me work here." He said, "You're the best worker we ever had. And you can always work here."

We played Lincoln in football. I'm not bragging, but I scored two touch-downs and I threw for two touchdowns. We beat Lincoln 27 to nothing. Saturday morning I went with Pa to the mine to get coal. In the *P.I.* there's a big picture of me scoring. And I pull up in a diamond T-truck. We had a good fancy truck.

And a guy at the chute says, *"Vene qua Boitano."* That means "Come here." I passed all the other trucks, he pulls his chute down. He says, "What do you want?" I said, "I want five ton of stoker." I pulled the chute down and we got five ton of stoker, and he says, "Hey, this is for you, kid, another five hundred pounds." That meant about five dollars more.

240 - John Boitano

I went to pay in the office, and five or six Italians were in there, and one guy said, "This is *figlio de* Boitano, that means son of Boitano. And, god, they all looked at me. My dad finally got respect for me. He thought it was something that these guys had paid attention to me, and my picture was in the paper.

The day is Thanksgiving day, 1940. We were playing football at the University of Washington. Twenty-two thousand people watching the high school game. The game ended in a nothing and nothing tie, but we had a better record, and so we won the championship. We had a good coach, "Heinie" Bendele. We had some good ball players: Tag Christensen, Jelly Andersen, Ray Ramsauer, and Bud Wheat — Wheat was tough, he was a good — Irv Wehde, who has passed away, Bernie Fredrickson in the back field, Dale Mitchell. I remember these guys like they were my brothers, 'cause we were together on a lot of things. That was Thanksgiving 1940, then we went home and had Thanksgiving dinner.

When war broke out, 95 percent of lower Ballard kids joined the service. Mrs. Wilborn, a Swede who lived across the street who couldn't talk English, brought me a silver dollar with my birthdate on it, 1922. She gave one to all the kids who went in the service. Wasn't that a nice thing? I went in the Air Corps and I washed out, so I went into the Navy, was on an LSM. And, there's not many of us left on that LSM. I ended up with cancer. I was in Sasebo, then I went to Nagasaki and Hiroshima. I could have picked up some radiation there. I don't know. The doctors don't know, but there's not many guys that had their arm amputated from a blow from the sun — or from the radiation that I picked up in Japan.

I went to University of Washington and got my degree, and I was a volunteer coach at Ballard for a couple years. I'm the only coach left of that Burnett-Bendele-Gasparovich bunch. Then I was head football and baseball coach at Garfield for 11 years. The first four years I coached football, I lost one ball game. Just one! We won the City Championship and the so-called State Championship. I wasn't much of a teacher, but I was a highly successful football coach. I was a teacher and coach for 22 years. And then I went to the Seattle Public Schools Athletic Office where I was Assistant Athletic Director for ten years. I enjoyed my coaching years. It was fun and I had some good teams because I had some good material. My boys are good coaches too, because they work at it hard.

My roots kept me in Ballard. I got a lot of friends that stayed in

Ballard. Why do people stay in a place? I could go to Issaquah or Carnation or someplace and build a nice flat house. We've got a two-level house. That's no fun. I built this house 48 years ago. I bought the lot 50 years ago. And I stayed here all these years even though I did a lot of building up on the hill by Swansons Nursery, over there on Greenwood. I built five houses in the swamp over there, but I stayed in Ballard. You stay because of roots and, yeah, my wife's here and my friends are here. That's what's kept me in Ballard.

John Boitano was born in 1922 in Ballard. His father, Giovanni (John) Boitano was born in Lombardi, Italy. His mother, Nina Angela (Boitano) was born in Utah to Italian parents, but when her parents were killed in an accident at the Kennicott copper mines, she was shipped to Italy to live in an orphanage. She grew up and married Giovanni (same community, no relation) and they come to the United States in 1900. They came to Ballard in 1904. Their children: Bill, Nino, Mazilia, George, John, and the twins, Lena and Gloria. John married Jane Andrew in 1947. Their children are John, Jr (1954), Jay (1956), and Sally (1964). After graduating from Ballard High (1941) and the University of Washington, John coached football and taught at West Seattle High (1950-54) and Garfield High (1954-66). He then worked in the Seattle Schools Athletic office until he retired (1980). John and Jane continued to live in Blue Ridge. John died in 2004.

Vicky Straumfjord Boyett

"Dad was like Honest Abe — he had integrity. He loved people and they loved him. He had a little blue and gold velvet sign, and it said to the customer, 'We hope to please you always.'"

Daddy's name was Johann Helgi Straumfjord. Quite a few that called him "Jo" for short. He was born on Hekla Island in Manitoba. And was delivered by his grandfather, a homeopath. Mother, Anna Maria Jonsson, was born in Harrickstada, in Eastern Iceland. My parents met, fell in love and married in Winnipeg in 1918. Dad got his training for watchmaking and jewelry repair and clocks in a Winnipeg department store called Dinglehoffer's.

He started as a watchmaker and jewelry repairman in 1925 on Ballard Avenue, just off of Market Street. He and Bjarni Johannsson had know each other back in the twenties after Dad moved here —[and after some years he moved his shop into Bjarni's Cascade Drug]. As you came through the front door, you'd come by the magazines on the right. Just beyond was Dad's shop, inside the drug store. It was like eight by twelve feet, and there was sort of a dutch door. The top part could be opened so Dad could serve the customers through there.

I worked in Cascade Drug with Bjarni and he taught me how to make cherry cokes. It had to be just like a chemist. He put his glass up like that and said, you know, "Not any more than this." He was delightful to work for. The soda fountain was a popular place. He had this wonderful marble counter there, and had these little wire backed chairs — Coca Cola chairs. He had two booths. He also had a large case where he had various kinds of candies. They were just wonderful, but I didn't nibble too much. And then of course his pharmaceutical work was done at the far end.

Dad was like Honest Abe — he had integrity. He loved people and they loved him. He had a little blue and gold velvet sign, and it said to the customer, "We hope to please you always." He was very meticulous, everything in its place. And he had a board, at that time in the forties, he must have had two hundred watches that were hanging up — wrist watches, pocket watches that he was working on.

He had a little blue book, and in there every single job was put down. Name and address and telephone number and what was done to the watch and how much it costs. And then he would do jewelry repairs the same. Very often when people would come in, old customers that were on limited income, he would sometimes not charge them. He'd have a big NC by their name.

Winnie Thompson, now Winnie Fairland, worked for my father. And the customers thought that she was the daughter. She was the first woman watchmaker in the state at that time. Dad had taught her.

Dad moved from that shop to the final shop, only a half a block away, in 1946. After leaving Cascade Drugs he moved to 5405 20th Avenue Northwest. And we helped to move him.

He retired in 1980. My son, Brian, learned the trade from his grandfather. He apprenticed two or three years or more, and then he worked alongside his grandfather. When Dad had health problems and could not continue, Brian and his wife Donna bought the store, and they work together as proprietor and wife.

Vicky Straumfjord, a life-long Ballard resident, was born October 13, 1925, to Anna Maria Jonsson and Johann Helgi Straumfjord (1896-1980). She joined a brother Hafstein (1921-1942 – he died in an auto accident), and Diana (1923). Vicky married Francis Boyett in 1946. They have three children: Brian (1947), Ann Marie (1948) and Vicky May (1951). Also six grandchildren and two great-grandchildren. Francis died in 1998. Vicky died in 2003.

Naomie Fredeen Bulloch

"I think my parents' generation all wanted to be American. They had a drive to become fluent in English, and to be seen as modern Americans. My mother particularly wanted to be identified not as a Swedish immigrant but as a young woman in 1920s America. That's how she saw herself."

My name is Naomie Fredeen Bulloch. I don't know why the "e" is on the end, except my mother put it there. My Swedish grandparents, both sets, came to Bellingham through different routes. My paternal grandparents came from Sweden to Nebraska, where my father, their youngest child, was born. Later they moved to Bellingham. My grandfather was a farmer. My maternal grandparents, Maria and Karl Hultgren, left Sweden for Winnipeg in 1905. My mother was less than a year old and her brother was two. My grandmother died in a typhoid epidemic that year and soon after the little boy died in a measles epidemic. My grandfather, left with an infant daughter, gave her up for adoption to a Swedish couple, Peter and Anna Axlund. They were the ones I knew as my grandparents. After my mother was grown, her biological father died in an accident at a logging camp in Oregon. This was several years after my adoptive grandfather died in a construction accident in Vancouver, B.C. I always felt so sad that my mother suffered all these losses and separations in her young life.

Peter and Anna Axlund lived in Ballard for a short time when my mother was little. In 1915, after Peter died, Anna and her child, my mother, moved to Bellingham, where she worked as a housekeeper.

I'm pretty sure my parents met at the Mission Covenant Church in Bellingham, one of the Swedish emigrants' churches, which still exists. In Sweden my adoptive grandmother was a devoted member of the Salvation Army, which she referred to as *Frälsnings-Armén.* I spent summers with her in Ballard in the 1930s. She played guitar and accordion, also played the drum in the Salvation Army band. Some times she took me with her when the Ballard Corps' conducted a Sunday afternoon street meeting in Pioneer Square. I followed my grandmother as she played in the band. She looked quite charming in her navy blue Salvation Army uniform, with a wonderful bonnet with satin ruffles under the brim, framing her face.

I'd walk to the Carnegie Public Library on Market Street. I would scoop up as many books as was allowed. After the library, I liked to visit the Sunshine Dairy. They made wonderful ice cream. I think a double-decker cone cost a nickel then.

We had moved to Seattle because my father hoped to find job opportunities here. Through the Swedish Covenant Church he met Mr. Strom and became his partner in his floor covering business, Strom Fredeen. Later my father owned the business.

At Ballard High I was taking a botany class when World War II came upon us. The garden behind the school immediately became a Victory Garden. I worked in the garden and have a picture which was reprinted in one of Paul Dorpat's *Seattle Then and Now* series. The picture, dated February, 1943, shows the Victory Garden with me and others working. The caption says we're harvesting. I think we were probably preparing for a new planting. The garden helped supply the school's cafeteria with fresh vegetables. Dorpat wrote, "The garden in 1942 produced 800 pounds of pumpkins, 300 pounds of tomatoes, cabbages, carrots, onions, beans, lettuce, beets, radishes, Brussels sprouts." At Ballard I was on the staff of the yearbook, the *Shingle*, and the newspaper, the *Talisman*. Both were terrific experiences. We went to the *Ballard Tribune* Tuesday nights to put the paper together. It would be typeset there, and we'd paste up the pages, then send them to the presses. It had news about new students, new teachers, what the Honor Society was doing, and lots of sports. Ballard had some very good teams including the city championship football team when I was there. Henry Bendele was the coach.

When I was 14 I started getting part-time jobs. The summer of '42 I worked at Mr. McWorter's Toothbrush Factory a couple of months, then moved to Ballard Plastics, which was making parts for the Navy. I left that job after several months because the acetone they used gave me headaches. So when I had the chance to become a movie theater cashier, I took it.

I worked at the Grand Theater on 85th near Greenwood. People were flocking to the movies for relaxation, since everyone was working so hard. Because their parents were both working, we saw huge bunches of kids at the theater. I'd get telephone calls at the box office from parents looking for their kids. "Is Betty in the theater right now?" Sometimes the sheriff came to round up someone reported missing. If the kids recognized someone coming in who might haul them home, they'd get up and run. We'd have kids darting out the door, behind the screen, trying to get out to the back. It got pretty chaotic sometimes, but it was kind of amusing — no violence involved, just silly kids trying to get away with something. It became a real problem on the street around there and the sheriff decided something had to be done about kids out on the streets at night. As a result, the Boys Clubs were organized. They started in Seattle and then spread around the country. Later they added the Girls Clubs.

Wherever we went — to the ice arena, to the Trianon Ballroom, a movie theater — we saw soldiers and sailors so it was easy to meet fellows from all over the country. When I went to the University of Washington, the Navy was using a lot of University facilities for the V-12 program. The young men in that Navy program had the rank of ensign, and wore their uniforms to class.

At the University I joined a group of what were called "town girls," who lived off campus and who created their own sorority, Phrateres. It was sponsored by the dean of women, May Dunn Ward. We sometimes volunteered at the USO downtown. And that's where I met my husband. I ran the soda fountain, served hamburgers, coffee, milkshakes, that kind of thing. A girlfriend of mine came up and said, "These two young Army Air Corpsmen would like to meet us." We went to a booth and she introduced me. They invited us to sit down and talk. Douglas Bulloch, from New York, was based at Boeing Field in the B-29 program. He eventually flew 35 missions over the Pacific and Japan. He was a gunner. That was very dangerous work.

During WW II, gasoline and food were rationed. We saved aluminum foil and rubber bands. We saved cooking fats and took them to the butcher shop to be recycled. Even pots and pans could be recycled. We couldn't buy silk stockings and dress styles reflected the shortage of fabric — everything was cut along skimpy lines.

And we worried about being invaded — I'd hear an airplane and think about Mussolini's planes — we'd heard they bombed Ethiopia, and they must be very powerful. Probably because of Boeing, we were terribly aware of the idea of air power. And after the Japanese bombed Pearl Harbor, I think everyone felt they might attack the West Coast. My mother volunteered to spot and identify airplanes flying overhead. Security was tight. After D-Day in 1944 everybody just prayed that it would succeed. We felt vulnerable. We didn't have any sense of being the "superpower" that we've been painted ever since.

I want to tell a little bit about Christmas. We always made Christmas cookies, spritz cookies. We still do. My sister cooks the *lutfisk* and we buy the potato sausage. My sister and brother-in-law have prepared the Swedish version of ham from scratch — they like to do that kind of thing. And I bake spritz every year at Christmas with my grandchildren. That's a lot of fun.

I think my parents' generation all wanted to be American. They had a drive to become fluent in English, and to be seen as modern Americans. My mother particularly wanted to be identified not as a Swedish immigrant but as a young woman in 1920's America. That's how she saw herself. My mother-in-law, of the same generation, emigrated from Scotland. They both had a need to be contemporary, to appear fashionable and to have a modern home and household. My mother was always researching things like vacuum cleaners and refrigerators. She would have loved to have an automatic dishwasher.

My dad was typical of a lot of men in that he tended to be away, very involved in his business and church activities. So his wasn't really a strong presence. And when the war came along he traveled a lot on business. At church he was on the board of deacons and was sort of a lay minister, too. He was invited to other churches to speak. It was a very important thing in his life. And he was one of the founders of Crista Ministries in north Seattle. When I came back to Seattle with my family, after I'd married, he was involved in starting King's Garden Schools, the living facilities and all the rest. He and Mike Martin were the movers and shakers who got it established. It's quite a monument to my dad. He died only last year, at age 97.

My mother liked needlework a lot. She embroidered tablecloths and napkins and she made quilt squares, lots of them. She had had a very sad life at times, and needlework is kind of soothing. She felt deprived as a young person, and in the '20s, fashion became a very big thing and she was just the right age to be a flapper. She disgraced the family when she had bobbed her hair. It was always clear that she loved beautiful jewelry, things like that — gold and rhinestone. One Christmas I bought her a sequined beret with a matching belt, both very bright and glittery — and my sister bought her the same thing. We both knew what would appeal to her.

We spent a lot of time in church, but it never became our life as it was my father's. We attended Sunday school and youth groups and service. My father persuaded Emanuel Church to sponsor a new branch church out past Lake City. For several years he devoted himself to organizing and building it up. And that was where we went to church. We made a lot of friends there, but I was more interested in my school friends and the school activities. To me, school was a refuge from many of the discomforts of home life.

Ballard certainly gave you a sense of place. I took a walk in Ballard recently. Ballard is becoming gentrified. I passed Kathy Casey's Gourmet Food Laboratory and a couple of art galleries and the Great Harvest Bakery, and of course Starbucks. I had the sense that Ballard is changing. It still gives me that sense: it's my place.

Naomie Fredeen was born August 28, 1926 in Bellingham, Washington to Karen (Axlund) and Axel Fredeen. They came to Ballard in 1935. Her sister, Natalie was born in 1932. Naomie graduated from Ballard High in 1943. She married Douglas Bulloch in 1944. Their children: Stephen (1947-1976— he died in an accident a week after he graduated from medical school), Christy (1949), Bruce (1951) and George (1956).

Robert L. Campbell

"My grandmother used to tell me when I was a young boy, that we originated from Danish royalty. But I don't even know what their name was."

The Campbells originated in Scotland and immigrated into this country through England and Canada. On my grandmother's side there's some Scandinavian history. My grandmother used to tell me when I was a young boy, that we originated from Danish royalty. But I don't even know what their name was. My dad was born in Nanaimo, B.C. My mother was born in Saginaw, Michigan, her dad was a salesman for a hardware store. He transferred to Seattle Hardware bringing his family with him. My father was probably in his teens, when he came to the United States from Canada. He was in the Merchant Marine for some years. Then he went to work for Seattle Hardware in their paint department. My parents were married while he was working there. Their first residence was on Boren Avenue. I was farmed out to the Seattle Day Nursery while my mother worked.

In about 1937 he and another Seattle Hardware employee, Art Cowman, started their own business, even though it was the aftermath of the Great Depression. Cowman-Campbell Paint Company began on 8th Avenue South near East Marginal Way. In 1946 they purchased the property that's known as C&C Paint, at 5232 Shilshole Avenue, next to Salmon Bay Sand and Gravel.

I was born in Seattle at the old Swedish Hospital on March 8, 1922. I was their only child. Later, my parents divorced. My mother married William Lamb around 1928 and I used the Lamb name.

When we moved to Ballard with my stepfather, I went to Whittier, then to James Monroe Junior High through seventh grade. My folks moved north and I graduated from Lincoln High in 1941.

Off and on I worked at the paint company as well. On Saturdays and part time I would help with canning and mixing and stuff like that, working with my dad. They were still 8th Avenue South. When they moved, I went to work for Isaacson Ironworks full time and then, in 1944, I was drafted. I served the United States Navy from 1944 to 1946.

After I was discharged, I went back to the paint company, working for my father. I worked there in the factory from 1946 to 1965, when I went into the hardware business. Twenty years later in 1985, I liquidated the hardware business and came back to C&C Paint in Ballard.

When they moved to Ballard in 1946 I think they had as many as 30 employees. There was an inside crew and an outside crew. The outside people were the sales people out canvassing the area. The territory C&C Paint covered in those days was Washington, Oregon, Idaho and Alaska. I think the military business is what gave the paint company its jump start. They were pretty well organized by the time of the second World War. They made a lot of Navy gray hull paint.

I'm retired from C&C paints and my connection there now is as landlord. The property is owned by three people: the Cowman Estate, and Harold Cowman and Bob Campbell. The company will be history probably by the end of the year. We are developing it into rental property mainly. There's about five parcels there, and three of them are warehouses.

I remember when Seattle Cedar burned down. That was a catastrophe for Ballard. It sure concerned us at the paint company. I think when I first noticed the glow in the sky, I was in downtown Seattle. That was a terrible, hot and big fire. They were only a block up the street from us and embers were flying all over the place. We sure as heck thought all of Shilshole Avenue, our paint company, Salmon Bay Sand and Gravel, and another company that made foul-weather gear for fishermen — Johnson Clothing, I think it was called — and the whole block was going to go. We rushed to the plant to see what we could do to help, and cinders were all over the place. The fire went along the old cedar drying shed, and I saw two or three firemen up there with hoses. I thought, boy, those guys are in a dangerous position. But they controlled it.

Robert Campbell was born March 8, 1922 in Seattle to Ruth (Mitchell) and Robert Campbell. He married Shirley Spencer in 1941. Their daughters: Shari (1942), Cathy (1945) and Becky (1947).

Alan "Moose" Clausen

(with his sister Myrtle and his wife Dorothy)

"Hey, I love my heritage and I love
Ballard and I always will."

ALAN: My dad, Christian, wanted to get ahead in life, and he wanted adventure, so that brought him over here. He was something of a maverick.

DOROTHY: The tragic story of the Clausen family was well known in Kvæfjord. Christian's family was very poor. Their home was so humble the floor was dirt, with no means to cook inside. The father, Arndt, was a blacksmith and there wasn't much work. He hunted to provide food for the family. They cooked outdoors. In 1902 the mother died. She was 34 years old. Nels was just four months old, Alfred was two, Christian was four, Andreas was five and Claude, the oldest, was eight. Arndt, also 34, died the same year, but before he died, Arndt placed his four youngest sons in the care of relatives. Claude, the oldest, was raised by the pastor. Christian — Alan and Myrtle's father — was placed with his mother's sister, her husband and their daughter, Kitty, who was close to his age. All the Clausen brothers remained close to one another.

Alan's mother Helene said, "I'll never forget the day when I left for America. My face was smiling, I was beaming, and I could hardly wait for that ship to come. I didn't shed one tear. I got on board that ship. I wasn't sorry, I wasn't sad. I was happy I was going to America" She was just filled with excitement. She said, "Here I was on that ship and at last my dream was coming true. I stood on that passenger deck so proud and waved to my mother and my sister, and I watched them, and finally I couldn't see them. Then, all of sudden, I felt all alone. I didn't know a person on the ship, and then I couldn't stop the tears from flowing down my face. I thought, what am I doing? Why am I leaving Norway?"

But once she was on that ship there was no turning back. Ten long days of travel in the worst weather. She felt like she'd made the biggest mistake of her life. The journey was almost over and the ship was nearing New York Harbor. A new excitement filled her heart. "And then I saw the most incredible sight — the Statue of Liberty. She was majestic, a proud lady. She held a torch of friendship in the sky. She seemed to say, 'Welcome to America, Helene.' All the fear and doubts were gone. I knew I made the right choice."

She told about how she met Christian at a Norwegian dance — he was a handsome fisherman, you know. They married in 1931. But in 1945 the Coast Guard came to tell her that Christian had died of a heart attack. Myrtle and Alan still remember that knock on the door.

MYRTLE: She told Alan and me to go down to the bakery and get a loaf of bread. She wanted us out of the house while she talked to the Coast Guard people.

ALAN: Mom always told me that Dad had told her, "Don't let Alan be a fisherman." It was a very tough occupation. I'm in the baseball business. I've worked for the Seattle Mariner Baseball Club, for 19 years. I played baseball at Ballard High School, and little league in Ballard, and played some baseball up in Fairbanks, Alaska, when Mom had remarried about four or five years after Dad died.

I got the nickname "Moose" from Ballard High School days when Tony Gasparovich and Don Burnett were our baseball coaches. They liked to have a big guy on the team, and I was only four feet, 11 inches, barely 100 pounds, and the smallest one to play baseball in the City of Seattle in those days. Tony and Don said, we've got to have a "Moose" on our team, and it happened to be me. The *Seattle Times* came out and took a picture of me looking up to our skinny six-foot, two inch pitcher named Bud Clark. He was all-city and a great athlete, and it says, "Little by little Al Clausen aspires to be five feet."

There's not a greater community that Myrt and I could have been raised in. There were others who stepped in as a father figure for me as a young boy. The next door neighbors, after church on Sundays, would take us to Thompson's Old Fashioned Freeze on 58th and 24th, or somewhere in that area. On vacations they took me with them up to Orcas Island. Many people took me under their wing.

In high school I worked at Ballard Zesto's, and that was *the* place to work when you were in school. I was a soda jerk. I made milkshakes and Boston coolers and hamburgers, and made enough money there to buy a '47 Club Coupe Plymouth car.

I went on to college, and Nelson Chevrolet had a job for me in Ballard. I held three jobs. One was at the Lapidary Equipment Company across the street, Nelson Chevrolet and Hill Auto Parts. I was trying to pay for my own college education. I'd be working 17 hours a day, and finally it got to me. I had a little virus so I had to stop a couple of jobs and just take the one. Nelson Chevrolet always had a job for me when I came home from school at Christmas time. I went to Central Washington, in Ellensburg. It was a neat thing to be a part of Nelson Chevrolet. When I graduated from college, Mr. Nelson offered me the parts manager job there. So I took it, and it paid very well. And for a young man just out of college, he took good care of me. I had a brand new car every three months, a demo.

Then I was approached by the New York Life Insurance Company — a friend of mine told them "You've got to get ahold of Al Clausen, and talk to him about selling insurance." I ended up being a New York Life agent for 14½ years. Then I was asked to be the director of sales for the Seattle Mariner Baseball team in 1982.

Right now I'm in charge of selling the suites for Safeco Field, and I had been in charge of selling season tickets in group sales. So, that's been my career. I'm starting my 19th season right now. I've been there for a long time, and have had a lot of fun in doing it. Scandinavians are known to be hard workers and self-starters.

I still go down to Ballard. I get my hair cut in Ballard, I've gone to Louie's since I was 14, and get fishcakes from the Norwegian Sausage Company. I still seem to come back to Ballard. Hey, I love my heritage and I love Ballard and I always will.

Alan Clausen was born September 20, 1938 in Seattle. His father, Christian Ror Clausen was born May 28, 1898 in Kvæfjord, Norway and immigrated when he was 25 (1923). His mother, Helene Halvorson, was born November 30, 1901 in Vålor, Norway and immigrated in 1928. They met at Norway Hall at a dance and were married June 30, 1931. They had two chidren, Myrtle, born March 12, 1932 and Alan. Helene, a Norwegian-trained nurse, worked as a Licenced Practical Nurse here for over 30 years. Christian, a halibut fisherman, died at sea of a heart attack in 1945, age 47. Helene then married John Hoberg. She died in Seattle in 1998, age 97.

Lorna Daniels Conrad

"I really feel like my whole life has been a miracle, because I don't remember how we managed, but we did."

We moved to Ballard in 1924 to 1737 West 58th and I was not quite eight years old. I thought I was in Heaven. The library was about four blocks away and I'd been reading since I was four, and I'd read all the stuff we had. You could only take two books a day from the library, but I always was a speed reader, so I went back one day to get two more, and they said, you've read enough today.

Right across the street from the library was the fire station. And my uncle, Joe Osborne was lieutenant. He was a big, jolly fellow, and he wore a white shirt with black elastic sleeve bands, because he was the lieutenant, and all the other fellows wore blue. In those days, there were nine of them down there. And they still had the old horses next door. One was named Dan — he was a big dapple gray. Once my uncle took me upstairs to show me where they all slept. And while I'm standing there looking around, he scooped me up under one arm and down the pole we went. Scared me to death. He had to hold me on his lap and console me for about a half an hour before I went home. I was eight.

I went to Salmon Bay school, Irving School and the Irving annex, they called it the Peanut College. Bardahl's is there now. It was a long way to go, so I went back to Salmon Bay. Then I graduated from Irving, because I was scared of the eighth-grade teacher at Salmon Bay.

We'd go down to the Locks for a walk or we'd go up to Woodland Park for a walk. They had a big merry-go-round up there inside the building, and a big Ferris wheel outside, and it's on the hill, anyway, you know. You know, you could see it all over Ballard. At night it would be lit up. But it all burned down one time and they never replaced it. It's near where the Norse Home is now.

We went to Ballard Beach. We didn't like it after they put that stupid marina there; all those boats mostly are owned by people on Mercer Island, anyway. They ruined the beach. They filled it all in. There used to be little tide pools and you could find shells and things, and back by the big rocks, there was nice smooth sand. I don't swim, but we went there a lot. My mother went to Ballard Beach when she was a kid, which was before 1900.

We went to movies at the Majestic then, which is now the Bay, and it cost ten cents. They had a different show on Saturday and Sunday, and you could buy a little popcorn if you had an extra dime.

There was still another old theater there called the Empress, and it had an organist that came up on an elevated platform and down again. It was triangular shaped, but it didn't last very long. Then they opened the Bagdad in the Eagle's Building.

Then one night, I was in a contest for kids at the Majestic. I was ten, then. And I was the last one, because I was very nervous. I don't know how I ever had the nerve to do anything like that. But this man, when he greeted anybody on the stage, always put out his hand to shake hands. And when they went to shake hands with him, he'd throw his hand over his shoulder. And I wasn't going to do that, so I slapped his hand. And then he asked me what I was going to do, and I said I was going to sing, so he went and wrapped himself up in the curtain at the side of the stage, and I sang a little song about Men and Andy Gump. At the end, anyway, we lined up and he put his hands over our head, and who got the most applause won the prize, and it was me. I don't think it was my singing; I think it was because I slapped his hand. So, when I got home, there was my father, who never was very encouraging. "Well, you little goof, I suppose you won first prize." "Yeah," I said, "I did." It was a big satisfaction to throw that box of chocolates in his lap.

My father was older and he worked for many years for the Great Northern Railway. He was a timekeeper. And he was let go by the railroad just before he was due to get a pension. By then, he was in his 50's. He'd never done physical work. He got part-time work for awhile, and we had to be on WPA for awhile. And he had to go up to where they dished out commissaries, they called it, like cheese and butter. That embarrassed him terribly, but he did it.

My mother worked at home all the time. She was just a little lady, not even five feet tall, but out here in the country, when he was gone, she did everything. She had chickens, a cow, a garden, and she didn't have any conveniences. No indoor plumbing, you know.

My brother worked at Kastner's meat market at one time, for awhile. They used to give him scraps from the meat they were turning into hamburger to take home for the cats. But the fellow that worked there usually gave him some of the better meat, and mama made soup, so we always said we had cat scrap soup.

256 - Lorna Arlene Conrad

I met my husband through my brother, really. He came down to the house to see my brother, and his name was Ladd Conrad. We just kind of saw each other quite often, mostly at my house. But, anyway, I decided he was pretty nice and he was pretty good looking, I thought, and he was strong. I liked that. So, we got married just before I was 17 — three days before, as a matter of fact. And we were married 64 years. But he wasn't a man who was able to solve problems, so it was all left up to me. I had to handle everything, and, of course, that made me a stronger person, but it also made him not like it, but that was too bad. If the captain won't run the ship, somebody has to.

Anyway, he was a hard worker and he did beautiful work. He could have done a lot better than he did financially, because he was more interested in having people like him, I guess, and doing favors for his friends. But he could build furniture, he could do perfect plumbing or anything, and very neat about it, too. But I would never have known it if I hadn't seen it at friends' houses.

I don't know how we managed. There were times when I went to the store with three dollars to get dinner, breakfast and lunch for ten people. Of course, I had a few staples at home, potatoes and stuff. But, I just learned how to manage, I guess, which is lucky. Nobody ever went hungry, and my kids were very nice about it. My oldest daughter, Arlene said, "But you're really the better cook, because you could make a meal out of practically nothing." I know I was lucky in lots of ways. I really feel like my whole life has been a miracle, because I don't remember how we managed, but we did.

I tried working at a restaurant when I had six little ones, but my husband was no baby sitter and I couldn't afford to hire a baby sitter. I worked from six in the evening until two at the restaurant in Ballard. It was called the Roxy. Well, up until midnight, it was fine. It was mostly family people for supper and after the show for an ice cream or something. But after midnight, they started coming out of the woodwork. Terrible people. I could have walked home; it was not far, but I was not going to go out on the street knowing there were that kind of people around. Those people were rotten, drunk, and good for nothing.

There was still a police station in Ballard then, and these two policemen used to come in about two in the morning for free coffee, and they would take us home, but I would never go with them unless the cook, whom I knew came too, and they would drop me off first.

The woman who owned the cafe paid a good-for-nothing cop ten dollars a week to let people spike up their coffee. If they kept the bottle hidden, they could do that.

I didn't work at the cafe for long, then I didn't really go to work until I was 45, and then I worked for the post office, downtown terminal. They said they were going to do a big hiring, and 700 people took tests. I found out later, out of the 700 people, I was third, so I went to work in two weeks.

I love my children very much. I've always called them my jewels, and they were the only jewels I wanted.

Lorna Daniels was born October 29, 1916 in Meadowdale, near Lynnwood, Washington. Her father, Harry Daniels was born in Cornwall, England. He immigrated to Canada in his late teens, and in his 30s to the U.S. He worked for the Great Northern Railroad. Her mother, Estelle Osborne, born in Iowa in 1884 came to Ballard in 1894 when she was 10 years old. Their children: Ida (1908), Henry (1909), Laura and Phoebe (1920). The family moved to Ballard in 1924. In 1933 Lorna dropped out of high school and married Ladd Conrad. She was 17. Their children: Arlene (1934), newborn boy, lived only ten hours (1935), Camille (1936), Rosalee (1938), Janice (1939), Laddie (1941), Karen (1942), Ralph (1945), Georgia (1946), Chris (1950), Terry (1952), Julie (1954) and twins Pamela and Angela (1957). Lorna wrote numerous essays and poems, some have been published. Lorna died in 2003.

Signe Heggem Davis

"My grandfather was very amazing. He was a designer of fishing vessels and many other kinds of craft."

M y story starts at the end of the Second World War. I was born in 1945. My father, Ole Johan Heggem, had been in the Navy but left after the war. He had a degree in fisheries from the University of Washington so he worked in that field all over the world. My mother, Ruth Aljean Ashment, my father and I went to the Philippines first, then to Hawaii for five years, then to New Delhi, India, and Karachi, Pakistan. After that, during the sixties, we were in Santiago, Chile, and Okinawa.

Somehow, I managed to sort of stay where I was supposed to be in school. When I came back to Seattle I graduated from Ballard High School and then went to the University of Washington and earned a degree in art. In those years I visited my parents on Okinawa during the summer when I had a break from school.

The first time I came to Seattle I was two-weeks old and flew here to meet my grandfather, Ingvald Marius Heggem and grandmother, Marit Johansdatter Westad. We stayed in Seattle for several months and didn't return to Coronado until the war was over and my father returned. But the first time I remember seeing my grandfather was when I was somewhere between seven and nine years old. My grandmother, Marit, died when I was about four years old so I have no memories of seeing her on her visits to Coronado.

My grandfather was very amazing. He was a designer of fishing vessels and many other kinds of craft. When he was a child he laid cod to dry on the the rocks in the sun. Making bacalao (dried fish), was a major industry in Kristiansund. When he finished *folkeskole* he was 14 and then he went to work in the largest shipyard in Kristiansund. His father, his uncle and his grandfather were all boat builders and they worked at Neddre Kranens Shipyard together.

My great great-grandfather, Even Knudtson Heggem, came from Bofjordan, Halsa to settle in Kristiansund. His birth name was Anton Knudtson Vassli, but like many other young men at the time, he took the name Heggem from the estate he worked on. So when he was in

Kristiansund he was known as Even K. Heggem. He married Ingeborg Olsdatter from Surnadal and had two sons.

Even Heggem's sons were Karl Magnus Heggem, who never married, and Ole Evenson Heggem, who married Britt Larsdotter Faksness. Britt died in childbirth and Ole began a courtship with the widow of a seafaring man, Patrine Madsvag, who had one daughter. Ingvald remembered that his father asked him to take messages to Patrine because he was too shy to do so. Grandfather Ingvald already had two siblings, Ingeborg and Lai, and after his father married Patrine they had three more children. Four generations lived together in the Heggem house:two brothers, Ole and Karl Magnus, Patrine, seven children and great grandfather, Even K. Heggem. All the men were boat builders and they could go to work by stepping out their front door on Ballast Wharf and, then, probably, rowing a short distance across the bay to the shipyard.

After finishing *folkeskole*, Ingvald started to work at the Neddre Kranens Shipyards where he worked with his father, uncle and grandfather. When he was 18, he served an apprenticeship at *Kristiansund Boadbyggeri* for eleven months and he managed to find time to serve in the military in Trondheim.

Ingvald did go to sea for three years until the end of 1903. He served as a ship's carpenter or *tømmerand* on various ships. While between voyages in 1902, he learned that his father had drowned at a boat launching. There he was, as age 20, with a stepmother and a large family to think about.

Grandfather went back to sea on another contract and then in 1904, he left for Bergen where he completed a six-month apprenticeship studying shipbuilding construction and ship's plans, at Brunchorst and Dekke. Ananias Christof Dekke was famous for the fast sailing ships he produced in Bergen. He had learned his trade in the United States from Donald McKay, one of the great builders of schooners on the East Coast. Dekke died twenty years earlier but his shipyard was still a magnet for young shipbuilders. Undoubtedly, Ingvald picked up some of Dekke's ideas.

Grandfather returned to Kristiansund and worked for two years at the Neddre Kranens Shipyard. In 1906, he bought passage and headed for Seattle. After he arrived in Seattle, he went to Eilert Ericksen's house (in Ballard). Ericksen had worked at the shipyard in Kristiansund and lived not far from the Heggem house there. He was about eighteen or twenty years older than Grandfather and came here in 1901. I think Grandfather probably had written to a lot of people here because there was a whole community of people from Kristiansund who ended up in Seattle working as carpenters.

Census records show that in 1910 the Ericksen household at 7013 22nd Ave. NW included Eilert with his wife and five children, a servant girl and six boarders all from Norway. They included, besides Ingvald, 29; A. Anderson, 46, a ship carpenter who also arrived in 1906; Anderson's wife, Eliza; Elias Linvog, 26, a fisherman who arrived in 1907; Ole Linvog, 27, also a fisherman who had immigrated earlier, in 1902, and Ole Robeck, 28, who came in 1903. Heggem and Ole Robeck were ship carpenters. In 1920 Heggem was living about a block away at 7016 23rd Ave. NW and was still at the address when he died in 1956.

By 1909 Grandfather had his name on some ships, the *Brac* and the *Hanna*. But his big debut was a large halibut schooner called the *Albatross*, built in 1910 at the Sunset Boatyard at the foot of 28th Avenue that was operated by Ingvald Heggem and Eilert Ericksen. This was a beautiful ship with quite a history; it just put him on the industry stage for ship-building. People admired that ship and talked about it. After that he built eight halibut schooners with Eilert at their shipyard, Sunset Boatyard. Ingvald was the master builder and many of these boats were his design. And then he built another eight halibut schooners when he became manager of the Fishing Vessel Owners Marineways when it was founded in 1919. Ingvald continued in that position until his retirement in 1946.

Ingvald would ride to work with Eilert and Anton Anderson. They would go in this little car and they would stop and Ingvald would say, "All clear starboard?" and the others would answer, "Yeah, all clear," then "All clear port?" "Yeah . . ." and they would move forward. They had this little ritual that everybody talked about.

A history of Marine Way, prepared by the Shipbuilders Council of America, says that the firm, still located at Fishermen's Terminal, is believed to be the Port of Seattle's oldest existing tenant and began building and repairing wood halibut schooners, seiners and trollers. "It has never lost touch with traditional skills of shipwrights and caulkers. The president of the company began as a shipwright . . . When steel fishing boats became accepted in the 1950s, the company adapted and kept up with all welding technology methods . . .FVO is known for its high quality service to tug boats and yachts – including some of the area's most historic vessels."

Grandfather stayed with Eilert for six years until he was married in

1912, to Marit Johansdatter Westad from Sekken, Norway who was also a boarder at the Ericksen's home. My father said that when he was growing up in Ballard all the children had to work very hard. He had to wash down everything – the windows, the floors – and work at the ships' chandlery. He was not allowed to go on a date unless his sisters went with him. The family included my father, Ole Johan Heggem, his oldest sister Mabel Bergliot, Katherine Ingeborg, Margaret Irene and Lillian Caroline. They were a very close family and remained so their whole lives. Grandfather Ingvald and Grandmother Marit Johansdotter Westad were founding members of Ballard First Lutheran Church.

Today the great, great-grandchildren of Ingvald and Marit are being born and the Heggem name is passing into legend from whence it once appeared with serendipity. There are five cabins at Heggembo, the summer place near Shelton, where they are remembered. I felt I had a great responsibility being the last grandchild with the Heggem name. My dad was an only son and I am an only daughter. Even into adulthood I imagined myself going back to Norway, finding some guy named Heggem and marrying him so I could keep the name. As it turns out I have learned that we only borrowed the name of a farm in Norway called Heggem for a few generations With women's liberation, I found I could keep my maiden name. I am an artist and for the last eight years I have been signing my paintings, Signe Heggem Davis. Sometimes life offers great gifts when least expected. My grandson carries the Heggem name as his middle name forward for another generation. Someday he will ask to hear the story of his ancestors.

Signe Heggem Davis is an artist living in Seattle. She paints primarily in oils but also works in other media. Her art has been shown in galleries throughout the Northwest and she says she often finds inspiration in the docks and industrial areas of Ballard where her grandfather built ships.

Jess L. "Hap" DeShaw

"I won a Model T Ford down at Wilson Motors for 99 cents."

My dad worked in the shingle mills. He worked in every mill in Ballard, except for Seattle Cedar. I was born up in Everett. We moved down here when I was two years old, out here in the north end when I was about four, I guess. It was my dad's work brought us here. He was a shingle weaver and also a packer. Packed shingles. As a matter of fact, when he was a young fella, he won the world's championship in packing. My dad was real burly. He was only about five-feet nine, but he was big and broad. Big, big barrel-chested. I knew when he paddled me.

When I was about 16 I won a Model T Ford down at Wilson Motors for 99 cents. Johnny Boitano was the kid who pulled my name out of the barrel. My dad was standing there talking to his friend. And he said, "Some 'scow-wegian' is going to win this car." And the third name out was my name. I thought it was some kid calling me, saying "Hi" or something like that. The guy looked at the slip, and it was me. My dad had 50 cents. That was during the Depression years. And the car was for 99 cents. He went around to his buddies down there and got the other 49 cents and I got my Model T. I put up a big sign on the back end of it: "Well, what do you expect for 99 cents?" On the way home, I had a couple flat tires.

You know, Bill Boeing owned all the Blue Ridge property out here. When we were kids, we used to go out there and camp — Ally Henderson, Emmett Blair, Don Bower, and a few other kids. We were roasting some potatoes, we had a fire going; and this fellow came up there. He was dressed in a business suit, and he came up and introduced himself as Mr. Boeing. Bill Boeing. We were getting ready to take the potatoes out of the fire, and Allie asked Bill Boeing if he'd like a baked potato. And Bill Boeing says, "Yeah." So he sat down there on a log, and ate that old dirty potato. He came two or three times, to see how we kids were doing up there. He told us, "You're welcome to camp here," and he says "Watch the fire." We had a fire pit. So I can still see Bill Boeing, — well, he was quite well-known at that time, you know, Boeing Airplanes.

That fish trap down at North Beach, the attendant had to come in once a week or so to get supplies to take out there. We'd wait until he came in to get the supplies, and we'd get a boat and we'd cat hook salmon out of the net. And we were getting quite a few salmon. My dad asked me, "Where the heck are you getting these salmon?" Well, I had to tell him. And he says, "You darn fools, you cut it out. You'll get killed." But everybody in the neighborhood was eating salmon.

You know how Loyal Way got its name? That was Harry Treat's daughter's name, Loyal.

When I first started working, I worked for a guy named Dewey Lott. Had a small auto rebuild. Then I worked for Frank Pantley for quite a few years. I got out of the service in 1946. I started my own business in '49. My brother Wade and I started in 1950. We got tired of paying rent, so we bought this property on 14th Northwest and Leary Way and put up a building. Ernst bought me out in 1968. I moved over on 46th, between 8th and Leary Way, for three or four years. Then, in 1978, when I got 62, I retired.

I remember the earthquake in '49. I was up at the gas station on 28th and 85th. Harvey Larson had his auto repair there and he let me bring my car in there to change the master cylinder. I got the master cylinder out, and was putting it in place, and my car started to shake. She was up and down, up and down, up and down, and I thought those guys hanging around there were shaking it. And I hollered at them, "Cut it out, cut it out, cut it out. I'm underneath here." And Harvey ran in there and grabbed me by the leg and he hollered, "EARTHQUAKE!" And he grabbed me and I was on the creeper. I got up and I was so cock-eyed mad, because I didn't realize it was an earthquake. I looked out, and saw the poles wiggling back and forth.

What the Golden Beavers is, there's about 1500 of us, been out of Ballard High over 50 years. And what we do, we give away scholarships. And we get together and have a luncheon once a year.

Jess DeShaw was born January 10, 1916 in Everett to Grace (Brown), from Minnesota and Gideon "Leo" DeShaw, a French Canadian from Toronto. The family name had been *des Champs d'Emmons* or the fields of Emmons. His nickname "Hap" came from his French grandmother, because she called him an "'appy *bebe*." His siblings: Jeanette (1908), Dave (1914) and Wade (1921). The family moved to Seattle around 1918, to Ballard 1920. Hap married Helen (Stroup) in 1941. They have one son, Glen (1949). Hap retired in 1978. Hap and Dorothy Leu Conrad initiated the annual Webster picnic in 1934. As a hobby Hap has built many doll houses for raffles over the years. He died in 2004.

264 - Jess L. "Hap" DeShaw

Domeneca Del Duca

"I always wanted to be a teacher. I can't remember when I didn't have that as my aim."

When I was a little girl my family lived in Black Diamond and my father worked in a coal mine. I started to school there and then my family moved to Seattle and I went to Beacon Hill Grade School and graduated from Franklin High School. I took teacher training at Bellingham Normal School [now Western Washington University], majoring in primary education. I was 19 years old when I got my diploma.

My first teaching position in Seattle was at Rainier School, which was torn down a long time ago. In 1931 I transferred to Whittier School to teach music. I lived on Beacon Hill, so every morning I took the streetcar downtown, then transferred to another streetcar to take me out to Ballard. Whittier is at N.W. 75th St. and 14th Ave. N.W. I taught music every day to 3rd through 6th graders. Often I went to the primary pupils [kindergarten, 1st and 2nd grades] to teach music to them too. Whittier School had two buildings in 1931— the one built in the late 1920s was called the "new building." We called the other the "old building." When I got there, the primary grades were in the old building and grades 3-6 in the new building, which was quite a bit larger. I had my own music classroom most of the time. Every pupil in the 3rd-grade through 6th grade had a half-hour [music] class daily. In years when there was a large enrollment, I didn't have a separate music room but taught music in regular classrooms. Some of my pupils say they remember seeing me pushing my little piano down the hall to the next class.

For children who wanted to learn to play the harmonica or song flute [a simple recorder], I had classes before or after school. For awhile I had a before-school accordion class. I always enjoyed so much helping my pupils learn new things in music. I always wanted to be a teacher. I can't remember when I didn't have that as my aim.

Sometimes we had a chorus that practiced before or after school. I never chose the pupils for the chorus. They chose to be in it.

We had many programs for parents and friends, especially near holidays. At Christmas time we'd sing all the old carols; they can't do that in public schools any more. Sometimes the Whittier chorus was asked to sing for various Ballard groups.

I was always glad to give extra help to anyone having problems in my classes. I recall one boy who loved to sing, but he sang like a crow. I took him aside and said, "Jimmy, you know, sometimes it takes awhile for us to find our singing voice. Would you like to find your singing voice? He said he would like to. So I said, "Would you like to come in here every day at recess and we'll work together till we find your singing voice?" By the 6th grade that boy was one of the class leaders in singing.

Outside of school sometimes I helped Boy and Girl Scout groups with their musical programs. I remember when a Cub Scout pack in Ballard asked me to organize an orchestra and I was happy to do it.

So many of my pupils' parents were just wonderful to me. They knew how far from school I lived so many of them would invite me to stay overnight at their homes, especially after evening programs at school or in bad weather. Some families even gave me a key to their house and said, "Just come in, put another cup of water in the soup and have whatever we're having and stay overnight." I did that a lot. So many people were so nice to me.

The Whittier Parent-Teacher Association had a party for me when I retired in 1962. The school auditorium was full. My pupils and their parents came, so did former pupils—some of them from years ago. I told them "I've spent exactly half my life at Whittier, and I enjoyed it all. I have such wonderful memories of the children I had in school, and the parents and the way we all worked together."

And then on my 97th birthday—34 years later—I had another party in the Whittier School auditorium. Some of my former pupils organized it and there was such a big crowd. They told me later there were 350 people there. Think of it, 34 years later!

My philosophy of life? Count that day as lost when I have not done something for someone, be that a smile, a kind word, a good deed. None of these cost even a penny, yet the good they do cannot be measured.

Domeneca Del Duca was born October 23, 1899, in Black Diamond, Washington, to Italian immigrant parents. She was very young when her family moved to Seattle's Beacon Hill, the neighborhood where she still lived in 2000, the only surviving sibling of her large family. She was interviewed in 1988, and again in 2000. The photo was taken at her home on her 100th birthday in 1999. Domeneca died in 2003.

Ed Egerdahl

"So there I was; Gordon Tracie's folk dancing group downstairs and the Canine College up on the third floor. As we were sitting in the mezzanine classroom we'd hear accordion music down below and howling dogs up above."

My dad was an immigrant from Norway. He came to America as a small child, the youngest of five kids, traveling with their mother and father.

My father's name was Ottar Egerdahl. His father was Hans Hansen Egerdahl. Hans's older brother Thomas was the first of his generation to come to the US, traveling with family members and a close friend to join an uncle in South Dakota. Tom was ten years older than my Grandpa. Hans was 17 when Tom had sent a letter to the family in Norway asking if there were any boys who wanted work. He and the uncle could set some of them up with jobs.

My grandfather agreed to that and traveled with a cousin to South Dakota. All of them signed themselves out of the church records, stating they were heading to North America. I'm imagining that Hans and my grandmother Julia had some kind of a "nuptial" understanding, as young as they were. When Hans took off for America it was Grandma's plan at any rate that he would send for her to join him.

However, Grandpa had been in South Dakota for five years while Grandma was still waiting in Norway working as "house help" for another family. I think her decision to emigrate was a combination of getting "itchy" -- five years is a long time when you're that age—and the date in history, just before the beginning of the First World War. People in Norway couldn't help but know that the rest of Europe was on the brink of something huge and awful.

One of Grandma's brothers, Jørgen, who had gone to South Dakota with that wave of young men, sent money to his little sister to come to America to join her intended. So, Grandma made it to New York City one month before the *Lusitania* was sunk and there would be no more safe travel across the Atlantic. Whether she had her hand firmly on the pulse of what was happening or she had just one gigantic stroke of good fortune she made it in the nick of time out of Norway and in record time got herself from New York to South Dakota. My grandparents were married in South Dakota within seven days of her having landed in New York City. I'm sure she grabbed her intended by the ear and dragged him down to the Justice of the Peace. They had a farm, I'm imagining, or they were possibly working on his brother's farm. Hans and Julia with their first three children decided to become naturalized as U.S. citizens just after the Armistice was signed in November 1918.

I assume that they had intended all along to return to Norway. The

Egerdahl family passport picture

Armistice was signed and two months later in January they had become citizens and were granted U.S. passports. In the early spring of that same year, 1919, they were buying their tickets to go back to Norway. The purpose of their journey was stated as, "To visit aging parents." With three kids in tow, they headed off, first to Bergen and then north to Egerdal, on a peninsula called Hamarøy, about 100 miles north of the Arctic Circle. They lived for a time with Grandma's parents while they made arrangements to build a house on top of the hill called Åsen. They moved into the house to the great celebration of their extended Norwegian kinfolk that was glad to see this young family back from America.

Hans and Julia's last two children, including my father, were born in Egerdal. Their US passport was valid for 12 months - they lived in Norway for nine years. Then in the late 1920s, America Fever hit the north of Norway. Grandma watched as one after the next of her friends lost their children to this powerful wave of emigration. Realizing that their first three children were technically already US citizens, Grandpa and Grandma decided that they wanted to keep their family together. They were going to pack up what would fit in the immigrant trunk and all seven would travel to America, again.

They returned to that same older brother of my grandfather, Thomas. They arrived during a horrible winter. By chance, Tom's wife had a sister who was visiting for Christmas from Seattle. She planted a seed in my grandmother's ear: "So you don't really have in mind to stay here in South Dakota do you? I come from Seattle where it's really quite a lot nicer."

That spring Hans and Julia packed up their five children and headed off to Seattle where there was already quite an established network of immigrants from Norway.

By now, in 1929, their oldest child is 13 and my dad is 6. Getting the kids enrolled in school was a bit of a challenge since none of them spoke English. It was especially awkward for Gladys, the 13 year-old, who didn't know the language and had just left all of her friends and family right before what would have been confirmation time in Norway. The teachers didn't know what to do with this girl and so they put her in a class for special-needs children. My aunt Gladys was so upset she told her parents she was going to quit school. That sent off all of the alarms in that household. Grandma and Grandpa said, OK, no more Norwegian at home. It has to be English.

My dad, being the youngest, was the one who had the least exposure to the Norwegian language. As a result I didn't hear Norwegian much at all growing up except when the five siblings would get together to sing and play music, especially at Christmas.

I was well acquainted with my grandmother but unfortunately she had suffered a stroke when I was eight. She was unable to speak from that time until she passed away when I was 16. The most dramatic experience in my own Norwegian history was my first trip to Norway when I got to meet and become very close with my grandmother's sister who was closest to her in age. They looked startlingly alike. When Tante Johanne spoke, out came this foreign language. That was my greatest inspiration to try and learn Norwegian - so that I could get to know my grandmother better through her sister.

By the time my grandfather Hans returned to the United States in 1929, he was almost 40 years old. While he was living in Norway for those nine years, he went back to the standard trade of people who live north of the Arctic Circle – cod fishing in the Vestfjorden and farming for their own sustenance. In Ballard, he got a job working in an ice factory that supplied the fishing boats. He was still involved in the fishing industry. He just didn't spend his time onboard a boat.

Soon after they had re-immigrated to the US, the family formed a musical group – the Egerdahl Family Band. I have my grandmother's notebook where she kept the calendar of all of their concert dates - all of their various radio programs, and what they were performing on each. They were a regular feature on KJR and KOL radio and on the

Egerdahl Family Band, 1938

Scandinavian Hour. They also performed at several immigrant churches
and other facilities. My grandmother and all five children were in the
group with guitars, accordion and vocals. They started performing in the
early 1930s and were particularly busy in 1936, 1937, 1938 and 1939.
Then the war comes and the two sons go off to serve their country. The
Family Band resumed in 1946 and continued strong until 1953. Hans
died in 1954.

When my dad got back from the Philippines after the Second World
War, he opened a record shop in Greenwood called the Music Spot and
ran it for several years. He met my mom, Naomi Jorgenson at First
Norwegian Lutheran Church. After they were married in 1953 and started
a family in 1955, he needed to get a "real" job so he worked at several
things along the way.

Grandpa Hans died the year before I was born. He was always the
quiet one from what I've heard. Grandma was the dynamo. She's the one
that had to put it together: To get to America and find him, to haul him
to the City Hall to get him married, to decide that it's time to get back
to Norway and to decide now it's time to return to America. She was the
go-getter in the bunch.

My mother's side of the family is one generation deeper into
the immigration experience. My mother's grandmother, Hannah
Thorstensen, was the immigrant. Her family was from Drammen, just

outside of Oslo. They were a shop-keeping family and fairly well to do. My great-grandmother was 19 when she decided that she wanted to make a voyage to the United States. She had an uncle in Minnesota who was the father of 13 children. They were looking for a part-time nanny. It sounded like an adventure and she and a girlfriend headed off. This was in 1890. A long letter she sent to her sister in Norway goes into great detail about preparations for the trip across the Atlantic, the ship ride, and coming into New York City, where there were "carriages with as many as four horses pulling them".

She mentions taking the train up to the St. Lawrence, following on through the Great Lakes and finally arriving in Minnesota to join her uncle's household. She came to a community where everything was in Norwegian -- the newspapers, the church services, the casual and social gatherings.

Hannah takes the job as a nanny and is enjoying it. Eventually, she meets Mr. Wonderful in the form of a Swedish immigrant, Johan Goransson (Jorgenson), and they marry. A summer vacation that turned into a temporary job has now turned into a marriage.

Hannah Jorgensen eventually had three sons. The middle one was my grandfather, Carl. The same sort of situation must have arisen as had in my dad's family. Hannah's husband must have intended all along to return "home". He said the rest of their family network was in Scandinavia and suggested they should move The problem was they couldn't agree on where "home" was. He was from outside Karlstad, Sweden. She had become a part of her uncle's family and had made more friends in Minnesota than she ever had in Norway (according to one letter).

She said to her husband, "If you need to go home, then you go." And he did. He left her with three children in Minnesota. She became a divorced single mother. That would be awkward at any time, but particularly in the early 1900s. Her youngest son died when he was only five years old. I don't know if this occurred before or after Johan returned to Sweden. Then her oldest son, age 22, contracted tuberculosis and died while he was a student at the University of Minnesota. Then came the Great Depression. Hannah does her best coping with the loss of two children and struggling to keep the farm.

My great-grandma Hannah in Minnesota faithfully wrote to her sister Ingeborg in Oslo as promised. She told about having fields full of potatoes but no customers because no one had money. She talked about the one who wouldn't be named -- the fellow who left her to go home to

Sweden. She must have been a strong woman to have survived it all and the heartache that went along with it.

Then my grandmother Rosa also contracted tuberculosis and was sent off to a sanitarium. Hannah had to move in and help my Grandpa with his three children, including his youngest daughter, my mom Naomi. At the same time, my mom's brother Clayton contracted polio. He had come home from school, laid down for a nap, and when he woke up, he was paralyzed. He was sent to another hospital. Here's this woman, barely five feet tall, who is trying to keep her one surviving son's family together with a daughter-in-law and a grandson in different hospitals. Hannah died the same month I was born but I am convinced that I know her fairly well through her letter writing and her faith.

Language always seemed something that I had some kind of an affinity for. I studied Latin at Ingraham High School and was named a Top Ten graduate representing the foreign language department. When I started at the University of Washington in 1974 as a math major, one of the requirements was to balance a science class with a class in the humanities. I decided I would take a Latin class in the Univ. of Wash. Classics Department.

Boy, was that a questionable call. Three years of high school Latin doesn't equate straight across to anything at the university level. I found myself in over my head. So I went back to the class-catalog and found a Norwegian language class listed under humanities. Soon after, in 1974, I made my first trip to Norway and came back very enthusiastic about continuing my Norwegian language studies.

My brother, who was (ironically) taking a Norwegian class at Ballard High School, mentioned to his teacher that his older brother had just come back from Norway and had pictures. I got volunteered to come to Ballard High and offer a slide show.

The Norwegian language program at Ballard was going gangbusters. To try to accommodate the long waiting-list of students who were trying to get in, the instructor talked me into teaching a class with her as supervisor. So, having been approved by the head of foreign languages for Seattle Schools, I was teaching one class a day at Ballard High at the same time that I was a math major studying Norwegian at the UW.

After a second trip to Norway in 1976, I had to make a decision. I was accumulating so many credits in Norwegian that it was starting to rival my major in math. I decided to change my major. I tried to get the College of Education to agree that Norwegian was a suitable major. It had never been tried before. They didn't know what to do with a student who was majoring in a lesser-spoken language from a department few had had any dealings with. I was rejected.

With the help of the chairman of the Scandinavian department and after we wrote a special petition, I was finally granted admission. I earned my teaching certificate and my degree in Norwegian Language in Literature through the College of Education. It was the only time that that had been done. It has not happened since. With foreign languages considered "electives", there wasn't much of a future in public schools. I hung my certificate on the wall, and went off to do something else – in a car-parts warehouse.

About a year later I got a telephone call from Seattle Pacific College. They had a program called Communiversity which offered classes to the general public taught by "local talent". I agreed to teach an evening class and for one session I taught a classroom full of enthusiastic second generation Norwegians. The following quarter, there was another bunch of people who were interested in taking the class. However, nobody in that first class wanted to quit. It came time for me to decide if I was willing to branch out on my own.

I contacted the Crown Lutheran Church, where I was organist at the time, and asked if they might have some space available. They said "sure" so I was teaching one class through Seattle Pacific downtown and another class in north Ballard at the church. The next quarter there was another batch of people who wanted to take a class, but none of the others wanted to quit. I was teaching several nights a week. If I was going to continue to do that, I needed to incorporate myself as a nonprofit organization compatible with the church's nonprofit status.

Since this is what I had trained myself to do and I was enjoying it a lot more than my "day job", I got several people together who would act as my board of directors. We incorporated as the Norwegian Language Learning Center. Soon after, I got a call from Our Redeemer's Lutheran Church asking if I might be interested in taking over an existing daytime Norwegian class. Do I give up my day job? I took a deep breath, plugged my nose, jumped in and said, "Yes, as long as I can teach another class at your same location, at the beginning level." They agreed. I was teaching two classes at our Redeemer's and three classes at Crown, with a children's class on Saturday morning. I've got maybe 90 students. So in short order, things are going very well. I received a phone call from one of my board members. He wanted me to know that a Nordic museum was opening. He thought it would make a lot more sense for me to be at the museum, rather than in Sunday School rooms in two different Lutheran churches.

Ed Egerdahl - 273

I came to a building that was pretty much empty and looked mostly abandoned. There was some scattered furniture with a roof and windows that leaked. Restrooms were another matter altogether. I picked three classrooms up on the mezzanine level, started teaching classes and very soon decided that it was really important for me to change the name of the Norwegian Language Learning Center to the Scandinavian Language Institute.

Marianne Forssblad, the museum director, and Issa Parker, the curator, taught Swedish classes for me. I was teaching Norwegian classes daytime and evenings. So there I was; Gordon Tracie's folk dancing group downstairs and the Canine College up on the third floor. As we were sitting in the mezzanine classroom you'd hear accordion music down below and howling dogs up above.

Soon I found Danish and Icelandic teachers. Now, I have been at the Nordic Heritage Museum for 31 years.

I was the breakthrough guy. I didn't have being born and raised in Norway as a teaching credential that I could hang my hat on. I had to convince people that it was the process of having had to learn the language myself that made me the better teacher.

When I first started teaching, I had students who were immigrants from Norway and were mostly looking for a forum where they could get together, hear the language and practice it. I found myself in this awkward position of having students who probably knew more Norwegian than I did. I was more the facilitator. I knew a lot about the mechanics and the structure of the language and that was a valuable asset in those early days. I was 23 when I got started. I had to grow a beard so I looked more professorial.

Now, I have people coming to me who are third, fourth and fifth generation Norwegians who have no idea where an ancestor came from. They just know that somewhere, some place, there was this immigration experience. It's interesting for me as somebody who helps these people who are searching out their roots.

Maybe 15 years ago, I had a student enroll who asked, "I am trying to learn Norwegian because my dad was an immigrant. Would it be OK if I brought him with me to class?"

I said, "Of course! A real Norwegian! Yes, bring him to class." I made him the default expert whenever we needed the answer from the perspective of a "real Norwegian." The next quarter, she didn't have her dad with her. I asked, "So, is your dad going to keep taking the class with you?"

274 - Ed Egerdahl

She answered, "Oh, Dad was diagnosed with Alzheimer's." Norwegian was his mother tongue. The doctor warned the family that he would eventually revert to speaking only Norwegian and they needed to find a designated Norwegian speaker so that somebody could communicate with him.

So, this daughter decided she wanted to make her dad part of the process as long as he could. When he wasn't physically able to come, she kept attending and after class would come with various questions like, "How do you say "swallow"? I can't get dad to swallow."

She learned the vocabulary that she needed. I knew right then that no matter if I ended up teaching for a hundred years, this was the most important thing I would do in my career. That woman needed to be able to communicate with her dad in the only language he was left with.

She needed to say some really important things, including "I love you, Dad" in the language that he could understand. That is essentially the value of my career; being wrapped up in those precious moments is a rare privilege.

Edward Egerdahl was born and raised in the Ballard neighborhood of north Seattle. He attended Whittier Elementary, Whitman Junior High and Ingraham High schools. Ed was named Top Ten graduating senior in 1973 by the teaching staff representing the Foreign Language department. Ed graduated from the University of Washington in 1977 with a B.A. degree in Norwegian language and literature and earned a teaching certification from the College of Education. Ed began his teaching career in the 1978-79 school year when he started the Norwegian Language Learning Center. In the fall 1981, he founded the non-profit Scandinavian Language Institute and moved the facilities to the Nordic Heritage Museum in the spring of 1982. In addition to teaching the Norwegian language, he also taught at and was the director of Crown Preschool from 1984-1996. He is currently the organist at Ballard First Lutheran; a position he has held since 1982. Ed has three grown children: Kjersti-Marie, Erik and Heidiann. He has been a resident of Edmonds, Washington for the past 21 years and lives there with his wife Laurie.

William Lee Engstrom

"The family life wasn't at home —
it was at the bakery."

My father's father's name was Erik Gustaf Erikson, but when he became a citizen in 1915, he changed the family name to Engstrom, which translates to "meadow stream." My father, Hilding, first worked in a grocery store in West Seattle. He also worked in a grocery store, Koll and Wicks, on 62nd and 24th in Ballard, in the late '20s. [See Long p. 355] He then drove a bread truck for Langendorf Bakery, 1930 to 1944.

My parents got married in 1931. They found this bakery located at 80th and 24th Avenue Northwest and bought it in 1944. A bit before then, my dad worked nights in the Columbia City Bakery to learn the bakery business — in addition to his full day at Langendorf.

He was too busy in the new bakery, Engstrom's Home Bakery, so my mother started decorating cakes there. One specialty was a doll cake. She made a round mound, cut a hole in the middle and stuck a toy doll in it. The cake was the doll's dress, and she'd decorate that. By the way, if you ever saw what goes into icing, you wouldn't eat it. Basically shortening and sugar. But those cakes really had a style.

My grandfather up on Whidbey Island, died on September 1st, 1952 — my grandmother had died about seven years earlier. The family farm was up there, and my dad and his five siblings each owned a piece of this farm, and there was a lot of timber on there. So my dad decided to become a logger. He sold the bakery, bought all this logging equipment, and he went up there and logged off the land for about a year.

Right after he sold the bakery, he had regrets. He had sold it to a Mr. Higgins, who developed health problems and needed to sell that bakery in a hurry, so, my dad bought it back in 1955. My folks continued to operate it until 1968, when they sold it to Helmut and Barbara Weise. They, in turn, operated it until around 1972 or '73. Then they sold it to the Larsen brothers, from Denmark.

I think about growing up in Ballard and working in that bakery — The family life wasn't at home — it was at the bakery. Before I worked there, I'd stop by after school. Sometimes my folks didn't come home until late, and we'd go have dinner at the bakery. It locked all of us into a lifestyle that dominated our lives. And yet, financially they made a good living in the bakery, especially at first. But my dad and mother were putting in a total between them of 15, 20 hours a day down there.

My folks put us to work. I really started working there when I was about 13. I started doing more serious stuff, frying doughnuts and so forth. I worked in that bakery nine years until I was 22. My sister Judith claims she started working in the bakery, collecting garbage or sweeping, when she was six years old. My older sister Joan says she started working there when they first bought it — she was about 12 years old then and they put her to work doing odd little jobs. When she was 14 she started waiting on customers. She worked there through high school, and some after.

The bakery became a focus for our social life. People would come in there, and a lot of times my dad would be doing something and he'd drop it and go talk to salesmen or customers.

Kids came in looking for jobs. In the time my folks had that bakery, they probably hired a hundred kids. My dad had this big spring paperclip hanging on the wall with names and phone numbers on it. Some kid would come in looking for a job and Dad said, "Give me your name and phone number." He would pin the note, along with all the other names and phone numbers. He probably had 40 or 50 there at any one time. He didn't hire more than four or five new kids a year, so he usually got the pick of who he wanted to work there.

My dad died in 1984, when I was 41, and that's about the time I started developing an ethnic interest. I suddenly realized I couldn't get all this information that I took for granted all these years. I started learning Swedish in 1988, and quite often I'd speak with my mother in Swedish for practice. But speaking Swedish was too slow, so we always reverted to English.

I remember one evening at home in the summer of 1964 — my dad was in his late 50s then. He was hot, so he had his pant legs rolled up a couple of inches. He had a drink in his hand. He was just burned out after another typical exhausting day. I was working at the bakery, but I was headed for another career and another life. And he said to me, "You know, Bill, you need to learn how to invest so you won't have to work like I do when you get to be my age."

I graduated from Ballard in '61, graduated in 1965 from the University of Washington with a B.S. in mechanical engineering, got a master's in '66. Then I worked for the Boeing Company and had a great career

William Lee Engstrom - 277

there. I loved my job, but I turned 55 and I decided that I didn't need to work any more and I didn't like commuting. So, I took an early retirement in 1998, and I haven't looked back since.

William Lee Engstrom was born in Seattle on March 27, 1943 to Signe (Anderson) and Hilding Engstrom. He joined two sisters: Joan (1932) and Judith (1938). Hilding was born in Clinton, Washington to Swedish immigrants. Signe was born in Ballard in 1907. Signe's parents, William John Anderson and Wilhelmina Maria "Minnie" Bjerkland, both Swede Finns, immigrated in 1895 and 1900, were married in 1907 at Emmaus Lutheran Church. Hilding died in 1984.

Anna Kristin Freyberg

"Something we have wanted to do as a gift for our children is to record some of the history that we've never shared and they've never asked. We just take it for granted that they know."

My mother came to the United States when she was 18. My grandfather came over to North Dakota because they had friends from Reykjavik, Iceland who established themselves in the Mountain/ Hensel area in northeast North Dakota. My parents were married in 1920 in North Dakota. She was 28 and he was 38. They lived in St. Vincent, Minnesota, for about two years, but he had asthma so bad the doctor told him to move to a drier climate or expect to die early. We moved to Bellingham in 1937 or '38 — my mother had a sister there. We only lived there nine months.

Friends in Ballard had a hotel they wanted to sell. Mom and Dad decided they could make a living on that, and we could live there. So in 1938 we bought the King Hotel at 5405 Leary Avenue. At that time the hotel had 20 rooms — actually 19 because hotels didn't have a room 13. We had the downstairs apartment; one bedroom for the six of us. Margaret and Sigrid, my sisters, slept on a daybed in the dining room. My brother slept on the sofa in the living room and I slept on an army cot in Mom and Daddy's bedroom. It's amazing how we were able to cope.

The hotel was mainly for men. A lot of fishermen would keep a unit, one room with a sink. They shared the bathrooms. They would keep them when they were out fishing. One man lived in Lynden, Washington, but kept a room. Two or three men were there for all the ten years Mom and Daddy ran the hotel, 1938 to 1948. Actually, Mama took care of the hotel and Daddy worked for Seattle Cedar. In a hotel at that time you made the bed every day. Once a week you changed the sheets, emptied the wastebaskets and washed the sinks. There was a sink in each room. We had to help my mother with that before we were allowed to do anything else. But mama did most of the work in the hotel.

I started the first grade in Hensel, North Dakota. Only the teacher spoke English — the rest of us spoke Icelandic. My sisters were 10 and 11 years older, and my brother was eight years older than I. In this

Icelandic community, everyone spoke Icelandic.

For the second grade I was at school in Bellingham. And I was in the third grade at Irving School, where Ballard Hospital is now. I went there one year, and Ballard Hospital was going to be built, so the whole school was transferred to Adams. The teachers at Adams were not very excited at getting a whole school of grade school children.

In the summertime, three or four nights a week we'd walk from the hotel to the Ballard Locks. That was our entertainment. We'd get an ice cream cone along the way, take the neighbor's dog and walk all the way to the Locks. We didn't take a lot of vacations — my dad didn't drive.

When I was in high school, as soon as I got through making beds on Saturday, my girlfriends and I would either walk down to Golden Gardens or take the bus up to North Beach. That was an everyday summer thing. Sometimes we'd walk all the way from North Beach to Golden Gardens, then home.

Margaret, my sister, and Lyle Hartje were married in 1947. They bought the hotel from my parents in about 1948. Jim Freyberg and I were married April, 1951. He worked for John Perine, a nut and bolt wholesaler. Lyle asked Jim if he wanted to go into partners in a second-hand store. So we bought the store on April 1, 1952, and opened April 5. They started buying surplus items and railroad-damaged goods and over the years Ballard Hardware became more of an industrial hardware store. They sell a lot to fishermen and mechanical contractors.

We bought the bowling alley across the street I think in 1965. Later we bought the building down the street where Berg Fuel had had a little office, and I.W. Harper. There are four lots, two on Leary and two on Ballard Avenue. Ballard Hardware is in the original building, the former bowling alley across the street, and the one next to it which we bought a couple years ago, the Robert Denny Watt Building. Some of these buildings are in the Ballard Historical Landmark District. I served on its board for many years.

Ballard has a large Icelandic community including a lot of young Icelanders in the north end, Queen Anne, Magnolia as well as Ballard. And Mama belonged to the Ladies Aid Eining through our church. Originally the Ballard First's congregation was primarily Norwegian, Our Redeemer's was Swedish and Calvary, Icelandic. Ballard is still a Scandinavian community. A lot of people from the Icelandic area in North Dakota have come out to live in Ballard and the north end.

Of course we keep Icelandic traditions. We still make *vinarterta*, Icelandic prune cake, and Icelandic *kleinur* all the time. There still is an Icelandic service at Calvary Lutheran Church at Christmas. The Icelandic Club has been good to keep that going.

I think it's really great that you are taking the time to go into the history. I wish I had taken a tape recorder and recorded things my mother could have told me about North Dakota, the good times and the bad times, and things that happened. I get bits and pieces from here and there. Something we have wanted to do as a gift for our children is to record some of the history that we've never shared and they've never asked. We just take it for granted that they know.

Anna Scheving was born September 30, 1931 in North Dakota. Her mother Anna Gudmundsdottir Johnson was born in Iceland and her father Steve Scheving was born in North Dakota to Icelandic parents. She joined two sisters, Margaret (1920) and Sigrid (1921) and a brother Steve (1923). The family came to Ballard in 1938. Anna married Jim Freyberg in April, 1951. Their children: Julie (1954), Kimberly (1957) and Douglas (1958).

Irma Goertzen

"If an opportunity comes along take it, because you never know where it's going to lead."

I was born November eighth, on my father's birthday in 1932, in Kenmare, North Dakota on my grandparents' farm. My father's name is Gudmund Agee Bernard Rundstrom and he is a native of Denmark. He came to the United States in 1926. He was twenty-two years old. My father is the only member of his family that came to the United States to live. My mother, Alice Marie Gissel, was born in Kenmare, North Dakota of Danish parents.

My father came with a purpose of going to school. He felt that if he was going to be anything other than a farmer he was going to have to get an education. So he came to the United States via ship and landed in New York in 1926.

He tells a story of how when he got to Ellis Island it was very depressing. He felt it was like cattle. So he and one of his friends decided they were not going to stand in this long line so they tried to get out. When they went out they apparently had to have a certain number on them somewhere and he didn't have his number. So he got picked up and sent back into the line and took his turn just like everyone else who came into America.

He landed in New York and he tells about with his friend how they stood on the streets of New York and they said, "Now we can take off our tie because we are in America and we have freedom." That was his idea of freedom.

He did have an aunt and uncle, Alma and Jorgen Peterson who lived in Chicago and served as his sponsor. They had no children. So he did have a connection with them. He first went to Chicago but then he went to Dana College in Nebraska to study there.

My grandfather, came to the United States from Denmark and my grandmother's parents came from Denmark. They lived in the Iowa area and she was one of nine children, I think, quite an extended family. My mother did go to school. She was quite an accomplished musician and a singer. My grandfather decided that he wanted her to go to this Dana College in Nebraska, because they had a choir which was going to be traveling to Denmark. He knew she would be able to make the choir. My grandfather's idea was that she could go to Denmark with the choir and meet his mother. That's the only way he felt he was going to have any connection with his direct family. There [at college] of course, she met my father and they took the trip to Denmark together. My mother did meet my grandmother, Serena, and did spend time with her while she was in Denmark.

My father then decided to go into the ministry. He went to Augsburg College in Minneapolis. There were a couple of years that my mother spent a lot of time with us two girls on the farm while my Dad was going to school. He used to write her lovely poetry, which I also have found and kept.

His first church was in Zahl, North Dakota. It's a very small community northwest of Williston. It's not far from the Montana border. He had four churches there, was ordained there, and was there until I was eight years old.

I was always a tomboy and I had a lot of friends in Williston, [North Dakota], girls and boys. I spent a lot of my time outside playing baseball, and climbing trees and things of that nature, and ice skating.

We lived in Enumclaw until I was sixteen and those were also very good years. In those days, when you played basketball you could only run half of the court and then you had to pass the ball over to the other girls on the other half of the court. That was a very frustrating experience for me, because I was very competitive and a lot of the girls were not.

One day one of the coaches was watching me. He said, "Have you ever thought about playing tennis?" Of course, I hadn't. I didn't know anything about tennis. He took me into the other gym and he painted a line across the back of the gym, which would be at the height of a tennis net. He taught me how to play tennis, which became my sport.

Of course, I was used to playing with boys so I wasn't threatened by the boys at all. He would stick me in to play with the boys and that gave me an advantage because I learned to hit the ball harder and take harder balls and harder serves than a lot of the girls did.

Following high school, I had an idea that I wanted to be a doctor, and my dad was very supportive. One of the things my father always said to me was, "You can do anything you want to do as long as you work hard and keep trying." In my high school days when I graduated women were not admitted to medical schools.

Irma Goertzen - 283

My mother also had a very famous saying that has been passed down to our children: I can remember saying something like, "Well I can't do this." My mother would say, "There is no such word as can't. You haven't tried yet, you just keep trying."

I went to the Emanuel Hospital in Portland and went through nurses training there. When I was ready to graduate, I got called in to the head of the school's office one day. We always stood when we were in her office. She asked me to sit down, which I thought was interesting. I remember being scared to death. She took out some papers and said, "I would like you to look at this and consider it. I've already made all the arrangements."

In those days very few nurses in the country had master's degrees and she was one of them. This was an application to Columbia School of Nursing in New York and she wanted me to go there. Apparently she saw something in me that I didn't see in myself. I had no ideas or thoughts about going on to school but she talked to me about this, gave me the papers, and I thanked her and left the office.

[I ended up] taking a job as the nursing supervisor [at the Ballard Hospital] and I was a supervisor from 1960 to 1964 in the operating rooms. Many times I would remember Mrs. McFadden who had called me into her office and told me I should get further education.

I went to the University of Washington and found out they had a program called the R.N.B.S. program. I signed up for the program. As soon as I finished my bachelor's, I went right on to get my master's degree in administration.

Don and I had children at the time and we were trying to build a nest egg. So I did go to school full time, took the job and I worked at the hospital and I raised, while working, the children.

I did get my degree and I got a call to be then an applicant for a job as the Director of Nursing at the Ballard Hospital. I was the Director of Nursing from probably 1969 to the mid 1970s.

I was there at the hospital and then was recruited to the Providence Hospital to take the Director's job there. Also, I was appointed by Governor Dixie Lee Ray, to chair the state board of health.

I went on to the University of Washington and took the job there as the associate administrator for nursing. While I was there, I had also over the years been very active in the National Nursing Association. I was pretty active, and I was known nationally in the nursing world, in the nursing circles. At the time, National Institutes of Health had appointed me to a committee at NIH on women's health grants, where I would get massive stacks of grants that were to be reviewed. We reviewed them and made recommendations for who got approval for grants, etcetera. It was another good opportunity to be able to add my knowledge base.

My boss was promoted to the corporate office. That opened up the position at the University of Washington for a new administrator and I decided to apply. My competition basically ended up to be four men and me. I did get the job. It turned out that I was the first woman in our country to lead a major university hospital.

I did work there and I got a call from the State Hospital Association. they had gotten a request from a physician in Pennsylvania. They had put out a call to different parts of the hospital field to ask if they knew anybody that understood hospitals and universities, because they needed somebody to do some consulting with them in Pittsburgh.

The CEO here at the Hospital Association, Leo Greenawalt, recommended they call me, and I went back there. I was there 15 years and we developed the largest women's health hospital in the country [Magee-Women's Hospital and Magee-Women's Research Insitute, Pittsburgh, Pennsylvania]. I created a research institute for women's health. When it started they had about $600,000 to $700,000 in NIH grants. When I left we had over $100 million. A big operation.

In that position also, we were asked by our government to develop a western-style birthing house in Moscow, Russia. It was just after Perestroika in the early 1990s. That was the second largest hospital complex in Moscow. I probably was in Moscow 25 to 30 times. The last time I went back there, I went into the labor and delivery room. They have private rooms and there were two staff in there working with ultrasound on a patient. A husband was in one room helping his wife. It was all very different. We were then asked to extend our programs to the Ukraine. We had 24 different educational sites in Russia.

Now I'm retired. Don and I have been able to watch our children grow and have their successful careers. They are all successful, in different ways. We have ten grandchildren. I've been to an awful lot of soccer games. Life is very good.

Irma Goertzen was the Director of Nursing at two Seattle hospitals from the mid-1970s to the late 1980s: Ballard Community Hospital and Providence Medical Center. Later she was the Associate Administrator for the Nursing Division at the University of Washington. Following a successful nursing career she bacame the Administrator of the University of Washington Hospital followed by a position as Chief Executive Officer and President of the Magee Womens Hospital and Research Institute in Pittsburgh, Pennsylvania. Since her retirement, Irma has been an active member of the Nordic Heritage Museum, and is the current president of the board of trustees. She is the mother of four daughters: Pegge, Kathi, Sara and Krista.

Irma has been the recipient of many awards and honors including the following: Order of Saint Anna Award from Her Imperial Highness, the Grand Duchess Maria of Russia (2010); Distinguished Daughter of Pennsylvania from the Governor of Pennsylvania (2003); Honorary Doctorate of Humanities, Thiel College, Greenville, Pennsylvania (2000); Honorary Doctorate of Public Service, Chatham College, Pittsburgh, Pennsylvania; National Association of Women's Health Professionals - Leadership in Healthcare, Clinical Excellence Award (1994); Distinguished Alumni Award, School of Nursing, University of Washington (1982).

Arthur D. Haavik

"At one time the church was called 'Haavik Church' almost as much as 'Ballard First Lutheran.' He started the Fishermen's Festival in 1927, and that's going on yet. Every year they meet at Fishermen's Wharf to bless the fleet."

My father, Olai Haavik, was a Lutheran minister. I was born in Spokane, but we moved here when I was five years old. I have a brother and a sister. We all went through school in Ballard, to Salmon Bay, and then to Ballard High School. My brother Obert lives here. He was a teacher, and then he was an industrial manager for Continental Can Company. My sister Carol went to PLU and was a May queen, and married Marv Tommervik, a big coach. He's a Little-All-American football player. Carol has passed away.

My dad came to Wisconsin from Norway in 1905. He was then about 18. He met my mother there and married her. I think it was for schooling that he wanted to immigrate, but I'm sure he had being a minister in the back of his mind. He always wanted to be a minister. He went to Luther College in Decorah, Iowa.

He was the pastor at Ballard First Lutheran for 27 years, and in the Nordic Heritage Museum you can see a replica of him in his vestments, standing next to the church at the end of the "Dream of America." We gave them the vestments. At one time the church, was called "Haavik Church" almost as much as "Ballard First Lutheran." He started the Fishermen's Festival in 1929, and that's going on yet. Every year they meet at Fishermen's Wharf to bless the fleet. They have a service in the church, besides. I still go to Ballard First Lutheran. After 27 years in the church my father became the director of the Josephine Sunset Home in Stanwood for several years after he retired.

When I was growing up, some entertainment was restricted because my father was a minister. He didn't want anyone to do those things, but when I got to be on my own, I did a lot of dancing. I went to the places where they had the Scandinavian dances. We did most of our athletics through the Ballard Fieldhouse, on 59th, between 26th and 28th, right next to Adams School. We played football and basketball, by moving around to the different field-houses and playing there.

I went to Pacific Lutheran College and that's what got me started teaching. I got a master's degree in education from the University of Washington. I played football and basketball at PLC and there, too. I was not that good an athlete, but I enjoyed it very much.

Reverend O. L. Haavik, 1944

I taught one year in Silverdale, then I taught at Monroe Junior High and was Vice Principal at Ballard for 40 years. There's no place harder to teach than in a junior high school. Especially around the eighth grade, but I spent many years there, teaching mostly P.E. I'm a math major, not P.E. When I first applied, I was quite an athlete, and they wanted me as the P.E. teacher. And so I stayed there until I became a counselor, and then a vice principal at Ballard.

Kids would get in trouble, and as a counselor I had to take care of it. I'm a firm, non-believer in corporal punishment. I don't believe in that at all. But I have a lot of tricks I would use to help some of these kids get along. High school's the same thing, except parents are different. In junior high they blame the school. But in high school, when a kid gets in trouble, they want help, and that's what we were there for. We saved a lot of kids by the things that we did.

If you know anything about teaching, you know we didn't have much money to live on. So every summer for 25 years, I would go directly to Alaska to work. I watched traps for seven years, to start with, then I went to the Bristol Bay area, and worked within the cannery, loading boats and whatever. I fished, too, from time to time.

A trap is anchored on the shore, and goes out for about three blocks, we'll say. It's built with layers of fencing [or netting] until it gets about eight [feet] deep. And the fish hit this trap, and then they come out, and they have nets all built there, too. And then they have "spillers," and all the fish go through different gates until they get up to the final log, and then they are brailed [removed with a dip net] out.

I was in charge of different traps up there for seven years. Those traps caught perfect fish, but they're no longer allowed because it's too easy a way to catch fish. These traps had to be inspected for holes all the time. We'd get divers to do that. We caught 140,000 fish in one day, one time.

It was the last day of the season. The fish came, and we had some boats there, and they keep brailing them out, until the season ended. I'll say it was in 1955, about there.

I took a couple summers off and I built my own home in Olympic Manor. They closed the golf course and started selling off the land for Olympic Manor. It took several years to sell it all. I was fortunate to get my spot in there. I was a good builder, so I built my own home. I hired certain things but I built it myself. I'm proud of that home. It's on 90th and 21st.

We were almost forced to put up [outside] Christmas decorations in those days, you know. Everybody had them up. It wasn't a closed community, but we had our own Olympic Manor covenants and there were certain things we could not do. We could only go 17-½ foot high, I think it was, on the main street. And we couldn't block somebody else's view. But it was a great place to live. Good for my kids. I lived in Olympic Manor for a long time, and then I came here to Cristwood [a retirement community] three or four years ago. This is mostly because my children thought it was time I should be here. I didn't really want to come, but we are glad we're here now.

I taught for 40 years in the Ballard schools, starting at Monroe Junior High School, and I ended up as Vice Principal of Ballard High School. I retired in 1982. If I had it to do over again, I'm not sure I'd go into education. It was never a well-paying job, and I had to find other means. I might have strayed away from it, but I did enjoy what I did, especially when I got to be vice principal of Ballard High School. I really liked the place. I didn't really want to retire, but 40 years is about enough. I think I helped the kids out. Because, even though I was the vice principal, and I learned to know a lot of them, and I think I helped them. I hope I did.

Arthur Haavik was born October 1, 1916, the son of Thora (Peterson) and Olai (O. L.) Haavik. His siblings: Obert (1917) and Carol (1919-1935). In 1942 he married Bea (Swanson). Their children: twins Janice and Joyce (1947) and Karen (1950).

Don Hansen

"I think that's one of the things our boats are noted for — they have a fair line."

My dad's name was Harold Hansen. And he was one of five children who came from Norway with their mother and dad, and their granddad. They came across Canada, first to Port Ludlow, but they landed in Ballard and they got into fishing and boat building almost right away. At first they were just building for themselves, so they could go fishing. They built skiffs.

My dad talked about beach seining with his grandfather up at North Beach, north of Ballard. My grandfather started purse seining with a rowboat. They had possibly six oars and they towed a really small barge with the seine on it. They'd set the seine from there, and follow the seine with the skiff, and then pile it on the barge to set it a second time. The first time my dad went purse seining, he was about 16 years old. He had to handle an oar the same as the regular guys. There was a steam tug that towed them from Ballard up to Point Roberts and back.

Things gradually got a little more sophisticated. My granddad built the first *Seven Brothers*. It was possibly the first or second seine boat with power in it. This was probably around 1905. That boat was maybe 30 feet long. We have some real old wooden models that they built those boats from. When my dad or granddad built those they used to make a half model and then they took measurements off of that to construct the boat. It's built to scale, maybe a half inch to a foot. But it's also just a half a boat in order to use the center of the boat as a center line.

I'm sure my grandfather had built skiffs in Norway. Whether he had built any bigger fishing boats, it's hard to say. In 1920, he build the *Valor* and the *Supreme*. Both are still operating.

They all were partners and owners in boats, except the youngest brother, Ingvald. My dad and Hans were together on a boat or two, and then Jake and Ike, Peggy's dad, were in a boat or two. [See Heinselman p. 274] My dad was usually the leader when it came to the building. But when they went out fishing, they were on their own.

The boats kept getting bigger. You see, when they first started seining, they didn't even have a winch to fully align those together to purse the bottom of the net. What they did was pull the net on in, hand over hand. And gradually, the first winch they had was hand- cranked to turn the drums. Then they figured out how to put power to it, and let the engine do it. It was a gradual development.

Dick and I were still teenagers when my dad started the yard, which was Harold Hansen Boat Company, over at Fisherman's Dock there. But we were around there a lot and watching what was going on, after school and Saturdays. And we went to drive nails, and getting into other things. I was always interested in designing boats and drawing lines, and at Ballard High, at that time, they had a boat drawing class. I knew quite a bit already, but I did learn to use the tools. And there were some things that were brought out that was customary in designing, what a regular architect would include. And it was a fun class compared to a lot of others.

I kept every boat magazine I could find in those days. In some of the boating magazines, I saw a sailboat that took my fancy. And so, rather than build it just like it was, I built it a little smaller, and designed it myself and built it myself. Of course, Dick came over and my dad came over. My dad was working at Olsen and Sunde at that time, which was another little yard at the Canal.

But he'd come around after work, on Saturdays, and help me bend frames and so on. And coach me as far as what I was doing wrong and what I was doing right. And we had that sailboat for a couple years.

And my dad built a few trolling boats during that time, too. And, of course, there was always some material left over — sometimes that's accumulated enough to build a boat.

In 1936, a fellow came and wanted a seine boat built for Kodiak. And that was really the first seine boat that I did. And from then, I would do most of it, design it, layout, and so on for the yard. In 1937 we built one boat called the *Loyal*, that was designed by H.C. Hansen, a noted boat architect in this area. In 1938, we built a boat for a brother of the man who owned the *Loyal*.

And so, then things just kept going. And we found a chance to get a yard over on the north side of the Canal, a little further towards Fremont. And we moved there in 1943.

I think we built better seine boats, and kept improving them simply because we were in that industry. You get a better insight when you go out and use them. Every boat we built, we could see something we wanted to do a little different on the next one.

In designing, you just have a few tools that are used for making lines, and measurements. And one of the things that our dad taught us was that you don't just slap these things together. We know that there were some boatyards that prided themselves in how fast they could do something, which was all right if they wanted to do it that way, that's their business.

But we felt that the boats were going to last a lot longer, and do their job a lot better if they were put together right. A boat has to have a fair line. You have to build a boat to really know what that means. It means you can't have a lot of humps and hollows and . . .

When you see a boat from a distance, and you see a funny sweep in it somewhere, you would say that it wasn't faired up very good.

I think that's one of the things our boats are noted for — they have a fair line.

Don Hansen was born 1915, in Ballard to Harold and Anna (Ellingsen) Hansen. His grandparents, Jørgen and Hulda Hansen came to Ballard from Norway in 1889 with five children, Agnes, Harold, Sarah, Hans and Jacob. They had six more in Ballard: Mamie, Isaac, George, Daniel, Rina and Ingval. Harold started the Harold Hansen Boat Company in the early 1930s. Don and his brother Dick worked for their dad beginning in 1933 and eventually took it over. Don was interviewed in April, 1988. The picture was taken in 2001.

Fishermen's Terminal
Port of Seattle

Home of the North Pacific Fishing Fleet

Designed to be the headquarters for the salmon and halibut fishermen, construction began on Fishermen's Terminal in February, 1913. The fishermen lobbied the Port of Seattle, formed in 1911, to provide a home for the 250 vessels in the Puget Sound fleet. In January 1914 a parade of 200 boats led by the fifty-four seine boat, *F/V Inga,* came through the entrance to Salmon Bay in celebration of the terminal dedication. Captain Chris Nelson commanded the *F/V Inga.*

Members of the Puget Sound Fisheries Association assemble at the dedication of Fishermen's Terminal on a cold day in January 1914. This group led the lobbying effort to build the terminal.

The Seattle fleet was joined in the parade by boats from the Tacoma fleet. Fleet owners in Tacoma were also lobbying for a publicly-owned facility in Tacoma.

293

Izetta Spearman Hatcher

"I don't like to speak to problems. I could relate to situations. And I'm not sure whether it was because I was black, or whether it was just a sign of the times. The schools were staffed by spinsters. Your spinster-type teachers were different, and they were strict, not very patient."

My parents were married and moved to Ballard in 1917, and built their home at 7334 12th Avenue Northwest. I'm the third child, and I was born at home. We all went to Whittier grade school, James Monroe and Ballard High. I graduated in 1941.

Were there any special problems because you were Black?

Well, when you say "problems," I don't like to speak to problems. I could relate to situations. And I'm not sure whether it was because I was black, or whether it was just a sign of the times. The schools were staffed by spinsters. Your spinster-type teachers were different, and they were strict, not very patient.

Basically, I think the teachers liked me. I always have been an outgoing, free speaker. I've never held back what I was thinking. I always spoke out and I think some of them resented that because I wasn't submissive. My older sister Florice preceded me, and she was quiet and never had much to say. And they would say, "Well, she's not as quiet as her sister." Well, I'm not my sister.

I think when I really started feeling pressures of my color, my race, was in junior high. My mother used to recite poetry. And she had this large book of Paul Robeson's work. I memorized one, through her tutorage, in dialect — I do not have an accent. I had worked very hard. And my English teacher said, "That'll be enough. Just go sit down to your seat." And I said, "Well, I'm not through." "We don't want to hear any more of that." And she gave me a C.

My father was a lather. That's the wood slats you put on the wall before you plaster. Before that, I think he tried to be a stevedore down on the waterfront. He was a hard-working man and a good man. He never drank. He never swore. He never mistreated my mother. And he came from a family of hard workers so anything that required hard work, he was willing to do. He was just kind of a self-taught man. If he really didn't know how to do anything, he'd work around and try and experiment until he could do it. He could shingle a house. I'm sure he could build one. His pride and purpose was to take care of his family.

Father was a laborer. His work was seasonal and he didn't have a lot of money. So, in order to be presentable, I taught myself how to sew. That had nothing to do with my race, it had to do with our economic status. In my sewing class I was thwarted by Miss Evelyn Anderson. I copied everything she told me to do, just exactly. If I was to make a flat-felled seam, one-half inch, I measured one-half inch. And I cut it and turned it over — it was just exact. But she never gave me anything higher than a C. I remember the teachers at junior high, patting me and saying, "Izetta, you're just fine. You're a C student, you're okay." So I was labeled as an average C student. And I found out much later that I wasn't. When teachers were a little more liberal, I did get Bs. I never got As. I got Bs and Cs.

I got more of my education because of support and encouragement at home. I firmly believe that living in an area where I went to school gave me more support than if I were a transfer student or a bussed student, because I had that defense. If someone would call me a name or make some racial slur, my mother taught me to be proud of what I was. And she described how we were as flowers in a garden, all different colors, and they're all beautiful. And she says, you are, too. And you can't help God made you the way you are and you be proud of what you are.

But she also encouraged us to to use our intellect and our behavior to present ourselves to other people well. Without that influence, I couldn't have made it here. Whenever I have situation or a happening in school, I was only moments from home, and could tell my mother what happened. And if it were necessary, she would get back to the teacher with, "Izetta tells me this." "I need to know" — get more information.

We were always encouraged to further our education. We had the idea we'd go to high school, graduate, and go to college. The promise was that we'd get our first year of college paid by our parents, and after that we were on our own. My sister Florice, being the oldest, went to the University of Washington for her year. I don't know why she didn't go on. My brother Austin was the second. He graduated in the School of Engineering. Then, I went, but only with the idea that someday I was going to get married. I started September of '41 and I went the full year. After that I went part time for three years. I took arts and sciences, dress making and designing.

I experienced more prejudice in college, and it was strictly racial. I recall my biology teacher saying that Negroes never advanced beyond the age of seven, that our brains didn't develop beyond that age. And I used to wonder, well, what am I doing in college if I hadn't advanced beyond seven. But you had to play the game, and in order to get a grade, I had to write down what he taught, whether I believed it or not. It was hard. At that time I was Miss Spearman, I wasn't a child. So I didn't come crying home to mom, like in grade school. I'd talk it over, but do the best I could, and continue on —don't knock it.

As far as being different? Sure I was different. I was Black. And not only was I Black, but I was dark complexioned. Black people, or Negroes in that day and time, were different colors, also. And like the flowers that my mother described when we were referred to as Colored people, I accepted that because we were all colors. There's the lighter Blacks, the darker, and all the shades in between.

Walking in Ballard in a predominantly Scandinavian area, where you have your blondes, white skin, blue eyes, naturally I was different. And people would look at me. "Oh, there's a dark cloud." And I never answered, because my mother always said, you have three names, first, middle and last. You only pay attention to that.

But certainly, it would make me churn inside. I learned not to be embarrassed. But you can't help but be bothered by it, constantly being pointed out as different. As I remember, it was mostly boys that did this. I can't remember girls ever pointing a finger at me and calling me a name or making me out to be different. They'd shun me, but they never made any overt, loud retorts. And just thinking back, that's quite interesting.

Now, my friendships; there weren't that many families or children my age. But the ones that were, and the girl that actually lived on my block was Betty Barrett, across the street, three homes down. She's a year to two years younger than I. But we were good friends. And it's probably because there was no one else around to be good friends. Her uncles were my uncles, my aunts were hers. She'd come and eat at my house, I'd eat at her house, we slept together, we walked to Woodland Park, we had picnics. We did fine until we went to James Monroe, the junior high. I think that's when I started feeling my hurts. Now I understand that age group and why. Everybody's having a difficult time. The changing hormones, puberty, the whole bit. The girls were noticing the boys. They didn't want to be different. They wanted to be accepted and certainly they didn't want a minority to be their friend if their boyfriends didn't accept them. So this girl that we'd spent all of our childhood together, and I met her in the hall, and I said, "Hi, Betty." And she didn't answer me.

I went home and told my mother about it. She tried to explain. I can't remember what she said, but, in essence, don't speak to anybody until they speak to you, and then you're not hurt. So I learned not to speak until — or I caught their eyes or some mannerism where I knew that they were going to speak to me first. But when did this change?

When we went to Ballard High. It was just like night and day. I'd see Betty in the hall. "Hi." We weren't quite as friendly, but we did resume the speaking relationship. And I noticed a big difference in everyone else. They didn't want to get real close to me, like going places with me, like Betty and I had. But we were on a speaking relationship, and we related in the activities that we did together.

I was very athletic and belonged to the Big B Club. And I was accepted for my abilities to perform, the talents that I may have had. I think the other aspect was we didn't have a lot of money. I don't know whether a lot of people in Ballard had a lot of money, but because we didn't, and I was minority, and we had to pinch pennies, I felt inferior from that standpoint. But it wasn't racial.

When I was much younger, I remember how kind our neighbors were over on 13th. They never really knew that we might have been bad off, but they'd bring a basket of food around Thanksgiving with fruit, which was a big item when I was a kid. Oranges were just like gold; and candy, around Thanksgiving and Christmas.

The uprising of the '60s, called my blackness to people's attention, where they had accepted before. "There's some Colored people living on 12th. They're nice people." But once these things started happening, then they began to look at us in a different light. I remember in the '60s, I had children on campus, and they were told to leave. And I remember as a sympathizer, my son was probably in junior high, and he was just there. And a policeman took a billy club and whopped him and said, get off the campus. It was just because he was Black. But it was a learning experience for all of us, because I came up being a Negro and Colored. It was during that time when we were to change, be Black. That's not very good English. But it was hard for me to change from being Colored, which I accepted, and being a Negro, which I accepted. I didn't want to be a Negra, but I went from being a Negro, to being Black.

I had arguments with my own family. My children told me how old fashioned I was, and if it had been up to me, that there would be no advancement in the world at all because I would sit back and just accept things as they were, that I wasn't willing to grow. And that was very hurtful. That came from my own children. I've changed, but not to the extent that they did. And I don't mean my kids, per se, but I mean, my race.

Izetta Spearman was born July 7, 1923 in Ballard. Izetta's parents were Ballard pioneers. Her father Elihu Spearman was born in Georgia in 1898 and homesteaded in the Yakima valley. Her mother Vivian Austin was born in Hannibal, Missouri also in 1898. She grew up in Rainier Valley. They married and moved to Ballard in 1917 to what is now 7334 12th Avenue Northwest. They had four children: Florice (1918), Austin (1920-2001), Izetta and Irene (1932). Vivian died in 1976; Elihu in 1978. Izetta married Melvin Hatcher in 1944. They have six children: Vicky (1945), Sharon (1949), Lorraine (1951), Mel Nolan (1954), Gloria (1957) and Mark (1960), twelve grandchildren and two great-grandchildren. Izetta's husband, Mel, died in 1993. She worked as an Registered Nurse at Harborview Medical Center until she retired in 1995. She still lives in Ballard. She was interviewed March 23, 1988. (Photo taken May, 2001)

Dwight "Bud" and Barry M. Hawley

"We grew up there in this wonderful neighborhood where we knew everybody and the kids were in and out of each other's houses just like they lived there. It was a wonderful place to live and wonderful people around us."

Dwight "Bud" Hawley

BUD: My dad was two years older than my mother, so I don't think they met at school. In those days Ballard was a very social place with lots of dances, picnics, get-togethers. Everybody knew everybody. Dorothy was quite an attractive woman and I think my dad was drawn to her at once. Dorothy and Dwight were married in 1923 and I was born exactly nine months after their marriage. I was born in the Norwegian Hospital in Fremont. We lived in a little one-bedroom house on the southeast corner of 115th and Greenwood. I went to Broadview School at 125th and Greenwood. I was cross-eyed and stuttered and was having a hard time in school. Then we moved here to Sunset Hill, and all of a sudden all these neat kids became my buddies.

I got a magazine route and I sold magazines. I'd say, "D-d-d-d-d-do you wa-wa-wan-wanna b-b-buy a-a-a *Liberty?*" By the time I got

Barry Hawley

done, they had their purse out, buying it. The first *Liberty* route I got, the guy gave me 20 magazines — I was seven years old. I didn't ask my mom or anything. I just said, "Yes, I'll do it." We had a little bag to carry magazines in, and I went home so proud. "What have you got there?" "Well, I'm gonna s-s-sell these ma-ma-magazines." I sold them all and ended up at my grandma's house, about three miles away, and it was dark. They were all worried about me. And they were calling back — "Buddy, where you been?" "I was se-se-selling ma-magazines. I've got one-one-one one more, you know." So grandma bought it, gave me the nickel. I put it in my pocket; it rolled down my pants and onto the floor. And I looked in my pocket and found a big hole there. I'd lost all 20 nickels. My dad came and got me. But they didn't tell me I had to quit, so I kept up the magazine business.

When the Depression came, half the people with a house lost it because they didn't have a long-term mortgage. They had a mortgage for a year or two, and when it came due, if they couldn't pay it, they'd lose their house. We never lost our house, but we couldn't sell it. My dad would sell it and then he'd get it back. Then he'd sell it again and get it back again. In the meantime, we lived in rental houses.

Charlie Snyder had platted a subdivision on Sunset Hill, between about 70th and 72nd, right on the bluff. He had built some houses there to sell and then the Depression came along and he got the houses back. We rented one of Charlie's houses for $25 or $30 a month. After a couple of years, he said, "You might as well buy it. Just keep paying the rental and we'll apply it on the purchase." I think they paid about $3200 for that house at that time, with a beautiful view of the Olympic Mountains. We grew up there in this wonderful neighborhood where we knew everybody and the kids were in and out of each other's houses just like they lived there. It was a wonderful place to live and wonderful people around us.

We played every game in season. The vacant lot across the street was a football field in the fall and we played baseball in the spring and summer. We had a basketball hoop on the back of a garage. We'd fish off the dock that went out into Shilshole Bay; it isn't there anymore. We'd go swimming in the Sound from about April till October. Sometimes we'd run a string of days, like 92 days in a row, without missing going swimming. We'd hike on the railroad tracks up to Edmonds and back when we were 10 or 11 years old.

We went swimming right down from our house at Ballard Beach. Some kids would swim by the ferry dock, where Ray's Boathouse is now, but the sewer outlet was there, and sometimes it wasn't too appetizing a place to swim. Sometimes we'd go to Golden Gardens, but it was a little too commercial and formal. We'd go there and swim back to Ballard Beach, almost a mile. And the water was just as cold then as it is now.

When my dad came back from the war, [WW I] he joined the Elks. The Ballard Elks in those days was maybe the second largest Elks Club in Washington state, and he became the club's secretary. Most of the business of Ballard was done in the Elks Club. The mill owners and business people went to the Elks Club every day. He got to know many people because of his job. My mother didn't like the Elks Club, because it was a drinking club and she didn't like that environment. She was always trying to get him out of it and she finally succeeded. About 1935 he went to school to learn the insurance business, then opened an agency on Ballard Avenue. The "soldier bonus" was finally paid that year — during the Depression, $1500 was a lot of money, and it was enough to stay in business for a year and buy a new car. He opened the business January 1, 1936. The first year he made $900. The second and third year he did a little better and a little better. By the time World War II came along, he had built a successful business. He worked hard, but he wouldn't have done it without my mother giving the prod. And the whole family shared in the ups and downs of it.

Ballard was covered with old grocery stores in those days. Every corner had a grocery store. During the Depression the grocers needed insurance, but they didn't have any money. So we would take the insurance premium out in groceries. My mother kept a list on the icebox door of those grocers and how much credit we had coming. She'd say, "Well, it looks like I'd better order from Whitney's this week." So that week Bob Whitney would deliver our groceries.

We went everywhere on our bicycles. I'd be down at Ballard a couple times a day. One day Mom said, "You know, I feel like having clams tonight. Bud, why don't you go down and get some clams." Sure, I'll go down and get them. She gave me a quarter, I went down to the fish market and I got a big bag of clams for a quarter. I curled the top of the sack around my handlebars and I was riding up Market Street toward 24th from the fish market. Of course, the sack got wet from the clams and all the clams dropped out onto the streetcar track. And here came the streetcar. I didn't have time to gather them up. The streetcar just crunched them all. Market Street was the stinkiest street you ever saw for three or four days. I went home and told my mother. She gave me another quarter and a cloth sack to hold them, and I went and got some more and brought them home.

BARRY: You asked how Dad got into politics. Maybe because his father was a city councilman for Ballard before it was annexed to Seattle. His dad, who was Lucien Hawley, was also a bookkeeper at C.D. Stimson Company. Dad was born and raised in Ballard.

BUD: My grandpa must have come out here around 1890. He married Emmaline, who was also out here. He probably settled in Ballard because he got a job at Stimson Mill. I think he was more like chief accountant than just a bookkeeper. He was close to the Stimson family but they had a falling out and he either quit or was fired, right in the middle of a panic in the 1890s.

To support his family, he went to work for the summer in the wheat fields near Calgary. He came back all skinny and tanned with a few bucks in his pocket. But I think it was rough going. Then he went to work for Seattle Boiler Works. He was still working for them when he died.

Their family included five children. My grandfather became a single parent, and raised the kids with the help of the oldest daughter. In old photographs, you can usually pick out the daughters, because they were absolutely beautiful girls.

BARRY: I went to Webster and then on to James Monroe and Ballard High School, graduating in '57. I first went to work as a sophomore, for Harold Nilsen at Food Town. He built a nice new supermarket on 63rd and 32nd, a forerunner of today's supermarkets. I learned a lot working for Harold. [see Nilsen p. 190]

Then I went to the University of Washington. And I worked at the Ballard Company, run by a mechanical contractor, Ed Milam. I worked in the office and learned I didn't want to work in an office the rest of my life. Then I worked two years for Foss Tug and learned I didn't want to be stuck away on a boat 24 hours a day, and only get paid for eight. When I graduated from the University with a Bachelor of Economics, I did it without having to take any math. I went in the Army Reserve for six months active duty. After my six months, I was down at Fort Ord, and didn't know what I was going to do. So Bud helped me figure it out. I had two choices: I could go to work for a bank or go into the real estate business. Bud knew Mike McDermott, who was setting up a Sherwood and Roberts office downtown. When I came back in November, I did two things. I got married to Dee Dee, who is from West Seattle, and went into the real estate business at Sherwood and Roberts with Mike McDermott. This was right after the World's Fair, and Seattle was very slow then. The top producing real estate broker in the city was maybe making $10,000 a year. Dee Dee, a school-teacher; she was making $4200 a year. My first year, I think I made $900 or $1000. I made two deals. I sold a property on Mercer Island, and a property in Ballard that my dad owned.

After being downtown for six months, I saw that if I was going to do it, it would have to be in Ballard. I wanted to feel that I knew what I was talking about. And I knew Ballard, had a certain confidence in Ballard. It took five years to get past the point where I felt I might be able to stay in the business, maybe longer, maybe seven years. It was long and slow, all the time learning how to do business and understanding it.

We have three children, Cindy, Christy and Brett. I've lived in the same house in Magnolia since 1965. I've had my office in three buildings: the office behind Bud and Dad over where the House of Fabrics is, which was the Wigwam Department Store; the Ballard Building, where my dad had his offices for years, and this building [56th and 24th Northwest] in one office or another since 1974, the same year Bud sold the insurance business which is why I moved from the Ballard Building. And it's been great.

BUD: I was away in the Army from about February '43 till February of '46. I'd had one quarter of college before I went in the service. I came home and planned to go the University of Washington and work for my dad at the same time, but my dad and I didn't get along. So I got another job, continued at school, graduating in 1948. I went in with my dad full-time when I finished school. It was slow getting started, but eventually we had a successful insurance agency, doing most of our business right in Ballard, both individual policies and commercial business. Our motto was "Everything in insurance." Later, when my dad got into politics, I took on more responsibility running the agency.

Dwight Hawley Sr. was born in Ballard 1896, graduated from Ballard High in 1914. He married Dorothy Youngblood in 1923. He sold insurance, and was a Ballard activist. He served in the State Legislature 17 years and worked on numerous projects to better the community. He died in 1981. Dorothy died in 1972. They had three sons: Dwight, Jr. or "Bud" (1924), Bob (1928) and Barry (1938). All three graduated from Ballard High and the University of Washington. After serving in the Army during WW II, Bud joined his father, selling insurance. He married Katherine in 1950. Their children: Sue (Dec. 1950) and Terri (1952). He married Helen Smith in 1968. She had two daughters, Suzanne (1960) and Jana (1962). They have a son Sam (1970). Barry became a real estate agent and married Valorie "Dee Dee" Masters in 1962. Their children: Cindy (1965), Christy (1968) and Brett (1974).

"The Shilshole Breakwater"
Bud and Barry Hawley

BUD: The way my dad told me, we had two ferries that came in where Ray's Boathouse is now. In fact, the state still owns the ferry landing there and Ray leases part of it. The Ballard-Suquamish ferry and the Port Ludlow-Ballard ferry came in there. This was back in the 1930s before the state got into the ferry business.

These were individual enterprises. Captain Payne owned the Port Ludlow ferry, and Captain Anderson owned the Ballard-Suquamish ferry. There was just one ferry on each run. One of the captains, a friend of my dad's, said, "We have such a hard time turning around to get in the ferry dock, particularly when it's stormy. I wish we had a breakwater out there."

Well my dad was kind of an activist. He was always interested in projects for Ballard. He felt this would be good for Ballard. He started in on this project by himself, and then enlisted the help of some friends. Over the years he accumulated a file and every chance he got, he put in a plug for the Ballard breakwater. It had been part of the original plan when they built the Ballard Locks, but it had been dropped by the wayside.

Then he formally organized the Ballard Breakwater Association and, with Congressman Tom Pelly and later with Senator Warren Magnuson, finally there was a chance to get some seed money to study a breakwater proposal. Dad met Maggie in Washington, D.C., and he said — I forget the numbers, but it was like — "We need $50,000 to start the study." "Hey, Dwight, you'll never get anywhere with $50,000. There's no way that that's going to do it. We'd better go for a million, and then we might get $500,000." And sure enough, things started falling in place.

I lived on Sunset Hill then, and I watched the breakwater being built. Every day barges came in and dumped rocks. This for maybe a year, and I thought, they're never going to get this built. Then one day, at low tide, I could see rocks sticking up. I thought, "My God, maybe we can even go to the moon some day if we can do this."

BARRY: As I recall, that breakwater cost something like $3,000,000. The Shilshole Breakwater Association was formed in about 1935, a long time ago. This was a 22-, 23-year process.

Peggy Louise Heindelsman

"Cliff went out fishing one trip. My dad didn't want my sister or me marrying a fisherman, because it wasn't a life for a family man. Cliff enjoyed it, but as soon as he come back, they called and asked him to join the fire department."

My father was born in Ballard in 1892. Ballard was a city then. His parents came from Norway with five children, and then had six more in Ballard. So I had lots of aunts and uncles, and cousins by the dozens. We all lived within walking distance of each other, and I just took it for granted that everybody had a cousin two doors down, or over in the next block. And my grandfather was two blocks away.

My dad's family came first to Canada. His father, Jørgen Hansen, had his shipyard in Ballard before the Locks was built, about where the railroad bridge is, by the Locks, the Hansen Boat Yard. Harold, with his sons Dick and Don, ran the shipyard after his father retired, more or less. Then they moved it up to Marysville. It's still Harold Hansen Shipyard. They combined ship-building with fishing.

My mother's family was here, too. I had a grandmother who lived on Market Street — the house is still standing, across the street from the new fire station. She had a rooming house. In 1934 one of my uncles converted it into apartments for her.

August is a fishing month for purse seiners. Mother spent her honeymoon on Lopez Island cooking for the fellows. They slept in tents on the island, then went out again on the boats.

I don't know if I should mention this, but before I was born my dad and three of his brothers were rum runners. They picked up whiskey in Victoria on their fishing boat. My grandparents were really religious, so it was kind of a black mark for the brothers to be doing this. But my grandfather said if these boys were going to do this, they were going to have the best boat in the fleet so they could get away from the patrol — and he built the boat. My dad and mother had only been married a short while when he had some whiskey to take down to Todd's Shipyard for the yard master down there. After my mother passed away my dad told me, "You know, your mother climbed into that old car. I had it loaded with booze. I had some in the front on the floor, and your mother climbed in, planted her feet on top of the case, and told me, 'If you're going to jail, I'm going to jail with you.'" And Mother's father was a minister.

You could keep chickens in Ballard, so during the Depression we had chickens, and one turkey. My dad won a turkey for Thanksgiving, and somebody gave him a live turkey. We kept the live one, and it turned out to be mean. In winter, it could go in part of the basement and it had a pen under the porch in the back. We had a big garden back there, so he couldn't have the run. He chased us when he got loose. The next year, the folks decided that we should eat that turkey, but nobody could kill it, not even my dad. We called my cousin Frank, and he chopped its head off. So we had this big turkey dinner. And none of us could eat it. We all just sat and cried. We had to call my Aunt Ruth and Uncle Jake to come down and get the turkey dinner. In the midst of the Depression, we couldn't eat that turkey.

Uncle Jake and my dad's boat, the *Yale*, was a gas boat — the engine would go putt-putt-putt. When we lived on 61st up there, mother could hear the putt-putt when he came through the Locks, and we'd go down to the Locks and ride in with my dad.

We went to USO dances at Fort Lewis almost every Saturday night. And my parents started inviting servicemen for Sunday dinner. One weekend my future husband Cliff and a buddy came out for dinner. Mother usually had leg of lamb because you didn't have to use meat stamps to buy lamb.

Cliff came from Oklahoma in 1936. They sold their farm. The grasshoppers had come in and ate everything one weekend. And the dust storms — they were just like the Okies that moved out here in '36, except they had a new truck. They had relatives up at Elbe. His great-grandparents had come from Germany. Cliff was in the Civilian Conservation Corps, stationed near when he graduated. They made $25 a month — the boys got $5, and the rest was sent to their parents. Cliff, the oldest of seven, had lots of responsibility. He had four brothers and two sisters.

We met in September, '42, we were engaged at Christmas and we picked September 22nd, 1943 to be married. Cliff had his leave all planned, but his captain told him, "If you're going to get married I suggest you do it today, because I can't tell you from day to day when we sail." We went down to Pastor Cleveland from Bethany Baptist. And he said, "I can marry you today, and if he's still here on Wednesday, we can go ahead and have a regular ceremony. But if he isn't here we can always pray for you two." My dad ended up being best man; and my sister was my maid-of-honor. My mother sat there and cried the whole time. I was married in my folks' living room — and we went down for dinner at the Captain's Table.

That was Saturday night. Wednesday was supposed to have been our wedding. The church was filled. No bridegroom. And then my dad and I were out in the vestibule. We were in a Lutheran Church because Bethany Baptist had no center aisle. Most of my cousins and I were married in this little Lutheran Church on 61st and 22nd [Ballard Free Lutheran Church]. Anyway, when Pastor Cleveland announced that he had married us, and Cliff had left, there was just, "Oh!" just a sound like that all through the church. When Dad and I walked down the aisle, I don't think there was a dry eye in the place. Cliff's brother, Ross, was there. He had gotten his leave, so he stood with me. Pastor Cleveland said a couple of prayers that everything would go right with Cliff and we would be reunited again.

Cliff came home later for ten days. For our honeymoon we took the boat to Victoria for one day. Then he was gone for two years.

After he was discharged in '45, Cliff went out fishing one trip. My dad didn't want my sister or me to marry a fisherman, because it wasn't a life for a family man. Cliff enjoyed it, but as soon as he came back, they called and asked him to join the fire department.

When the Stimson Mill caught on fire, Cliff was at Fremont Station, Station Nine. They were one of the first that got a call. Cliff was the driver and hose man. They pulled in and saw no sign of a fire and they walked in and just about then it exploded. The flames just started shooting up. We could see from the home here on 27th. The kids were already in bed, but I got them up and we went down. They wouldn't let us go any further than the foot of 24th and Market Street.

About midnight my sister and I were on the phone talking, worried because we had heard several firemen had been hurt. Her husband, Vic Martin, was also a fireman. We had the radio on and the commentator said, "Oh, here comes a fireman now, let's interview him." The minute this firefighter opened his mouth, I knew it was my husband. He still had kind of an Oklahoma twang. He's all right! — and I turned off the radio and went to bed. Cliff was a hydrant man and he had to stay by the hydrant which was right outside the fire there. The water was boiling in his boots, and when he passed away, he still had scars on his legs from that. It was so hot, it broke the windshield on the fire engine.

Peggy, the groomless bride

Anyway, Ballard's a nice place to live. And the neighbors were all nice. My mother's friends, their kids were our friends too, because we all lived in Ballard together on Sunset Hill.

Peggy Hansen was born May 26, 1923 in Ballard to Edith (Giles) Hansen and Isaac "Ike" Hansen. She had a sister Betty (1919) who died at age four, and a sister Gloria (1926). Ike was the fourth son of pioneer fishing boat builder, Jørgen Hansen. Peggy married Clifford Heindselman September 18, 1943. After he returned from service in the Navy, they settled in Ballard. Cliff joined the Seattle Fire Department in November 1946. Peggy and Cliff had three children: Cheryl (1946), Shirley (1949) and Bill (1953). Cliff passed away March 17, 1997. Peggy died in 2007.

Helen Pekonen Hill

"And they couldn't speak English anyway. Not very well, just a little bit, you know, a little 'Fin-glish,' as we called it."

I was born in 1926 in Ballard in a house near Market Street. My father went out to get the doctor and by the time they got back, I was there. My father, Victor Pekonen, was a carpenter, and we didn't have a whole lot of money. We moved to a little house in a great big lot near 32nd and NW 85th, three houses from our only relatives in the area. I think a lot of babies were born at home. Medical care wasn't that available then. And they couldn't speak English anyway. Not very well, just a little bit, you know, a little "Fin-glish," as we called it.

When I was four, we went to Finland, because my mother, Lily, was lonesome for her parents and her family. We came back to Ballard when I was seven. I had to go to school, but I couldn't speak English, only Finnish. It took me about six months to learn English. As a young child, you just kind of absorb things as they go.

My parents spoke very poor English, so, when I got a little older, I was their interpreter. All through their life I interpreted for them when they were stuck. They got better, because they had to get their naturalization papers. They had to study all this stuff. They knew more about our government and how it works than I did by the time they finished going to school and taking all those classes.

Three times a week my parents would go to a dance, right on 15th, the Veliaseurra Hall. It was a Finnish hall. In those days you'd take your kid with you. They would almost always have live music. Somebody knew how to play a violin or a piano or something. My mother and dad would be dancing, having a good time, and I'd be sleeping right next to the band. If the band stopped, I would wake up. As long as it was playing, I slept like a baby. They loved to dance. That's where they met all their friends.

By the time I was old enough to walk, I was out there dancing with my dad. That was fun. They had a stage in that old hall where they put on plays. I used to crawl around back stage, going through all these powder puffs and lights, and pretending I was a star.

In Ballard they have a Finnish Lutheran church, on 85th and 13th Northwest which is very active with Finnish gatherings. I go every November to the Nordic Heritage Museum and get all my coffee bread for the Christmas season, because there's some woman there that can bake that coffee bread so good. I buy every one I can find, and I put it in the freezer. Cardamom makes the difference.

Golden Gardens was my really fun place to go with my mother and father and all their Finnish friends. Finnish people, like a lot of people, are clannish, mainly because of their language. They would all contribute something to this big pot of stew. Go down there in the morning, bring their kids, bring their cards, and cook this stew there at the stoves, which are still there, and play pinochle. This was during the Depression days, so you just didn't have a whole lot. That was a great activity for those people. They all got there, and laughed and joked, and told stories. And that's where I learned to swim, because I didn't want to sit there watching them play cards all day. I'd go down to the beach and paddle around. Pretty soon I was able to swim all the way out to the raft, which they had at that time.

Because my father needed work, we got a free ride and went to Alaska on a halibut fishing boat. Bag and baggage, off we went over the mountainous stormy waves. We ended up in Sitka, where my father built his first house in Alaska on a street called Finn Alley. We lived there awhile, then moved to Juneau, and then to Anchorage.

I was in the first year of high school when the war began. There were 3,000 residents in Anchorage and many thousands of soldiers. My parents didn't think it was a good place for a young woman to be, with all those men. So we moved bag and baggage back south. We had to get a special permit to get out of Alaska because my father and mother were aliens. We came down on an Alaska Steamship.

After some time in California, we came back to Ballard. Dad started building houses and I finished high school in Ballard in 1945. Ballard was nice school. My favorite subject was horticulture, a gardening class. I spent a lot of my extra time working in the greenhouse. When they tore the building down, they were giving out bricks of the old school, and I said, "I want the brick from that greenhouse." It's sitting right over there.

Then I went straight to the University of Washington, paying my own way. I worked in an insurance company during the afternoons, and went to school in the morning. I almost graduated, but I met Melvin at one of those Hub dances. His grandma, who brought him up, couldn't speak any English, and the two of us could communicate in Finnish. I used to kid him about it, "That's why you married me." We got married up at Phinney Ridge Lutheran Church.

Eventually we scrounged up enough money for a down payment on a lot in Ballard, on 3rd Avenue Northwest and 47th. There was an existing garage on that lot. Mel fixed it into our first home where our daughter was born. We lived there a year, while he finished the main house on the lot. When he got that finished, we moved in, with sawdust on our feet. Before you know it, I had another child, who didn't live past 18 months. But then comes Norman, like gangbusters. So the two of them were brought up pretty much in the early years right there on 3rd Avenue.

Helen Pekonen was born in Ballard April 9, 1926 to Victor and Lillian Pekonen. The family went to Finland in 1930 for three years, then came back to Ballard. They moved to Alaska for a few years, then to California a couple years before they again returned to Ballard in 1944. Helen graduated from Ballard High in 1945. She and Melvin Hill married in 1947. Their children: Diana (1949) and Norman (1953). Helen died in 2002.

Ruth Ouillette Hughbanks

"When I came here in '28, the Ballard Bridge was on 14th Street. I just loved that bridge. When you came along, there was a great big key across the top of it, a great big house key, and it said, 'Welcome to Ballard the Key to the Locks.'"

I didn't come here until 1928, but my husband's family had been here since the turn of the century or before. My husband's mother's family came from Italy. My mother-in-law was Clorinda. Her father was Frank Borzone and her mother was Louisa. He bought a piece of property on Shilshole close to the waterway, and he was still doing a little ship caulking. They built this house there, and that's where Clorinda was married. My father-in-law [Dan Hughbanks] had this house up on, what we call 17th and Market now, but it was Broadway then. My husband used to carry milk jars down to his grandparents' where the Ballard Hospital is now. Down there to Dock Street was all woods. He said it was a pretty brave thing for a little boy to carry the milk down through the woods to Dock Place.

My father-in-law was working in mills. He got cedar poisoning, so he made a change. He bought this farm out on the other side of 85th. It had been a cabbage farm and it hadn't been very successful. Right down in that wonderful bog land, all the ditches and pipes and everything were wooden. They went into a log house on the corner of Third Avenue Northwest and 88th and he started truck farming. He raised carrots and all the good things. They didn't have trucks those days, so he had horses and a wagon. The windmill on the place pumped up their own water. There wasn't anything in the Northwest like that windmill. Later they got the water from the line at 85th.

Grandmother Clorinda, a delicate little lady, had a strawberry field going from Eighth Avenue up Ninth. Her father didn't think that was a very ladylike thing to do, but she did a real good job of it. Her friends called her Chloe.

When my husband came back from World War I, he first worked for Frye & Company, and then went into some insurance business. Then he met his Navy friend, Mr. Jasperson — they knew each other as younger boys. So they thought they'd go into business together. They bought the corner at Market and Leary. At the same time the Eagles in Ballard were building the Eagle's Building [now the Ballard Building]. Where the service station property was there's a hole in the ground. So, they hauled the dirt in the basement of the Eagle's Building across the street to where they built the service station. They had that service station and the two of them ran it. It was the only service station north of the Canal open 24 hours a day, never locked.

Mr. Jasperson and his wife had two little girls and my husband gave up because they couldn't both work in the station. He was also working for Prudential Life Insurance, and they sent him up to Bellingham. He gave up the office there and came back to Ballard. We were married in Bellingham and I came here as a bride in 1928. My husband bought a lot before I knew him. It's near the railroad tracks on 62nd and 37th and looks over Shilshole. We raised two children on the first floor here. We had a good architect and he built it to take in the view, and it was a conveniently laid out house, very comfortable. My children had never known any other place.

The children tell me they felt they were privileged to have been brought up in an area like this, where everybody knew each other. Every mother knew the other kids' mothers. Ben and Carol Lafferty started a drugstore across the street when we started the gas station. And I think Dan Bergen was on the corner over there. To me, it will always be Dan Bergen's Place. It's never going to be Bergen Place. All along Market Street, I think of all those people.

When we first moved here, the first ferries came in here. I used to sit and watch the traffic going up through the Locks. There were two ferries a day, one that went over across the Suquamish, and one to Port Ludlow which went early in the morning and came back loaded with milk trucks from the dairy farms because that was the dairy country up that way. That's where Ray's Boathouse is now.

My boys used to fish off that dock where the Home Port is now. Tregoning's Mill was down there, too. Right over toward the condos is where Tregoning's Shipyard was, and that was a huge place. It burned down. The boys would go down to the beach, and they'd get the pollywogs from the ponds along the railroad tracks and put them in fruit jars on the back steps until they grew into tiny frogs. I had a police whistle that I blew when it was time for them to come home to eat, or in the afternoon, if they'd been down to the beach long enough. It's a wonderful place to raise kids.

Ruth Ouillette Hughbanks - 313

When I came here in '28, the Ballard Bridge was on 14th Street.
I just loved that bridge. When you came along, there was a great big
key across the top of it, a great big house key, and it said, "Welcome to
Ballard the Key to the Locks."

Mr. Hopkins and Betty Hopkins had the big boiler works between
Ballard and Fremont, and they lived right up here on 32nd. One day
she said to Mr. Hopkins, "Ice skaters have to go down to Crystal Pool
downtown. And he's said, "Well, I'll build you one and you take care of
it." And that's exactly what he did. He bought it for a practice place. It
was there for years, and we had some real good skaters came from out of
this area.

The service station was there about 34 years. My husband had to give
up the station because of his health. Mr. Jasperson was a retired Navy
officer, and he was called up right away after Pearl Harbor. Running
the station like we did, my husband put in some pretty long hours. The
doctors told my husband that he just had to get off his feet. He sold out
to his partner. We went south for his health for the winter, and I got
somebody to stay with my children.

When we came back, Mr. King called him from the savings bank, Dad
King, we called him. He said, "I'm getting in my wife's hair and I can't
stand it. I've got a lot on 24th, what you say I put up a little office and
we go in business together, sell some insurance, sell some property, and
then put a sign on the door 'Gone Fishing' whenever we feel like it." So they

The gas station at the corner of Leary Way and Market Street, circa 1926.

314 - Ruth Ouillette Hughbanks

did. My husband said at the time, "I wish I'd done this a long time ago."

It got to be a pretty good business because Dad King was so well known, and my husband had been so well known. And the boys that used to come in on Saturday night with their little cars and get a few gallons of gas, and they were treated like they were full-tank customers, never forgot it. So, if they were going to take out some insurance on a house or a car, or going to look for a house, who are they going to go to?

And then Mr. King got tired of it, and my husband bought him out, and when he died, he was still running that little real estate office on 24th. My husband and Dad King, when they sold a house, would always gave a tree to the people who bought the house. And every Washington's birthday he pruned every tree that he ever gave away. My husband planted too much stuff, and then his health got so that he couldn't take care of it.

I've been in Ballard since 1928. And I feel like I'm about the luckiest person in the world that I still can remember all this and see all this, and see all the progress that we've made in it. It's a great place to be.

Ruth Ouillette was born March 24, 1904. She married Clarence Hughbanks in 1928. They had three children: James (1933), Nancy (1934) and David (1936). Clarence died in 1955. Ruth died in 2001.

Phoebe R. Jewett

"I loved the library. And I still love it.
When I go in, I feel like it's a magical
place, and I forget everything else.
And I just wish I could read all the books.
And I felt like that then."

My name is Phoebe Jewett, and I am the younger sister of Lorna Conrad. We lived in just a simple little house, with a living room, dining room, kitchen, bath, three bedrooms, and a hall. For many years we had a cool cupboard in the pantry area on the north side of the house. It had windows up and down and screened little openings. And then, eventually, we got an icebox out on the back porch. We didn't heat the house, hardly. The kitchen was sometimes the only comfortable place because the stove was always being fed in there. It was a big old wood range. My brother's job was to chop up the kindling and any wood we got. He really liked to do that, and he'd chop down any tree that was handy. Every now and then we'd order a load of wood, but it could be in big blocks.

I went to Salmon Bay Grade School on 63rd and 20th. My first grade teacher was very nice, and at the end of the year, I was happy to hear her tell us that she traded classes with the second grade teacher every year, so she would be our second grade teacher, as well. I went there through the fifth grade. There was a teacher there named Miss Thompson, who was very nice —they used to send around inspectors every so often to watch the class — Miss Thompson had us all standing up doing a little exercise; simple things, because they didn't have a gym and she had us so well organized, she got a call to be a physical ed teacher, so she left us. That wasn't too good.

I had to go to sixth grade down to Irving school. At Irving School one teacher found out I printed well, so she had me do some of that at times. And I think she was the one who also oversaw the lunchroom there where they just served soup, milk and simple things. I worked in the lunchroom for a while. I was probably 10 or 11. They had several kids do that. I think we helped with the dishwashing. They didn't have automatic things for everything then.

Then I went to James Monroe Junior High. I loved it. It was clean.

It was light. The lockers weren't in the hall, they were in a locker room. They had a gymnasium, and all we did was change our shoes to go in and play basketball or something and I loved that.

The one thing I really enjoyed, is they separated you according to the grades you got. They had one and two and three, and even sometimes five different groups of us. And the slower children went at a slower pace. We just went a little faster with the same math. And yet, they had the problem that some of the teachers aren't that good in imparting their information. They may know exactly what they're talking about, but they don't tell you as well.

The girls wore whatever they could afford. Some people could afford nice clothes. I never could. We had to wear a skirt and a blouse. And I can remember washing my blouse at night and ironing it in the morning because that was the best I had.

Actually, we were quite poor. And at that time you were getting things from government if you, wanted to sign up for them. You could get some groceries, just staples. I got a couple pairs of shoes, but they were this tan, buck kind of shoe. But an Oxford, and I wore them. I didn't have anything else. I didn't like it, but it made a great impression on my mind — that I wanted to finish school, to learn something I could get a job at and earn some money. I wanted nice clothes, and I wanted things at home to be better.

When we got bigger, I used to walk down to Ballard almost every night because the library was there, and I always went to the library. I loved the library, and I still love it. I feel like it's a magical place, and I forget everything else. And I just wish I could read all the books. And I felt like that then. The children's department was up the stairs. And so we'd have to clatter up the stairs. And usually old maidish type women were working there, if you made any noise, they would say, "Oh, shh." And so we watched our step. They were nice — you just had to get used to them, and they to you.

I remember the drug store on the northwest corner of 20th and Market. They had a little soda fountain, and so did the one kitty corner. When my sister Ida started working at Sears Roebuck down on 1st Avenue and Lander Street, she had a little money. Occasionally, she'd give me some money, so I could run down and get a quart of ice cream. And they had to make it up in a quart. And then I'd run home with it. That was a big treat for us. Because we didn't have a refrigerator, we had to just sit down and eat it.

I remember at Penney's they used to have the little things, you know, where they put the bill and the money you gave them in this little clip of things, and then they pulled the cord and it sailed across the room to the office. And then they'd send it back. And I used to think that was quite interesting.

I was 13 and my sister Lorna was 17 when she went off and got married. I can remember how unhappy it made my mother and father to think that she was already beginning such a tough life. And the times were very poor. You know, the Depression was a real depression. And it affected me very, very much. I simply didn't like it.

For a long time during the Depression my dad did find odd jobs. But he finally couldn't find work, and became very depressed. It was really a bad time for me. I was in high school, and I wasn't too sympathetic because I thought that my mother was going through the same struggle. My mother was a natural-born optimist and survivor. And I think I inherited that, too. And she was always there for us. Without her, I don't know what we would have done.

I was 18 when I graduated from Ballard, in 1939, and I was doing some work for the *Shingle*, the school yearbook, typing it and whatever came up. I would just do it, maybe till noon. And this woman who had graduated called in to the head of our department and said they needed somebody part time to typewrite. He asked me if I would be interested. And I said, oh, certainly. So I had a job.

They made window curtains there on 8th and Virginia in a big old building. And they had a small office where they needed some extra typing done. And I made the grand amount of $15 a week, and I went home and gave my mother ten of it, which left me a big five for any new clothes and my carfare and my lunch. But the streetcar was three tokens for a quarter. So I could go the week for a dollar.

Ballard was a nice, friendly place to grow up in. When you walked down to Ballard, for many years, you saw the Reverend Wilhelm and his friend sitting on front of the library. And they always spoke. He always would get up and take off his western hat, and made you feel a little bit at home. All right.

Phoebe Daniels was born December 14, 1920. Her father, Harry Daniels, was from a family of Methodist ministers in England. Phoebe married Glenn Jewett April 23, 1942. He died in 1959. Three children: Leslie (1943), Jeffrey (1948-1992) and Danielle (1952). Phoebe died in 2010. [See also Lorna Conrad, page 255.]

"The Organ Grinder"
Lorna Daniels Conrad

One time, when we first moved there, the organ grinder came along with a little monkey. It was so cute. Just like you'd read about, you know. There was only a couple of years, I don't know, he gave up, I guess. Then there used to be a scissors-grinder come and holler, "Scissors to grind!" You know, and he'd sharpen the knives and whatnot. I didn't see him again for years until, oh, about 20 years ago, I saw a cart that said that. It was down at the beauty shop down in Ballard. They don't do that anymore, but they did.

Woodland Park in 1924

Photo of Seattle's Woodland Park taken on July 4, 1924 by Asahel Curtis from the roof of the zoo's primate house (still standing in 2001, but not for long). This view to the Northwest shows the Seattle-Everett Interurban and Ferris wheel at the Park's entrance on Phinney Avenue.

319

Harold Leo Johnson

"I have really enjoyed my life till now.
There's never been a moment that I wasn't
busy with something."

My name in Icelandic, is Hallur. I go by Harold Leo Johnson. I was born in the Ballard Hospital on May 13th, 1929. My grandparents immigrated to Canada about 1877. They homesteaded in the area called New Iceland. My mom was born in Arborg. My mom immigrated to Seattle in 1923. She stayed in her Aunt Vega's boarding house in Ballard, on 26th Northwest and Northwest 70th.

My dad immigrated to Seattle in 1924, with his brother Steini and his family to be carpenters. My dad bought a small three-room house on Northwest 86th Street, just outside Seattle city limits, near 28th, and that's where I grew up. Across the alley from us Jess Jackson had an old Richfield gas station, with two old pumps with the glass on the top. Robert Twigg had worked for him but had gone into the military. I'd been hanging around there so Jess asked me if I'd like to come work for him. I said, "I sure would." He said, "You talk it over with your mom and dad." And they said, "Fine, if you think you can handle it, go ahead." I had to get a work permit because I was just 12 years old. I worked there for something like five, six years.

I worked there all during the war. And, for a young man, that was an education. The gas station had a counter with candies and cigarettes and snuff and so on. All along the sides were benches, because this is where a lot of the men came in the daytime. And, if they weren't working, they sat and talked about this, that and the other thing. Lot of it had to do with, oh, "I have a son in the Navy, and a got a letter from him." And he'd share it with the others, and so on. It was really a good education for me to see how these people were worried about their family, their children that were in the service. And, the funniest thing of all was, you're familiar with the snoose can? They'd come in, and the first thing they'd do is say, "Jim, you got some snoose?" He says, "Yeah, I just put up one here." So they'd go over and look on the bottom of the can for the date. So the freshest can, they took snuff out of it. And on the street corner you'd see the shingle weavers and snuff. They couldn't smoke in the mill. But they could use snuff, or tobacco. That's why Ballard got the name of Snoose Junction.

My dad and my uncle were the contractors who built the Northminster Presbyterian Church on 25th and 77th. It was the [Icelandic] Unitarian Church. It was built back in the Depression time. They added a chapel on the north side. We had a real small chapel on the 25th Street side. But anyway, that church was there for a long time, and my wife and I joined the church. My parents were married July 28, 1928, in Seattle. My wife's [parents] were married in Chicago on July 28th, at the same time. So we decided we would get married on July 28th, 1950.

My mother belonged to an organization in the church called Eining, an Icelandic group of women, during the different times of year, they would do all of the Icelandic cooking, *polafest*, and *vinartertas* and all of those things.

In January 24th, 1951 I joined the fire department and went through the recruit school. We had a graduation, and Chief Fitzgerald came down. And I told my supervisor, "I lived in Ballard all my life, had paper routes and other things, I know Ballard almost like the back of my hand," I said, "I'd like to be stationed at Station 18."

The cook at the fire station was leaving, and when he left, I took over. Some of the wives called me, saying, "You're feeding our husbands too heavy. We put nice food on the table and they're too full." So I had to cut it back to just soup and some bread and crackers in the afternoon, and that was enough to fill everybody up. I was the cook on our shift for 17 years. And I drove for 18 years. Never had an accident.

I was the only one who was hurt in the Seattle Cedar fire. I was on a kiln with a hose. I had four or five guys behind me, it was high pressure on the water, so high it could lift you up if you were just by yourself. Anyway, we were on a dry kiln, and it dropped a foot underneath us, because the fire was burning underneath us. We didn't know that. The people behind me took off and just left me, because I had a hand on the shut-off here. I couldn't get it shut off fast enough. My helmet went into the fire, knocked off with the hose going back and forth. The doctor said to me, "Well, it's a good thing you were a square head 'cause you might have got hurt otherwise."

That was the largest fire Seattle's ever had. There was an airplane 2,000 feet above, that saw timbers and two-by-fours going around in the sky. The heat had taken it up like that. And there was a white cone right out through the middle of it, where all that cedar that was stacked. They

Harold Leo Johnson - 321

were stacked in 55-foot piles. We were there for two or three weeks or more. Still fighting little fires.

When I first joined the Seattle Fire Department, I was stationed at Station 18 on Russell Avenue and Market Street. At that time I wasn't aware of all of the history that building had, where the horses ran out of the station. They had the doors on the back, and when they got a telephone call, they'd push a button to open the doors automatically. The horses came out and would stand in front of the fire rig. They loved to go to a fire. The firemen came down the pole. The harnesses were hung from the ceiling with ropes, and they'd just unclip them and put them on the horses. The horses were chomping at the bit, and they'd head off to where the alarm was.

I worked as a driver there for 18 years. And then I went on to become an officer. All those little squares in the floor were so that the horses didn't slip when it was time for them to go. We could wash out the station in the summertime and we could still smell the horses. So horse manure was still in the cement.

At the time that Ballard was new, the station itself was a place where people could come — there's an attic there where we used to play ping pong. They had a piano and an organ, and different things on the second floor. Of course, we, the firemen, had our bunks, and each fireman had his own designated bunk and they slept there at night until an alarm came in.

I have really enjoyed my life 'til now. There's never been a moment that I wasn't busy with something.

Harold Johnson was born in Ballard on May 13, 1929 to Inga (Bardarson) and Skafti Johnson. His grandparents emigrated from Iceland to homestead in an area of Canada called New Iceland. His parents met and married in Seattle. Harold married Rose Marie L. Melsted in 1949. Their children: Susan Lee (1951) and Becky Marie (1958). Harold died in 2004.

322 - Harold Leo Johnson

Isabella Backman Johnson

"I want the Nordic Hour to be remembered."

Have you heard of the Nordic Hour? It was a radio program that Gus Backman, my uncle, had. It was an hour program, in English, dedicated to mostly Swedish music. It aired Sundays between seven and eight for quite a few years.on KVI and then KOL. I want the Nordic Hour to be remembered. I was about 18. I helped him write script. But he was a good radioman, very good voice. Mother had a commercial on the program and once my uncle gave the wrong address. Mother came running from the kitchen and she says, "That's not right, that's not right, that's not right." She had a store, Backman's Novelty Shop, on Sixth Northwest at 77th.

When she opened it in 1929, she called it the Maybe Shop because she didn't know if it was going to fly or not. She changed the name to Backman's Novelty about '32 or '33. She was in business until '40, '50 — she sold it once, got it back and stayed in business for another few years. She was one of the first ones to import.

Dad worked for a machine shop, and it burned down. After that he just did odd jobs and the bookkeeping for mother. He was too conservative. He did not want to charge as much as the traffic would bear, and sometimes he didn't want to sell certain things that wouldn't go well. Mother was stronger than he was, as far as merchandising was concerned.

To begin with, we lived in the back of the store, half of it was store and half was residence. Sunday mornings were havoc. Seven o'clock in the morning someone would knock on the door — they knew we lived there. They were going to Catholic Mass and didn't have any hosiery. We finally rented the adjoining store to live in and that put a stop to any Sunday stuff._

When mother first started, people were interested in inexpensive gifts. She gradually improved her merchandise. One Christmas, Manfrid, my husband, worked at the store to help out. He said the Swedish merchandise was not marked high enough, so he changed all the prices — and they sold.

My uncle, Gus Backman started the Scandia Buffet at 1109 Virginia and a bakery on Olive Street. The old Swedish Club was up the street from the bakery on Eighth Avenue. It was a hangout for Swedes. It was called Snoose Corner — Ballard was Snoose Junction. The lumbermen and fishermen gathered there. The boys working in lumber mills stayed weekdays in a number of boarding houses on Capitol Hill. They got their laundry done and they got a bed for the weekend. The rent was not very much, so that they were able to keep themselves together.

The Vasa Order bought property on 24th and Market Street on the northwest corner. It was an old schoolhouse they converted into a lodge hall, and they met there for quite a few years, the Frihet Lodge. I remember going there to meetings with my mother and father. I sat through the meetings, I knew the ritual by heart. And it was coffee, and a dance — always a dance afterwards.

And at Christmas parties at Vasa Hall in Ballard, they always had a big tree, children dancing around the Christmas tree, and maybe 10 or 12 adults who knew the Christmas songs and the Christmas dances, so we all learned them.

For about 10 or 12 years we had Swedish school on Saturdays and conducted a meeting in Swedish. That was called Snödroppen. We had a dance group — we had costumes and danced Swedish folk dances. We spoke Swedish — some better than others.

Isabella Backman was born July 19, 1918 in Seattle. Her parents, Gunhild (Karlsson) and Leander Backman were born in Sweden. Isabella graduated from Ballard High School in 1936. She married Manfrid Johnson in 1939. They had one daughter, Linnea (1952).

Johann Isak Johnson

"There was an oil well at the foot of 32nd Avenue Northwest"

My parents came out of northeastern Iceland and settled in Winnipeg at first. My mother taught school on the prairie. My father Isak was a builder and architect. Eventually they came together, and they moved to Victoria, Canada. From there they moved to Seattle and Sunset Hill. He built the old fashioned huge homes with porches. My mother, Jakobina, was really deep into the literature. She could translate anything that came her way from Icelandic to English or English to Icelandic.

In those days, if you wanted to meet some real Icelanders, you'd go there and see Big Jake. He ran things at the Ballard City Hall as he thought they should be run. He was a great giant of a man and he kept the peace on Ballard Avenue. A lot of tough guys had to be handled, saw mill workers. Big Jake was a policeman at that time.

We were not all Icelanders. There were Italians named Fiorito. Immigrants, they came over with their picks and their shovels ready to go, and they helped dig the gas lines in the streets, and the water mains. I knew them very well. It was just hack away with a pick and a shovel and pour all that cement, do everything by hand.

We had horse-drawn fire trucks which ran all over Ballard if they needed a fire to be put out in a home. Six horses to the wagon, running and running, maybe a mile or two to get to the source of the fire. Sometimes I'm afraid that some scalawags deliberately pulled the handle to signify where the fire was — we had to see those horses run, and they were beautiful. Nobody seemed to mind.

The athletes at Ballard High, a fellow that was five foot or over was considered a big guy. He could be five foot six or seven or eight or nine, he was okay, but the little guy got banged up too much. I know. I was one of them. We had football and we had good teams.

I wound up going to sea for awhile. After high school I went to sea on a ship to Japan and China and the Philippines. I was in the steward department. I was only 17. I got out of the school and ran down and got a job. That was on a Friday, and on a Saturday I was on the way to

China. It was a passenger ship. It had accommodations for about 250 people, and there were missionaries. Haraldur got the job about the same way I did. But he signed aboard as a cadet, a junior officer, an officer material man, which he proved during World War II. Imagine sailing across the Atlantic about a hundred times. Thousands of ships were sunk. He survived. Never talked about it.

There was an oil well at the foot of 32nd Avenue Northwest; across the street, which was North Street in those days. A fellow named Harry Treat came to town. I'm not too sure about it, but he sunk a well there and made a lot of money. We've never seen a quart of oil, but plenty was splashed around to make it look like it was full of oil. I don't think the intention ever was that they were going to get any oil, it was a stock swindle, that sort of thing. You could get very greasy and oily if you went down there, which I did. We climbed to the top of the derrick because nobody was around the office. It was torn down, and I guess everybody left town.

This fellow, Harry Treat, had a huge home up around 85th. And a huge barn. In the barn he had horses and maybe 15 carriages. They originally came from England. We little kids could get through the cracks at the bottom of the sidewalls. We couldn't understand what he was doing. This was about a mile from his home. Now that was rich man's row up there, the bankers, the sawmill owners. Bolcom was a sawmill man. Taylor Mill over there in that area that overlooks the Sound in there. Wally Casler, banker. Ned Stone, Stimson Mill. That's how Ballard grew.

Johann Isak Johnson was born November 24, 1915 in Ballard. His parents, Isak and Jakobina, were from Iceland, and had first settled in Canada. Their children: Kari, Ingolfur, Konrad Ari, Haraldur Bjorn, Gudrun (who died young), Johann Isak and Stephan Jon. Johann Isak died in 2004. Photograph from 1973.

Robert David Jones

"My dad always said Ballard was the best place to have a market because Ballard had the biggest industries in the whole northwest, principally lumber and fish."

My father, Johan Johanson, was born in Småland, Sweden. My mother, Anna Jansson, was born in Norrland, Sweden, on the same day, the same year, 1884, January the 3rd. They met in Chicago. In Sweden my dad, Johan, and my Uncle Anton were helping on the farm. He recalled once that he and Uncle Anton were to kill a bull. They tied the bull to a post in the barn. Johan held a spike to the front of its head and Anton gave the bull the blow, but missed. This infuriated the bull, who tore himself free from the post. Anton ran out and closed the barn door — with Johan inside with the bull. Johan shimmied up another post until Anton came to his senses and let the bull run out. They sold the meat there in the central square.

Johan could not see any future in Sweden, and he was also due to go into the military. So, at age 20, he thought this was time to leave Sweden. At Ellis Island, he found so many Johansons and Johnsons he decided to choose a more uncommon name. He chose Jones.

Johan came to Chicago in 1905 and got a job in a meat market. In 1909, he and Anna Johnson married and came to Seattle. He first worked as a conductor on a cable car on James Street, going up First Hill. After that, he went back to the meat business again. He had a market on Greenwood which he later sold to the Skaggs brothers. The Skaggs brothers became Safeway. And look where Safeway has gone, and we Joneses have just been spinning our wheels.

My dad always said Ballard was the best place to have a market because Ballard had the biggest industries in the whole northwest, principally lumber and fish. On the northern side, it was lumber, and on the southern side it was fish. And the Norwegians, the catalysts of the fishing industry, would have to drive their boats through the log jams the Swedes had constructed for the lumber industry.

My dad was on the southeast corner of 20th and Market Street. He did so well there, that he decided to sell his business, use the money to take the whole family to Sweden. This was in 1922, before I was born. I'm the afterthought in our family.

My dad came back to Ballard again, and put up a shop on the southwest corner of 20th and Market, Fair Price Market. You know, at some time or another there was a Jones working in a meat market on each of the four corners of 20th and Market.

During the war years it was harder to get meat. Meat and butter were rationed. Everybody who went to buy meat or butter, had to have their red and blue stamps. Businesses had to think about keeping up their ration coupon account, as well as their dollar account. And if you fell short in your ration account, there was no one to help you. You would just go out of business if somehow those ration stacks got lost.

Beef, pork and lamb were rationed, but not chicken or mutton. My brother found that the Swedes and Norwegians really enjoyed mutton. And he could get that quite easily. People came from all over Ballard. They liked the mutton that he handled, because he got it with lots of fat on it, like choice steer, but with mutton flavor. He'd have long lines of people coming in to get their meat.

People were buying lard in those days instead of shortening. So if the animal was fat, we'd just render the lard. But we were next door to Mittelstadt's funeral chapel, and our fragrant odors came through the walls into his chapel. This was a point of discussion on the street out there. Mittelstadt would smoke big, long cigars, I guess to suffocate the next door smells.

E. E. Mittelstadt had the biggest funeral business in town. His son, Otto Mittelstadt, was the county coroner. He would bring the bodies always into Mittelstadt Funeral Home. Not just those who were killed on the highways and things like that, but the street people and those they couldn't identify real quick. They were stored in the county morgue freezer, and as soon as they found identification, they would come to Mittelstadt's Funeral Home for a funeral. I daresay Mittelstadt's was doing about the biggest funeral business in Ballard.

There was a clergyman who took care of most of their funeral services. He had a special contract to come in and take care of the burials. They called him Marrying and Burying Sam. He had a long, wide-brimmed hat, black and pointed up at the top, and a nice smile for everybody who came by.

Now my dad had a big yard with a chicken coop. He was killing about a hundred chickens every Friday. Some of those chickens'd be running around on the grass with their heads cut off. Dad would take the chickens and put them in that big lard kettle in the basement full of boiling water. Those feathers would come right off; then he'd chill them as quick as he could. He would do this on a Friday night.

Other times during the week, he would bring home fat from the store, get the lard kettle going, and render it in the basement of our house. My mother had to go through all the smell of the lard coming up into the main part of the house. Dad used to smoke these big cigars. And Mother would rather smell a cigar in the house than to smell all that lard. So she was running around the house blowing on a cigar, getting the house full of cigar smell to cover the lard smell.

Dad didn't want to spend extra money to wash the coats and the aprons and things like that, so he'd take them all home to Mom, and put them in that same lard kettle after he cleaned it out for each time. And all the bloody, stained, greasy coats and aprons would be thrown in the lard kettle. She would soak them first, and then mix in soap and boil them. Then we'd have the white coats and aprons hanging on the line up and down the backyard.

My dad took his car down to the Fishermen's Wharf on Elliott Bay, picked up his fish, picked up his meat, put it all in the back part of the '32 Ford. You could smell the meat and the fish on Sunday morning when the folks took us children to Sunday School.

For Thanksgiving and Christmas my brother bought turkeys from a turkey farm on Whidbey Island. He'd sell about a thousand birds at a time. He even worked with competitors, like John Kastner, who had a meat shop on 56th and 20th. Together they would get these turkeys and bring them in for Thanksgiving and Christmas. So that's how it was in the time 1945 up to 1952 or so.

Robert "Bob" Jones was born January 25, 1925 near Green Lake to Johan and Anna Jones, their youngest. Lillian was born in 1911, Bill in 1912, Harold in 1915, and Kenneth in 1918. The family moved to Ballard and Bob went to several north-end Seattle schools, and graduated from Ballard High in 1943. He went to Bob Jones University where he met his wife, Janet Wildy. They worked in missions in Italy from 1951-1976. They had four children: Janilee (1952), Cynthia (1957), Jonathan (1960), and Jared (1962). The family returned to Ballard 1976. Over the years his father and three brothers had many meat markets in Ballard and other parts of Seattle, the last was located in the Sunset Hotel building, which was destroyed by fire in April, 2000.

Bernice Jonson

"I used to go up to Saint Alphonsus and kneel and ask God to send me clients, whether they could pay or not, just send me a client."

I was born June 12th, 1914 in Quincy, Washington, out on the prairie. My father was born in Småland, Sweden. My mother was born in Minnesota. Her parents came from Norway. My mother was a high school principal at the time she married my father. At about the age of eight I came here to Seattle with my family. I attended Olympic View Grade School and Lincoln High School, graduating in January of '31. I entered the University of Washington. My mother died in 1933. At that time I was going to be a teacher, but my father, an attorney, promised me he would send me to Bellingham Normal after I finished law school if I still wanted to go. I had three younger siblings so I stayed home and kept house while I went to school, with the cook in charge of the day-to-day.

I graduated from law school, passed the Bar in August 1936 and made up my mind I would practice law one year and then I'd go to Bellingham Normal. I've been practicing law ever since. I spent one year with my father, Axel E. Jonson. I had worked in his office all through high school and through college, which was a wonderful thing because at law school I understood the practical aspects of the law as well as the theoretical.

When I graduated from law school, the top law school students were being hired at fifty dollars a month. Seven women began in that class and three of us graduated. There were very few women lawyers. One of the girls I went to school with ended up working as a legal secretary. I did not want that. I opened my own office, and the rest was saying my prayers. I used to go up to Saint Alphonsus and kneel and ask God to send me clients, whether they could pay or not, just send me a client. [St. Alphonsus was the only church open weekdays.]

There was a Depression existing in 1936. Also, people had not accepted the fact that a woman could be an attorney. I had many a person come into my office and look at me and say, "I want to see the lawyer." I would say, "I am the lawyer." Fortunately, very few of them turned around and walked out. So, I was able to build a practice. I would say it took me about ten years to build a practice and to have a steady flow of clients and referrals. Gradually I drifted into being a family law specialist, and that's what I am right now.

I moved from home in 1937. I rented a room with a potbellied stove on 50th between 15th & 17th Northwest for $7.50 a month.

At one time the Commercial Club sponsored a dinner for the Mayor and the Council people, and as chairman for that committee, I hired a secretary who went along Shilshole Avenue and listed every business and the number of employees, the gross income and the details of that business.

Then we hired a bus and we plotted out the course that the bus would take to show Ballard to the Mayor and Councilmen. Of course, the first stop was Fishermen's Wharf. At that time, it was piers and fishing boats, but no real buildings of any consequence. Emerson Street didn't exist. The University-Ballard highway didn't exist. Shilshole, where the breakwater was, was filled with rocks, the support was rocks, and then the sand might drift down. After we took the Mayor and the Councilmen to Fishermen's Wharf, we went along Shilshole Avenue, telling them what Ballard really was — there was a tremendous amount of industry, and there were a lot of employees. It was a self-sustaining city actually, with the hospital, the doctors — we even had our own precinct station. Then we took them down along Shilshole where the breakwater was subsequently built, the Golden Gardens part. Some of those Councilmen didn't even know that this existed in the City of Seattle, so we showed them where all the schools and the parks were.

They were impressed. Out of that dinner and that exhibition of what the assets of Ballard were and how much we needed to do something came seven projects, including the University-Ballard highway, the Emerson Street bridge and the Shilshole breakwater.

The Ballard Commercial Club was extremely active. We met above the *Ballard News* building, Harold Kimball's building, and we'd fill it. At least 50 to 75 men would meet — and a few women.

And then the district sponsored the Lucia Bride Festival. There were three of us who ran it. For three months we planned and schemed and held the Lucia Bride Festival, which brought a tremendous amount of individuals, finally culminating with crowning of the Lucia Bride in the Civic Auditorium. We had a program that consisted of accordionists, in the stores in the afternoon and the evenings; we had smorgasbords throughout this period of time to which the public were invited. We had a real fun parade sponsored by the merchants. We had an evening choir parade marching and singing with flashlights in the month of December.

It was interesting to watch a whole community, Lions Club, Rotarians, Kiwanis, Commercial Club, BPW [Business and Professional Women], churches, everybody — gathered around and just went to work. I didn't practice law for three months, but it was a lot of fun. Also involved were the Scandinavian organizations, the Swedish Male Chorus, the Norwegian Male Chorus.

It was really a celebration. And I think the Seattle Chamber of Commerce got an award for having an event that received more publicity throughout the United States than any other event that year. We had gone to *The Seattle Times* in the very beginning and asked them if they would give us news coverage. They agreed that they would if we would furnish them with something of interest for each day. And so when you opened *The Seattle Times*, Ballard was on the front page of that issue.

The International District people came to my office and talked to me. Would it be possible for them to do the same thing? How did we do it? And I said yes, it would be possible, and in fact, I encouraged them. The next year, then, the International District had a festival and out of this came Seafair. It was contagious. If you have an idea and if you're willing to devote the time to that idea, and if you're willing to give people the credit for the work they have done, they'll work.

I was president of the Ballard BPW Club. Then I was a director of Ballard Commercial Club.

I married Art Olson in December of '49. Art had three boys and I had an adopted boy, and then we had two more. But with that and a busy law practice, all my activities with the Commercial Club came to a grinding, screeching halt. I used to get up at five o'clock in the morning and come down and work and then go home and serve breakfast and get my kids off to school. I worked Saturdays and Sundays. I took my work with me to the cabin over the weekends. While they were fishing, I worked. Those things I don't do any more.

I think I had an advantage when I started out because I had my father's assistance, and my father had given me the "no's" and the "don'ts" and the "do's." There was a time when, I didn't want my briefcase carried by anybody; I didn't want doors opened for me; I didn't weep or cry. I can vividly recall times when I walked out of the courtroom wishing that I were a man.

There was a time when basically King County lawyers were hated in every county in the state. I frequently went to Snohomish County and Judge Bell would look down at me and say, "Miss Jonson, are you from Seattle?" and I'd say, "No, Your Honor, I'm from Ballard."

The real difficulty is that although the back door is open and employment open and the professions open, women have never earned as much as they should earn commensurate with their ability. But I think that nothing good happens unless something bad comes along with it, that is the demand that women had to be treated equally. There's a fine line between demanding that you are treated equally or working so that you're recognized as an equal, performing. It's true, I could walk into the courtroom and I could try a case. My brother lawyer on the other side of the table could commit error after error, ask the wrong questions. If I did it, the judge would look at me, and the eyebrow would go up because he knew I knew better and at times, I felt that. At other times I took it as a compliment. You just did your very best. And gradually the judges came to accept women because it didn't make any difference whether you were men or women or who you are as long as you managed to do your job. Over a period of years you gain respect, you gain your reputation.

I'm astounded and really thrilled at the number of women and the quality of women that have entered the legal profession and the medical profession. I walk down to a courtroom now, there are so many women lawyers, I do not know them. When I first started I think there were maybe five or six, seven in the county.

Today my two sons, Mark and Eric Olson, practice law with me. I don't think I would ever quit because as long as my sons are with me, I enjoy practicing law.

Bernice Jonson was born June 12, 1914 to Axel and Karen (Gilbertsen) Jonson. She graduated from law school, was admitted to the bar in 1936 and set up an independent law practice in Ballard. When her sister Corinne died, she adopted her orphaned nephew Ralph. She married Art Olson December, 1940 in Our Redeemer's Lutheran Church. Art had three boys, Tom, Marshall and Jerry. They had two sons: Eric (1950) and Mark (1952). Art died in 1979. She was interviewed April 30, 1988 and photographed in 2001. Bernice died in 2005.

Jon Marvin Jonsson

"My sisters called me broðir. *The kids couldn't pronounce that and they ended up calling me Bobo, and the name Bobo stayed with me."*

Mother came from Iceland to Canada as a five-year-old at the turn of the century. Father, Thorbjorn, came about 1914. They met and married here. He was older. He left Iceland, went to Hamburg, Germany to go to cabinet making school.

He also lived in Switzerland, and had a bit of a life. He was there long enough to learn to speak German. Germany, apparently, had a non-conventional draft where they could pick up single people, whoever they were, and put them in the army. WWI was on the horizon − and his friends advised him to return to Iceland.

So he left to return to Iceland. In England, he found no boats going to Iceland, but one was going to New York, so he took it. He had a cousin who immigrated some years before to Winnipeg, so he went to New York, then to see his cousin Eggertson in Winnipeg. Eggertson suggested he should build and sell houses. And he did, ultimately, in Seattle.

In Seattle, Thorbjorn visited an Icelandic lady, Hilda Siegel. He saw a young lady walking up the street. He asked Hilda, "Who's that walking up the street?" She looked out and said, "That's Brynhildur." She went to the front door, called Brynhildur in, they met, and they married very shortly thereafter. I think that was April of 1920. They went where there was construction. Once they returned to Ballard, they stayed. My sister Kristin was born in San Francisco, and Elin and I were born in Ballard.

After grade school, I spoke both Icelandic and English, but prior to that time, just Icelandic. We weren't allowed to speak English in the home, only Icelandic. If we accidentally forgot, we'd get slapped with a wet dishrag or spanked, and that continued until I was maybe 14 or 15. Then I started speaking English, but my mother still only spoke Icelandic. At that age I knew everything and could get away with it. My dad spoke Icelandic because he was more comfortable with Icelandic. But I think my mother sort of ran the show.

I went to Adams. I could not speak English − the only students who

Back Row: Kristin, Jon Marvin, Elin,
Front: Brynhildur and Thorbjorn Jonsson, 1940s

would associate with me were the "Indian Johns" (that's what they were called). They lived in an Indian village north of the Locks; they had lived where the Locks are, but when the Locks were built they were required to move. And they moved to the north − Ballard − across from the Locks. We walked to school. At recess we would chase the soccer ball, and if we were lucky, we could kick it if we caught up to it. We also played marbles. There were two kinds of marble games. One, a big ring, and then one with a pie-shaped ring — that'd be for two people. When you played with the big one, to get the marble, you'd have to hit the marble and knock it out of the ring, And I lost every marble I ever got. And I'd hope that the recess bell would ring so I could grab all the marbles I could get a hold of, and say, "Grab dates and run," and run.

But at the end of the fifth grade I was expelled. I went to Webster for the last year, and there I met a whole new group of people who are still good friends: Robert Hawley, Herman Johnsen, Cal Nerdrum.

About my nickname, Bobo, my sisters called me *broðir,* [ð is pronounced 'th']. The kids couldn't pronounce that and they ended up calling me Bobo, and the name Bobo stayed with me, all the way through law school.

There was an Icelandic church on 70th and 23rd and the sermons were in Icelandic. And they had an Icelandic organization called Vestri, which means westerners. Sometimes I had to go with my parents to the Vestri meeting. Vestri had a book society. You could borrow books in

Icelandic. Vestri was strictly social and it continued until around 1960. At that time, I incorporated the Icelandic Club of Greater Seattle, which took over what Vestri had been doing.

I built a kayak at home when I was in junior high school. And I would say that I built it properly and correctly. I took the plans from *Boys' Life*, and spent the winter building the kayak. It had ribs 12 inches apart, and they varied in size because they started as a point, came out to the cockpit area and again diminished down. I did all the steps you're supposed to do, shrink and coat the canvas and make it water tight and then paint it. And Andy or Bud Hjellen, who lived across the street, he too built a kayak. But, as it turned out, his kayak was a foot shorter than mine because the ruler he used was only 11 inches — he thought it was 12. But you know, you don't throw away a ruler if you break it, you just cut off the end..

When I was in junior high school, I had a *P.I.* carrier route. And I would get up at 3:30, would get my papers, and I'd always be there. I didn't sleep in. And then, when the war started in 1941, most of the boys who were *P.I.* carriers were seniors in high school. It was a desired job

Jon Marvin, age 14, from a P.I. *ad*

because you'd get money. There were no other jobs. The war started on Sunday. On Monday, three went down and joined the military. All of a sudden their slots were empty, including the shack manager. And I was then made the shack manager, which meant I got paid ten dollars a month, maybe. It would be my job to make sure that everybody was there. And if they weren't, I'd go wake them up. And if I woke them up, I would get to charge them 50 cents.

If they were noisy or caused a disturbance, I would then tell them to be quiet. And if they weren't quiet, I could assess them 50 cents. Now, here I am a kid in junior high dealing with people in high school. Do you see? Do you see the problem? Okay. So the next thing that happened is I would get pantsed. Do you remember that procedure, take your pants off? Okay. I would get pantsed. And I would put up resistance, but you can't put up much of a fight with — and it wasn't a serious fight, no one's getting black eyes. You know, it was more a tussle, yeah, and I would get pantsed. And I would then charge them each 50 cents. And then I concluded, I can make money from this. So what I would do is, I would wear a pair of pants I didn't care about and hide a good pair. Then, in case they took my pair and threw them up in the telephone wires, at least I had another pair to put on.

And then when I'd be through with the route, I would go by Kannitzer's Bakery on 24th and 63rd. And I would go in there and I would give them a newspaper, a *P.I.*, and I'd get four maple bars. I'd bring the maple bars home, and I'd wake up my parents and I'd give them each a maple bar and I had two for myself.

Then, another thing the *P.I.* had going, was solicitation for new subscribers competitions. And if you got a new customer, you would get something. I forget what you'd get. And I would — I just don't know, maybe 25 cents or 35 cents for a new subscriber. But then they would throw in the prizes, too, later. And for example, if you could get 20 new subscribers, you would, for example, be able to go on a train to the rodeo in Ellensburg.

I used to go down to Ballard Avenue and hit the apartment houses down there and get the fishermen to subscribe because they would subscribe and put their name on anything. They wouldn't be there when it came time to pay the bill. But that wasn't my problem, all I had to do was get the subscription.

I graduated from Ballard High in January of '46. The war was over August 14, 1945 but service people were still showing up at school with their programs to encourage people to enlist in the Army and the Navy. And then in October, the Navy came with a program called V5 and V12. A program that if you enlisted, you would go to a regular university, like Stanford, for a two-year program there. Then, if you were in the flying bit, (V5), you would then go to flight school and finish your four-year enlistment as a pilot.

That was very attractive to me. There was a three-day test and just a few were accepted. Then you were sworn in the Navy, though you're still in high school. And when you graduated, the Navy would send orders where to show up. So I graduated in January, and was waiting for the Navy to send me my orders. Well, I received a letter from the Navy, saying in so many words, "We don't need you. Here's your discharge." But that made me a World War II Veteran before I turned 18.

After high school, I enlisted in the Marine Corps; I served for 14 months. Because of the Marine Corps service, the G.I. Bill permitted me to enter the University of Washington. My high school grade point was not a factor to entering the U.W.; only the G.I. Bill. Thus I entered the U.W. and the G.I. Bill took me through to the first quarter of law school. The G.I. Bill also compensated; so, when I married in 1948, I was paid $110. a month. I then had a job managing the Neptune Theater building — not the theater, but the building, on 45th Street and University Way.

I practiced law in Seattle, doing criminal defense work (appointed by the judge at the arraignment hearing to defend a person charged with a felony). After five years of doing criminal defense work, I decided to move my office to Ballard — where I was born and raised.

Lawyers could not advertise then; the Bar Association said advertising was unethical. So, prior to my move to Ballard, I ran for the State Legislature as a Democrat. I did not expect to get elected. I was running against Dwight Hawley who had been a State Representative (in the 44th District) for twelve years. To my surprise, I was elected. Thus, I had to go to Olympia — and deferred opening my office in Ballard.

I don't know that there were any big issues. The [Shilshole] breakwater was coming in and Dwight Hawley was primarily responsible for it. In spite of that, he lost the election, which didn't make sense, but there was an issue on the ballot when I ran that bothered the Unions — the right-to-work — so they got the Union vote out, a Democrat vote. I came in on that Democrat sweep. The next time around, that issue wasn't there, the Democrats stayed home, the Republicans voted, I lost and Dwight Hawley came back in.

In 1965, I was appointed Consul for Iceland, and in 1984 I was promoted to Consul General. My wife and I have been to Iceland maybe thirty times, if not more. My dad was the only one of seven siblings to come to America. The rest are in Iceland. I was raised in Ballard and I didn't have any cousins. Never had any family, except my mother, dad and sisters. And then to go back there, and I have just a vast number. Maybe 200.

Jon Marvin Jonsson was born in Ballard March 22, 1928 to Steinunn Brynhildur Erlendsdottir (1883-1961) and Thorbjorn Jonsson (1877-1947). He has two sisters, Kristin (1921) and Elin (1925). Jon Marvin graduated from Ballard High 1946 and from the University of Washington Law School in 1954. He has practiced law as a sole practitioner in Ballard since 1954. He was elected to the Washington State Legislature 1958-1959. He married Marlene Pedersen in 1948, one son, Dwight Gilman (1950). Jon Marvin married Joanne Sivertsen in 1960. Their children are: Bryndis (1965) and Geir Thorbjorn (1972).

Alf Knudsen

"Our sponsor, Frank Daquilla, said, 'You're not having these kids marching in a parade' and I said, 'Oh, yes, I will.' I had seen in the store a beautiful double-bell euphonium. I'd never seen one in Norway. He said, 'I betcha.' I told him, 'I really like that euphonium. How much you want for it?' He said, 'No, I'm not going to sell it to you. But if you get the band in the parade this year, I'll give you the horn.' I said, 'OK, it's a deal.' I have the horn today."

My name is Alf Lunder Knudsen. I was born in Brooklyn, New York, USA. I stayed there for two and a half years, and then my mother took me back to Norway. We went on *Stavangerfjord* to Stavanger. I lived at my grandma's house. At that time it was my grandmother and my grandfather. He died two years later, so I grew up actually with my grandmother on my mother's side. They were Inga Ragnhilda Lunder and Sverre Lunder.

My mother went back to the United States, I think to try to make some money to bring me back to the States. The reason we went to Norway in the first place was my father deserted the family. It was hard for her to support a son and live in New York.

So I stayed with my grandparents and, luckily, in the house my uncle and his family lived upstairs. During the war we had renters both upstairs and downstairs. So actually there were four families living in that two story house.

[During the war] there wasn't any real action in Stavanger. There were German warships coming into the harbor and the Germans occupied most of the schools. When it came time for me to go to school, I started off in my teacher's home. We had classes there for the first year. Then I had to walk across town to get to another elementary school.

There were air raids from time to time and we had to leave town. There were evacuations. Luckily, my grandmother came from a farm on the island of Finnøy. That was our refuge where we went and spent most of the time during the five years of occupation.

I was working on the farm when I was there. I suppose my education was inadequate. I didn't put in my seven years of elementary school like I should have. But I survived.

I remember the last few weeks before the war ended there were rumors going through. You never knew if it had come to an end or not. The day I remember the war was supposed to end, it so happened I had an American flag and a Norwegian flag in the attic. I took those out, and somehow I ended up downtown with those two flags. We started improvising a parade down there. My flags were up front. Of course, when it started getting dark I had to tell everyone I needed my flags to go home for dinner. I started the parade and I ended the parade.

After the war, I still had two years of elementary school to go. The family insisted I continue and at least finish middle school. So I went on with that. I started dabbling in music. I didn't know which way to go. I decided well maybe I get my middle school exam and see what happens then. So instead of taking five years to get my examination I took middle school for three years, then three years to get my examination.

Well, our family: There were 13 brothers and sisters on my grandmother's side. And most of them lived in the area. And we would go from one family to the next, visiting. There was always music, song and music. So music seemed to come naturally. On the paternal side there was a different kind of music, piano music. So I don't know, it started with string instruments, mandolin, guitar, that stuff. But pretty soon when I was a YMCA Boy Scout – *Ynglingen* - they had instruments available, brass instruments, and I got involved playing on brass instruments.

Unfortunately, in 1945 I did not have the chance to be part of the instrumental music program at my school. I only had two years left and they felt, "We can't use him for anything, he won't be ready to play in our band so we won't let him in. We are not going to bother to teach him." So this is why the YMCA bands there were a great help to me.

They say I'm a natural. They told me the story about coming across on *Stavangerfjord* in 1936. They had dance bands on board. And most children weren't allowed around the bandstand. But I'm told that I spent quite a bit of time sitting next to the string bass on board the ship any time they were playing. So, maybe that's where I got my beginning

A lot of [my music] was self-taught, although, I met a lot of people from the church organist to the man who later was my conductor, Jon Wold. He was the first trumpeter in Stavanger Symphony Orchestra. And I had a feeling that he is the one that was behind inviting me into the symphony orchestra when the time came. I was 17 years old, and I ended up playing trombone in Stavanger Symphony Orchestra. And again, back to Ynglingen, the YMCA, they had an orchestra as well. And wouldn't you know that, in one of the back rooms, they had an old bassoon laying around. So I got a hold of the bassoon and of course, that was an instrument that was always in demand. And I started fooling around with that. And, pretty soon, I was playing bassoon.

And it so happened that the oboe player in the Stavanger Symphony, Jon Vik, he was trying out for the position with the Oslo Philharmonic. And he was also the director of the YMCA orchestra.

And when he was trying out, he had the Stavanger Symphony Orchestra director substituting for him. And when he heard me playing the bassoon, he said, "Hey, we need you to play the bassoon in the orchestra."

Anyway, things just fell into place. And I just rolled along with it. And that's also one reason why I was uncertain whether I should stick with school. And I thought, you know, a 17-year-old kid, playing in a professional orchestra. You know, "What? I don't need schooling." But the family insisted that I do it.

And, of course, schooling seems to have been part of my life all along. I was older than most of the students when I got my bachelor's degree at the University of Washington. And when I got my master's degree at Seattle University, I was almost as old as the professors. And when I got my doctorate at the University of Washington, I was older than my professors.

At that time, when you reached 18, then you were called in by the military. I received my papers from New York. I was to report for military duty. And I was in Stavanger, and I didn't have any money to go to New York. I sent the letter back and I said, "Send me a ticket and I'll be more than happy to report."

Well, they refused that, of course. But they said, "As soon as you reach American soil, then you report for duty here."

So, in the meantime, the Norwegian military called me in, too. Through our music acquaintances I'd been more or less promised that I could get into the Norwegian military band. And I thought, well, that'll be right up my alley.

When my papers came, they said, "Report to *Kløvhestkompani Nord-Norge* ." And I thought, that is strange. Here I am, playing in the symphony orchestra in Stavanger, and they want me to sit on a horseback and perform on bassoon or trombone or whatever.

So, I thought, no, this isn't right. There was no band there. Pretty soon, I decided that there's got to be someplace where there's American soil around here. This was after the war and America had bases all over Europe.

The closest I could find was in Zweibrücken and Frankfurt in Germany and on the day that I was supposed to report to the Norwegian military, I stepped on a plane from Sola and flew in down to Zweibrücken.

I said, "This is American soil, this military base?"

They said, "Oh yes this is."

And I said, "I am reporting for duty."

And they put me on a troop ship pretty soon and I ended up in New Jersey – Fort Dix, New Jersey – for basic training. Then they sent me out to Fort Lewis in Washington and that is how I ended up on the West Coast.

After I was done with my military service I found out that the rule was that you can demand to be discharged at the same place where you enlisted.

So I went to the orderly room and I told my first sergeant, "You know what, it's coming time for me to be discharged. I'd like to go and be discharged where I came in." Which was Schleidweiler in Germany. From there I knew my way up to Stavanger. The second bassoon position was still available. I ended up back in the orchestra there. [But] I had met lots of people in the Seattle area, a lot of Norwegians, and they took really good care of me, invited me into their homes. I had good experiences. I had to think of the future and I didn't have the same perspective as I had as a 17- year- old. I ended up going back to Seattle in 1957.

Well, I had to make a living. I got a job at Boeing. I was the Materiel Investigator. Don't ask me what that is. None of the planes that used the parts that I sent have ever fallen down. So my conscience is clear. But then, I wanted to do several things. Of course, I wanted to play, there wasn't anybody in the Norwegian community that played in any bands or anything at the time.

I applied at the University of Washington. I had the idea that if I go in as a pre-major, I can take a lot of the basic courses that I need for any major, any degree. Regardless of where I started or what I aimed at, I seemed to end up in music. Of course, that's where I [met] Professor [Walter] Welke who was the one who sort of helped me along. Played in a band, and so on.

I managed to get through and got my music education degree from the university. Well, I had taken education courses and whatnot, and I had enough credits for a teacher's certificate. Although in my senior year I had played in a Seattle World's Fair Band in 1962. In order to do that, I had to drop out of the last quarter. Then I would come back in the fall and graduate in December instead of June. Of course, Alma wanted to learn Norwegian. Alma's my wife. She is Swedish. They tell me that mixed marriages don't last and we've been married 52 years now.

So anyway, she was taking Norwegian and she had piled up lots of credits. I had to just take some easy courses or whatever. I decided, "Well, I'll take some Norwegian courses."

After graduation, I got the music position at Webster and Whittier elementary schools. Then, I spent 30 years with the Seattle Public Schools.

[In the late 1980s] there were rumors that Henning Boe, editor of the Norwegian newspaper *The Western Viking* was going to sell it when it reached its hundredth anniversary in 1989. He had several buyers that were interested but Henning didn't want to let it go to just anybody. Then he came and asked me if I would take it over. Of course, my journalistic experience was as sports writer for the Western Viking, covering the Norselander Vikings, or whatever name we had for the Norwegian soccer team. Anyway, I got a group together of friends that felt that we should have the paper continue in the Seattle area and we bought it.

Western Viking, founded in 1889, was the oldest Norwegian newspaper in the country. I took over in 1990. We kept it going for another thirteen or fifteen years.[Alf's daughter, Kathleen, succeeded him as editor-publisher in 1997.]

I had the Norwegian Male Chorus [that] I joined in 1960 and I kept going until, oh, I guess, 2006 would probably be my swan song. Although last year I directed the Grand Finale at Sangerfest and they've asked me to do the same thing this year.

Then I had the Ballard Youth Band, I felt that the community bands in Norway had done a lot for me. What do the kids do here when they are through with the school bands? They didn't have a lot of community groups around at the time. Now, today, they're stumbling all over each other. So I decided that all of these students that I have should have some place to go. So, in 1968, I talked to some parents and I talked to some kids. We decided to try this band business. It is sort of a Norwegian tradition we are trying to make here. At the time we had a music store in Seattle named the Stan Boreson Music Center. I talked to them and said,

"How would you like to do that?" They said, "Sure, that's a good idea." So we started the Stan Boreson Youth Band.

It was sponsored by the store. It was not Stan Boreson [longtime Seattle comedian-entertainer] who owned the store. He let them use his name.

Well, we got the band going and I decided that you had to have uniforms. I subscribed to some music journals and there was a school band back east someplace that said that they were getting new uniforms. We'll give you our uniforms. Well, we scraped together the money and, got the uniforms. Of course, they come in all sizes. Most of them were too large for my little kids. But, we got them into uniforms and we marched through the streets of Ballard and practiced like mad getting ready for first 17th of May parade. We played in the Seafair Torchlight Parade. It must have been about 1970.

Of course, our sponsor, Frank Daquilla, said, "You're not having these kids marching in a parade," and I said, "Oh yes, I will." I had seen in the store they had a beautiful double-bell euphonium, which I'd never seen in Norway. He said, "I betcha." I told him, "I really like that euphonium, how much you want for it?" He said, "No, it's not for sale. I'm not going to sell it to you. But if you get the band in the parade this year, I'll give you the horn." I said, "OK, it's a deal." I have the horn today.

At first the uniforms didn't fit that well and pretty soon we decided if we just had blue pants and if the girls wanted skirts, dark blue, navy blue skirts, and just a red pullover and white long sleeve T-shirts. So, that's the uniform we've used. It's lasted almost 20 years.

In 1973, we made a concert tour of Norway. Here Henning Boe was very helpful. He and his wife Randi, they had a travel agency. He knew that the the Oslo Philharmonic used little vessels called Brand VII to travel from Oslo up to the northernmost part of Norway and back down again to play concerts for the people up there. So, he said, "Well, this will be OK for us, maybe." We said, "Sure."

We traveled around from Bergen all the way around to Oslo, and stopped in for concerts here and there and everywhere. We happened to be in Stavanger on the 17th of May, 1973. We led the American school in the parade.

In 1978, we participated in the Copenhagen youth band festival. And we traveled quite a bit around Seattle. The city would call us and say, can the Ballard Youth Band play at so-and-so? Once a Swedish war vessel came in here and they wanted the band to play the Swedish national anthem. So we did. Even if they were Swedes, we played for them.

I led the Norwegian Male Chorus here for close to 50 years and I'm still on-call you might say. They asked me last year to come in and direct the grand finale for the Sangerfest. Now, they asked me to do it this year in July. So, we'll see if I'm still alive in July. You never know.

Yeah, we did some big concerts in all those years, but here, again, there were so many moments that were memorable. For the Sesquicentennial, we performed in the Seattle Opera House. We invited all the ethnic choruses in Seattle. The old Opera House had three stages plus the orchestra pit. We had the Ballard Youth Band in the pit. At the time, I directed the Swiss Chorus also. So they were there. The Germans had Arion mixed chorus; the male chorus. You had Swedish, male and female, and you had Norwegian male and female. Then we have the Latvian chorus and Icelandic chorus. You had Latvians, You had Finns. You had the Runeberg chorus. So, you had a little bit of friction. Memories. These people had gone through terrible things.

I was involved in the 17th of May Committee and Henning Boe and I are the ones that managed to get the parade moved from around Norway Center. We decided that it belonged in Ballard because at the time, in the 70s, Ballard was a Scandinavian stronghold. And the Ballard Youth Band was the official 17th of May band.

Alf Knudsen was born in Brooklyn, New York, and grew up in Stavanger, Norway. He moved to Seattle in 1957. Alf and his wife Alma have a son, Alf, two daughters, Lisa and Kathleen, and two grandchildren. In addition to his work with the Ballard Youth Band, the Norwegian Male Chrous and the *Western Viking*, Alf was president of the Norwegian Commercial Club, president of the board of Norway Center, received a Man of the Year Award from the Norwegian-American Chamber of Commerce and was dubbed Knight, The Royal Norwegian Order of Merit by King Harald V of Norway.

Ingrid Elizabeth Knudsen

*"It was an interesting life out fishing.
I wouldn't have given that up for anything."*

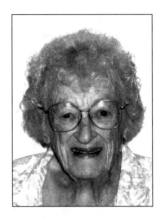

I was born in Chicago. My parents came from Larvik, Norway. My mother was 15 or 16 when my grandmother came over with her family. Her husband had passed away and she took the children to America, got them all settled in and then she went back to Norway. Some of my mother's brothers were engineers like my dad was, and that's how they met. When my mother and dad got married, he worked in Chicago. He was a mechanical engineer or a draftsman, and he got over here working and we lived on Bainbridge Island while he worked in Seattle, in Tacoma, in Salt Lake City. Most of my school years we were on Bainbridge Island.

I met Ed Knudsen there. He had relatives there, and he was clearing some land for them. We met at a St. Patrick's Day dance. After we got married we rented an upstairs in a house in Interbay

In the mid-1930s we rented a place in Ballard, but the place was sold and we had to move, so we bought a little place we thought would do us for awhile, but then we lived there all our married life. We paid $750, maybe $850 for it. We paid down on it monthly, I think $10 a month. It was a lot of money in those days.

We didn't have much, and Ed, being a fisherman, we didn't know what our income was going to be. But we did a lot of work to the house and we lived a very happy life. We added to the south end there, making a big utility room. At the end was Carl's bunk bed from the boat. And we added a complete bathroom — we only had a toilet bowl. We had hot water, with coils in the wood and coal stove. So later on, when we remodeled, we put in an electric water heater and a gas range.

Young's Grocery was on the corner behind us and Almquist Grocery was down the block across from Ballard First Lutheran Church. They had a butcher shop there, so I did most of my shopping there. Otherwise I'd have to walk to Ballard. [see Almquist p. 212]

All three of the kids went to kindergarten to the old Webster School, then across the street to James Monroe and Ballard High.

When Ed was going to build his own fishing boat in the wintertime, I thought, well, the kids are in school, I'll see if I can get on at the school lunchroom. Then I'm home when the kids are home. I thought at least it'd help the kids with nickels and dimes they needed. So I got a job across the street as a beginner helper, and when the cook retired, I ended up being the cook. I thought, well, I might just as well be the cook as getting somebody new in there. I'd have to show her, so I might just as well cook, myself. So I did.

It was always hamburgers on Thursdays and fish on Friday. And maybe spaghetti, toasted cheese sandwiches, and stew or soup. I didn't have to bother with anything but cooking. We had a manager who took care of the ordering and whatnot. I think my kids went home for lunch. They fixed sandwich for themselves.

After the kids graduated from high school. I went fishing with Ed — trolling. Sonja was working and still living at home; Carl had just graduated and was living at home, so I quit my job and went fishing. I've seen the coast. I've been from Santa Cruz Harbor in California to Sitka in Alaska. I used to get seasick on the first day or two out, and then I heard of some good old Norwegian fishermen, who took seasick pills for a couple of days. So I took seasick pills for two days and then I was all right.

Ed had built his boat some years earlier at Interbay. A friend of his had the property, they got together and put up a big shed and they built their boats there. Ed's was 40-foot. He built it down on 15th, just by the Magnolia Bridge. Then they took it to Fishermen's Wharf and launched it. And he worked on finishing it there and he did a good job. That was in 1952. He was interviewed by a fishing magazine, *Pacific Fisherman.* We didn't want to name it after somebody and someone suggested, "Why don't name it the *Reward,* the reward of your hard work?" So that's what it is.

Ed had fished on other boats, halibuting, purse seining. He went sardine fishing in the wintertime in California until we saved enough money to start the boat. He went out on other boats until he finished his own on the off seasons. It was a struggle, but we managed. Then after he built his own, and he tried purse seining on the Sound, the hot spots that he used to know weren't there anymore, so we went trolling. He fished alone, but I'd go out with him maybe one trip or two in the season, and my mother would stay with the kids I did that for quite a few years.

When the children were grown it was several years that I went out with him steady. We did salmon trolling together, just Ed and I. He

Ingrid Elizabeth Knudsen - 347

had four bunks down below. We slept in the top bunk. One lower bunk was full of tools, and the other one was full of our clothes. A trip would be about a week. Then we'd go in, sell our fish to the fish buyer, get cleaned up and visit a little bit. Then we'd fill up with water and fuel and groceries and go out again. We were gone several months, from February or March till September or so. Sometimes the meals were kind of quick and easy, but I enjoyed it. There was bad weather, but generally, if it got too rough to fish, we'd just anchor up in a bay someplace. The main thing was Ed and I were together.

We kept the boat in California most of the time. Ed wanted to overhaul the engine, and we brought it home. When he got it over-hauled, he said, "If you want to see Alaska, this is your last chance." So we spent three years up in Alaska. Then he had his heart attack. He was in the hospital in Petersburg for six weeks. We took it easy going home, and I steered part of the time Of course, he was there when I drove the boat. We fished again in California, but Ed finally decided we'd better sell the boat. He was getting kind of tired, and he couldn't take much more. So we sold the boat in California. He made up his own mind, and I didn't say anything.

It was an interesting life out fishing. I wouldn't have given that up for anything. Of course, Ed and I were together. That was the main thing. It wouldn't be everybody that'd like it, but I enjoyed it.

Ingrid Evensen was born October 10, 1912 in Chicago. Her mother, Borghild Tellefsen was from Larvik, Norway and her father, Carl Evensen was from Shien near Larvik. Ingrid's sister, Ragni (Osterberg) was born in Tacoma in 1917. Her family moved to Bainbridge Island. She met Ed Knudsen there and they were married. They moved to Ballard in the early 1930s. They had three children: Sylvia (1932), Sonia (1938), and Carl (1942). Ingrid worked at the school cafeteria, and later went fishing with her husband. Ed died February, 1999. Ingrid died in 2010.

Anna Jensen Kvam

"There were no streets, just a wagon trail, winding in and out, and then trees all over."

My father had lots of houses and lots, and would rent them out or sell them. I imagine my mother had an education to eighth grade in Denmark. She took care of all the business end of it. He built a little shack to live in. They didn't have water and they didn't have a toilet. So you imagine it wasn't much of a house. Later on, they built this house. They had kerosene lamps. We had to wash that chimney every day and fill it up and sometimes snip the wick so it would be straight.

You had a toilet out in the back, a ways out, you know. And you didn't have any toilet paper. I never heard of that in those days. You had a Sears catalog and they'd cut that in pieces and hang it up on a nail. They did have a chamber pot if you had to go in the night.

When my father built this house, there were no streets, just a wagon trail, winding in and out, and then trees all over. He came to Ballard because somebody he knew had told it's nicer here. He found a job at the Ballard Stimson Mill. We were just two children, my brother, 91 last June, and me, I was 90 in September. I was born at home. You had just a midwife. She'd just come for that time. You couldn't go to the store and get a loaf of bread. You baked all your own. You baked everything. And you canned vegetables. They had kind of a root cellar to keep all their vegetables and things. They raised everything, from potatoes and fruit. We had apples and pears and peaches and prunes.

In the summer we went barefooted. We never wore shoes in the summer months, unless we had to go someplace. We had to help with the work, too. There was berries to pick, loganberries, blackberries, currants, gooseberries. And the garden to help with.

My father had chickens and ducks and there were streams going through. And they had pigs and they had cows. My mother sold quite a lot of chickens, young fryers. And they'd come and get them and she'd kill them right while they were there. There were some Jewish people living in Ballard. And they'd want big, fat chickens. Then they'd take it to the rabbi, and have it blessed. This would be the only place they would buy their chickens. Later on my father sold milk. He had regular customers. He just had a little wagon he pulled, and sold the milk by the quart. They had a regular little milk house where they had water and everything to sterilize the stuff with.

We carried in every bit of water we used from the pump. We had no washing machine. Clothes had to be washed on the board, and we always boiled the clothes. We used wood in the stove. If you bought it in the summertime, you bought it wet. And you had to haul it in and stack it up outside to get dry, then put it in the woodshed to have it for winter. Here on the hills there were bears around even. They weren't that plentiful, but there were bears.

FRANK: My grandfather told me down here, where 52nd and Eighth Avenue is, every two years a bear used to have cubs in an old stump. There used to be a spring on about 56th just above Third. And there were Indians around where Blue Ridge goes down. They had summer camps there and at North Beach and up on the hilltop.

When my grandma came out here, she had to come across in a boat from Denmark to Ellis Island. And then they put her on a train and they had a tag on her — her destination, name, and nationality. And at the stoppings, a lot of times they'd have somebody who could speak Danish to reassure them, let them know they were going the right direction, and ask them if they needed things, and just cheer them up a little bit. She came by herself.

Anna Jensen was born September 1897. Her parents were from Denmark. She married Ben Kvam. Their children: Mildred (1922), Frances (1925) and Frank (1929-1999). Anna died in 1999. Interviewed February 27, 1988 at 326 NW 51st Street in what was Ross, a Ballard suburb.

Lawrence (Larry) Bryan Linnane

"In 1958 I had the world by a string with all my skiing, all my music and a good job."

My grandparents were from a little town called Valley Vaughn in County Cork, Ireland. There were those renegades, the Linnanes. They were just working people, whereas Katie Byrnes's family were property owners. She's getting too thick with this Pat Linnane, so her family sent her to Boston to a brother who had immigrated. She worked as a nanny and a housekeeper, and she saved her money and sent for Patrick. They migrated to Jackson, Michigan, where he worked in the federal penitentiary. It was sometime in the 1880s. And this was the time when the Northern Pacific was coming west to Tacoma. So Patrick and Katie came west and he went to work for the Northern Pacific in the South Tacoma shops, where they built and repaired different types of railroad cars.

They were in St. Leo's Parish in Tacoma. The seven siblings all went to school at St. Leo's. They all went to work right out of high school. My father, Bryan, they always called him Barney, worked in a grocery store, which had a horse and buggy for deliveries. He met my mother, delivering groceries to her house.

Their name was Harrington. She was an only child. Her father died quite young. She and her mother came west. My mother's mother met John Duffy, big hulk of a man. And they married.

My parents were married around 1912. I was born in 1914. His father helped my dad get a job with the railroad. Dad was working at Northern Pacific in B&B, that's Bridge and Building. If he'd move to Seattle, he could get a better paying position in operating, so we came to Seattle around 1916. In 1918, they bought a three-bedroom house at Third Northwest and 70th, really out in the boondocks.

We were in St. John's parish. I was an altar boy there. I went to school at John B. Allen for first and second grade, 1921 and 1922. In the meantime they built a church and a school, which opened up in 1923. So I shifted to St. John's, and right away I became involved with serving mass. The Sisters of the Blessed Virgin Mary were the teachers.

Lawrence Bryan Linnane - 351

Because the school had just opened, the Sisters lived up on the top floor since they started out with only the lower grades. By the time I was in seventh grade, the Sisters were down the street in a large house, which they converted to a convent and the seventh and eighth grades were on the top floor. We had classes in writing, arithmetic, history and of course religion — you know, the basics. Going to Catholic school, we had homework. After dinner every night we gathered around the big table to do our homework. There were five of us. Marie, Eileen, Betty, and then another redhead, Jackie — but Jackie died of meningitis when he was seven years old.

We had spelling bees about once a month. All the school went to the auditorium and Father Quigley gave us a spelling test.

My dad worked for the railroad during the Depression. As I recall, he was the only father on the block who had a steady job. There was no welfare or food stamps in those days.

After St. John's I went to O'Dea for two years. And then my junior year, my mother condescended to send me to Ballard High. I was up early in the mornings and out at night collecting. It meant I could peddle my paper route and come home and go to bed for a couple hours and then go to school. Well, Ballard High School wasn't much of a challenge compared to O'Dea. No study periods at O'Dea, no gym periods. Ballard had two study periods a day, and if they gave me any homework, I'd have it done before I came home. I graduated in 1932. However I found it was permissible to stay in school, and at no cost. So, quite a few of us did. In 1933 and 1934 over 200 graduates were still in school. There was no work, and there were subjects I wanted to take. I took commercial arithmetic, commercial law, public speaking, a capella choir and typing. In 1934, and I helped Dick Munson, the basketball and baseball coach.

I tried out for football. I weighed 135 pounds in 1931, and I was up against all those Ballard Swedes and Norwegian boys who could go hunting bear with a stick. I did manage to make the track team. I wasn't a star, but I was always good for a second or third.

There was a brother and sister, Mamie and Harry Gruber, who had a grocery store down on 60th and Fifth, and I used to work there Saturdays for $1.50 a day. And I sure ate a lot of sauerkraut. Then I got a job at Hastings Grocery Store in the Pike Place Market. In 1934, I had an early dismissal and I'd go down and work in the store for from three to six or so. In 1935, I worked there steady, $15 a week.

I was paying $5 a lesson for voice lessons, but I was still saving money, and buying all the groceries for the family, a big family, nine people, including my mother's parents, the Duffys. In fact, we had free deliveries, and I used to have the groceries delivered.

Around that time 1935, 1936, there were Metropolitan Opera auditions. I won, which entitled me to go to New York. But, Depression days, my family was just getting by on my father's salary, and I certainly couldn't afford to go back there so that was the end of it.

Around September, 1936, the railroads hired, and the first five persons they hired since 1928 were sons of railroad men. I enjoyed railroading, and I never felt bad about going to work. It was always interesting. Every day was different for 40 years. I was in the operating department, switchman. And later, with my seniority, a yard conductor. Everything on the railroad is seniority.

I was starting to ski. And I was singing out at St. John, mainly benediction. The next year, 1938, I started teaching skiing up at Milwaukee Ski Bowl. I'd go up on the train Friday night and teach skiing Saturday and Sunday. Mid-season Father asked me what's going on. I said, "I get paid $5 a day for teaching skiing." He says, "We'll pay you $5 if you come home and sing," which I did. I was developing my liturgy, the Gregorian music, the chants. And I was singing weddings and funerals in almost every church in town. I worked afternoons in the railroad for many, many years because I had one or two singing jobs every morning. I was paid by the mass, $5 every time. I also worked on the railroad and in the grocery store.

My high school friend Jim Bennett and I rented a cabin up at Mount Rainier for the whole winter, for $30. And that's where we went. The next year I went back to work for the railroad, but again I got laid off come late fall. So, I went back to the mountain and spent most of the winter, except now I had a room in the inn with two other fellows, Rusty Morris and Rex Clay, with running hot and cold water and maid service, for $60 for the season. I also ran out of money so they let me run up a tab.

When the summer season opened up at Rainier, I had a job because that was the only way they were going to get their money back. And I got $30 a month, room and board, and a dollar for every night I sang on the program, which was almost every night. But then after a month or so, the railroad called me back to the railroad. By 1940 I was teaching skiing, working on the railroad and singing. I worked at the railroad in the afternoons. I had weekends off. I only taught skiing on Saturdays and came home on Sundays to sing at church. I was living at home but I got married in 1941, and in 1942 was a father. So, because of my occupation and the fact I had an infant I was exempt from the draft. During the war, we were short on help and I worked two straight years without a day off. My marriage ended in divorce, around 1944, 1945. I moved back with my folks. I was still singing 20, 30 times a month.

During the 1950s, I joined the Seattle Star Singers, who did concerts and conventions and stuff like that. We gave concerts, sponsored by the Seattle Park Board at Volunteer Park for a few years. The Aqua Theatre was empty and we did the *Desert Song* there. When we did *Oklahoma,* Robert Joffrey did the staging for the ballet and the choruses. We did *The Vagabond King* in 1950; the *Desert Song* in 1950, and I did *Tosca* with the Seattle Symphony. In 1951 we did a Cole Porter night at the Aqua Theatre. We did four shows a summer. And we sang on the Christmas ship, which started during the '50s. It consisted of members of the Seattle Symphony and six singers. It was pretty much just around the Sound and Lake Washington. We did *Oklahoma* in 1954. Larry Linnane was Will Parker. *Guys and Dolls, Damn Yankees, Oklahoma, Carousel, Kiss Me Kate.* I didn't have a favorite — I loved them all.

In 1958 I had the world by a string with all my skiing, all my music and a good job. I worked on the railroad till 1976. I was a yard conductor — with runs inside the city. My son is still in railroading. Superintendent. And my grandson, Scott Linnane, is a yardmaster at Everett. And my daughter-in-law works in the ski school. My son grew up in Ballard and graduated from Ballard High. Most of the ski instructors who went through the school with me for so many years were his pals from Ballard High School. And one of them is still with the ski school. He's been with them since the beginning. I'm still involved with the ski school today, as Director Emeritus. So, everything's still in the family.

Lawrence "Larry" Linnane was born July 4, 1914 in Tacoma to Stella (Harrington) and Brian "Barney" Linnane, the oldest of five children. Stella and Barney were raised in Tacoma. Barney's father's parents, Patrick and Katie, were from Ireland. Stella was born in St. Louis. Larry married (1942) Angeline Harrison. They had a son, Ronne (1944). They later were divorced. In 1964 Larry married Jean (Malcolm). Jean died August 22, 2000. Larry died in 2008.

Margaret H. Long

"During the Depression, my father, having the store, said, 'We'll always have plenty to eat, but you may not get new shoes when you think you should.'"

I was born in Ballard, the youngest of three children to Alex and Hannah Koll. Both were immigrants from Finland, but Swedish speaking. They moved into this home when they were married in 1910. We three children grew up there when it was very undeveloped. There were homes, but dirt streets, and we three kids used to stand at the window and watch the horse-drawn carriages bringing wood or milk. I lived at 6534 25th Northwest for 35 years.

All the ethnic groups started their own Lutheran churches. We went by a Swedish Lutheran Church, a Norwegian Lutheran Church, a Finnish Lutheran Church, until we got to our Swedish Finnish Emmaus Congregation up on Second Northwest. That building is still there, but it's been sold to another church group. My father was one of the charter members of that church. That was in 1909.

My father came from Finland in 1903. He worked in grocery stores in the Ballard area for other people till he got his own store. He joined with Alfred Wicks, and they formed Koll & Wicks Grocery. They each owned their own separate stores under that name. Father's was on 24th Northwest and Northwest 62nd. He closed it in 1943.

I got out of high school in 1932, in the Depression, and my father had to let people go. I worked full time several years 'til he closed the store. I did everything — waited on customers and filled orders. My brother drove the truck and delivered the orders to people's homes. A customer came in and stood at the counter, and we did all the running. If they wanted a can of peas, we got a can of peas. If we got telephone orders, we shelved them, boxed them and delivered them in the truck. But nothing was all bagged and boxed like it is nowadays. We weighed up sugar and beans and dried peas and the like in 25-cent, 50-cent, dollar bags. We had chicken feed. We had big sacks of flour. Our warehouse was in the back.

We walked to the Ballard shopping district, but all the stores were on Ballard Avenue. Nothing much was on Market Street until the Eagles built a big hospital building; which is now called 2208 Market Street Building [The Ballard Building]. It's a four-story building on the north side of the street. There was nothing there before. And Ballard Hospital started in that building.

Life was simple in those days, and yet we didn't have all the modern conveniences we have now. My mother had a washing machine, a big copper tub washing machine. She boiled the clothes. As children, it was very simple. We didn't have to go to this and go to that. We made our own fun in the neighborhood with other kids. My mother used to say, "You kids have cheap fun." Nobody had any money to spend, and we did it on our own.

Most of us went to the same school, Adams Elementary and Ballard High School. We walked. Our music teacher at Adams was Miss Lillian Foss. Her father was a Lutheran pastor. She taught music and some gym class. They didn't allow married women to teach until during the war when they couldn't get enough teachers.

My husband was in the war. He went over in 1942 and came back in 1945. We were married in 1946, but we grew up in the same church, and our families were friends. We never got very far from Ballard.

I remember going to *Julotta* early on Christmas morning. It was dark, and when you came out, it was daylight.

My father being in business was trying to be as American as he could because he had to deal with English speaking people. He enjoyed giving speeches. He could get up and give a talk at Runeberg in Swedish or at the grocer's meeting or convention in English.

During the Depression, my father, having the store, said, "We'll always have plenty to eat, but you may not get new shoes when you think you should." We didn't suffer, really. We managed to keep things going, but my father did lose money in the store. He would credit customers who couldn't pay. Some were very honest and paid all they could for as long as they could.

During the war we had rationing. In the store we had to get the stamps from people so they could buy certain things. And then we had to paste those stamps on a big sheet of paper so we could buy wholesale and there were times when you couldn't get butter, and coffee and sugar were scarce, things like that. It wasn't easy.

Margaret Koll was born Mar 24, 1914. She had a brother Eugene and a sister Florence. She and Runar Long were married in 1946. They had two sons, Kenneth and Russell. Margaret died May 31, 2001.

Rose Louie

"More people line up for Chinese food than for American food because they can cook American food, but they can't cook Chinese food."

The restaurant, Louie's Cuisine of China, opened in 1954 at 1471 Northwest 85th, and was there for 21 years. We have been here at 5100 15th Northwest almost 23 years. We see the grandchildren of people who used to come to our old place. We've had to expand. When we first opened, the only Chinese food the customers knew about or would even try would be fried rice, chow mein noodles, things like that. Gradually we have expanded and included spicy dishes and more ethnic [Chinese] dishes. At first people were skeptical, but they tried it and liked it. So we kept adding to it.

More people line up for Chinese food than for American food because they can cook American food, but they can't cook Chinese food. One time a customer come in and said, "I'll never cook Chinese food again." She took a course in Chinese cooking and decided to have a party. She shopped for three days and cooked for three days. By the time she had her guests in, she was so exhausted she didn't enjoy her dinner. She said, "From now on I eat Chinese out."

George was born in Seattle. His father came over from China as a teenager. He worked on the boats and worked his way to America. About 1904, he worked in restaurants up to the level of bartender for the Lincoln Hotel, downtown. It's no longer in existence. He learned English very well, considering he never even went to grammar school. He was intelligent enough to have picked all these things up. I guess if you apply yourself, you can learn.

It's interesting how his father and mother got married. In China they had fixed marriages, where the parents pick the wife or husband for you. In those days there were people who went around fixing you up with a bride or groom. They had books of pictures of available women and his father picked his mother out of a book. He was short and he said, "I don't want short kids." So he picked a tall woman. And his kids turned out tall, except for one.

He was very interested in opera. A Chinese opera company wanted to come to Seattle, so he built an opera house in Chinatown. And then came the Depression and there was no opera to go to and no money to go. So he opened a Chinese restaurant with live music and dancing. Some famous people come there, including Bob Hope and Nelson Rockefeller. They would come by limousine, driven by chauffeurs. That was when Seattle didn't have much in the way of combination dining/ dancing. He continued working in the restaurant but the Depression was a tough go, even for the restaurant.

Then he had a heart attack and his son George took over to run it until World War II came. After the boys were drafted, their father, being elderly and not well, couldn't run the place, so he sold all the shares except he kept one share. When the boys came back after the war, the one share wasn't enough for all of them. George ran [his father's] restaurant before the war, so he went back into it with his dad. He kept the one share. All this was in Chinatown. Gradually the one share wasn't enough to spread around, so he sold it.

Then George decided to strike out on his own, and came out to Crown Hill. From there things went fairly good. He knew people out here. People would talk about this area needing a Chinese restaurant, so he came out and surveyed it and found the spot and put up the restaurant. And people said, "Oh, George, you'll never make it out here. The Scandinavians don't eat Chinese food."

But it worked out okay. He became acquainted with the merchants in the neighborhood. In those days people had time to know their neighbors. He joined the Ballard Rotary Club and became a trustee at Ballard Hospital for nine years. In the meantime, the restaurant on Crown Hill was becoming very old. It couldn't be upgraded without improving the sewer and electrical. If you upgrade a restaurant, you have to redo everything to suit the city. It was too costly to put that kind of money into someone else's building, so he looked around for property and found this place.

We built this place for [our son] and he worked here for five years, and then he was killed in an airplane crash. He was 31 years old. Actually, the restaurant opened and got so busy, he couldn't finish at WSU, and he came here to work. He was going to get his degree at UW — he had only about a year left to finish. This place was very busy at the time, because it was the only restaurant in Ballard big enough for a Chinese restaurant. In the meantime, he took a trip to Costa Rica, there was a plane crash and he died. Very, very tragic because he was a very dynamic kid. Then here we are.

358 - Rose Louie

Another son was in California. He came up to take over. He was headed to New York to work, but his father wanted him to come. George had congestive heart failure, he couldn't work full-time. He could oversee things, but not day-to-day hands-on type of work.

It's a lot of hard work and very expensive to maintain. We close one week every year to scrub the place down and paint and repair or add new equipment, whatever is needed. We've been here over 20 years and things do fall apart when you're open as many days of the week as we are. I don't take vacations anymore because I've done a lot of traveling and don't have a desire to travel anymore. Like they say, I've been there, done that. I get plenty of vacation at home just not having to come to work.

When we opened this place, we had a traditional lion dance. The people of Ballard had never seen anything like it. They were lined up along the street watching the parade. We had a three-day party for the Ballard people.

George's parents had five children, all boys. I have several members of the family working here besides Art, who is George's brother. And my son works here, my nephew works here, and Art's ex-wife works here. Once in a while we need extra help and my niece or nephew will pitch in for a day or so here and there.

A lot of the art and decorations in the restaurant are from the family heirlooms. George's parents and my parents had a lot of things. Before we opened this restaurant, my son and a friend and the architect, went to Hong Kong and bought some of the things we have here. These chairs came from there.

There's really nothing too exciting. We're laid-back people. We don't stir up a lot of trouble or try to make a lot of hoopla. We just go to work and take care of business. That's about it.

Rose Yaplee was born in 1922 in Pasco, Washington. George Louie was born in Seattle in 1910. His father was born in China, his mother in San Francisco of Chinese parents. George died in 1990. Rose continued to run the restaurant with the help of many family members until her death in 2010.

Marie A. Malone

"Any kid that had a dime had a lot of money then."

My parents came here to Ballard in 1908. They both came from the Skee parish in the Bohuslan province of Sweden. My father came to North Dakota and my mother came to Chicago. They did not really know each other in the old country, although their families were known to one another.

He was 35 and she was 28, and she didn't know if she should get married because she didn't know him that well, but she said, "Oh, everybody says, if you've got a chance to get married, get married, because that was about the only way women had."

They were married December of 1904 in Minneapolis. They were four years in New Rockford, North Dakota. She had the one child and was pregnant with the second one when she made the trip here. She remembered the lights of the city at that time and she thought it was wonderful, because she didn't care for a small town.

They rented a place for four years; then they moved to the home where I was born and five years later they moved next door. It was all woods up there when they came here. There were not even gravel roads, just dirt roads and no sidewalks at that time.

My parents didn't go to church but I went to Sunday school. I started when I was five, It was a Swedish church. At Christmas they had a Swedish service, *Julotta.* My mother thought she'd like to go to *Julotta* when I was nine years old. At five o'clock in the morning we walked to church in the snow. Of course, I didn't understand it.

As a small child we played together and when we were probably about ten, eleven, we played ball in the street. We had what we called an indoor ball. It was bigger. There was so little traffic in the neighborhoods that it wasn't too hard to play in the streets. Dad didn't care much for it because they broke our kitchen window once. After we got side-walks, I was about six or seven years old, we used to play hop-scotch. We some-times used a rock to play. And in a game called Squares, we used a tennis ball.

There was at one time an old school house that used to be on the corner of 24th and Market. People rented out for parties or for recitals of music students and dance students here in Ballard. I took piano lessons for a long time from a woman who lived in Ballard. I started when I was nine years old, and I took until I was about 16. For recitals we couldn't have any music — we had to memorize it.

Several little corner grocery stores were within four or five blocks of home. When I was around 12, there was this small chain of Piggly Wiggly Stores. They had groceries and fresh vegetables and I guess meat. One was on 65th and 24th. One other store, called Skaggs, seemed large in comparison to the little neighborhood stores. Most were not much larger than a good sized living room. The grocery store near our school had a lot of penny candy. Some were two for a penny and some three for a penny, like little gum balls. Any kid that had a dime had a lot of money then, you know.

My brother Bus started working for Mr. Jackson at the grocery store on 68th and 32nd when he was 11 years old [1919]. People would call in their order and he delivered with his wagon. Later he had the whole store and he ran it. Bus's store had fresh vegetables, and for ice cream they had a two-hole freezer. Ice cream would be in two flavors. When people bought a quart of ice cream he had to scoop down, and he had these paper cartons that he put the ice cream in. He probably gave more to people he liked by tapping it down a little bit more. A little later the ice cream came in blocks, like a quart of ice cream. Bus would go down to Pacific Fruit, down on Western Avenue, to pick up the fresh vegetables for the day. For meat, they dealt with Kastner's. The [customers] would call Kastner's to have them deliver it up here so when the people got their groceries they could get their meat there, too. Kastner's meat market was on 20th and 56th in Ballard for years and years. It was a Kastner family store, run first by the father, and then his three sons continued on. They did a lot of orders for fishing boats and they had many steady customers. They had as many as four or five butchers working there. Bus sold his store to Victor Anderson in 1939.

In 1931 Ballard High School had a class in retail selling for the first time. They took in 33 students. The teacher, Marion Candee, worked with the downtown department stores: Frederick & Nelson's, Rhodes and J.C. Penney. We had to give a reason why we wanted to work for a store; I wrote something like, "My father was a painter and there wasn't any work and I could use some money."

I worked for the J.C. Penney on Saturdays from the middle of October till Christmas. I was in the women's glove and hosiery department, and the pay was two and a quarter a day. No social security. We got our lunch hour, but no coffee breaks at all. At Christmas they gave us white tissue paper and red ribbon. If [a customer] would like [something] wrapped, we would wrap. There was no such thing as scotch tape then, and we had to tie with this red ribbon and make a bow right at the counter. Of course, there was no pantyhose then, there was silk hosiery and they did carry some cotton. The silk stockings were what we call full-fashioned cut with a seam in the back of the stocking. In the cheap hose, the stitch was tightened at the ankle, then larger at the calf. They really didn't fit. Full-fashion hose was 59, 79 and 98 cents a pair. A little later they had a very sheer hose. It was only two threads of silk. And they were $1.19 a pair. They were surprisingly strong for being so sheer.

I started in 1931, I worked there until I graduated from the University in '36, and I continued working there until January, 1937 when I got a job with a lumber broker.

I took French in high school from Miss Beulah Russell in my senior year. She took me aside one time and she said, "You know, Marie, I really think you should go to college. Even if you get married the day you graduate, I think you should go to college."

I never thought of going to college. My brothers didn't go. One day I told them what the teacher said. And Bus, says, "Well, would you like to go," and I said, "Well, I guess I would," And he thought I should go. I graduated from the University in 1936.

After he sold the store, Bus drove a truck for the Carnation Milk Company. Then he had to go into the service. In 1945, he didn't want to go back into driving, so he took a test for the post office. He thought that's the job where you don't have to collect money from people, so he did that until he retired My brother Rosey worked at Seattle First National Bank as a bookkeeper. And then he had Parkinson's, his eyes went bad and he didn't work after that.

I love it here in Ballard. I really like it here, and I like being close down at the water. And I thought, whenever my husband and I went shopping, we always went down along the water to come home. And I bet if I could have a nickel for every time we went down along the water I'd be rich.

Marie Anderson was born May 27, 1915 in Ballard to John Anderson and Hilda Gustavsson. She had two older brothers: Clarence (1906) or Rosey, and William Howard (1908), or Bus [short for Buster]. Marie married James Malone in 1938. They had four children: James II (1941), John (1944), Thomas (1946) and Jana Marie (1949). Marie was widowed in 1999.

362 - Marie A. Malone

Carl Henry Moen

"I can remember that the boat went underneath the trees and my hat got caught in the limb of a tree and we had to land the boat and I had to walk back about a block and crawl out on a limb and a log and get my hat back again."

I might say a few words about my early rowboat life. Shortly after we moved up on what is now called Sunset Hill, which was all woods, we wanted a rowboat. And we found a boat. We paid three dollars. That was our first rowboat, and right away we wanted to try it out fishing. We kept it on some logs on what is now called Ballard Beach. I can remember our trolling session. The boat was so narrow we couldn't change places hardly. We had to crawl between our legs to change them.

Anyhow, we got up to what we call Meadow Point, just north of Golden Gardens, and we hooked onto a big salmon. And we played him, and played him, and played him out. We didn't have any gaff hooks or landing nets or anything, so we rowed to shore and towed the fish into shallow water, and got him on the beach and hit him on the head. That salmon weighed sixteen pounds. So we went out again and right away we caught a four-pound salmon. That was our first experience.

We never used reels, always hand lines. My father worked at Balcombs Lumber Mill at the time and I can remember Ed and I going down there in the middle of the afternoon to tell him we caught two big salmon.

I can remember distinctly those first two fish we ever caught. Later on we bought a nice rowboat. I think we paid a dollar a foot for the boat. It was a nice cedar boat. We called it Bubbles.

At first, before there was any boathouses around there, we kept the boat right on top of a bunch of logs on what we called Ballard Beach. Later, when Johnny Jacobsen built a boathouse where Ray's Boathouse now stands, we used to keep the boat there. We made many, many trips, like blackberry picking in the summer time or going up to Lake Washington and down the end of the lake and down the river.

Back when I first got the camera [1908 or 1909] Ed and I took a trip around the loop as we called it. We rowed up the canal to Fremont and pulled the boat over to Lake Union and then we rowed through the University District and got up to the portage and we took the boat across the portage and into Lake Washington.

From there we rowed down to Seward Park for the night, and in the morning we hauled the boat across the slip, before they lowered the lake, into the lake and rowed down to the end of the lake looking for the river. We couldn't find it and we saw some fishermen there and we finally asked them where the river was and they pointed where it was.

That was the Black River. The Black River ran out of the south end of the lake. So we went slowly down the Black River and all of a sudden we heard the Cedar River. The Cedar River comes into the Black River.

And we went down just like a bullet. We thought we could just sit in the back and just steer the boat. We found out soon enough that both of us had to row to keep the boat in the middle of the river.

I can remember that the boat went underneath the trees and my hat got caught in the limb of a tree and we had to land the boat and I had to walk back about a block and crawl out on a limb and a log and get my hat back again. From then we had to sit there and row the boat to keep in the middle.

But after two or three hours it widened out and we got down to this wider river, the Duwamish. And we went down two or three miles it seemed like and back again and we could look across the river — in them days. Now they have it straightened out. I remember that night we stayed where Boeing is now. Nothing around there, no farms or nothing, the river and just empty land.

We went from there the next morning. No Harbor Island at all at that time, just right out past Luna Park over to West Point and back to Ballard, to make the whole round trip in a weekend.

In the early part of the last century, boats were a more common means of transportation for the people of Ballard than they are now. When Henry and Ed Moen were young men, they would row over to Bainbridge Island to picnic with girls who lived there, to Discovery Bay to dig clams, to Sequim to hunt, and one weekend, they rowed around the outskirts of Seattle. This account is edited from transcripts of audiotapes, recorded October 9, 1977, of conversations with Carl Henry Moen by his son, Morris Moen.

Ed and Henry Moen in boat

Ed and Henry fish camping

Ed and Henry camping

Carl Henry Moen - 365

Morris Moen

"[Lars Brekke] wasn't a huge fellow. He was only about five seven or eight, but he was quite muscular. He had big, strong hands and could pound all day on the anvil."

All four of my grandparents came from Norway. And they are a part of the now-vanished generation. So all we have is my memories at this point. My mother's father was Lars Olsen Brekke, and her mother was Kristianne Marie Arnesdatter Fosnes. The Brekke farm and the Fosnes Farm were both located in Oppstryn, Norway. Lars and Kristianna went to the same church and the same school. Lars's father was a blacksmith. Lars said he marveled at how his father could make a threaded nut and bolt, not to any standard size, but that would fit each other.

Kristianne Fosnes was the seventh of eight children. She wanted to go to school so she could be a teacher, but her father figured she'd just get married and it would be a waste of money. She said if she couldn't go to school, she'd go to America. Lars decided if she was going, he would go, too. About 25 young people left to go to America, so they had a church service and a party for them.

They took the *SS Catalonia* from South Hampton and arrived in Boston on June 1st or 2nd in 1884. They each brought one piece of baggage. On the voyage Kristianne changed her name to Christine. They took the train to Minnesota, where Christine lived near Blue Earth for five years. She moved to Seattle shortly before the fire of June 6th, 1889. After four years in South Dakota, Lars moved to Seattle in June, 1888. He worked on the tugboat *Blakeley* for 11 months. Then he got a job at Westermann's shop. While he was working ten hours a day and six days a week there, he built a house all by himself on Charles Street [near Dearborn, north of Beacon Hill], as a home for Christine and himself. Lars and Christine were married July 5th, 1890, in the basement of the Norwegian Lutheran Church, which was still under construction.

In 1900 the workers had a strike at the shop, so Lars decided to go to Alaska as a blacksmith to sharpen picks and shovels for the gold miners, leaving Christine with six small children and $10. There was no work left in Alaska, so he came back. He took a paddle wheeler down the Yukon and missed the steamer, the *Islander,* which sank just a short way out of Skagway. Christine didn't know he missed the boat and when she saw the paper showing the *Islander* had sunk, she fainted. A few days later they got word that Lars was not on the boat.

In Alaska, Lars noticed that anybody with a trade had something to do during the day even if it wasn't very much, so he decided to open his own blacksmith shop. He started the shop in Ballard. He got his steel from Schwabacher, near Pioneer Square. He walked two hours to get there and walked back with 40 pounds of steel — to save ten cents in streetcar fare.

When he first started blacksmithing, Lars collected rainwater in a puddle outside to quench the steel. He knew how to temper the steel so that it would not be so brittle that it broke and not be so soft that it wore out. Picks and shovels were a big part of the business in those days, as well as things for the fishing industry.

The family moved from Seattle to Ballard in 1903. Before that, Lars commuted to the shop from Charles Street, a long walk, or by streetcar. And when Olaf, his oldest son, was seven, eight years old, he would come out to the shop after school to help his father. He was so small and young, the streetcar motorman wouldn't stop for him alone, so he'd get on where a group of people were waiting to board. He became an expert blacksmith and was the backbone of the shop.

Lars was a good blacksmith, but there were three important people working at the shop with Lars who really made it go. One was his son Olaf. The other two were Bill Andersen and Howard Keenan. Ole's son Darold, when he was grown, became an expert like his father and grandfather. Norm, Lars's other son, became business manager succeeded by *his* son Eugene. Now Eugene's son Marshall also works at the shop. The shop continues today, under grandsons Eugene Brekke and Darold Brekke, although it has moved from blacksmithing to welding.

The shop made a lot of hatch-cover staples. A hatch is an opening in the deck of a ship where the cargo goes in. Hatch covers were made of heavy, heavy planks. The hatch-covers had a semi-sphere cut out of the plank, with a staple across, so they could put a hook under the staple and lift the hatch cover off, usually with a winch. Those staples from Ballard went all over the world wherever there was salt water.

Christine was about as tall as Grandpa and very dignified. She was a hard worker, keeping up the house, especially with Grandpa's dirty work. The dirt was ground into the palms of his hands, so his palms were always black, his fingers black.

One problem with living so close to the shop was the nearby Seattle Cedar Lumber Mill's burner — the sawdust turned to charcoal in the stack and it would get through the screen at the top and go all over south Ballard. They called it "Ballard snow." It was black and it would drift like snow against the steps, and it was just an awful mess. It left marks on the laundry whenever the wind was from the south, which it frequently was.

Lars was very outgoing, loved to tell stories and jokes. He repeated his jokes over and over, and he always laughed at his own jokes. He wasn't a huge fellow. He was quite muscular, but he was only about five seven or eight, but he had big, strong hands and could pound all day on the anvil. Eventually he got a trip hammer which he would operate with his foot and that would do the heavy pounding. He called it his "best girl."

In 1930, Lars and Christine were going to go to Norway, take a trip to see their families. Both Norm's wife Martha and Laura were expecting at that time so Grandma Brekke thought she would rather stay in Seattle. But Lars went back to Norway. He had never left Norway in spirit. He wrote constantly to people there. Almost 50 years later, we were visiting there and heard several people remark, in Norwegian of course, "I remember so well when Lars Brekke came to visit from America in 1930." I think Lars Brekke was more satisfied that he had made the right decision in leaving Norway after he made that trip.

When I was 12 years old, I worked at the shop for a week. They only let me sweep the floor and such until the last day. Then Lars let me pound some steel on the anvil, red hot steel. I learned how to start fires in the forge and that kind of thing. I did that in the morning when I came in. But at 12 they didn't trust me to do much blacksmithing.

In 1950 my cousin, Eugene, and I were at Grandma and Grandpa's house. I had my wire recorder and we asked Grandpa to tell us about the old days and he talked for at least an hour. Later I had that wire recording transferred to tape. Excerpts from that tape can be played in the Nordic Heritage Museum's "Dream of America," in the Ballard section, near an image of Lars Brekke.

Lars worked at the forge until he was 86 years old, but when his beloved Christine died, he never went back to work. She died March 18th, 1951. He died a month later, April 20th, 1951.

Morris Moen was born in Ballard August 2, 1925 to Henry and Laura (Brekke) Moen. Henry's parents, Ole and Anna (Henrrikson) Moen were born in Norway, met in Minnesota and married and raised their children in Seattle, Ballard after 1894. [See Wylie p. 478] Laura's parents were both from Oppstryn, Norway. They married in Seattle and lived in Ballard from 1903. [see Smith p. 442]. Morris attended Webster, James Monroe Junior High, DeVilbiss High in Toledo, Ohio, and graduated from the University of Toledo and worked as a chemist in the paint industry. He retired in 1990. Morris married Marilyn "Lynn" Rolie in 1958. They have four children: Martha (1959), Keith (1961), Arne (1963) and John (1965), and six grandchildren.

Richard Philip "Dick" Nelson

*"I didn't picture myself as a politician.
I pictured myself as someone who . . .
was interested in current affairs."*

I was the last of five children. I grew up
in lower Ballard in a working class
neighborhood. Down the street were
Norwegian families, including the Brekke
family. Their blacksmith shop went back
even before my parents came. And I grew
up with Brekke children. It was a mixed
Protestant and Catholic neighborhood. I
remember going west to Adams Grade School while my childhood
friends went east to St. Alphonsus School. And somehow that led to
perceived differences between us. They had school uniforms, we didn't.
And I think there was some childhood animosity that developed. They're
different from us. Unfortunately that wasn't unusual in those days. I
think it's changed now.

My father died when I was in junior high school, and we moved to
85th and 32nd Northwest. I was closer to the Sound then, so I spent a
lot of time at Ray's Boathouse. In those days it was a center of sports
fishing with boats to rent. We went there to see the big salmon come in.
As a kid, I watched that and fished through the cracks in the dock there
for perch. Now it's a restaurant.

Before my father died, he and I were fishing buddies at North Beach.
An old Portuguese gentleman operated a boathouse there. The boats he
rented looked like they had seen their best days long ago.

In those days you could catch bottom fish. My father was into fishing
to put food on the table, not as sport. That was how they fished in the old
country. He came from an area on the west coast of Sweden, right on the
Kattegat Sea. A lot of small fishing boats there went out and harvested.
He enjoyed fishing. It took him away from real work, but it was still
fishing for a purpose. We would bring back boxes of flounders and sole,
and occasionally, some other fish. We caught them on drop lines with four
or five hooks on them, so when you pulled up your line, you pulled up four
or five flounders at a time. Really catching fish the most efficient way.

First we found sand worms for bait in an area between Golden
Gardens and North Beach. They were maybe five inches long, thick

worms, ideal bait. We also sometimes found a few clams to use.

Then we would go out. I bailed to keep the boat from sinking. When we got home we cleaned those fish, which was quite a job. I think that my mother canned some of them. We ate a lot of fish for a few days. And we gave away quite a bit, too.

I remember exploring the old jail and City Hall in Ballard. We'd try to sneak in when it was operating. We didn't get very far, but then it closed down by the earthquake in '49. Some of my friends and I were probably in junior high school then. We went in to check out the cell. We had never gotten as far as the jail, itself. Once they had officially closed it, we could see the jail. It was kind of a satellite building for the City of Seattle. And they had a holding cell there because once it was the jail and the City Hall for Ballard. It was where 22nd meets Ballard Avenue.

I graduated from Ballard High School, class of 1954. I grew up in a family that was very attuned to current affairs. And so there were a lot of discussions about the war and about government and politics and other issues of the time. I think that those family discussions lead to an interest that I have in our system of government; and eventually was responsible for me getting involved in politics and running for office. I served eight terms in the Legislature for 16 years.

I went to the University when I was living at home for four years, and then I went to graduate school in Massachusetts. I spent four and a half years at M.I.T. in Cambridge, Massachusetts. After I got my graduate degree I went to Sweden, and lived there for a year and a half and worked at a Swedish research institute.

I had an uncle there who was married to a Norwegian woman. They lived in the fishing village where my mother grew up. They actually lived in the house where my mother was born, a beautiful spot. One of my relatives was a lighthouse keeper, just a few hundred meters away.

It was very difficult not to stay, but I had to decide between two cultures. And Sweden was still a very different culture. As much as I knew about it, some of the language, some of the customs, I was not prepared to become a Swede. Swedes are somewhat different than Americans. They're less outgoing and I found myself still feeling not quite at home there.

After a year and a half, I had to make a choice. I wasn't prepared to change my life that drastically. And I needed to go back. That was my interest in government and politics showing up. And I couldn't do that in Sweden.

I was working in high temperature chemistry. I got my graduate degree in materials science. My first degree was in ceramic engineering. I was working on what are called inorganic materials, including a kind of high tech materials. One of my interests was in nuclear materials. I went from Sweden to Hanford and worked there in the nuclear materials industry. Our job was to try to make nuclear reactors safer by understanding the properties of the nuclear fuels that are at the heart of nuclear reactors. I spent five years at Hanford, at the Battelle Memorial Institute there.

I didn't picture myself as a politician. I pictured myself as someone who, because of my family experience, my family was interested in current affairs; and my college experience — I got involved in some of the issues during that time. And after that, when I went to Richland and Battelle, I got involved more directly in the political scene over there. But I was not yet an aspiring politician. However, in 1970, I made a life choice, that I was going to leave the profession that I had been trained for and be more directly involved in politics. So I came back to Seattle and worked for a candidate who was running for the U.S. Senate in that year. And then I got involved in a statewide political organization.

A couple years later I decided that I should run for the state legislature. I lost my first try, but I succeeded the second time.

Now I have a consulting firm. And I do what I call urban dynamics, which is, I work on public policy issues involving transportation and land use. Yeah, it is a sticky wicket.

Richard Philip Nelson was born May 1, 1936. His parents, born in Sweden, emigrated in the 1910s, came to Ballard 1918. He has four older siblings. His father was a shipwright, and before coming to Seattle, worked in Texas and at Yellowstone Park. Dick served as a state legislator 1977-1992.

Stanley Nelson, Jr.

*"The dealership is still in the family.
My three daughters have it and they run it."*

My great-grandfather had some property in downtown Seattle. Then he moved out to Ballard. He had a hotel called the St. Charles. It had a bowling alley, a bar, rooms, and a dining room of some type. Both my parents grew up in Ballard. They lived about a block from each other near the Ballard Playfield by Adams School. They went to Salmon Bay School and when Adams was built they went there.

I remember them saying that there were 21 shingle mills along Ballard, and just as many beer parlors or bars. My mother graduated from grammar school, but I don't think she went to high school. She used to work in a box factory where she made little wooden boxes. My dad went to Ballard High School, only for a year, I think. They got married young, they were both 19, and I was born the next year. He worked around, then a little gas station in Ballard on Leary and 20th came up for sale, and they paid a couple hundred dollars for it in about 1920. It was a small building, and a hand pump that pumped one gallon at a time. When they got gasoline, it was brought in by a team. There was a tank in the ground and a team of horses would bring the gas to the station. They probably only took 150 to 200 gallons. There just weren't that many cars around. They also had garages where people would leave their cars there overnight. Some people were scared to take them home; they didn't want to put them in their barns for fear of fire from the gasoline. My dad built seven or eight garages just to hold cars. People would leave them in the garage and then walk home. That lasted maybe three, four or five years.

In those days when you'd have a flat tire, instead of replacing it, they'd repair them. They had real sharp knives and they'd cut the sides out wherever the hole was. Then they'd put this raw rubber over it. They would put a "boot" inside the tire and then they'd rub these big heavy rollers over this raw rubber. Then they'd put it into kind of like a steam chamber the size of the tire, heat it up and that would cure the rubber. That's how my dad and my uncle did it. This was the first gas station in Ballard.

The first car that my dad had was the Overland. In those days cars were new. They had very few parts. And then, when he got into the Chevrolet business, there was a fellow by the name of Kellogg, who I understand was a logger. And he and my dad were partners in the Chevrolet business in 1922.

There was an old stable at 4918 Leary Avenue. And they went in there and put a plate glass window in by the front part of it and made a showroom. In the back, where there had been stalls, they made a little parts department. They had a mechanic, and that's where they worked on the cars. A very small operation at that time. He had maybe three, four cars.

For a long time, the cars came in railroad freight cars, or a regular boxcar. And they would come down to Seaview and they would park the boxcar there. When I was a kid, they'd go in there with a block and chain. And they had wood which would hold the cars up. They'd hold up one and then drive another one under. Maybe there'd be four cars in a boxcar. And they would use this block and chain, lift it up and unload them and push them out. And then they'd get them to run, and we would drive them up to the car dealership.

Today, we're one of the oldest family-owned dealerships — I know in Seattle— and probably one of the few in the whole United States. The dealership is still in the family. My three daughters have it and they run it. And Pam has a dealership up in Mt. Vernon. She has a Toyota, Buick and Pontiac. Barbara has the Acura dealership in Bellevue. And Frederika had always been a homemaker. And she's in there, too. All three of them, now.

Stanley Nelson, Jr. was born July 11, 1915. His mother was born in 1895 in Ballard. Her parents, Mr. & Mrs. Bloomsness, were from Norway, came to Minneapolis in the 1880s. His father's family came from Sweden, to Canada first. All were in Ballard before 1900. Stanley attended Adams, Webster, Ballard High. Attended the University of Washington for one year, married Janet Barry. They had a son, Stanley Nelson, 3rd. Janet died in her late 20s. He then married Ann, who was widowed with a small daughter, Barbara. They adopted each other's child, then had two more daughters, Fredrika (1949) and Pam (1952). Stanley Nelson, Jr. died August 24, 2001.

Harold L. and Alice (Tangen) Ness

*"I really bonded with my grandmother
in that year. I am so happy that I had
that opportunity to meet and get to know
my grandmother."*

ALICE: My father grew up in the
Sognefjord near Høyanger. He was
orphaned when he was three years old. I
think his brother was a year and a half. They
were raised in two different families. My
father's name was Lasse Tangen, and his
brother Øystein took the name of the people
who raised him, Berge. Lasse came to America probably when he was
19 or 20. He went to Alaska for the gold rush, and when he was about

48 years old, he went back to Norway. My
mother grew up in Leirvik i Sogn and was the
oldest of six children. I think they probably
met in Bergen. She was 29, and he was 48.
He wanted to come back to Seattle. And she
said, "Okay, if you take my three brothers."
So they came here, in April of 1923, and I
was born in June. My mother, more or less,
ran a boarding house for her brothers and
cousins who came. It seemed like there were
always a lot of people around. But sadly,
she took ill, and she died at the age of 34,
when I was five years old. That was a very
sad time, and my father tried to be both mother and father to me, and
even though he had to work very hard, he would spend his weekends and
every Sunday with me. And one very hot day when he was working, he
suffered a stroke and he died. He was 56 and I was seven.

A month earlier, my mother's oldest brother, Leidolf Systad, had
married Christine, who was the oldest of ten children. They moved into
my house, at 4318 Greenwood Avenue North. And Christine, just 22
years old, inherited a seven-year-old and two brothers-in-law, Toralf and
Oscar, who also lived in the house. She did all the cooking and washing,
and it was not a very easy time for her.

Then, my grandmother in Norway, my mother's mother, wrote, saying,

"Alice is my only grandchild and I really would like to see her before I die. At least you'll have food if you come, because we live on a farm." In 1934, Uncle Leidolf, a carpenter, didn't have any work because of the Depression, and by this time they had a two-year-old son and I was 12. We gathered together enough money for the fares, took the train from Seattle, took a steamship from New York and went to Norway for a year on my grandmother's farm. I went to school there. I really bonded with my grandmother in that year. I am so happy that I had that opportunity to meet and get to know my grandmother. The Christmas we spent there was really wonderful. We went around visiting all the neighbors for a whole week and we had all this good Norwegian Christmas food. The children went around the Christmas tree, and it was a very nice time.

When I came to Norway, my grandmother spoke no English, and I spoke no Norwegian. We got there in June and by the time I started school, I was quite fluent in Norwegian. And just before we came home, June 1935, I noticed I was thinking in Norwegian. So then I had to come home and reverse that.

So we came back to Seattle, and my uncle decided to build a house at 6215 Second Avenue Northwest. We moved in when I was 13. I went to West Woodland Grade School for a half of year, then to Ballard High in 1938. I graduated in 1941.

HAROLD: My dad, Hans Ness, immigrated to North Dakota to homestead, to get this big free land around 1910, but he went back to Norway with his brother. He received an invitation to come back to the United States, to form a partnership with Bartleson, a bricklayer. My father was a carpenter and he also set stone. So Bartleson and Ness became partners. This was in the middle west.

I was born in Green Bay, Wisconsin, where they were building the YMCA Building there. They moved from job to job. Whenever there was a big crop, the first thing people wanted to do is build a church. And it had to be bigger than the other one down the corner. So, as contractors they developed a relationship with labor, and when they would move, they would set up camp and put up platforms and erect tents. The wives and children would be there. The kids loved it.

They were low bidders on the R. A. Long High School in Longview. That was their first job in the Pacific Northwest. Then they bid on the Civic Auditorium [in Seattle], which later became the Opera House. And they were low bidders on that. That was right before the big crash. That's how they got out here.

And then my mother wouldn't move again. We were living on

Phinney Ridge, 6220 First Avenue Northwest, and I went to the eighth grade at John B. Allen, then half of the class went to Lincoln and half to Ballard I graduated from Ballard High in 1941.

The construction business was hard during the Depression. My dad didn't have a job for five years. There were two of his cousins, fishermen, who lived with us, Sig and Tryg Petterson. They paid room and board, and they brought a lot of fish home.

ALICE: We both went to Ballard High School, and, of course, Harold and I knew of each other. Harold's parents were charter members of Harmony Hall, because it was started by *Nordlandslaget*, and they were members. Harold was the cashier at the dances and I had my eye out for him.

HAROLD: I thought you said I was snooty.

ALICE: You were, in school. He'd take his glasses off and when he walked down the hall, he couldn't see to say hello to people. Well, anyway, we began dancing together at Harmony Hall. It was a really nice place — the Norwegian people would bring their sons and daughters, and it was an opportunity to dance. I think we grew up knowing how to do the schottische, the polka and the hambo and everything. And then the ladies would have this wonderful lunch to serve at intermission. All the good sandwiches and coffee cakes and things like that. And it was just such a treat to go there.

Then we went dancing at the Swedish Club every Sunday night. And we'd just have so much fun because there was just a great group of people that went there. And we went up to Bert Lindgren's out on the Bothell Highway. We did a lot of dancing in those days. Then the war came and Harold was drafted and went in the Army in 1942. We became engaged then; we were both 19. And then he went off to war. We were married in August 1944, when he was on a furlough. When Harold was discharged from the Army, we lived with his parents. During the war, his father had bought about seven lots in the north end of Seattle. When we came home, he said, now you can choose one of these lots — at that time they cost like $750 for a lot. We chose one over by Green Lake on Fremont and North 77th. So Harold, his brother and his father built our first house. We lived there for 22 years and had three boys.

HAROLD: My brother was partners with Aksel Fiksdal. They built the Crown Hill School, and the aviary at Woodland Park. And then they were low bidders on the Bear Grotto which was built the same time the Feline House was built. The Bear Grotto was designed to be concrete, cast in place. And it required a concrete pour of every third day. And

Harold and Alice (Tangen) Ness - 377

when it came to hoist it, they took bids, and O. A. Gordon, who had the first crane mounted on a truck, did the job. He said he'd like to sell his two cranes. I didn't know much about cranes, but I thought there might be a chance to get a start. This was in 1950. That's how I got launched into the crane business.

I didn't know anything when I started. We've been very fortunate. And I had very good men working for me. You have to try to satisfy the customers, and get the repeat business. It was hard breaking into it. When you have competition, friendship helps.

Alice and Harold Ness
August 12, 1944

ALICE: We bought our cranes in May of 1950, and Larry was born in 1947, and Eric was born the 31st of January, 1949. The "office" of the crane business was our home. And when the phone would ring, that would excite the children and they'd want to make a lot of noise and run around the house because Mother's on the phone. And so it was kind of a hectic time. At first we had so few jobs, it was easy to write them down and keep them in a book.

But then things got more complicated because there were tax statements and reports that I wasn't familiar with. One of Harold's old school friends from John B. Allen and Ballard, Einar Bugge, was an accountant, and he would come over at night and do bookwork.

As the business became more successful, we moved the crane business down to 1125 Northwest 53rd, a building which was built and bought by Fiksdal and Ness, Harold's brother and his partner. Eventually, Fiksdal pulled out and it was just Ness, and so the two Nesses merged into business, Ness Construction and Ness Crane. And then Harold's brother, Fred Ness, died very young at the age of 57 of emphysema and lung problems. So that's that story.

When the children were seven, eight years old, and during summertime, Harold would sometimes take them down to the yard and give them a bucket of black paint, and they would stand there painting boom sections. Come home all covered with paint. It was a way they could earn a little money. As they got older, they would work down there during summer. Our youngest son Randy and his friend set up the

378 - Harold and Alice (Tangen) Ness

computers for Ness Crane. They all graduated from the University of Washington, and are Eagle Scouts.

The oldest one, Larry, was a crane operator, so he knows the business on both ends. He now runs the business and will soon be its president. Our middle son, Eric, worked for Ness Crane, but his original dream was to become a minister, and he is finishing up going to seminary. He's 51. [He graduated June, 2001 and is chaplain at St. Peter's Hospital in Olympia.] Our youngest son, Randy, got a bachelor's degree and his M.B.A. at the University of Washington, and has worked for Price Waterhouse since he graduated. And we have four grandchildren.

Alice Tangen was born June 3, 1923 in Ballard to Lasse Tangen and Hansine "Sina" Systad, both from Sognefjord, Norway. She graduated from Ballard High 1941. Harold Ness was born in Green Bay, Wisconsin on August 7, 1923 to Hans Ness and Agnethe Caroline Pettersen. His parents were both from the Vesterålen Islands in northern Norway, Agnethe, the oldest of six children, and Hans the oldest of eight children. Hans immigrated to North Dakota to homestead in 1910 but returned to Norway in 1916 to marry Agnethe. They both came to the United States in 1917. Their children: Fred (1918), Margaret (1920) and Harold. When the boys were grown, they worked for their father until they started their own businesses. Alice and Harold were married August 12, 1944 when he was on furlough during WW II. They have three sons: Larry (1947), Erik (1949) and Randy (1950). Harold died in 2002 and Alice in 2012.

Harold F. Nilsen

"We worked at the store day and night; me, my wife, and my three daughters, too. It was a family affair. Sometimes the daughters worked 'til midnight on a Friday to get ready for Saturday."

We moved from Astoria to Seattle in 1928. I was born with asthma. The doctor told my dad they'd better get me out of Astoria to a drier climate. So they tried Seattle first, and my asthma left me. We had a lot of relatives who lived in Seattle. The fishermen came to Seattle from Norway. Halibut fishing was big in those days. The people we lived with temporarily [the Surland Ness family] came in with 75,000 pounds of halibut. They got three cents a pound for the best grade, and one cent a pound for the other. And each man had to divvy up $75. They went in the hole. That was the Great Depression of the 1930s.

When I was about 13, I was a *P.I.* carrier from 65th to 85th and from Third to Eighth Northwest, a big route. Then I got a job at the Safeway store on Northwest 75th and Sixth Northwest. They had no delivery service. I had a wagon and I delivered to some of the women. I got a dollar for the first day I worked on a Saturday.

I worked there until Franklin D. Roosevelt came into office — no more child labor, you had to be 16. So I got laid off. I went back to being a *P.I.* carrier again. And then when I was 16, I went to work for Safeway. And when I graduated from Ballard High School, I got a full-time job at the Queen Anne store for a couple of years. Then, I became a Safeway manager on 105th and Greenwood. On Christmas Eve in 1940 I became manager of a new store on Greenwood at 71st. I had 12 people working for me, one man, all the rest women, because it was the war years. But I still was 1-A and was going to get drafted, so I quit. I shouldn't have, because I flunked the exam.

In 1938 I had bought a brand new Chevrolet. And I went down to show it to some good friends, and I met Evelyn Tomren there. And on August 23, 1941 we were married. She was born in Ålesund, Norway, but grew up in Ballard.

I decided I would try something else, so I went tuna fishing with my brother-in-law, John Vatn. [see p. 380, 464] Later I bought a little grocery store at 75th and 32nd Northwest on Sunset Hill, just a little "mom and pop." I had a very rich customer, a retired lumberman from Juneau, Alaska, who lived on that lookout on 75th and 34th. He used to come in and see how hard Evelyn and I worked. He said, "You should have a new store." I said, "Well, I know I should, but I don't have any money." So, he said, "Well, you find a location and I will help you." I found a vacant lot in a good location on 63rd and 32nd Northwest, and bought it. And he gave me all the money I needed — just made me take out a big insurance policy. We broke ground in 1950, and on April 5th, 1951, we opened the new store. It really was a big event. We gave away a new live baby at the opening. My cousin, [Ragnhild Wulff-Nilsen, now Mrs. Henning Boe, see p. 143-146], had just come from Norway. She was a nurse and gave it away in her uniform. It was a baby pig. We also gave away a TV set.

We worked at the store day and night; me, my wife, and my three daughters, too. It was a family affair. Sometimes the daughters worked 'til midnight on a Friday to get ready for Saturday.

At that time, self-service meat was illegal in the Northwest. You'd have to wait for the butcher to cut and wrap it, and put the price on, and take the package to the check stand. I had heard that self-service meat would be allowed the following February in Washington state so I chanced it and bought self-service fixtures. We were the first in the Northwest to have self-service meat. And we were the first store to have a Van de Kamp Bakery in-store. We took in the money, and hit a certain key, to show what we'd pay Van de Kamp.

6306 32nd Ave. N.W.
BALLARD'S MOST MODERN SUPER MARKET

Nilsen's Foodliner, from a September 16, 1954 ad.

Harold F. Nilsen - 381

I was also the first one to have these speedy checkouts where the customer unloaded the groceries, and then we had this little thing at our hip. We just touched it and the table went around. They said it would never work. The customer won't do it. I had four boxboys for three check stands, they were so fast. And, lo and behold, that's what they all have now.

A lot of Scandinavian immigrants shopped at our store because of our name, Nilsen's Foodliner, that's a dead giveaway. And that's when they were really coming from Norway and, thank goodness, with my wife being the checker, she understood them. We both speak Norwegian fluently. The hardest part for the Norwegians was spices, because there's no correlation at all between the name of something in Norway and here. To this day, we talk to people who remember coming in to our store in the 1950's and asking about spices — like, oh, cloves are *kryddernellik*, and cinnamon is *kanel* — stuff that like, in Norwegian. We had a lot of specialties from Norway — there was a [wholesale] company that had all the specialties. We carried all the Norwegian stuff in a special section, so they didn't have to look for it.

We had credit and delivery, I'll never forget the big snow of 1949. My delivery boy didn't come home till 7:30 at night. He was stuck in the snow delivering down in North Beach. We had a delivery boy, afternoons and the Saturdays. We were closed Sundays, of course.

I was in the grocery business until 1962. Then I sold the store. By that time I was in the travel business big, as a founder of Holiday House Cruise & Travel Service, and as a tour leader for groups all over, until I retired in 1988.

Harold Nilsen was born November 18, 1917 in Astoria, Oregon. His father emigrated from the Lofoten Islands, Norway in 1914 and his mother in 1915. His father was a commercial fisherman in Astoria, Oregon, then moved the family to Seattle in 1928 where they had relatives. He graduated from Ballard High School and entered the grocery business. On August 23, 1941 he married Evelyn Tomren who had been born in Ålesund, Norway. They have three daughters, Patricia (1942), Nancy (1944) and Beverly (1955) who helped them in their businesses. Harold died in 2008.

Scandinavian-American Bank

The **Scandinavian-American Bank** was formed in 1892 and ultimately had branches in Tacoma, Seattle and Ballard.

On July 8, 1921, the *Ballard News* reported that the bank, with deposits of more than $10 million, had been placed in the hands of the State Bank Supervisor. The failure was attributed to over expansion of loans and unwise managment. Residents of Ballard had over $1 million on deposit in the Ballard Avenue branch.

Washington's guaranty fund collapsed in 1921 under the failure of the largest bank in its system, the Scandinavian-American Bank of Seattle. Losses associated with this failure consumed the entire fund as well as a special assessment that was levied. Rather than continue to exact high assessments on banks remaining in the fund the legislature repealed its deposit guaranty fund. This action left depositors with 75 cents on the dollar from liquidation of the assets of the Scandinavian-American Bank and only 10 cents from the guaranty fund.

The Scandinavian-American Bank building at 5300 Ballard Avenue was occupied for many years by the Starlight Hotel. The building was restored and is now known as the Ballard Inn.

George and Elsie Norman

"We really enjoyed our home in Ballard. Our children say that was their favorite home."

ELSIE: I came to Seattle in 1942 to work at Boeing as a machinist. I was the only woman working on milling machines, both here and in Wichita. After I finished high school, a friend had told me about the National Youth Administration. I applied, and got in. They asked me if I'd like to learn something to help the war effort. I said, "Sure, why not." They gave me a math test. So I became a machinist. It involved a lot of trigonometry and so on. After I finished my course I was offered several jobs. I had relatives here, so I came to Seattle. I think we were 18 young girls who came here.

I worked at Boeing until 1945, the end of the war, earning money for college. I met George at college and we came to Seattle in 1951, during the Korean War. He got a job at Boeing. George and I had been married three years. He had graduated and started his masters degree. I had been in nurses training. I'd had three and half years of college. By 1957 we had two children. So we bought a house in Ballard and moved in there.

We were involved with the Danes all the time. We were active in St. John Lutheran Church. It was then composed of Danes, primarily. A lot of our friends were Danes. There was a Danish old people's home out on Des Moines Way. When it was sold, the proceeds went to buy a building and it was decided to establish a Danish Foundation. My husband and I were both on the committee to get the Foundation started. Their primary purpose when they bought this three-story office building — part of it is a culture center — was to keep elderly in their homes as long as possible so they don't have to go into retirement homes.

Our children were both involved in Scouts, and we were also involved. And for several years our daughter represented the Danes in

384 - George and Elsie (Molby) Norman

the Swedish Lucia pageant. There were representatives from each ethnic group, Norwegian, Finnish and so on. I'm sure the queen was always Swedish, but she'd have her attendants. So we went to all these events, to listen to them sing the Santa Lucia song.

We were also involved in many Ballard activities, like the festivals. When the Nordic Heritage Museum was started in Ballard, we were in on getting the Danish Room organized. The museum organizers wanted representatives of the Danish community. So we had big parties and fundraisers and that type of thing, I'm the archivist for the Danish Room. We collect all these artifacts and have them catalogued, and so on. Nora Olsen worked with me on that, too.

In 1964, I went back to school to Seattle Pacific University, and earned a BA and masters degrees, and started my doctorate. I became a reading specialist in junior high for a while, and then moved to elementary in the Highline District. I taught remedial reading. I quit because they wanted me to go into administration. They offered me a job taking charge of 19 schools. I'd rather work with children.

We lived on Sunset Hill, 75th and 31st Northwest. We bought the home from Gene Mittelstadt, who was a mortician. When we moved in, we found he had left behind a lot of ribbons and things such as baskets for floral arrangements. Our kids thought that was wonderful. They told their friends, that's where he kept the dead.

We really enjoyed our home in Ballard. Our children say that was their favorite home. One of the best things was we had such wonderful neighbors. The neighborhood was full of Norwegians.

When the pastor of St. John Lutheran Church, Richard Sorensen, came to Seattle in 1957 or so, the parsonage wasn't ready, so they moved in with us. It was cozy. They had three children; we had two. And one bathroom. A morning schedule outside the bath-room door listed who got in first. George was first, because he had to go to work at Boeing, and so on down the line. They stayed three weeks. That was rough having one bathroom for nine people.

I don't really cook Danish foods. One Danish custom is at Christmas you put an almond in the rice pudding. And whoever gets the almond gets an extra gift. Well, we didn't like rice, especially me. So we put it in the mashed potatoes. We still do that to this day.

Although my grandparents and my father were born in Denmark my mother was born in this country, so we ate American foods. One time my daughter's Girl Scout troop had an ethnic progressive dinner. And she announced the night before, "Mom, the Girl Scouts are coming to our house for dessert, and it has to be Danish." Oh, wow, you know, here I'm working. So I thought, I'll make *rød grøt* — that means red pudding. It's made with berry juice and a thickener and you serve it with cookies. So I quick made that up the night before to serve the 12 Girl Scouts. And they liked it. They really didn't care for the Norwegian fish balls they got at another home.

GEORGE: We've been busy in retirement, much more than I thought we'd be. We travel a lot and have many activities. We're not a bit bored with being on our own.

ELSIE: We both belong to a Danish singing group that meets once a month. It's anywhere from 25 to as many as 60 people, with more singers at Christmas. We get together and sing Danish.

GEORGE: People may question talent of the singers, but we have a good time. And nobody gives us a hard time.

ELSIE: I was thinking about the masquerades. That was part of the *fastelavn's* party. People would dress in costume, like they do in New Orleans. And that was always a lot of fun. It was a Mardi Gras thing. One year George went as a German admiral. He wore a wig and shoes that must have been size 15. And no one knew who he was all evening. Another time George went as a lady. He and another man came dressed as women wearing high heels and wobbling all over the place. It was hilarious.

GEORGE: This other man and his wife lived in West Seattle and we were from Ballard. He and I agreed we were going in costume — people wouldn't know us at all, dressed as we were. But he was worried about what would happen if he had a flat tire on our way to the party and he had to change a tire dressed as a woman. I was smart. I didn't dress up until we got there.

Elsie Molby was born (1924) in Askov, a Danish community in Minnesota to Marie (Johansen) and Aage Mølby. Aage was from Denmark. George Norman was born (1920) in Chicago to Thyra (Ammentorp) and Leif Norman (from Norway). Elsie and George were married in 1948. Their children: James (1949) and Janet (1955). They came to Seattle in 1951, Ballard in 1957. They are active in the Danish community and the Nordic Heritage Museum. George died in 2007.

Captain Gunnar Olsborg

*"Tokyo Rose was twelve different women.
I read a lot about Tokyo Rose, and strange as
it may seem, she is a friend of mine
today."*

Gunnar Olsborg, ca. 1965
University of Washington
Libraries, Special Collections,
Negative UW 33417

I am born in Seattle. My mother and father
spoke Norwegian at home and I was reared
with the language, the customs, the food and
the traditions. I was at least seven years of age
before I began to speak English. I spoke only
Norwegian during that time.

[My father came from] this area called
Olsborg. and some of his family took this name
and others took the name Ericksen. My mother
was from Tromsø. She was the twelfth child in
this particular family. They met in Chicago, married in Chicago, and then
came westward. Dad had a wealthy uncle in Chicago who sent for him
and was going to put him through school. Dad was a clerk in the Russian
Consulate in Tromsø. He was a popular man in Tromsø and he performed
in theatre, in the small village theatre that they had.

Because my father lacked an English education, he had to take work
as a laborer. He was a roofer, tar-paper roofs, and he fell from a roof
when I was about twelve years of age. He injured his lungs badly and
developed a cancer in the lung and died from it before I was fourteen
years old.

Except for the roof overhead, I actually supported myself since the
age of ten. I caddied on the golf course out here at the Seattle Golf and
Country Club, 25 cents an hour, which was big pay then.

I was twelve years of age when I decided on a seafaring career. I was
the oldest of four boys and we were an impoverished Norwegian family.
I knew that when I wanted an education that I was not going to have,
and I had to plan on a career that I figured I could handle. I chose the
sea. Three years later I started to sea on a tugboat in Tacoma, where I
was hired and fired in thirty days because I refused to wash the captain's
long-handled underwear. He would put a bucket of water on the stove,
then he'd come. I wanted to talk; we'd go ahead and wash underwear.
Well, I couldn't say, "No." At the same time I never agreed that I would,

but I just let the water boil there all day long. The next day he gave me the same order. Again I refused to wash his underwear. Then he knew I just wasn't going to accede to his request or order - it was really an order - so he fired me, and, well - I expected it.

My first job was on the *President Madison* going to the Orient. These were big ships in those days. They were set aside to become passenger ships carrying about 200 first class passengers, and about 800 steerage passengers, to and from the Orient.

It took a number of years to become qualified, between three and four years before I could get a 3rd Mate license. Then one year as a 3rd Mate, eligible to take a 2nd mate's license. One year as a 2nd Mate which is also the Navigating Officer, eligible to become a Chief Officer. After one year experience as a Chief Officer, then you are eligible to become a Ship Master, the Captain of the ship. In my case, it took about seven years after I started before I finally qualified as a Captain. Now that doesn't mean that you become a Captain, you have to then wait your turn to get the job, when you are inexperienced.

It was the depression years and it wasn't until the war came along that the opportunity opened up for so many of us, not just myself. In my case it took seventeen years to become a Captain.

What happened, we [Gunnar Olsborg and Evelyn Torwick] were both young. We were twenty years of age when we met. We were married in Seattle on September 19th. This year, in just another few days, if we're still here on the 19th, we will have been married 64 years. We had two girls. She reared two girls during the depression years, living up on 64th, up on Phinney Hill. Evelyn suffered from jealously of other people. She was a good looking young woman and people suspected her of running out when I was at sea, which I knew was not the case.

And the strange thing is that I never got involved in a shooting war although I was involved in bombs falling only a half mile away on the beach. I remember the bombs falling and naturally I was concerned and frightened too but luckily we got away from that. I might say that when we left Guadalcanal we had only been out about half a day – it was around midnight – and we got word from the U.S. Navy Intelligence that there was a submarine lying ahead forty miles.

And we got an order to go hard left and get away from the area and we would have gone for the Panama Canal…Now in order to go hard left we had to go through an area of low-lying reefs and small, low islands. And it was a smooth sea. If it had been a rough sea, it would have been easier. We had to depend on our navigation and luckily when we changed course we were able to go through an area where there weren't reefs. So we escaped that submarine and we went on to Panama, arriving in Panama some ten days later. It was a thrill you might say to get into Panama Canal and have the protection of the port and the installation. It was a protection that I didn't realize at the time was going to be available only during World War II and probably would never be available again. When we left the Panama Canal we actually went through the Caribbean Sea, an area where during World War II the Germans sunk five hundred ships. Of course, that's an area of a thousand square miles, or more, I just forget now. But it's a good size.

We were very lucky. I didn't realize myself that that many ships were being sunk in the area and in that particular position. So we went from there to Cienfuegos, a sugar port in Cuba where we loaded sugar for Philadelphia. Arriving Philadelphia we were still in the area where ships were being sunk, right into Philadelphia. When we got to Philadelphia I thought that I had received warning, sort of a "Dear John" letter. We had been away for seven months. Everybody got mail, except the Captain. Evelyn was also without mail all during that time because she was a Captain's wife. I came into the office in Philadelphia just as she was calling me on the telephone. She knew I was in port, but she was calling me and she wanted to know what happened with the mail. I told her, "I have the same problem; I didn't get any mail from you either."

That was an experience we had at that particular time then, while I was being transferred back to Seattle to go on a troop ship from Seattle to Dutch Harbor, Adak, all of the Alaska ports, military ports, and then back, Seattle, San Francisco, and Los Angeles. We had an experience coming back one time from Dutch Harbor. We had only been out less than a day and they wanted to know what time we'd get into San Francisco. They were going to put this in the paper. It had nothing to do with ship security. They asked what time we would get in, and they had to get that information from the Captain. I said, "If the weather continues, we will be at the pilot station at six o'clock in the morning, some five days hence" and I said, "two hours later," and I knew what the current was, "we'll be underneath the Golden Gate bridge," and one hour later at 0900 I said "We will be at and finish the engines at the dock." And so help me, five days later that's the way it came out. Six days' time. I couldn't believe it. I was amazed myself.

It had to be luck, the fact that the weather agreed we made it in those days. This was a comparatively slow ship, you see, for a troop ship. The faster a ship goes, the easier it is to maintain your position. The same like the airlines, they - the faster the plane goes the easier it is for the captain of the plane to estimate what time you're going to get into San Francisco, Seattle or wherever.

I'd like to mention another incident we had going to Guadalcanal. The 3rd mate and I were on the bridge together and we saw a submarine underwater – I know this is hard to believe - that was crossing from port to starboard, commencing at a distance of maybe two or three hundred yards. This was at night time... It came across the bow at a distance beneath the surface and crossed so close that I thought we were going to hit. But we were that close that there wasn't anything we could do.

But this submarine cleared our bow and then kept going, and we saw the submarine disappear, maybe another two or three hundred yards to the right. Then we looked to the right and now we are looking at a flotilla of ships about five miles down the moon glow. Luckily we were in the dark part of the moon, but regardless of that, we turned a hard left in order to present the smallest target to this flotilla of ships. I was convinced that this flotilla were Japanese ships, the reason being that the Japanese never had radar at any time during World War II. If they had had radar they would have seen us on the surface, and they would have fired and sunk us.

I'd like to mention another thing that happened up in Alaska, in Unimak Pass late in December, 1944. It was getting late in the evening, just before darkness, and we observed from the bridge a submarine that went across the bow about one-half mile away with the telescope up. We broke radio silence, we were that close. I didn't know if it was a Japanese submarine or an American submarine, but we were that close. So I broke radio silence to report to Dutch Harbor, roughly 150 miles away, the presence of a submarine. They acknowledged. We got into Dutch Harbor about eight or nine o'clock in the morning, and immediately Navy Intelligence officers were boarding the ship to investigate me for nervousness, and they didn't believe it, no. But there's no question about it.

However, that night, Tokyo Rose, one of twelve women that actually operated as Tokyo Rose, came on the air and reported the torpedoing and sinking of the *Carl Shurz*, that was the name of the ship I was on with 1500 on board, and not only the destruction of the ship but the loss of many men including Captain Gunnar Olsborg! Now that went over the air! My wife, living in Poulsbo, came in on the Bremerton ferry that morning and as she was walking up Madison Street, a seaman crossed the street — she recognized him as a seaman but didn't know his name.

390 - Captain Gunnar Olsborg

The seaman came across the street, doffed his hat and he said, "Mrs. Olsborg, I'm awfully sorry what happened last night." My wife had a special telephone number to call the American Mail Line, which she did, to find out that the report regarding Tokyo Rose was correct but luckily the ship was safe in Dutch Harbor.

I've read a lot about Tokyo Rose and Tokyo Rose, strange as it may seem is a friend of mine today. She was born in Los Angeles, graduate of the School of Music at University of California at Los Angeles. She went to the Orient to help her aunt who was ill. Tokyo Rose's mother would have gone there herself if only she had been well, which she wasn't. So Tokyo Rose took the assignment to go there in August of 1941 and was well accepted and received by the Japanese people. When war was declared, Tokyo Rose was evicted from her aunt's home. Here she is, a young woman, very attractive woman, she's out on the street. She was arrested and put in prison.

You see, she actually volunteered to leave Japan and return to the United States, and to face a court, knowing full well that she was innocent. But the court system was so angry, everybody in the United States was angry with this Tokyo Rose, or one of a dozen Tokyo Roses, and she served six years and eight months in federal prison before being released. In 1976 when President Gerald Ford, who was appointed to the office, was asked to give a pardon to Tokyo Rose, President Ford gave some excuse that she could still have a pardon if she wanted to, but she would have to request it. I wrote to Mrs. Ford and asked her to intercede on behalf of Tokyo Rose. Regardless of that, President Ford, as you know was defeated on November 4, 1976.

She was hooked, you might say, but she was one of a dozen. She wasn't working or broadcasting every night. And she may not have been broadcasting the night that I was on the ship that supposedly sank.

November 4, 1976, I had been in communication with Tokyo Rose and her nephew had told her, after reading my letters, this is one letter you must answer. That's how it was that Tokyo Rose answered my letter in the middle part of the summer in 1977. On Nov. 4th, after Ford was defeated for the presidency, Tokyo Rose was in San Francisco and I came home that particular night from Port Angeles to find that she was being taken on the steps of the San Francisco court house. I was only home a short period of time, somewhere around eight or nine o'clock in the evening, and I get a telephone call. Who was the telephone call from? It was from Tokyo Rose! She called me, she said, "I've been trying to reach you for five hours. I got in here this afternoon and you are the only one, with the exception of my girlfriend that I'm visiting with right now, you are the only one that I have been trying to reach." I said, "For goodness sake, I didn't realize that you've been trying to reach me. In fact I just saw the paper; you were in San Francisco last night." She said, "That's right, I'm up here [in Seattle] visiting right now."

I said, " It's so late now, we can't meet tonight, nine o'clock, but I want you to come in here tomorrow at noon and we will meet up at the Space Needle and we will have lunch there and my wife too, I'll bring her in from the country and we will have lunch together." We had a visit there for a couple hours, and then I have to drop the subject at this point, but also refer to January 19th in 1977 at which time, just the day before Ford left office, he gave her a full pardon. Now, this is what would have happened, if he had given her a pardon in April when I asked or at least not later than July when I asked Mrs. Ford to do the same. I said Ford would have been elected. The reason he would have been elected President would have been because of his help to this particular lady. Now the Japanese-American people are the strongest ethnic force that we have here in the United States, and had the Japanese-Americans, the other, all of the black people, would have gone for the pardon, all the Chinese, all the Oriental people would have backed that particular pardon, and Ford would have been elected.

Tokyo Rose is in Chicago today. We exchange Christmas gifts and cards every year. Occasionally we telephone one another.

[I've worked at sea for] 57 years plus 8 part time years, a total of 65 years. The eight years that were part time, this was up in the Bering Sea as relief Captain on the processors, on the large processors.

The Japanese-American people were badly treated when they were taken out from our west coast and moved east or inland to these various detention camps. You may wonder why, when they removed them here from the West Coast, why didn't they do that same in Honolulu? No, they didn't. You know happened? There was never a case of sabotage. Most of the Japanese people were doing the longshore work on these ships. I was down there, I saw them. These ships cleared port and were never sabotaged.

Then I'm going to finish up with one last story, and that is down here at Shilshole Bay when before 3,000 people I was the MC, introducing the various officials, the Governor, the Senator - two Senators, the Mayor, and so forth. The people that were down there, they were surprised with the way things went and I did have my brother-in-law's mother down there. She was a woman that really had not had much of an education but she said something like this to her son and daughter out in the center field, you might say, "Well, I see that Gunnar Olsborg is master of ceremonies, and he's introducing the Governor, the Mayor, and the Senators, but which one is Leif Erickson?"

Gunnar Olsborg was born in 1909 in Seattle, and died in 2000. He and Evelyn Torwick were married September 19, 1930. They had two daughters. Olsborg served in the Merchant Marine for 20 years. During World War II, he was a shipmaster on American Mail Line vessels in the South Pacific. After the war Olsborg became a Puget Sound pilot, retiring in 1982, but continued delivering ships to and from Alaska, Honolulu and Seattle. He was a longtime member of the Norwegian Commercial Club, the Council of American Master Mariners and the Leif Erickson League of the Seattle Area. As league secretary, Olsborg played an important role in the installation of the Leif Erickson statue overlooking Seattle's Shilshole Bay. During World War II, Olsborg became sympathetic to the plight of Japanese-Americans, later becoming active in the Japanese-American Citizens' League and campaigning for the presidential pardon of Tokyo Rose Iva Toguri. He also served as the president of the congregation of Immanuel Lutheran Church of Seattle.

Mae Olsen

*"The entertainment we had
in Ballard was quite interesting."*

My mother and father were both born in Norway. My dad homesteaded in Crosby, North Dakota. He had met mother's brother, who had a big farm there and he worked for him. Mother came out to cook in the cook car, and this is how mother and dad met. They married and then dad sold his homestead and moved to Aliquippa, North Dakota, which was six miles from the Montana border and nine miles from the Canadian border. And this is where my brother and I were born.

In the early 40s my parents moved to Everett, Washington. My father and brother commuted to Ballard and worked at the Stimson Mill. And when the war broke out in 1942, we all had to go to work. My dad, my husband Vic and my brother all worked at Stimson Mill in Ballard. My sister-in-law worked at Frederick & Nelson and I worked at Seattle Cedar Lumber Company. We moved to Ballard, to 624 West 44th, just off of Eighth Avenue. We lived there together for awhile 'til we could get other accommodations and my mother was the cook for all of us working.

For awhile I was running trim saws, but I was very afraid of that. They said I didn't do good at all because I was too scared, and took too long to cut anything. So then I was put on the green chain, and I was the smallest person in the mill, and there were a lot of us women working there. They put me loading boxcars, and I had to put the shakes and shingles into boxcars. That was a horrible job. But I survived it for some time. Then I decided to go to work at the Old Home Restaurant in Ballard as a waitress.

At Stimson Mill my dad first started on the green chain, where the logs first come in out of the water. He slipped on a log and got both legs broken at the same time, so, he spent some time in Ballard Hospital. My brother also worked there, and then he went on to something else. My husband Vic was a mechanic there. And this is when he worked on these big lumber carriers. They were big and high, and they'd go right over the top of the lumber and just pick it up underneath. Vic then worked at Wilson Ford for 26 years as a Ford technician.

The entertainment in Ballard was interesting. I was working at the Old Home Restaurant at that time, and the Chinaman came in there and told everybody that they were going to start a Chinese lottery and lotto. It was spooky but a real fun thing. It was in some building way back from the restaurant. We had to go way down the back streets to get there. The first night that I went there, Vic went with me and I won $70, which was a big amount of money at that time. So then my dad, my brother, his wife, we all used to go down there. And after a month or two this same Chinaman came up to the restaurant and said to me, "Not tonight, not tonight." We didn't know what he meant but we didn't go that evening. It was raided that night and many of the people there were put in jail that night. This was illegal then. And then it was closed for about two or three weeks, and then he came and he said, "You can come tonight now. You can come tonight." So we did. Not too long after, it was raided again, and they moved to Greenwood.

Vic was in the Civilian Conservation Corps beginning in 1934. He served in eastern Washington for awhile, then he went over to Sequim, Washington in the CC camp there. The CCC was a program started in 1933 during President Roosevelt's time. It was a very bad Depression time, and there was no work. Parents were on a program called the WPA, the Works Progress Administration. The fathers would have to go out and work on the roads and things, and be gone many times for a week at a time. Mrs. Roosevelt had started a program in New York for young boys who were homeless and were on the streets. She was the one who really had started this.

President Roosevelt started the CCC for the sons of the people on the WPA; ages from 17 to 25. These boys were given $30 a month and they had to send $25 home. So the CC boys got $5 a month. They built our state parks and built roads, and did all kinds of conservation work. One example is at Deception Pass State Park. The Deception Pass Bridge was built by a construction company, but the CC boys built the approaches to it. The log and rock railing — that's all built by the CC boys.

I saw a little article which said, "Were you ever in the CCs? Did you ever know anyone that had been in the CCs?" And, of course, I thought this is my magic moment. There must be something I can do to get some of these guys together. We sent our $5 in. Then Vic and I started a chapter in the Everett area of the CC boys in 1983. It wasn't long till we had 100 members. And then they started bringing me all these mementos and pictures, and so I said, now we've got to get a museum. And my husband says, "Oh, no, that's too big a job," but we did it. The museum at Bowman Bay in the Park has been open since 1988.

Mae Olsen - 395

Vic passed away just a year ago, but I still kept the museum open this past year, and I will be doing it this coming year, too.

Mae Rukke was born, 1916, on a homestead in Aliquippa, North Dakota close to the Canadian border. Her parents emigrated from Norway; father, Ed Englebrit Rukke, from Hallingdal, mother, Gunda (Thon), from Vickersund. They met and married in North Dakota. The family moved to Puget Sound in the 30s. In 1937 Mae married Victor Olsen whose parents were from Denmark. Vic died in 2000. She now lives in Mount Vernon.

Allan Osberg

"My parents were Axel Osberg and Hilma Olson Osberg, both of whom were from Sweden. My dad emigrated in 1912 at the age of 16. His family lived in a little town called Östanbäck. They were farmers, but boy I think they grew more rocks than they grew anything else."

Allan and Inger Osberg

My dad emigrated in 1912. He went from out of Trondheim over to England and then he went from Liverpool to Halifax, Canada. Then he took the train across Canada to Edmonton where he had a cousin that had emigrated three years prior.

Dad found work building the railroads at that time. He worked on a railroad near Jasper. He said they had to wade across the river, and when he was doing that, he lost his suitcase. And in his suitcase, he had a Bible and that was the end of his church-going.

In 1915 he immigrated into the United States, through Montana, through Sweetgrass, I believe. At that time he changed his name from Erland Lundberg to Axel Osberg. About 1916 he wound up in Seattle. He worked some in the shipyards, for a time but then he got involved with building logging railroads in this area.

I understand that sometime shortly after he crossed the border in 1915, the border station burned down with all the records in it, so they had no record of him having entered the United States legally. He decided he better go back and make arrangements so he could get his citizenship. He had to go back to Sweden and re-enter the U.S. legally, which he did in 1939.

My grandfather, on my mother's side, and his family came first to where his brothers were in the Skagit or the Cedarhome area [which is near Stanwood]. They lived there for a short while and then went up to British Columbia and they farmed for seven years. My mother learned how to count in Hindu because there were a lot of Hindus around there.

In 1912 they moved back to the States and my grandfather bought a farm out west of Mount Vernon. He paid — and I've seen the deed — six thousand dollars in gold coin for the 22 acres. I don't know how you can make a living on twenty-two acres with seven kids but they seemed to do fairly well. He was just a hard-working farmer. He was able to buy a car, and they lived pretty well. And so that's where my mother was raised.

She and my dad were married in 1920. And I can remember him telling me that all the money he had at the time he got married went to buy a case of Sunnybrook Whiskey.

Sometime in the late twenties we were all moved up to a little house in North Bend. My dad was building a logging railroad up there on the middle fork of the Snoqualmie River. That work ended in 1930 with the onset of the Depression. So, Dad and Mother decided to move to Mount Vernon, where she was raised. He got a chance in 1932 to take over a logging operation up on the coast of British Columbia that was owned by some people that lived in Anacortes. And so, in 1932, we moved to Vancouver.

After coming back from Canada in 1935, we lived in Seattle. I went to the University of Washington in 1942, graduating in 1945. I stayed out a year, and then I went back to Harvard for another year in 1946. I was just there for one year. I graduated in civil engineering.

Inger I met at a dance at what used to be the Palladium Dance Hall. She had a date with another fellow, and I had a date with another gal. During that evening, I asked her "How about a date next weekend?" She said, "OK." So, I told her I would be out of town until the following weekend.

When I came back, I called her up. I said, "This is Allan." She said, "Allan who?" I said, "We were supposed to have a date tonight." "Oh," she said, "I've got a date." So, she said after a while, I'll break it. So, we went out to the Town and Country Club. That was probably the best place in town for dinner and dancing at that time. So, we went there and sure enough she ran into the guy she had the date with. She introduced me as her cousin. That was kind of a rocky start. Anyway, that was probably in June, I suppose, of 1953. We were married January sixteenth, 1954.

Shortly before we were married, Dad took Inger aside, as she tells it, and said that "No Osberg wife was ever going to work outside of the home." And she never did. Except for when she started volunteering in the gift shop at the Nordic Heritage Museum. If dad knew that she was working there, that would bother him some, but if he realized she wasn't getting paid, that would be even worse.

Sometime in the late 1990s Ken Jacobsen — my state senator — contacted me and wanted me to go with him down to see the museum. I went with Ken to meet Marianne Forssblad, the museum's director, and the three of us went out for lunch. I had a tour of the museum at I guess the same time. And it wasn't long after that Marianne put the bite on me to become a member of the Board of Trustees. So I said sure. So it started.

Allan Osberg was born Seattle, Washington, on July 25, 1924. He graduated from Lincoln High in 1942 and from the University of Washington with a B.S. degree in civil engineering in 1945 and was the Presidential Medalist. In 1947 he received a master's degree. also in civil engineering from Harvard University. He is president of Osberg Construction Company, a firm founded by his father. He has twice served as president of local chapters of the Associated General Contractors of America.

With the charitable trust that his parents left, Allan and his brother, John, have donated to the Mountain to Sound Greenway, the Nature Conservancy, the Museum of Northwest Art (LaConner) and Washington State University, to name a few. Allan and Inger Osberg are supporters of the University of Washington College of Engineering, endowed a professorship in civil engineering and a Presidential Graduate Fellowship. They are lifetime members of the President's Club and have been recognized with the status of Laureates. Beyond the University, they are supporters of the Woodland Park Zoo and the Nordic Heritage Museum. Allan was first elected a member of the Board of Trustees of the Nordic Heritage Museum in 2000 and served as President from 2004 to 2008.

Edward Palmason

*"Music has enriched my life no end.
I've been very fortunate that when I went
to medical school they paid me to sing
at a big church [in Portland]."*

My father was born in northern Iceland
July 6, 1874. Times were very hard
in Iceland in those days. At that time the
Canadian government was interested in
having immigrants and settlers. My father's
father, Palmi Hjalmarsson came out of a
sense of adventure. He and his wife and
three children left Iceland in 1875 and came through the Great Lakes, by
train to the Red River region of Dakota territory and by boats up the Red
River into Lake Manitoba.

A storm began to brew and the master of the boats refused to take
them any farther. He dumped them on the shore. That night the snow
fell and the first baby was born in what they called New Iceland. They
had a terrible time. They had no shelter. They had to dig themselves
in and prepare for the winter. The local Indians were friendly and
taught them how to fish through the ice and so on, so they were able
to survive. In the spring, they proceeded northward to a much better
area — Gimli, now a large Icelandic settlement in Manitoba. In 1876 a
terrible smallpox epidemic took the lives of my grandmother and two of
the children. In 1880 my grandfather and his family came into Dakota
Territory in what is now called Pembina County. They homesteaded a
farm. My father came into the Ballard area with other Icelanders from
North Dakota in the early part of the year 1902 and worked as a laborer
for a few years. In 1905, he joined the Ballard Post Office. He worked
there for 35 years, most of that time out on a route.

Our mother's parents came from northern Iceland also. They
immigrated to Winnipeg in the mid-1880s. My mother's father, Magnus
Olafur Sigurdsson, changed his name to Smith. My mother was born in
1891. Her family moved to the Seattle area in 1909 to the see the Alaska
Yukon Exposition and decided to stay here.

Shortly after that, my mother and father got married and built a home
on 75th and 18th Northwest. Five children were born to them between
1913 and 1919. Also living in our home was my widowed grandmother

Halldora Smith, formerly Thorlakson, and her sister Gunnlaug Thorlakson — nine of us in this modest home.

I had an older brother and sister, Victor and Victoria, who were twins, I was the middle child, then two sisters, Elin and Doris. My brother and I were raised in what was a tough neighborhood. I was very bookish and I carried a briefcase full of books, and Vic had his violin case. And I think our mother dressed us kind of funny — we wore knickers like the golfers used to wear, and black stockings down below. And we were set upon more than once by neighborhood rowdy kids who'd tease us and follow us and taunt us and even try to hit us. My brother tells me I had a big mouth and I would talk back to these guys and then expect Vic to protect me. But that was part of growing up in Ballard. When we graduated from grade school a good percentage of the students didn't go onto high school. That was 1928. I would say that 30 percent didn't go to high school.

Music has enriched my life no end. I've been very fortunate that when I went to medical school they paid me to sing at a big church in Portland. I sang on the radio and I sang for funerals. I did this sort of thing on weekends or evenings, and it didn't take much time. My wife Vivienne worked in the shipyards as I went through medical school. This was 1940. But there never was a time when she made more money than I did.

In 1940 I started school at the University of Oregon in Portland. There was no medical school here at that time. When I was a sophomore, the war broke out. They decided that they would run the school all year round. So I graduated a year early, in 1943. Then I went back to Baltimore for a very truncated internship. In fall, 1944, I went into the Navy. In 1946, I started practice in Ballard. I practiced there until 1970. Then I worked in the emergency room in the Ballard Hospital for five years. In 1975, after 29 years of practice, I got a job as a medical consultant for the state's Department of Social and Health Services. I worked there for 12 years. We monitored for the Medicaid program, authorizing surgery, reviewed hospital bills and so on. It was interesting work.

I joined the Ballard Kiwanis Club and in 1952, I was president there. I served 14 years on the Seattle School Board. I was a trustee for the Seattle Symphony and the Seattle Opera Association. I also sang in the Opera Chorus. I enjoyed that. I sang in about ten or 12 operas. Very time consuming though. You know, when you're doing general medical practice and delivering babies and so on, it becomes very difficult. By the time I was 60, I was not in very good health. That's one reason I left

Edward Palmason - 401

practice and took a job with the state — much easier, less stressful.

When I began to practice in Ballard, I got an office on the second floor of the Ballard Eagle's Building. A couple of the older doctors had a lot of surgical experience, Dr. Devor was a surgeon and Dr. Chris Melgard had had a lot of experience in obstetrics and gynecology. They were pleased to help the younger doctors like myself get started. In those days, the family doctors made a lot of house calls and delivered babies and also did what they might call bread and butter surgery, tonsillectomies and simple appendectomies.

In the late 1940s we realized that the hospital was inadequate, and so we started talking about building a bigger hospital. The property that seemed to be the most adequate for our purpose was a vacant lot over on Tallman Avenue, but it was owned by the school district. It was where the old Ballard High School used to be before it moved to the present location in 1916. Before the school district could sell it, they had to have a referendum. So they put it on the ballot, and the people voted that we could buy it.

Congress had passed a bill called the Hill-Burton Act, which enabled Congress to provide matching funds for communities that would raise money. Ballard Hospital was one of the few hospitals in this area that really met the criteria of the original Hill-Burton Fund.

The hospital here cost a million and a half to build. We raised the $750,000 locally. The big contributors like Ole Bardahl gave $15,000, and Nelson Chevrolet gave us $10,000, but most of the contributions were smaller. The doctors raised over $100,000. The younger doctors, like myself, gave $3,000, and the more established doctors gave $5,000. So, we built the hospital and it was formally opened I think in December of 1954. I was the first chief of staff in 1955. During those growing years, we were very proud of the hospital. It was built as a general practitioner's hospital, and we attracted a lot of doctors who were general practitioners. But then it became evident that we had to have a broader base, and so the surgeons came and the obstetricians and the gynecologists and so on. We had some pediatricians. We had a pediatric wing in the hospital for a while, but we couldn't compete with Orthopedic Hospital, so that was closed down. So that's the story.

Edward Palmason was born October 4, 1915 in Ballard to Jon Thorstein & Lillie (Smith) Palmason. He had an older brother and sister, twins Victor and Victoria and two younger sisters, Elin and Doris. Jon was born in the Hunayatnsysla area of Northern Iceland. Lillie was born in Winnipeg, Manitoba to parents from the Skagafjordur area of Northern Iceland. Ed married Vivienne Fireoved, also from Ballard. They had four sons: Ed, Jr. (1942-1990), Dennis (1945), Richard (1949-1956) and Jon (1951). In addition to his medical practice and his music, Ed served on the Seattle School Board 1956-1971, and as its president in the 1960s. This interview was recorded March 19, 1988. Ed died in 1997.

"The Ballard Hospital"

Dwight "Bud" Hawley

My dad, Dwight Hawley, was also initially involved in the Ballard Hospital. In addition to being secretary to the Elks and the Commercial Club, he was also secretary of the Ballard Hospital when it was upstairs in the old Eagles Building, and he was one of three or four founders in the community effort to raise money to build a new hospital. None of us ever worked more on anything than we did on Ballard Hospital. It was a Herculean effort where many people spent most of their time for two years on the hospital fund drive. He was one, along with Dick McAbee, Ole Bardahl, Hans Lehman and many others. Ben Lafferty worked so hard that hospital people said, "Ben, you're cutting your own throat because all the doctors are right upstairs. They come down and buy this stuff from your pharmacy." He said, "That's okay, it's good for Ballard." His son Barry, also a pharmacist, opened his pharmacy next door to the new hospital.

Ruth Hughbanks

A lot of the doctors, and the professional people were in the Eagle's Building. When they decided to build a new one, they decided that they'd just have to ring doorbells, so they called themselves the knuckle knockers. They used to meet after work, and the whole group of the businessmen did that and got their families involved. Several evenings they took high school students, paired off with them, and asked for donations. It was wonderful how the people responded. When you go through the Ballard Hospital now and see all that, it makes you think what the community can do when they work together and that was good.

C. Arthur Pehling

"You've got to know what you're doing, that's all. At one time I was the biggest house moving concern in the state of Washington"

In the midwest in those days I don't think the economy was that great. An awful lot of people came out to Ballard. The people I remember from my early age were German. The Norwegians came later after they had separated from the Swedish people. They came out to do fishing. The Swedish people came later on. Most of the Swedish people were carpenters or builders.

My father was in the house-moving business. Before my birth he had first worked in a shingle mill, but that wasn't to his liking. So he got himself some horses and hauled things. He hauled garbage, and then he hauled sand and gravel for Salmon Bay Sand & Gravel. Two of the horses were "Chub" and "Trammy". When I was young, especially on Sundays or weekends, it was my job to take the horses outside to drink water. And I had to shove hay down from the barn loft and give the horses some oats too. My grandfather was in the wood and coal business, and he got most of his wood from Seattle Cedar. He had his horses, my dad's horses and some other horses — eight horses in all in a barn alongside our home. He delivered wood and coal in horse and buggy and a wagon. When I was small, I'd run outside to see my grandpa bringing his horses back for the night. I'd run down the street and my grandpa would pick me up so I could get to ride maybe a block. After I got old enough, I cut lots of wood.

About the end of World War I we got our first Model T. Then my dad bought what today we'd call a pickup. And later on he raised a lot of houses, then dug out the dirt from underneath to make basements. He had a good old shovel.

My dad built the house I was born in especially for my mom. The house was pretty much finished by when they got married in 1911. It had one bedroom downstairs and one bedroom upstairs, a full basement with a dirt floor. My mother used to do her washing in the basement. In those days you didn't have an electric furnace and we always cooked with wood. We had electricity and a modern home, with a bathtub and toilet and all that. Down in the basement, Mother had a gas plate so she could boil the clothes in a copper tub. You heated your irons on the wood cook stove; usually you had two or three cast-iron irons to keep hot.

The house is still there. My dad owned where the house was and 75 feet below where the barn was. And there was a little house my dad and his two brothers built for my grandma Pehling. It was a one-bedroom house with bath. My grandmother and grandfather Hensel's place was at 1707 West 57th. At first, they had what we called a backhouse. Later they built a bathroom on the back porch.

The first school I went to was kindergarten, at Washington Irving School, where Ballard/Swedish Hospital is today. I was on the Board of the Ballard Hospital when we built it. I went to Salmon Bay School, which was between 63rd and 64th on 20th. Then my mom got into a little fight with a teacher, so my sister and I went to Whittier School for a couple of years. Then Whittier got too full of students, so my sister and I graduated from Webster, where the Nordic Heritage Museum is today. From there I went to Ballard High School and graduated in 1931. I also went to the University of Washington for a couple of quarters.

How did I meet my wife? Well, that was in the first part of 1935 and we had quite a bit of snow. We were sledding on 71st from Greenwood Avenue down to Green Lake. And I broke my leg hitting something. So I had a broken leg, using a cane and whatnot, and went to a dance out at Parker's. I went with a fellow who worked for my dad. At Parker's he introduced me to his cousin. And that was the last of me going out with any other girl. She was for me, and we were married in June, 1936.

I worked for my dad. Before I got married, Dad paid me and most of the fellows working for him 45 cents an hour. When I got married, Dad says, "Oh, now that you're married, I think I better raise you," so he gave me 50 cents an hour. I've never worked for anybody but my dad. He passed away in 1942. So I took over the business and ran it for a good many years. You've got to know what you're doing, that's all. At one time I was the biggest house moving concern in the state of Washington. My son was in business with me. He did not like house-moving, so we went into the remodeling business. Our company is Pehling & Son.

There was a gasoline service station on Leary and Market called Hughbanks and Jasperson where we bought all of our gasoline and all that type of thing. After I took over my dad's business, Clarence Hughbanks wanted me to join the Kiwanis Club. I went to a couple of meetings and so in February 1943, I joined the Ballard Kiwanis Club and I am still a member. I was president in 1948. Later my son joined and

30 years later he was president of the Ballard Kiwanis Club. I was on the Scout Board, the YMCA Board, the church board and I was on the Ballard Commercial Club board.

The Stimsons owned a lot of property where the Olympic Golf Course was. When they built the golf course, there was a lot of trees that they cut off there, and then they would blast a lot of the stumps. My dad had a Fordson tractor with two winches on it, and he used to pull those stumps out. Well, the golf course went out of business. The Ballard businessmen tried to buy that property from the Stimson family, but we just couldn't raise enough money. So then they platted it into housing, the Olympic Manor. The property that is now Blue Ridge belonged to the Boeing family. That was platted and sold.

I became a member of the hospital board, I think in 1948 and continued for 10 or 12 years. There still was the small hospital in the Eagles' Building. We'd go out pretty near every night and knock on doors, asking people to pledge money to build a new hospital. Finally, in 1954, the hospital was dedicated. The original contractor went broke building the hospital; somebody else finished it. [See "The Ballard Hospital" p. 403]

Arthur Pehling was born December 4, 1915 in Ballard, near Salmon Bay Park. His father's parents were born in Germany. His father, born in Springfield, Illinois, was the second oldest of nine. The family moved to Ballard in 1900. His mother's family, named Hensel, came to Ballard in 1890. Arthur Pehling died January 2001.

Ruth Elizabeth Peterson

"My husband Ted talked about coming from Bothell with his mother and one cow, walking. He said they walked 22 miles, but that's hard for me to really believe."

I think Albert, my husband Ted's older brother, and his two sisters were born in Michigan. [The Peterson family] came out here together. They bought five acres when they came to Ballard. That was between 1900 and 1902. They built a home on Sunset Hill, about 1902. When their house was first built, it faced 77th. They wanted the house to be on just one lot so they could sell the other lots, so they moved the house to 31st Avenue, on another of their lots, but I don't think they changed the address, 7710 31st Northwest.

When his father, O.G. Peterson, first came to Ballard, Ted said he worked for a dollar a day — day labor of some kind. The Locks weren't built yet, but O.G. had an opportunity to work as a hard hat diver. They said something like, "Oh, you've got a tough head. Why don't you try it." And he did. From then on he did submarine diving work for many, many years.

Hulda Marie [Ted's mother] was quite a gardener. She loved flowers and made use of the ground space they had, And she always had corn and other vegetables, and they had an apple tree. She grew beautiful chrysanthemums. She would take them down to church — she was real proud of those chrysanthemums.

Ted needed his tonsils taken out, so he and his mother walked down to the doctor's office, on the top floor, where the Ballard Bell Tower is now, and Ted didn't want to go in. He ran away with his mother after him. She said, "Well, come on, Teddy, now. We have to go up there and have your tonsils out." My father-in-law's dad lived with the Petersons, and he died there at that home. It was before I met them, so I never met him. Ted recalled he cried when his Grandpa passed away, and his mother said to him, *inte gråt,* which means "don't cry."

I never saw any livestock there, but my husband Ted talked about coming from Bothell with his mother and one cow, walking. He said they walked 22 miles, but that's hard for me to really believe. So that's the only cow I know they had. They milked the cow, and Ted delivered milk to several families on 32nd. I still have the milk can.

They had chickens too. And Ted used to tell how his mother sent him out to wring the neck off a chicken. They'd have fried chicken on Sunday. He talked about those chickens because they dipped them in boiling water to get the feathers loose, and he had to pluck them.

The Peterson children went to Webster. But Webster didn't have manual training and Adams did. So Ted finished the eighth grade at Adams, and then to Ballard High School. While he was at Ballard High, he worked a lot on the side. His teachers said, "You better not work all night because you can't do your work here at school."

They walked to school. They walked across many empty lots, including Ballard Baptist Church, which always was their church in Ballard. Ted used to tell how his dad would carry the youngest on his shoulders down to church, and they'd walk across all the empty lots, probably more empty lots than there were homes in those days. The church was their main interest in life, and the parents were Christians before they came here. My father-in-law was the superintendent of the Sunday School Department, I remember.

They were a very close knit family. The children all went to Sunday school and church; that was their main activity. Even during the week, I know the girls had different clubs at church.

I was there many times for Sunday dinner. They would come home from church and there'd often be a big roast. The whole family would be there for dinner. And dinner was at 12 or one o'clock, maybe as late as two.

When we lived there the few years after we were married, there was no sidewalk, but we had two planks. We would walk from there to 28th, where the streetcar ran.

Ruth Frank was born November 17, 1907, in Bothell. Her parents, Albert Frank and Alma (Blomdahl) Frank were both born in Sweden. Ruth came to Ballard at age 14 to live with an aunt after her mother had died. At Ballard High she met Ted Peterson, the son of Olaf Gustav Peterson and Hulda Marie (Anderson) Peterson, also from Sweden. The Petersons had built a home on Sunset Hill in 1902. Ted had an older brother Albert and two sisters, born in Michigan. Ted was born in Ballard in 1904. Ted and Ruth were married in 1931. Their children: Ted, Jr. (1934) and Karen (1936). Ted owned the Peterson Beauty Supply Co. He served 20 years in the Washington State Senate (1955-1975). He was a Ballard activist all his adult life. Ted died in 1993. Ruth died in 2005.

Robert Preston Pheasant

"My dad met Olaf Wiggen, and they formed the Pheasant and Wiggen Mortuary and Funeral Home in Ballard."

I am Bob Pheasant and I was born in Ballard December 28, 1918. I was born in our house at 22nd Avenue and 56th. My dad came with his family, five boys and a girl, from Nebraska. They settled in Wenatchee and later moved to the Seattle area. When he first came to Seattle, he worked for the Seattle Streetcar Company. He was a conductor and engineer on board, running streetcars through Seattle, going from downtown Seattle out to the Lake, up the Counterbalance and also through Ballard. Later, for a few years, he worked for Bleitz Funeral Home, then in Fremont. He met and married my mother in Fremont. My dad met Olaf Wiggen, and they formed the Pheasant and Wiggen Mortuary and Funeral Home in Ballard some years ago.

That's when my dad and mother moved into this home on the corner of 22nd and 56th. The business was downstairs, and the living area was upstairs. There was a third floor they nicknamed the Castle. I remember seeing an old telephone control up there, so it may have been used for that at some time.

About 1923 they built a building, still standing, on the [northeast] corner of 22nd and Market, with the business downstairs, and apartments on two floors above. We lived there for a number of years, including when I was going to school.

I remember as a youngster, before Market Street was paved, I would stand and watch when a fire was called and the fire engines started up. The pump left first, then the fire engine, going as fast as they could. Three horses pulled the pumper down Market Street.

I went to kindergarten at Irving, and later to Adams Elementary School through the eighth grade and to James Monroe Junior High. I think we were the second class into James Monroe. After Monroe I went to Ballard High School. I graduated in 1937. For a couple of years I tried to work and go to school as well. Then the war came along and I spent almost three years in the Army. When I came back — and God bless the Army and the GI Bill — I finished the University in 1948. It took me 11 years to get through college.

I met Helen, Mrs. Pheasant in the building on 22nd and Market. She was staying there with her aunt. After I graduated from college, I got a job in what I was supposed to know something about — transportation and/or international trade. We got married in 1948 and I went to work for Pacific Northern Airline up in Alaska. I finally retired after 33 ½ years. When we moved out of Alaska with our family, both my father and mother had passed on. We have been here ever since. Our kids all graduated from Ballard High School.

My dad passed away in 1937 and then my mother took over the business. She had no experience whatsoever, but she brought in my uncle, Clyde Pheasant, who had worked at Bonney-Watson and Home undertaking. Several years later the building was sold. Pheasant-Wiggen Mortuary and Pheasant-Wiggen Company ceased to exist.

My dad was a staunch member of the Eagles and the Elks. The Elks' main building was down on Ballard Avenue. He, Dwight Hawley, Joe Helsley and two others, as a committee decided to build the Eagles Building [now the Ballard Building] on the corner of Market and 22nd. [see Hawley p. 338,] When completed; it had a hospital up on the third floor, two floors of doctors and offices. On the ground floor a drug store on the corner, a men's furnishing store and the Bagdad Theatre. At one time that building had a big bronze plaque in the entrance, a memorial to the people who started the building. As I recall, it had at least five names on it. I have tried to find it, but I have not been able to.

Robert "Bob" Pheasant was born in Ballard December 28, 1918. His father, Jack Pheasant, was from Nebraska and his mother, Ethel Preston, from Minnesota. They met and married in Seattle. Bob graduated from Ballard High in 1937. After service in WW II, he graduated from college in 1948 in International Trade. Also in 1948 he married Helen Johnson and took a job with an airline in Alaska. After over 33 years in Alaska he retired and the family returned to Ballard. Their children, John (March 1956) and twins Julie and Joann (December, 1956), also graduated from Ballard High. Bob died in 2006.

Arnold Sverre Reinholdtsen

"And then, when you come into the dock, and you've got the boat full of fish, you know that you had caught those fish and you had worked to get them. That's a good feeling, you know."

My mother came from Leikanger, Nordfjord in the western part of Norway. She went up to the Lofoten Islands to work as a housekeeper for my father's family. They were engaged in Norway. My dad came to this country probably 1923. He worked for a couple of years to get enough money to get my mother over, I think in 1925. My sister Lorraine was born in 1926. I was born in 1928 in the Norwegian Hospital in Fremont. It went bankrupt during the Depression. The Depression was hard on the immigrants. We had to move in with my dad's uncle until my dad finally accumulated enough money to buy a home in Ballard. My mother didn't want to move to Ballard because she didn't want to live with all those Norwegians, but my dad says, if you want a house, you're going to have to move to Ballard. We've been living in Ballard since about 1939.

My dad fished 12 months out of the year. In the summer he went halibut fishing, and in the winter he went down to San Francisco — we called it sardine fishing, but actually it was for pilchards, big sardines used for fertilizer. We moved to San Francisco in the wintertime, and then, in the summer time we'd move back up to Seattle. In those days it took 21 days to make a halibut trip and then they were in for ten days. We would go on picnics and have a good time when my dad was home.

I remember canning halibut in the summertime. When my dad came in, my job was to run around the neighborhood with some halibut and give to the neighbors. In winter we had a halibut soufflé, *fiskegrateng*. The best part of it was a firm brown crust on the outside. And, we had canned salmon during the hard times. They would get the dents, the cans that had dents in them, real cheap. And we had salted codfish. We never were hungry. We didn't have money, but I never felt deprived. If we needed something, there was always a way to get it.

During the Depression, my dad made $365 in three years. My uncle, George Leikanger, would half-sole my shoes when I was little. My folks brought him over around 1930, and he made one fishing trip on the same boat my dad was on. He didn't make any money, he did it for nothing, but the crew went in the hole 17 cents. He decided that fishing wasn't very profitable, so he went into roofing. He was a roofer for the rest of his life.

At school they were going to put me in the dumb class — for slow learners. My mother was upset because she knew I wasn't dumb. The principal told her I was behind in spelling and reading, and I talked with an accent. My mother knew the superintendent of the schools, Mr. Knutsen, a Norwegian so she told the principal to call him. Mr. Knutsen said it was good that young people know two languages, so I didn't have to go in the dumb class. They gave me glasses instead. And, of course, I broke them. I think I was 70 years old when I realized I was probably dyslexic. I still have problems with reading backwards, but I was way ahead of my class in mathematics and history.

I think back on those years in the fishing industry. We had to earn the money before we could spend it, and that's why most of the fisherman of my generation and before were self-sufficient.

In wintertime the fishermen in Ballard worked in the sawmills. They put the Norwegian fishermen at the hardest job in the sawmill, where the logs come out of the water. That was in the 40s.

Before they had navigation equipment on the boats, all they had was the compass and the log to tell them how fast they were going. Coming across the Gulf [of Alaska], they knew they had to change course three times coming from Kodiak Island, so they timed it because that was the variation on the compass as they came across the Gulf. And when they came near, twenty-four hours before they were supposed to reach land, they started sounding by hand with a sounding lead if it was dark or rainy or thick fog [to determine the water depth]. As soon as daylight came or when the fog lifted and they could see land, there was always someone on the boat who had fished there, and could recognize it. Then they'd just find Cape Spencer and go down the Inside Passage. They didn't have the lights or buoys or anything they have now. It was mostly dead reckoning and listening and watching. That's how they did it in those days. I started fishing in 1946, the year I graduated from Ballard High School. Then we had an old surplus Fathometer and an old direction finder that they used to find the outlaw radios during the war. Now with sophisticated instruments, you know exactly where you are anyplace in the ocean.

Well, begin when I was dragging out of Seattle here. The greenhorn had to go on the poorest boats. I slowly worked my reputation up so I could go on any boat at the last. Finally, my dad got me the job on the boat he was on. His was the highline [got the biggest hauls] boat on the Pacific Coast fishing shark livers. That was the *Seabird*, with Jack Cleveland. The skipper told me after I'd been there a while, "You know, the only reason I hired you because I knew if you couldn't hack it, your dad would pick up the slack," But he says, "I found out that he didn't have to pick up any slack."

It's all trial and error [to know where the fish are]. I figured if I made more than 50 percent good decisions during the season, I'd have a successful season. The main thing on fishing is keeping track. Where did we get the fish today? Where did we get the fish yesterday? Where have we got them this morning? And try to find a pattern. When we got direction finders, I used to take bearings on the boats of people I knew were compatible to our fishing, and we could have some kind of an idea what was going on in that area. When we didn't hear anything from that area, then we'd better get there. Nobody ever calls out when they're pulling fish. And when nobody's getting any fish, I used to try and figure out where there weren't any boats. There might be fish there.

The first time I went out fishing with my dad, the trip was over and we were coming in. So we're out there, just the two of us on deck. And he says, "You know, I shouldn't tell you this — you might get swell-headed, but you did better than I thought you would." That was the biggest compliment I ever had [from him].

It's a good thing that our women understood us. Between the fish oil, fish slime and diesel oil and lube oil, it stunk to heaven, you know. We didn't smell it on the boat, but it went into the clothes and everything. We'd come home, and when I first started, I went down to the basement one time where the washing machine was. My sister was down there picking my clothes up with a stick to put in the washing machine. She said, "They stink, I'm not going to touch them." When my daughter was big enough to help wash clothes, she'd come up from the basement. She was using the stick too, to throw the clothes in the washing machine. She told her mother, "Daddy's clothes smell." And Sonia says, "Don't worry about it, just wash them, that's money smell."

The wives were glad to see spring come. They said the spring was the worst for the fishermen's wives. First of all, income tax came due. And we had to outfit the boats. Of course, we never had enough money to do what we wanted to do on the boats, in the spring to get them ready. And they were so glad when the men would leave. My mother was the same way. And then three days after my dad left, she used to say, "Oh, I wish daddy was home."

Arnold Sverre Reinholdtsen - 413

One time we — we almost were full, and we were running up the coast. And I told my dad, you go lay down now for you'll have the first watch when we get through tonight, we're going to run all night. So he went down and went to bed.

And the cook and I were back on the stern and we hit fish. And we started pulling fish, and finally the cook says, "You better call your dad up. If we fill this boat up and he isn't here, he's going to be mad." So I went down and I called. "Come on! Fish!" And finally, we had no more room. When I hauled the gear in, the ones that didn't have fish on the hooks would be chewed off. There was no hooks on them. So you could imagine how much fish was there behind the boat. We couldn't take it. We got to get a bigger boat. But that's when fishing is fun.

And then, when you come into the dock, and you've got the boat full of fish, you know that you had caught those fish and you had worked to get them. That's a good feeling also, you know.

Arnold Reinholdtsen was born August 13, 1928 in Fremont, the son of Emma Marie (Rasmussen Leikanger) and Leif Gordon Reinholdtsen. He joined a sister, Lorraine (1926). Arnold married Sonia Stenvaag in 1951, also born and raised in Ballard. They had four children: Linelle (1952), David (1954), Paul (1961) and Eric (1963). Sonia died in 1983. Arnold died in 2005.

Thorun Johannsson Robel

"So to me it was the age of innocence because everything was family oriented."

Vigdis Finnbogadottir, the President of Iceland, came to Seattle on a tour and they had a reception at the Calvary Lutheran Church, the Icelandic Lutheran Church. It happened to be near the time of my mother's 100th birthday so she was taken to the church to meet the President. My mother, Aleph Torvaldson, had quite a conversation with her and she told my mother that she spoke the purest Icelandic of any Icelander in this country that she had met. My mother was a scholar even though she had had very little schooling. I don't think she went beyond the 12th grade, but she translated from Icelandic to English and she loved poetry and did a few poems. She was a calm woman, very concerned — she was sort of a mother confessor for the Icelandic community. People would come to her if they had problems.

I went to Ballard High School and I graduated in 1931. At Ballard High we had a little clique that went in for everything —hockey, basketball, and we all voted for each other. So you had to be on the inside in order to get on all these teams. You had to be really good in order to break into it. A lot of us came from Webster and we had been together with sport. Also we used to have these assemblies. The principal, Mr. De Vilbiss was kind of an old fuddy-duddy. He wore his hair parted in the middle. He would stand up on the stage when he introduced the assembly and he'd put his hands behind his back and he would rock up and down on his toes as he talked. He was there a long, long time.

Mrs. Dorman was the girl's advisor. When we were playing games and athletics, we had great big pantaloons, real full bloomers, with a middy and our socks and our shoes — and if there was an inch of flesh showing between these bloomers and anything down below the ankle, boy, she'd call us in. And once she called me in the office because my dress was a little short. She sent a note home to my mother that this was not quite proper. My mother sent a hot note back, "I've got three daughters; I'm busy putting up hems, taking down hems and I'm not going to worry about it."

We had some real good teachers, like my French teacher, Mr. Ryan. He was tall, slender, kind of romantic looking. And Mrs. Nicholson, who taught literature always seemed to be so sort of other-worldly. Her nice soft hair, always flying around her face, she was a very gentle woman. All those women were single because they couldn't be married and teach.

We often put on plays. Mrs. Stronach taught what they called Oral Expression where you'd recite and learn to feel a little more at ease. Often in assemblies somebody would recite or somebody would sing. They had a dapper music teacher and he put on some really elaborate operettas. Everybody came and we paid a little admission and they used that money to maybe get some new instruments. They had a school orchestra — well, maybe more a band than an orchestra.

My mother learned to repair stuff and paint and everything else. My dad was never handy so my mother learned to do all of that. He worked long hours in the drug store and he didn't have time to do that sort of thing. He closed it up at eleven at night. He was so regular that people used to set their clocks by him. He'd walk from 72nd down to Ballard to the drugstore every morning.

I remember working late and coming home with my dad — we often walked home. There was quite a bit of goings-on down in Ballard. A lot of people didn't have cars for one thing, so there were theatres there, there were restaurants, there were taverns. And that's why he stayed open late. People would be coming in for ice cream after the show. We'd always have a rush at the ice cream counter. I was sixteen or so and still in high school when I helped at the ice cream counter.

My dad used to have a big bowl of Spanish peanuts with no lid on it. It was part of the ritual. You put your hand in and helped yourself, then went into the booth and ordered your treat. You could get a soda for ten cents, or a dish of ice cream or a sundae. You could get a banana split for two bits that had three kinds of ice cream, three toppings, whipped cream and nuts — oh boy those were the days.

At Christmas time, men who hadn't bothered to shop would rush in 'cause my dad usually stayed open 'til eleven o'clock Christmas Eve. They'd buy a box of chocolates or some of those little perfume sets or some toiletries. That's when he did his best business.

He also had hard candy in these glass jars that had a lid with a handle on them. He had licorice, he had what they called rock candy — it was on a string, clear — and jelly beans and horehound, all that

416 - Thorun Johannsson Robel

stuff. It was lined up in rows by the soda fountain and the kids would want to spend one penny or two. And then beyond that was the patent medicines counter and there was the partition in back where he mixed his prescriptions. He also made the chocolate for the fountain so we had to stir up a huge batch of chocolate on the burner back there.

During Prohibition Virginia Dare Tonic and Lydia Pinkham's were restoratives recommended for ladies. It was good for whatever ailed you if you were anemic. They were very popular. Elixirs, that's what they called 'em. And the ladies would drink them to supposedly help themselves. There was a lot of alcohol in them.

And of course there were bootleggers around. I was visiting a friend, and next door a guy who was bootlegging offered us a drink. I was a teenager. Of course, we were scared stiff — ran out of the house. Oh they went to prison. If they were making liquor illegally they went to prison. They'd smash the still and send them off.

Amongst the Icelanders there were no bootleggers. Some of the older Icelanders drank but where they got their liquor I do not know. Like the Icelandic parties where if you had a dance the whole family came, the kids and all. You had coffee and cake and all that sort of thing. The kids slid all over the dance floor and got in everybody's way but they were there and everybody was having a good time.

We had a lot of gatherings like that in halls around Ballard. They couldn't dance in the Lutheran Church so they had to go rent a hall. To me it was the age of innocence because everything was family oriented.

Thorun Johannsson (1913-1998) was born in Ballard of Icelandic parents. Her siblings: Lincoln (1908), Sigrid (1910), Wilma (1915) and Alice (1918). Her father, Bjarni Johannsson, a pharmacist, owned Cascade Pharmacy with Gunnar Mattiasson, another Icelander. Thorun graduated from Ballard High in 1931. She married Eugene Robel in June, 1938. Their children: Karen (1940), Kathleen (1943), Laurel (1945) and Stefan (1953). Thorun was interviewed March 11, 1988. She died January 5, 1998.

Gordon Ekvall Tracie
by Richard Sacksteder

Gordon Ekvall Tracie was born on March 20, 1920 and died in late 1988 before he could be informed that he was a Governor's Heritage Awardee. He devoted more than four decades to the study, teaching, enjoyment, and promulgation of Nordic traditional music and dance. At his death in 1988, Gordon bequeathed his music, dance and text collections to Skandia Music Foundation, with the request that the collections be kept together and made available to the public. That request was honored by the Foundation in 1993, with the cooperation of Marianne Forssblad, Director of Nordic Heritage Museum, to which Gordon Tracie's estate materials were donated and where those materials are housed. In March 1995 the Gordon Ekvall Tracie Music Library was opened as a research archive of traditional Nordic music and dance, available to the public at Nordic Heritage Museum. This chapter contains the recollections of Richard Sacksteder concerning his friend, Gordon Ekvall Tracie, and the origins of the collection contained in the Gordon Ekvall Tracie Music Library at the Nordic Heritage Museum.
— Gordon Strand

Gordon Ekvall Tracie grew up in Seattle. They lived in the University District, and his dad was a haberdasher. When the Depression came [1930s], he lost his job and he was never able to get back to work again. Gordon's mother took him and they went over on Bainbridge Island, where she was cooking in a boys' school. Gordon went to work in the weekly newspaper there and I think he lived all through high school on peanut butter sandwiches. And the problem was, exams were on Friday and the paper was put to press on Thursday night. So he'd be up all night and he'd try to take the final exams and so forth. So it was pretty tough on him. And he played in a Grange band, played guitar. And he wrote columns for the Grange, and of course he was very off to the left, and everything over there were to the right.

And when the war [World War II] came along he joined the Coast Guard. He was working in the print shop ... for the Coast Guard. And when he joined the Coast Guard they put a suit on him and he stayed right there in the same job. He started the Coast Guard Band. So they finally decided they were gonna send him to sea. So he was on a small Coast Guard boat for a month. He was seasick twenty-four hours a day, and they finally took him off. And he had a choice of going to Hawaii or to Alaska. Well, he doesn't like hot weather, so he went to Alaska. Most people would go to Hawaii. And up there, while he was editing the newspaper, he started up a band there. And he found out later on that it wasn't seasickness: he can't tolerate onions and garlic. They had an Italian cook on that little boat, and the whole thing was filled with garlic, and that's why he was sick.

Actually it starts with President Roosevelt and the WPA. We lived out here in the country, and so I learned all kinds of folk dancing, and then there used to be a place called Bert Lindgren's up north. Saturday night we all went to Bert Lindgren's. Then the WPA had a second thing: it was free guitar lessons, down in University District. I went down there for a free guitar lesson, and here was this guy with a blond guitar... and he could really play, and that was Gordon Ekvall Tracie. So there were a couple of sisters there and we walked them home, the Sheltons, and they were a very musical family, and we'd have a jam session. Their mom would bring out a huge pile of sandwiches at midnight, and coffee. And so that's where Gordon and I got aquainted. And then we went into the service and we wrote some letters back and forth, and after the war we got together, and I said: "Gordon, what you're doin' ?"

"Democratic politics."

I said "Hey, did you ever dance?"

"Nope, I never danced."

"Well, come on up to Bert Lindgren's with me."

So he went. He was very shy and he stood and watched, he didn't do any dancing, and then later on, we found the women's group called *Promenaders* [at the University of Washington] and they wanted a demonstration dancing and they needed some men. So we went down there, and Gordon started to learn to dance. One of the girls, who's still part of our group, said that Gordon was probably the guy least likely to ever learn to dance.

The *University of Washington Daily* one day said they're having a summer school for American students at the University of Oslo. I said "Gordon, I'm gonna sign up." And that's the first time he ever mentioned Swedish background, because of his grandfather on his mother's side. He wanted to go, too. So we both signed up and were accepted and went to the University of Oslo. I went on down to central Europe to visit with my relatives, and he went to Sweden to go to school. And there's where he learned all the dances. When we both came back nineteen months later, he had this whole bunch of records that were shipped over so we took his old model A Ford and went to Tacoma to pick up this great big box of records. He wanted to teach people dances, so we went back to the University, got a bunch of the gals and guys that we danced with there, and went over to Green Lake Fieldhouse, and he started teaching some of these dances. And then we moved to the University of Washington, and once he'd taught us a bunch of dances we started doing demonstrations around Seattle. And there was another dance group, Swedish, that was dancing, but we were younger, and we had more enthusiasm and we had new dances. They were doing the same old thing. Before we knew it, we were "The Demonstration Dance Group in Seattle." And we did that for almost a year or so.

Gordon was always lamenting the fact that over in Sweden they thought we all wore zoot suits and swung a chain and had no folk culture. He was saying, "We should go over there and show them our folk culture." Well, a fellow named Bertil Krogh, who was working for Riksforeningen watched us put on a dance out in Everett, of Scandinavian dances.

This was 1948-49, somewhere in there. So, Gordon was always good at finding the top people. And so he went up to see Bertil, and said "You know, we would sure like to go to Sweden and demonstrate American folk dance," and Bertil said "Hey, I'll set it up for you with the Folk Parks." So Bertil went back and completely forgot about us. And we got the group together, and one time we were dancing for a group and Bill Holm, who does Indian dancing, was on the same program. And he was so good, he was really professional. But we got up our nerve and said to Bill, "Hey, you know we're gonna go do this. Would you like to go?" Well, it turned out his grandfather was Swedish, he said, "Yeah, I'll go." He was great, on all the dances that he could do. And so we kept practicing. We were collecting money; I was the treasurer, and we were collecting money. Gordon got ahold of Bertil Krogh and says "Hey, you know we're all ready to come over," and he'd forgotten all about us. So he got busy, and actually got us the tour, and we paid our own way over. And we danced in twenty-two different cities, and our first one was at Göteborg, and we had a couple of thousand people, and I think we did three sessions there. And we went all over. We would ride on the train, we'd come in, they would meet us, they would take us to show us the town. And then we would have a great big meal, and then we'd put on the dance, and then we'd dance with the local people 'til midnight. And then the next day we would take off, and do it all over again. So we were there for about, six or eight weeks, covering Sweden which was really wonderful. And so then Gordon stayed on there and... we went on down into central Europe.

So when we finally got back here, there was no Skandia Folk Dance group at that time Gordon got things shifted over to [the] YMCA [in] the University District, and that's when the folk dance group started.

By that time Barb and I were married and we'd had our first child and I was teaching up in Arlington so we kind of dropped out. We raised five kids, and Gordon and I still stayed doing things but I was not involved any more in Skandia. Two or three years before he died, he was having trouble with the [Skandia] board, and he said, "Won't you come on the board?" So I was on the board, and I think I was treasurer for a while and one thing or another, kind of supporting him. And then when he got sick, he stayed at our house 'til he was getting well.

Richard Sacksteder

Finally, when he really got sick he phoned us up and said "Hey, come down. I got to write a will." So we went down, and he said well, maybe he should write it, because if we wrote it down, maybe it wouldn't work. So he wrote this up, and then we got hold of Phil Williams, who is his good friend also a lawyer, and Phil said, "That doesn't work, you've... it's gotta be official. You have to have... witnesses and all." So Phil spent five hours with him, with a laptop, and got his will all written up, and went back home. Well, Gordon called and he really wasn't doing well at all, and I called Phil and said: "Hey, you know... if you don't get this will done, there's not gonna be one... and we don't want Gordon to go away with the state taking over, you know." And so Phil got it done, and I brought it over, and then the problem was, you have to find witnesses... well, the hospital is not gonna get involved in anything, they won't witness it. Whenever Gordon had a stomach ache, he always liked mint. Our daughter was working in a little store up the street, and I went up there and of course they had the mints and I said, you know "Here it is Sunday afternoon. I don't know where in the world to get witnesses for this thing." My daughter says,"My girlfriends live in the apartment across here. I'll call them. I bet they will." And they said they'd come down. So they came down and he signed it, they witnessed it, and the next morning he was gone.

I was executor of his estate and everything went into the Skandia Music Foundation. And here's Gordon, who lived as a pauper all his life, never spent any money, and by the time I sold off his property and everything we had over two-hundred thousand dollars in Skandia Music Foundation, and it's been invested rather wisely. And so you know Gordon didn't get a chance to enjoy all this stuff because he grew up during the Depression, they had a very difficult time, and he couldn't realize that he was basically wealthy. He didn't wanna look at it that way, you know. But a lot of it, of course, was property. Gordon, as far as I'm concerned, was one of the brightest people I've ever known. I think he was kind of basically a genius.

When he went into a class he'd start questioning the professors, and within a week he and the professor were good friends. And you know... but he was a perfectionist. One time, I think it was on his graduation, or something, he was taking a course in political science, and he's writing his thesis thing for the course. But he didn't have it the way he wanted it. The professor said: "Look Gordon, just sign your name on a piece of paper and I'll pass you!" "No, I gotta get this thing done." He fooled around, and finally got an incomplete. And you know, he had his head so full of stuff, he could tell you stories about where the music came from, and how it fits, and how all the dances fit. And he was supposed to write a book. We couldn't get him to write the book. Then he got a computer. And whenever he got something like that, my job was to learn how to use it and take it down to show Gordon, and so that crazy computer went from me to one of our kids and, finally, a month before he passed away, John finally got him to use it and, man, he was a whiz. But it would have been the greatest book on earth, in this area, if we could have gotten him to write this stuff.

He never learned to play the fiddle. Yet, he introduced the Swedish fiddle to probably fifty or sixty people playing it around here now. He brought them in. The music was all in his head, and he played the mandolin, which is fingered just like a fiddle. There's no reason on earth that he wasn't one of the best fiddlers here, except it was up on a pedestal and he wasn't good enough, so he wouldn't do it. There were more women who would have jumped at the chance to marry Gordon. But they were all on a pedestal and he couldn't.... well, he never felt he had the income, proper income, he couldn't support somebody.

422 - Gordon Ekvall Tracie by Richard Sacksteder

Gordon was interesting. We figured he taught at least ten thousand people to dance in his life. When you look around Seattle, half of these folk bands got their start with Gordon. And half of the dance groups got their start with Gordon, and they spread out [to] different ethnic dances. But he left a big impression, and he taught all round the United States. He would go to these big dance things, like down in California, and he would always be on the program. He would teach and meet people there.

I've got a letter, in his file from the Swedish consulate down in San Francisco, saying that Gordon had a lot to do with reviving the folk music in Sweden. You go down to Stockholm and they say: "All those old fogies up there with that music. Who cares?" Well he went up there and met Knis Karl. He started at the top. Knis Karl was number one, and got things going. He brought the fiddlers down and, with Gunnar Hahn, they started producing records with these fiddlers. And pretty soon it started to spread. And now there's a lot of that going on in Sweden. But when he got up there in 1947, there wasn't much happening, except up in the Dalarna area. And so he was kind of a ... catalyst for getting that stuff going, and they recognized that.

Some people got a little upset with him, because when you dance, if your hands have to be this way you couldn't have them that way, and it had to be just the way it was. The interesting thing, though, we used to dance what we called "The Seattle Polka," two steps, two steps, and then pivot. And when he went over to Sweden, they put on a polka, and he started dancing that way, people said: "We haven't seen this since about nineteen five." The Swedes coming over here brought that with them and it never changed. Over there it changed.

And then he would go through old stores and he brought back sets of books that are no longer in print. Down at the Nordic Heritage Museum they're very happy to have that as part of their thing over there. Because they were things that nobody was interested in, except Gordon, and so he bought all this stuff up. We took a year to clean out his house. I took forty truckloads to the dump. But out of that, there was so much good stuff. He saved everything. There were a lot of seventy eights, and forty fives and... well, a lot of the stuff is down there now, because I built shelving for him. And fortunately I did that before he passed away, and he brought stuff up from the basement and he actually got it in shape. Otherwise we just would have found box after box of mixtures of stuff. But at least that did help when we got over there, this kind of segregated out.

He had over a hundred three ring notebooks above his desk. Each one had things in it that had to do with something or other. But, you know, he did the Midsummer thing, and he did the Skandia Ball, all by himself. And now they've got committees, they've got three committees doing what he used to do. One on dance, one on music and one on special events, and each committee has a bunch of people. But he used to do that all by himself.

And the radio programs he had... I've got one series when he talked about his first Christmas in Dalarna, and they got up at four o'clock in the morning and they went out through the snow. And the horses bringing the sleighs and with the torches and all this stuff. And so he'd discussed that and then the music when they got to the church. And so, he had a lot of drawings of wall hangings of things that parallelled that. So I photographed them all, and so, as you see these photographs you hear him describing this stuff.

But, you know, he did so much, for so many people. The number of people that met and got married thru' Skandia, we don't know how many they are, but there are lots of them. Gordon and I, at the beginning, we did everything as a team. But after that, he was doing everything and we were just dropping in as anybody else would drop in and dance.

Archivist Mary Mohler and volunteer Joanne Jonsson in the Gordon Tracie Library at the Nordic Heritage Museum.

Richard Sacksteder was born in Dayton, Ohio in 1922. The family moved to Oregon and then to Seattle, where Richard eventually attended the University of Washington (where he met Gordon Tracie). After both travelled throughout Europe, he returned home and joined the Navy (1941). After WWII he earned his degree at the UW and toured Sweden with Gordon and the Western American Folkdancers.

He married Barbara Steele in 1951. They had six children. Richard taught various grades and held principalships in the Shoreline School District. He spent the rest of his career as Director of the Instructional Materials Center, being named WA State Administrator of the Year in 1975.

After retiring, he travelled the world with his wife, taught high-school English in Japan, learned classical guitar, and created artisic works in various media. He also served on boards of several musical organizations.

Alice J. Sagstad

"They were trying to get the streets paved, and they had workers there. So I sold lemonade."

I've lived in Ballard all my life. What I remember most is from when I was young during the Depression. When I was about nine, my dad had a hard time finding work and we ended up living with my grandmother on 25th Northwest, between 70th and 73rd. We lived upstairs, sharing the one bathroom downstairs on the porch. Any cooking my mother did was in the kitchen on the main floor. The streets were not not paved. They were trying to get the streets paved, and they had workers there. So I sold lemonade. Mother made lemonade for the workers, and I sold it and made some money.

During that time, a neighborhood couple got married. After the wedding, all the kids went together and had a shivaree. We took pots and pans and stood out in front of their house and banged them. Then they came out and gave us coins. They don't do that anymore. I was just a little kid, and I thought it was neat.

One year we picked raspberries at a farm in Sumner. I wasn't real good at picking berries. My sister Helen, my mother and dad picked most of the berries. Then my dad got a year-long job as a carpenter building a new Sumner school. We continued to live in the tiny shack we lived in when we were picking berries. It had room for the four of us. We took our baths on Saturday night in a washtub.

We moved back to my grandmother again until we found a house my dad could buy. Around 1934 we moved to 3017 Northwest 66th and I went to Webster School. My mother hated that house because the family who owned it had painted big polka dots all over the bedrooms. My dad painted over them, but my mother still had a fit. I lived there until I married Howard in 1946.

When I was 12, 13 years old, we played kick the can, baseball, football, or whatever. A minister and his wife, who had a couple children, had a huge garden in the lot next to theirs. We kids would go at night and steal peas from their pea patch. We'd camp out overnight and we'd sit and eat these green peas. We had so much fun.

Mothers were home all the time. One time my mother was really ill and I had to wash clothes — my sister was gone by then. We didn't have a washing machine. We used a scrub board and a hand wringer. At the time I thought it was awful. Now everything is so easy for us, and nobody knows how hard it is to wash sheets by hand when you're 12 or 13 years old. We had two laundry trays in the basement. I scrubbed them on the scrub board in the first one with soapy water, then I put them through the wringer into the rinse water in the second. The wringer sat between the two laundry trays. Then I dumped the soapy water in the first tub, and filled it with clean water and wrung the sheets into it for a second rinse. Then, I dumped the first rinse water, and rinse again with bluing in it. And then I wrung the sheets again and hung them out to dry. It was a long process.

My mother was a seamstress, so she made a lot of our clothes. When we got older, we didn't want homemade clothes. We wanted something bought, so we would go to Penney's, down in Ballard.

My sister and I always had a big fight every time we had to do dishes. Helen would do anything to get out of washing dishes, but she would dry them. She'd lock herself in the bathroom until she was sure I had washed all the dishes, then she'd come out. When she finally left home, I ended up doing all the dishes almost all the time. We had to keep our rooms clean, and the house was always meticulous. Mother always kept it clean.

During the war when meat was so hard to get, my dad had a big two-car garage. He left his Buick outside, bought baby chicks, and raised them in the back of the garage. When they got big enough he killed them and we had chicken every Sunday. I got so sick of chicken. I think my dad also grew vegetables — carrots and potatoes.

My dad had always been a carpenter, but during wartime he went to work for Seattle Ship. In fact, I christened one of the warships that was down there when I was 19 or 20 years old. Sagstad's was near there, and they built wartime ships, too. A lot of bigger ships were built in LaConner. There was another shipyard near there too, Tregoning, but it was out on the saltwater side of the canal, and Maritime was on the other side of the canal.

My father-in-law, Sievert Sagstad, started Sagstad Shipyards in 1909. He had a little boat yard right below the train trestle. He was there for a long time. He built a Viking ship out in Bothell for the Alaska Yukon Pacific Exposition in 1909. From there Sagstad Shipyards moved to the foot of 20th to what was called the Ballard Boat Works. He didn't own the property because he said he couldn't afford it. Finally he purchased it in 1936. It continued as a shipyard up until the boys, Howard and Stan, took over. In 1959, when the fishing industry was not doing that well and they weren't building many fishing boats, they put in the boat marina [Sagstad Marina].

Sievert Sagstad was born in Norway, in Lysekloster near Bergen. Howard and I visited the place in Norway where he had built boats. When he came here, he had a long career of boat-building. Howard worked for his dad. Howard and I were married in January, 1946, and Sievert died the following November. He was sixty-six years old. Howard's brother Stan became ill in 1948, and was not able to participate much at the shipyard, so Howard maintained it. He took in another person, Odd Johansen, for 10 percent of the business and they worked together until it was changed over to the marina. Stan's wife, Margaret worked in the office, taking care of the books and everything.

My son Steven worked down there when he was 16. By then it was a marina. He worked at the gas dock and did things like that until he went to college. The marina was sold in 1994. From 1909 to 1994 is a long time.

Alice Svenslid was born February 23, 1923 in Ballard to Olaf Svenslid who emigrated from Eidsøra, on the west coast of Norway in 1912, and Alta (Johnson) Svenslid, born in Michigan of Norwegian immigrants. She joined an older sister, Helen (1919). On January 12, l946 she married Howard Sagstad. Their children: Steven (1948), Cathi (1951). Howard died in 1990.

Charlotte Erickson Sandusky

"Mr. Erickson, you have built the biggest dry dock in the world. You have done the heavy grading in Seattle. The only thing remaining to round out your career in the Northwest is to build a railroad on the Olympic Peninsula." Typically, the man of few words said, "I tank I might. …"

M y grandfather, Carl Johan Erickson, was born to Jonas Erickson and Kajsa Bengtsdotter June 22, 1852 in Hudene, a farming community in Västergötland, Sweden. In 1862, when Carl Johan was ten years old; his father left the family to fight as a mercenary in the American Civil War.

Back home in Sweden, Carl Johan learned to take responsibility; he herded sheep for neighboring farmers, and worked as a straw boss on the Göta Canal project. The canal crosses mid-Sweden from Göteborg to Stockholm, passing the city of Karlsborg as it enters Lake Vattern.

In time Carl Johan's family moved to the nearby small farming town of Jallby. There he met Anna Ericka, daughter of Lars Anderson. My grandma Anna told me, "I had two suitors, but your grandpa was more earnest than the other. We were married on Midsummer's day in 1877."

Carl Johan continued work on the canal and took small contracts in railroad construction on the Borås Herrljunga Railroad. A daughter, Jennie, was born to them in 1879. In 1880 Carl Johan brought his family across the Atlantic to Carver County, Minnesota. He joined his father Jonas, who worked in railroad construction there. Jonas worked in railroading until he retired and moved to an old people's home. After C.J. became prosperous he brought his father to live with him in his big house on Capitol Hill in Seattle.

In 1882 another girl, Ellen Christine, was born to C.J. and Anna. Two years later, on December 20, 1884, my father Charles Edward and his twin brother, Levine, were born. Levine lived only a few months. Another baby girl, Hilda Cajsa, came into the family on February 13, 1889. The family lived in Minneapolis several years and were members of the Swedish Baptist Church.

There were business reverses in Minneapolis. C.J. heard "wild tales of fortunes to be made on the West Coast," so he and his family and some friends from church took the Canadian Pacific Railroad to Seattle.

On June 6, 1889, while Seattle recovered from the Great Fire, C.J. and the family settled at 1922 Terry Avenue. They later moved to an area where C.J. built several houses.

C. J. walked all day over muddy streets looking for work. One day he landed a job building small brick chimneys. Later, walking the streets, he found a partner and organized a company. The Erickson Company built the Union Trust Building, Globe, Smith and Walker Building and Piper Building and the Svea and Shirley Hotels. He owned the hotels for a time.

In 1897 he and his workers went to Grays Harbor and built a stone lighthouse there. An Aberdeen newspaper described it as "the tallest lighthouse on the Washington coast."

C. J.'s firm was one of eight chosen to level Denny Hill in Seattle. The Denny Hill dirt was flushed by hydraulic gusher through an elevated culvert and dumped into barges which were emptied into Elliot Bay. City Engineer R. H. Thompson wanted the irregular harbor reshaped to create space for the downtown business area. It was delicate work done around the surrounding buildings but Great Northern was also building a tunnel under the area at the same time

Dad [Charlie] told me: "Your grandpa came to the United States penniless; unable to speak the language, yet he made a good go of it. He either had a hundred dollars in his pocket (a lot then) or nothing. If a project went sour, he was always ready to start a new one in the hope of better luck next time. He never mulled over problems. When he brought his work for critical analysis, C.J., bereft of persuasive words, would depart from the meeting without ceremony. He'd hurry to the nucleus of his work force and galvanize his efforts wholeheartedly into getting the job done. It was less frustrating than trying to explain his plans to the city engineers."

Charlie wrote of his father: "Like a compulsive gambler, C.J. wanted to 'get with it' and his men found his enthusiasm infectious. Repeatedly an inspector would report at his engineer's desk with, 'Do you know what? That change, that repair, that emergency has been handled — that Swede did not want wasted time here on the job.' 'Who knows what comes tomorrow!' was all C.J. would say.". . . "My father was a contractor specializing in road and street grading. His equipment? Many, many horses, kept at a stable at Seventh Avenue and Olive Way."

Under the direction of R. H. Thompson, the Erickson Company built the North Trunk Sewer. In 1913, at the outbreak of World War I, the 827-foot dry dock made of granite and concrete was completed. A 1945 issue of *The Seattle Times* called it the "largest dry dock in the nation and a major repair base. It held over thirty million gallons of water when flooded in one and one-half hours." Navy Secretary and future President Franklin D. Roosevelt praised the work.

Lake Washington Ship Canal: The government made a contract with him to dig and dredge the Montlake section of the Lake Washington Ship Canal, a major undertaking that aroused nationwide interest. New York newspapers compared the ship canal to New York Harbor and a 1916 international marine engineering periodical stated, "Even New York took notice of the energetic pursuit of the uniform ship passage to make Lake Union an important distribution center.

They cut down the earth of the Montlake section on a slope from Lake Washington to near the level of Lake Union. This involved excavating two hundred seventy thousand yards of dirt at the Montlake neck of land between the lakes at a cost of fifty-six thousand dollars. The excavated earth filled the shoreline northeast of the cut. A May 17, 1911 article in *The Seattle Post Intelligencer* referred to the Montlake Cut as "the Erickson Ditch."

Mr. Bilger of Hunts Point filed a suit against the state of Washington to prevent the excavation on the ground that lowering the lake eight feet would damage his property. The county court denied a temporary injunction on the ground that Bilger could not be damaged by ditch-digging unless the ditch was connected. At last, when only a few shovelfuls separated the lakes, the court by its final decree enjoined the state and the contractor, C. J. Erickson, from making connection. But the U.S. Engineer in charge of the work is said to have ordered Erickson's foreman to dynamite the remaining earth, which was done and the lakes were joined. Because the county and state were responsible for doing the canal excavating, the United States was secured from liability.

Soon after that incident, President Roosevelt contracted with C.J. to build nine steel vessels for World War I. C. J.'s daughter, Hilda, like Grandpa, a staunch Republican, deplored that her father would have to deal with Democrats. Gust Embom, an Erickson employee, told me:

"For these vessels, your grandpa built the Seattle North Pacific Shipbuilding Company at the original site of the Lockheed West Waterway on Harbor Island. It was a beautiful shipyard. Several ships were launched in 1919, but your grandpa lost of a quarter of a million dollars when World War I ended and the contract was broken."

Adelphia College: C.J. built Adelphia College at 1122 Delmar Drive East [Seattle] in 1907, a pleasant departure from his larger developments, Dad said.

The school not only taught the recent settlers, but became to them a home away from home. By allowing Swedish immigrants to make an easier transition from lower schools to U.S. universities and colleges, it gave those young people from Sweden educational opportunities C. J. missed.

Because expressing himself in English was difficult for C.J., Charlie must have helped him put his words to paper: "Having come to a new and strange land, without money and with the most limited schooling, it has long been my hope to do something for others in like circumstances."

The school operated successfully until World War I after which Swedish immigration ceased.

King Gustaf of Sweden not only knighted C. J. but conferred on him "The Royal Order of Vasa First Class" for this endeavor. In 1919, Seattle Preparatory School acquired the forty thousand dollar edifice. It fell to the wrecker's ball in Ferbruary 1971.

First Baptist Church: C.J. regraded streets and built several homes in the Denny Regrade area. He also built the First Baptist Church on Capitol Hill. Originally he belonged to the First Swedish Baptist Church, which in 1906 wanted to build a new church. C.J. would have built it, but decided not to when one man donated a large amount of granite for the construction. The church hired an architect with differing tastes than C.J.'s. He reasoned, "I want it to look like a church, not a library." which is where he felt granite belonged.

A rumor circulated through our family that he and the board didn't agree on certain parts of the Bible. Whatever the reason, C.J. withdrew from the Swedish Baptist Church to join the First Baptist Church. The First Baptist Church survived only until 1908 when grading of Fourth Avenue began. In *Our First Baptist Heritage Book 1869-1984* the story was told thus:

"During the early years, Fourth Avenue was a narrow dirt road on a steep hill rising from Puget Sound and climbing into the forest above. When population reached 240,000, the City decided the street needed to be regraded, as streets lower on the hillside already had been improved. Realizing the regrading would leave the church at the edge of a deep cut, with salvage impractical, the congregation decided it was time to move. But where? From the congregation of five hundred sixty-two, a committee was appointed early in 1906 to look for a new location.

Several months later, it came in with the recommendation of the Northwest corner of Broadway and Madison, which was accepted."

"Real old-timers among local Baptists are those who attended preaching on Fourth Avenue in 1908, before Brother Erickson's steam-shovel operations concluded the services." [said] E. Meacham, who grew up at First Baptist and now lives on Mercer Island. . .

Erickson transferred his membership to First Baptist in the spring of 1908 and was named to the building committee within a month, together with Rev. Mr. Jones, who is believed to have provided some of the financial backing Erickson required for his projects

Lake Crescent, Port Angeles, Milwaukee Railroad: In 1912, and the church completed, a Milwaukee Railroad agent, Mr. Calkins, persuaded C. J. to build an east-west railroad line from Port Angeles.

Mr. Aldwell, an entrepreneur in his own right, had pioneered a dam to provide power for the Port Angeles area. He said to C.J.:

"Mr. Erickson, you have built the biggest dry dock in the world. You have done the heavy grading in Seattle. The only thing remaining to round out your career in the Northwest is to build a railroad on the Olympic Peninsula." Typically, the man of few words said, "I tank I might."

Building the railroad around Discovery Bay wasn't easy. The daughter of Mr. Siedenbaum, a local homesteader, remembered, "Mr. Erickson built the railroad from beyond Maynard to Fairmont. As a young girl, I heard the elders saying that because of the changing tide and the wind, some people doubted he could build it around the bay. By using the tide to his advantage, he did it."

After construction, C.J. sold the railroad, as he'd planned, to the Chicago, Milwaukee and St. Paul Railroad. At that time, he acquired large timber holdings south of Sequim and in Indian Valley. He built a mill for processing the lumber and named the town Carlsborg after Karlsborg, Sweden, a town where he had worked as a young man.

In her book, *Now Tell Me This*, Charlotte Erickson Sandusky wrote about her father, Charlie, with a chapter about her grandfather, Carl Johan Erickson. This is from that chapter, reprinted with her permission.

Hilda M. Schmitt

"People didn't talk about being Indian very much when I was young because there was lots of prejudice. There were signs in stores and places that said 'No Indians Allowed.'"

My father was born in Tranabo, Sweden, the oldest of eight or nine children, mostly brothers. He came to this country when he was 18. His father died fairly early, but he was alive when he left. His mother lived to be 96 years old. Now this is not directly from his mouth, this is family talking that he didn't want to be in the service and he did not want to be forced to go to church. He didn't like church. He was a very lovely, honest, nice man, but he wasn't interested in church.

All of his brothers except one came here as they got to 18 or 19. His brother Arvid Peterson had a nursery and was a gardener. He had a big place near the entrance to Golden Gardens.

My mother died when I was three months old. I always wondered why my dad quit fishing. Well, I'm sure that's why. He had four children. He couldn't go fishing with that many children to take care of. I'm sure that was it. He became a longshoreman. My mother was born in Neah Bay. She was a Makah Indian. He was up there fishing, and she helped him with something to do with fishing, and they fell in love and married. It made a lot of people in Neah Bay unhappy because they didn't want to lose her. She moved to Seattle, but when I was three months old she contracted pneumonia — that was before penicillin and all that — and she died.

When I was growing up, I was totally away from that culture, but after I became an adult, I decided I wanted to know them and find out. I've had two wonderful aunties who are now gone, but when they were alive my whole family spent a lot of time with them. My aunties, Mabel Robertson and Helen Peterson were lovely, lovely ladies. They would not talk about my mother very often because Indians don't like to talk about someone who is dead. But they told me she was a very friendly lady and was popular in Ballard. When the police had a little lost Indian person who didn't speak English, they brought her to my mother, so she'd help with them.

People didn't talk about being Indian very much when I was young because there was lots of prejudice. There were signs in stores and places that said "No Indians Allowed." My aunties wouldn't go to a lot of places because they knew they weren't welcome there, but a lot of those places didn't have signs. I remember the taverns. If you went to go dancing, and there was live music. There was also liquor available, and there would be signs, "No Indians allowed," because it was illegal to serve liquor to an Indian when I was young. But I was just going to tell them I was Swedish if they had asked me.

We had picnics at Golden Gardens. It was an important part of our family social life. My dad and Uncle Arvid had a lot of friends, and they would get together. They were like extended family.

Occasionally we'd go out to Vasa Park to the Swedish picnic. There's dancing, schottisches and polkas. And it's funny, because people from Sweden told us they don't dance like that, and they didn't even, way back then, that they were corny. We danced schottisches and hambos. I liked the Swedish Waltz the most. They always had really good food at those picnics. They swam and had a great day.

I tried to find out some things when my dad was getting older. He would get emotional and couldn't seem to answer the questions.

However, I found out this thing about the Matsuda deal from a niece. And I failed to ask her how she knew that unless my brother knew it and told her, because she's my brother's granddaughter.

Okay, that was really horrible. All of a sudden the Matsudas were ordered away. They had no time to prepare, no time — even I, as a child, I was fairly young, I think probably 11, 12 could see it was horrible. They were just taken away. My dad was very proud to be a United States citizen, always voted, was very patriotic, but that horrified him. And this niece just told me that my dad and a neighbor, and I'm sorry I don't know the neighbor's name, were at the Matsuda's house so that when they came back from the internment camp they would have their house. Most Japanese lost their homes.

We lived at 2853 Northwest 69th Street, and the Matsudas lived across the street and two houses down from us. Mrs. Matsuda was a seamstress and she did some sewing for mom. Mr. Matsuda was a gardener and they just did neighborly things. Kitty, their youngest daughter, and I were very good friends, went to school together. But when she came back from the internment camp, she was always very polite, but very cool. She was really hurt. I think she was the one that was hurt the most. The Matsudas themselves seemed to just settle back in when they came back, like it's passed.

434 - Hilda M. Peterson Schmitt

I remember the Metropolitan Life Insurance man came every month or so and collected maybe a dollar or two for everybody. We all were insured. When I was an adult, I got to cash it in. The Fuller Brush man was very popular and there were a lot of ways to not have to go to the store. A corner grocery store just a block away. My mother used to send me there, sometimes every day for fresh vegetables or for a little bit of meat or something. And my dad had fisherman friends, and when they came in with a big catch, they'd share with everybody, and we had lots of wonderful fish to eat.

My girlfriend Elaine's parents were from Norway, I believe, and they charged things. To my mom and dad, this was just horrible, but it seemed fun to me. You just went to the store and said charge it. Their butcher was down the street a ways, and I would go with Elaine every month when she paid the bill. And they would give us each a really wonderful nice wiener or a pickle from a big pickle barrel. And then, occasionally we went and bought quarts of cow's blood, and Elaine's mother made blood sausage and we would always get people that weren't acquainted with Norwegian stuff to eat it, and then tell them what it was and they would just be horrified.

My mother believed in recycling way before it ever came up. She did a lot of recycling. Then it was called being cheap or thrifty. She was thrifty.

Well, there were a lot of people who did the same thing at Christmas. As far I know, Scandinavian people celebrate mainly at Christmas Eve. Christmas day is church. And we would have *lutfisk*, fruit soup, the adults all had *glögg* and it was served to them with a flame coming out of the cup. And my Uncle Arvid always had Christmas Eve. My momma had Thanksgiving. Uncle Arvid was a nurseryman and he had a living tree growing in a pot and covered with candles, and he lit them on Christmas Eve. We never had a fire.

Hilda Peterson was born June 11, 1929 in Ballard to Ann (Peterson) and Karl Peterson. Her siblings: Karl (1919), Frank Albert (1921), Ginny (1922). Her mother died 1929, in 1932 her father married Cecile Chapin from Paris, France. Hilda married Milton Schmitt Dec 31, 1951. Their children are: Gary (1956), twins Dennis (1956) & David (1956-1977) and Brian (1959). They have five grandchildren. After ten years at home with her children, Hilda worked for Kelley's, an answering service.

Laura Joan Seznick

"Everything in that house was done by Finns, except the plumbing. There weren't any Finnish plumbers."

We lived in Ballard near 24th and 64th. I was like two or three then. My dad then worked at the Stimson Mill. Then the Finnish people built a new hall down at 1239 Washington Street, just north of Jackson. My folks became care-takers of the Finnish Hall, so we lived there for about three years. I learned to speak Japanese at that time. I played with the little Japanese children whose parents owned a nearby Japanese grocery store. I started school at Pacific School, on 12th and Jefferson. We moved to Capitol Hill and I went to Horace Mann School. We lived in one duplex and then on 26th and East Union in another. In both we had the top floor and other Finnish families lived on the first floor, good friends of my mother and dad's.

The Finnish people are very friendly. I spoke Finnish before I spoke English but my mother and dad made sure I knew how to speak English and could read before I started school. Then we moved to the Madrona District and I went to Madrona Grade School and Garfield High School. I graduated from there in 1937. I was 11th in my class of almost 400, and I got a University of Washington scholarship from the teachers at Garfield.

The war started and I met a sailor, Peter Seznick, on November 9th. We were married February 20, 1943 in Los Angeles because his ship had gone down there. After the wedding, we went to the Biltmore Hotel where we spent our first night. Ozzie Nelson and his wife, Harriet, were performing at the Biltmore Bowl. They announced our wedding there and sang a song to us. Peter went to fight the war, and I came back to Seattle. When he came back after the war, we found our lot in Blue Ridge. We bought the property in 1947 and started building. Our house was built by the Finns here in Seattle, friends of the family. Everything in that house was done by Finns, except the plumbing. There weren't any Finnish plumbers. We had to go to others for that.

We joined Vasa Hope, a Scandinavian lodge in Ballard. We still belong to Vasa Hope. Both Peter and I have been chairman of the lodge. In 1953 I became the first woman to be chairman.

I don't want Ballard to change. That's just me being old fashioned I guess. I do think it's nice that we have the Nordic Heritage Museum and Vasa Hope, and the Sons of Norway trying to keep their heritage. I think everybody should keep their heritage.

I also believe that anybody who comes to America has to learn the language. They should go to school and learn the language like my mother and dad did. When my mother came, she just knew "bananas," and my dad knew "ham and eggs." Those were the words that they knew. My dad said he got so tired of eating ham and eggs on the train from New York. They came into New York to Ellis Island. My mother went to Ironwood, Michigan, where her uncle had a big farm. She worked on the farm cooking and washing 'til she paid off her debt to her uncle, and then she went to Duluth. My dad went to Missoula, Montana, to his aunt's. He worked in the mines for just a few months, and decided that's not for him. He didn't like being underground. He then went to Duluth, and that's where they met.

Peter and I have been all over the world, and I have not found another place that I would go to. This is the best place to live. The weather is good, even if it rains. That's what makes it nice and green. We don't have the horrendous heat or that terrible cold or tornadoes or hurricanes that people have other places.

Laura Maki was born December 7th, 1918, in Rossland, BC, Canada to Jack and Hilda Maki. Both emigrated from Finland. They met in Duluth, Michigan. Hilda (Ristimaki) came from Kauhajoki, Finland. The family lived in Ballard for three years in her preschool years. She and Peter Seznick were married February 20, 1943. They built a home in Blue Ridge in the late 1940s. They have three children: Joan (1943), Nancy (1948) and Jack (1950). Laura died in 2006.

Henry Theodore Simonson

"In the summer's long twilights, we played kick the can, hide and seek, and capture the flag."

My mother, Therese Marie Ingvaldsen, was born in 1890 in northern Norway. Her mother died when she was very young, so she and her older sister, Inga, lived with other families. Their father remarried and had a daughter, Jennie. My Aunt Inga came to the United States about 1912, and eventually to Seattle. She sent a steamship ticket to my mother, who came to Seattle in 1916.

My father, Hans Martin Simonson was born in 1887, about 55 miles south of where my mother lived. But they never met. My father was a second son. The custom was that the first son was given the farm if it could not be divided to support more families. My father immigrated in 1907, landing in Boston. Working at different jobs, he eventually arrived in Seattle about 1911. He became a fisherman, a job he knew best from his work in Norway. In 1917, after a fishing trip, he brought fish to his friend, Ivar Sather, met Therese there and eventually married her. Therese was fabulous. Although she became a citizen by marrying Hans, she studied and passed the exams and received her own U.S. citizenship. She was very proud of her accomplishment, and I was proud of her doing it. She never said a bad word about anyone. Everybody liked her. Our neighbor, Bob Bailey, when he was about ten, made a small May basket with flowers for her and left it on our porch. She chased him down the street and gave him a thank-you kiss. I think her early death was partly due to her grief over my brother's death in World War II.

Hans's first job in Seattle was on a halibut schooner. They were large boats that sent out smaller, two-man sailboats over the fishing grounds. Fishing changed since the Norwegians built smaller boats, 50 to 100 feet long, similar to the boats used in Norway. My father and his partner bought a boat. Then about 1927 they built a 57-foot boat, the *Unimak*, which they fished until they retired about 1950.

My parents spoke English at home except when they did not want my brother and me to know what they were talking about, or when Norwegian guests visited, they usually all talked Norwegian.

My parents were active members of the Sons of Norway, Daughters of Norway, Nordlandslaget, a club for Northern Norwegians, and the Masonic orders, Eastern Star, Amaranth, and Masons.

In summer my mother would take my brother and me on trips while my father was out fishing. Seattle had the Mosquito Fleet, fast, slick, steam-powered vessels that plied the waters of Puget Sound and Lake Washington. The restored *Virginia V*, still active, is an example. The vessels made stops about every three miles. A typical vessel, the *Hyak,* sailed from downtown Seattle to Port Madison, Agate Pass, Suquamish, Keyport, Lemolo, and finally Poulsbo. For two summers when I was seven and eight, my family camped on a small farm at Lemolo. We slept in a tent with a wood floor, cooked on a wood stove, and hand-pumped water from a well. My brother and I had great fun climbing trees to pick the fruit, swimming in the cold water, combing the beaches and hiking the narrow roads. As cars became more popular, car ferries replaced the Mosquito Fleet. Ballard had a car-ferry dock where Ray's Boathouse restaurant is now. One small ferry sailed to Suquamish on the Indian reservation. The larger ferries sailed to Port Ludlow, which had a large lumber mill and is now a resort community.

Immigrants from Europe were a large part of the population of Ballard in 1918. They were attracted to local industries such as fishing, boat building, lumber mills. There were many nationalities: Norwegian, Swedish, Finnish, Icelandic, Danish — also Irish, Yugoslav, Greek, Italian, Chinese, and Japanese. A high school friend of mine, whose father was Greek, and I were in business together after the war. In my neighborhood, one of my best friends was Mathew Tomasovich, whose father came from Yugoslavia. Two streets away and living across from Matt's family, was the Matsuda family, of Japanese descent. When the Matsuda family was sent to a relocation camp in Idaho in 1942, neighbors watched the Matsuda house and stored their belongings in their basements. A few houses away were the Hansens, who were Norwegians, with Corrinne and Jack and Helen. Behind us on the next street were the Johnsons, who were Swedes, with Holger as part of our gang. Across the street were the Baileys, whose Bob was with us; that family was English.

My brother and I liked to fish. We used hand lines with a weight and a small hook. A popular place was at the government locks. A long wooden pier extended on the north side of Salmon Bay towards the railroad bridge. We crawled under the pier and onto the supports and fished for small shiners. For bait we used mussels which we found on the pier. We crushed them with our feet and cut small pieces for the hook. My mother reluctantly took our catch for the cat and at the proper time she threw the fish into the garbage.

We lived four blocks from the bluff overlooking Puget Sound. In summer the gang would go to the bluff, crawl across a saddle of sand called the Camel's Hump, walk down a trail through brush and trees and cross the Great Northern railroad tracks to reach Ballard Beach. The road from the ferry terminal had not been developed, although it was possible to walk to Ballard Beach. We swam, built bonfires out of driftwood, ran the sandy beaches, and threw a football.

We played on the paved streets — touch football and softball, with third base a telephone pole, and first base a water meter cover; hockey on four-wheel roller skates with goal posts of cans or rocks. Usually we had a rubber puck, if not, a piece of wood was okay. We learned to check with a hockey stick. After tennis season, we played on the tennis court at Ballard Playfield, using park benches for goals.

In the summer's long twilights, we played kick the can, hide and seek, and capture the flag. One vacant lot had a basketball hoop and backboard on a pole. We played one-on-one, two-on-two, horse, and 21, the same games played today.

We made scooters with a roller skate, an apple box, a two-by-four, two stick handles for steering, and canning lids for headlights. We made stilts out of two by fours. We patched softballs and baseballs with friction tape when the covers were torn.

When we lived on Sunset Hill, we were under the flight path of a new airline. Mr. Boeing formed a company to fly mail to Victoria in a small seaplane. The open cockpit plane took off from Lake Union, flew over the canal to Puget Sound, then north to Victoria. On bad-weather days, the plane flew very low. We stood in the street waving and yelling to the pilot, "Give us a ride." He surely heard us, for we screamed so loud.

In the late '20s, young boys built crystal sets to receive radio signals. It was simple: buy special crystal from a store, scratch a wire across the crystal and a sound would come from a local radio station. Every home had a radio; some could even get overseas stations. Local stations presented sports; a favorite announcer was Leo Lassen who broadcast baseball games. Radio theater was very popular, presenting mysteries, detective stories and soaps. Every Sunday evening we listened to *One Man's Family*, a soap about a family in San Francisco. Other shows were *Amos and Andy*; *Sam Spade, Detective*; *The Green Hornet;* and *The Shadow*.

There was no organized soccer, but there was an unorganized recess period at grade school. A teacher would throw out a soccer ball and 20 or more small boys would chase it, anxious to get at least one kick before the bell called us back to class. On Saturday mornings, we participated in athletic programs at Ballard Fieldhouse. In season, we played basketball. We were grouped by weight, with divisions of 90, 100, 110 pounders. Our ages were nine, ten, and 11. We were also grouped by ability.

Every other Saturday, I was on the travel squad. We reported to the Fieldhouse and Coach Pete Peterson would say, "Henry, today you're the captain. Take the team to Collins Fieldhouse." He would give us instructions and directions, check that we had our lunch and two nickels for the streetcar fare and wish us good luck. He stayed at the fieldhouse to referee the games with the visiting teams. There were six fieldhouses all over the city in this program and we visited them all. We developed self-reliance, ability to follow directions, and a knowledge of Seattle and its diverse population.

Henry Theodore Simonson was born in Ballard September 7, 1918. His father, Hans Martin Simonson, born 1887 near Harstad, Norway, immigrated in 1907. His mother, Therese Marie Ingvaldsen, born in 1890 in Sørreisa, near Tromsø, Norway, immigrated to Seattle in 1916. His brother Justin (1920-1945) died in WW II. Henry graduated from the University of Washington in 1940 with a B.S. in Fisheries. After serving in the Air Force during WWII, he and a partner owned Covey Laundry until 1955. He sold his interest and bought a major interest in the Anderson and Thompson Ski Company. In 1975 they sold that business. He was consul of Austria for Washington State from 1960-1984. He was elected a Port Commissioner for two terms, 1974-1986. In 1986 he retired. He married Lois Parker in 1943. Their children: Gary (1946), Nancy (1949) and Susan (1948).

Helen Brekke Smith

"It was fun growing up in Ballard. I remember when I was a kid, sometimes as it was getting dark in the afternoon, I'd stand out on the porch and just smell the smells from the Puget Sound waters, up at Golden Gardens. That special water smell. I think it must have been from the clams and the seaweed."

My parents, Kristianne Fosnes and Lars Brekke were born in Oppstryn, Nordfjord, Norway, in the 1860s. Kristianne talked to her father about the possibility of her going away to school, and learning to be a teacher. But her father said, no. One of her brothers, Anton Fosnes, came home for a visit. Many of the young people from her valley returned with him to the United States, and she joined them.

When Lars found out that Kristianne was going to the United States, his life plans changed. He was in love with Kristianne and he wanted to marry her. So he gave up his right to the farm to his half-brother, and came to the New World with the group from Nordfjord.

After the ocean voyage, they went on the train into the midwest. Lars worked on a farm in the Dakotas. He learned that in the west he could earn $30 a month. So he went to Seattle. He had written to Christine [she Americanized her name] that he was going to Seattle, he wanted her to marry him and he would send for her when he had enough money. He got a job at Westerman's Machine Shop and worked hard and soon became a foreman. Each day, after work, he went to Charles Street [south of Dearborn] where he built the house he hoped to share with Christine. There was a garbage dump nearby, so the odor wasn't too good, but the price had been cheap. When Christine arrived, smoke was still rising from the July, 1889 Seattle fire. On July 5, 1890 Christine and Lars were married. The house was almost finished.

The men at Westerman's went on strike. Although he then was a foreman, he went on strike in sympathy with the laboring man. When the strike was over, he no longer had a job — as part of management, he was supposed to continue working with the company executives. He found other work. On the University of Washington campus, he took his tools and a forge out to the foundation of Denny Hall, the first building on the campus. With deer and a bear occasionally wandering around him, he sharpened tools for the builders.

Then in 1901 Papa left what money he could to Mama, and went to Alaska in the gold rush. He came back with only a few little nuggets that the family turned into money in Seattle. He didn't make a fortune, but the Alaskan expedition was successful for Papa in one way. He always had enough to live on with the money he made sharpening or making tools for the people who were panning for gold.

Mama was so glad when he came back, because she had run out of money for food. We always blessed Mr. Jensen, who had a corner grocery and gave credit. My sister, Bertha, used to go up to buy groceries for the family. She was so miserable when she had to go up there. Mr. Jensen would always give her the groceries Mama asked for, but he'd always say, "Can you ask your mama if she can pay a little on the grocery bill?" Mama didn't have any money.

I also went to summer school while I was going to Salmon Bay. When I was 12 years old, in the middle of the year, I went to a beautiful new Ballard High School. Nonetheless, I had several classes each semester in a dumpy little portable. They didn't have enough money to build a big enough school for all of us.

The sports in those days were very different from today. We wore big, floppy bloomers, black, so they wouldn't show the dirt, long black stockings, a white middy blouse and tennis shoes. We used Indian clubs and dumbbells to build up our muscles, and we climbed ropes that hung from the ceiling. I played basketball, volleyball and tennis. I again went to summer school, so I had just turned 16 when I finished high school. And, surprise of surprises, I was a salutatorian. After I graduated from Ballard I went to Whitman College. I had a $150 scholarship, which paid my tuition and lab fees for a year. My expenses for going through school were so little that only in my junior year my parents gave me $25 a month.

When I was young, I sometimes took lunch to my father at the blacksmith shop. The trip hammer was immense. It'd take two men, one to hold the iron to be pounded, and one to work the machinery. That was noisy and scarey. The forge was always glowing, full of red coals, with iron heating in it, giving off its own special metal smell. And the emery wheel which smoothed down any roughness on the iron pieces, shot off beautiful little sparks. You had to be very careful not to get too close to it because if the sparks got in your eyes, they'd ruin them. You were supposed to wear glasses if you were working with it. I would just stand a good distance away and admire it. It was kind of exciting, too, when a piece of iron that had been pounded while it was red hot, and began to lose its color, was pushed into a pail of water. It would hiss and the steam would rise. Always something to surprise and scare you.

My father would take time to look up from what he was doing and he'd say, "Now don't go until I've finished." And when he had finished it, he would give me a nickel and say, "Now you take this and go home and tell Mama you found me working." That was a big joke, because he worked 10, 12 hours a day, every day of the week.

It was fun to hear the way my father spoke English all these years, always with an accent: Bah-LARD, See-AT-leh, and Ya-KEE-ma. Many other names were given a new twist. [See Lars Brekke's image and hear his voice, recorded in 1950, in the Ballard section of the "Dream of America" at the Nordic Heritage Museum.]

It was fun growing up in Ballard. I remember when I was a kid, sometimes as it was getting dark in the afternoon, I'd stand out on the porch and just smell the smells from the Puget Sound waters, up at Golden Gardens. That special water smell. I think it must have been from the clams and the seaweed.

Helen Brekke was born in Ballard March 7, 1907. Her parents, Lars Olaf Brekke and Kristianne (Christine in the U.S.) Fosnes, were born in Oppstryn, Norway. They immigrated to the U.S. in 1884, they were married in Seattle July 5, 1890, moved to Ballard 1903 when Lars started the Brekke Blacksmith shop on Shilshole Ave. Their children: Emilie (1891-1991), Bertha (1892-1953), Olaf Fritjoff (1895-1964), Laura (1897-1964), twins Dorothy (1900-1990) and Norman (1900-1978) and Helen (1907). Christine died March 1951, and Lars died just a month later. Olaf and Norman took over the shop. Helen graduated from Ballard High in 1923 and from Whitman College in 1926. She taught school for many years in Longview, Washington. She married Reg Smith in 1950. They adopted two children, Jean and Dale. Reg died in 1982. Helen died in 2006.

Thomas Andersen Stang

"The first thing that happened when I was consul was that a Norwegian seaman was hit by a truck on Alaskan Way. I went to the hospital and saw him. I said: 'Everything is going to be OK.' During the night he died. Then there's the problem of what you do with arrangements. Actually we don't ever notify the family directly. We notify the Seaman's Directorate in Norway. . . Then right away we had another Norwegian seaman who was unconscious at the Marine Hospital due to an aneurism. I authorized the doctors to stabilize him and later received permission to escort him home to Norway. . . I received notice that Crown Prince Harald was coming to Seattle from Canada. That was the week before I received a letter from the foreign ministry that King Olav V was going to be here in May 1968 and to start making preparations. That was my baptism as a consul."

My name is Thomas Andersen Stang but when I was born my name was Thomas Stang-Andersen. Because my parents were Norwegian citizens, I had dual citizenship as a Norwegian and an American. I retained dual citizenship until age 22, when I was serving in the U.S. Army.

Sometime after my sister Ingri and I were born my father got tired of signing his last name as Stang-Andersen so he changed our last name to Stang with Andersen as a middle name. My father was Christen. He never used Chris. It was Christen or C.A. Stang.

My father immigrated to Seattle in 1920. He took a leave of absence from his job to visit his mother in Brooklyn and his uncle in Seattle and was going to go around the world. But he didn't have enough money to go all the way around the world back to his job, so he stayed in Seattle.

He represented the Norwegian American Line as an agent in Oregon and joined the Grieg Lodge, Sons of Norway, in Portland. Eventually he came back to Seattle and joined his uncle in the Thomas Kolderup Insurance Agency. Sometime prior to 1933, my dad had been appointed Kolderup's vice consul. When Kolderup died, it was decided that they had to have an established businessman, so Einar Beyer was appointed consul. When Norway was invaded [in 1940], Beyer resigned and my dad became consul.

Kolderup had emigrated to the United States in 1901 or 1902. When the dual monarchy of Norway and Sweden was terminated in 1905, one of the reasons was that Norway wanted to have its own foreign service.

Kolderup had come to Seattle because he knew someone would be appointed consul in Seattle. I think that's it. I don't know. I never met the man, because he died before I was born. He was first appointed vice consul of Norway in Seattle in 1906. Then of course somewhere along the line he became consul, and started his own insurance agency. Kolderup died in 1933; his wife, Dina, lived until 1968.

My dad took over the insurance agency and they had an arrangement where Dina Kolderup shared in the income from the agency.

My mother was a foreign student at Bellingham Normal and attended a Norwegian Male Chorus concert, where August Werner [a music professor at the University of Washington, who directed numerous choruses] introduced her to my father. My mother's name was Hedvig Alice Simonsen, but nobody knew that because everyone called her Lillemor, which means "little mother." I assume she got the nickname in her family because she had three older brothers. It stuck for the rest of her life, but she signed checks Hedvig A. Stang.

I remember when World War II started because when my dad and I came home the house was completely dark [and my mother was crying]. During the war there were a lot of Norwegian ships that were stuck outside Norway. My dad told me that he received orders from the Quisling government to direct the boats — all shipping — back to Norway. Of course he didn't like that. Then later he received another directive from the Norwegian government in London — the government in exile — that said: "The King is here and all Norwegian shipping is to report to an allied port." That he liked.

He didn't pay any attention to the Quisling government. [Vidkun Quisling was a Norwegian politician. On April 9, 1940, when the Germans invaded Norway, he seized power in a Nazi-backed coup d'état.]

The way my father told it to me, was that the ships didn't do anything. They just went up and down the coast. Then it was a rule apparently that if a ship runs out of fresh water they can come into the closest port to get water. These guys just pumped out their tanks and came in to get water.

In 1958, my mother became a U.S. Citizen. The reason she became a U.S. citizen was that we had an Alien Land Law in the State of Washington. That meant aliens could not own title to real estate. My dad, of course, was a Norwegian citizen. They figured at least one of them should become a U.S. citizen just in case, since they owned land on Whidbey Island and in Seattle

The Alien Land Law is no more, but it was at that time. My dad was kidding around with the director of immigration at the time. Dad said: "If I become a citizen, I have to sever all my ties with my former country. I intend to stay as consul." And that was that.

When I started as consul, my mother was my secretary. She had worked as a secretary at the consulate for my father until he died. She had actually worked as a secretary for Thomas Kolderup a little bit in 1930, before she went back to Norway. [She returned to Seattle in the fall of 1933 to marry my father.] There was no way I could have done the job as consul without my mom. She knew exactly what had to be done in most instances.

My father died in July 1967, and I was what they called "acting consul" until September 1967, when I was confirmed as consul. Actually my father and I had talked about it before he died. He had petitioned that I be appointed his vice consul because he was pretty sick. After his death, I was appointed vice consul and consul on virtually the same day.

The first thing that happened when I was consul was that a seaman was hit by a truck on Alaskan Way. I went to the hospital and saw him. I said: 'Everything is going to be OK.' During the night he died. Then there's the problem of what you do with arrangements. Actually we don't ever notify the family directly. We notify the Seaman's Directorate in Norway. . . Then right away we got another seaman who was unconscious at the Marine Hospital due to an aneurism. I authorized the doctors to stabilize him. I got permission to escort him home to Norway. . . I received notice that Crown Prince Harald was coming to Seattle from Canada. That was the week before I received a letter from the foreign ministry that King Olav V was going to be here in May 1968 and to start making preparations. That was my baptism as a consul.

First of all, I had to make arrangements for escorts here and at the airport and get up there to meet Crown Prince Harald at Blaine. I'd just left the prosecutor's office so I knew the state patrol. . . I got the state patrol to ferry me up to Blaine so I didn't have to drive my car up there. I met him and brought his party down to SeaTac and then he left for Norway. I had met him before when he was here in 1965 when my father was the consul, so we knew each other a little bit.

So my mom says: "Gee you've had more stuff in the last month than your dad had in almost all the time he was a consul. The only thing he didn't have was a royal visit."

After the war everybody was coming to my dad because they wanted to return to Norway. Because my dad had been a Norwegian American Line representative, he thought it was a good time to start a travel agency.

He and my mother started Stang Travel Service in 1946. Now it's just Nancy, my wife, doing travel arrangements from our home. At one time we had about five, six employees. Lillemor worked until she was about 85 years old as a secretary for the consulate.

When my dad died, I was assistant chief criminal deputy in the King County prosecutor's office. One of the things the [U.S.] State Department insists on is that consuls register as an agent for a foreign government.

I could not be employed by an American agency while registered as an agent for a foreign government. One of the conditions of me being appointed consul was that I formally resign from the prosecutor's office. I did like my job.

After I left the prosecutor's office, I think it was Mayor Wes Uhlman who asked me to serve as a judge pro tem in municipal court. I said "I have this problem of being registered as an foreign agent." He said, "We'll overlook that."

For the next 20 years I served as judge pro tem in Seattle Municipal Court, which meant I would sit in when a regular judge couldn't be there.

If you look at the job of a consul basically it is whenever someone needs to contact the Norwegian government. So people who need assistance contact the local consul. The consul is expected to be an expert on Norwegian pensions, land regulations, law and everything else. Well obviously he or she isn't.

During my time as consul we had something called a maritime inquest. It's an inquest if something serious happens on a ship. My first inquest was a seaman that died off the Mexican coast trying to fix some pipes — the chief engineer — he was gassed. We had to have a regular inquest. You have to record it and send a report back to the Norwegian Maritime Directorate.

When I became consul, I inherited Kolderup's files, my father's files and then built up my own files. It's about one file drawer per year from 1906 to 2006, when I officially retired.

When I closed my downtown office, I put the files in storage. I was billing the consulate general in San Francisco $175 a month for storage. They finally sent an archivist from the foreign ministry to sort through the files that had accumulated. It wasn't my property. I was acting as an agent for the Norwegian government, so those files belong to the Norwegian government.

The archivist looked at the storage locker and what I had in my basement at home. She said: "We're going to pack up the whole thing and ship it home." Which she did. I guess they are sorting through it in Norway.

Thomas Andersen Stang was born March 12, 1935, in St. Luke's Hospital, now Group Health Cooperative in Seattle. His father, C.A. Stang, was born December 17, 1896, in Oslo, then known as Kristiania. His mother, Hedvig Alice Simonsen, was born March 12, 1909, in Tromso. Tom is a graduate of Garfield High School. He earned a bachelor's degree in business administration with a major in insurance, and a law degree from the University of Washington. Tom's wife, the former Nancy Schroder, was born in Sundoy, Norway; her family immigrated in February 1949 after World War II. Nancy and Tom were married September 1, 1961. Tom served as Honorary Consul of Norway from 1967 to 2007. When he retired, the Norwegian Consulate had been served by his family for more than 100 years, beginning with his great-uncle, Thomas Huntington Kolderup, followed by Tom's father C.A. Stang. Tom has been active in Leif Erikson Lodge, the Norwegian Male Chorus; the Pacific Northwest Chapter of Nordmanns Forbundet, an association of Norwegians living abroad, and the Seattle Consular Corps. In addition he served on the advisory committee for Trollhaugen Lodge, built in the Cascade Mountains by District 2, Sons of Norway lodges. He has received two of Norway's highest civic honors, Knight First Class of the Royal Order of St. Olav and Commander of the Royal Order of Merit.

George J. Stimac

*"I've found Ballard's been good to me,
and I really can't complain. I wouldn't want
to do anything different than I have done."*

It was a roundabout way of getting here to
Seattle, but my dad came to this country
probably about 1910 from Croatia, which
at that time was part of Austria. He came
over married to his first wife. They had five
children. He started in Illinois, Michigan and
Minnesota working in the mines. Then to
Montana, and to Ronald, Washington, where
he finally ended up. Ronald is in eastern Washington, Kittitas County. It
had the largest coal mine in the State of Washington. My dad was in the
mining industry, moving from one state to the other to different types of
mines. They were copper mines, and I think there were some zinc, and
coal mines.

His first wife died and he wrote for my mother, Eva Abremovic,
from the same area in Croatia that he was from. I was born in Ronald,
Washington in 1930. I went to school in Ronald and graduated from Cle
Elum High School. My dad passed away in 1937 at the young age of 47
from a combination of emphysema and pneumonia leaving her and me
alone. Those were tough times. It was during the Depression and she
couldn't speak the language.

I graduated from Cle Elum High School in 1948. I went to
Washington State on a track scholarship, and I worked my way through
pharmacy school that way, and I graduated in 1953. It looked like the
opportunity was best in Seattle, so I came here.

I started with Art Olson back in 1955, the Art Olson Pharmacy on
the corner of 20th and Market. Art was married to Bernice Jonson, the
attorney. [See Jonson p. 330] I thought I'd stay one year, and it's been
45 or 46. I worked for Art from about '55 to '59.

In 1959 I married a Norwegian Ballard girl, Beverly Olson. We had
three children: John, Susan and Vincent. Beverly passed away in 1989.
Beverly grew up in Ballard. She graduated from Ballard High in 1950.
She was working at the Seattle First National Bank, and I just happened
to meet her, and that was it. We got married and raised our family here.
She was involved in the schools. She followed the kids through the

schools and was very active with them. I didn't have the time to do that, but she did. The football games had those card sections. She laid out the first card sections for Ballard.

I started with one store here in Ballard. I had several others in different areas of the city. At one time, I was owner or part owner in five different stores. We had to work hard, because an independent has to put in a lot of time.

I ended up here with Market Street Pharmacy, and I've been there for 38 years. My second wife, Evelynn and I bought out Marshall Olson's store here in Ballard, the Ballard Plaza Pharmacy, known as Olson's Plaza Pharmacy. So, I've been here at the Ballard Plaza Pharmacy for four years. We are compounding pharmacists. That means that we go back to the old style of practicing pharmacy where we take the raw materials and put them together and make a compound out of a tablet or whatever — liquid, or whatever a person needs for their use.

I've found Ballard's been good to me, and I really can't complain. I wouldn't want to do anything different than I have done.

You have a choice sometimes, to be a family man or a socialite, and I chose to be a family man. I stayed primarily with the family, and with a business — you can only do so much.

George Stimac was born April 22. 1930 in Ronald, Washington. Both his parents were from Croatia. He graduated from Washington State College in 1953 as a pharmacist. He came to Ballard in 1955. He married Beverly Olson, Ballard-born. Their children: John, Susan and Vincent. Beverly died 1989. George married Evelynn Cava in 1996. He died in 2011.

Ted Swanson

"My dad said, 'There's some flowers coming and we've got to sell those. That's going to be your job.'"

We came to Ballard on a Sunday morning in July of 1922. My mother, my dad and I made the trip. I was just 11½. I believe my father was 64, and my mother ten years younger. After breakfast, we got on the Phinney streetcar. Then we transferred to the little electric streetcar that ran from there to Ballard, commonly called the Dinky. We got off at 85th and 15th. There were two stores there, a grocery store on the northwest corner, and a drugstore on the south-east corner. We started walking [north] to our new home on plank sidewalks. Very few homes were between 85th and [97th]. And of course, no Holman Road. To the west we saw nothing but woods.

At 95th, a street went up to Crown Hill School. There was no 100th Street. That was the end of 15th. It got smaller and they were nothing but dirt roads. They called them gravel but there wasn't much gravel to be seen. Between 95th and 96th there were probably two or three houses. What's Blue Ridge now was old stump land.

Anyway, there were a lot of corduroy roads, for logging use. The logging was finished, but some big trees were left and a lot of stumps. There were trails through there. In the summertime, there were wild berries to pick and lots of places where young people and kids could have fun, but not many people got out there. That's about the way it was when we came to this place. It had been the Martin's summer home. Mr. Martin had passed away, and Mrs. Martin traded it for the house we left in Pasadena, California.

That's how we got this property here. They were called five-acre tracts, but they're 500 feet of frontage and went down to what was a platted but not a developed street, 17th Northwest. That was vacated by the city a long time ago

Dad started building a greenhouse that first summer and finished it by that fall. Oh, it was about 30 by 100 feet in size. My mother and I helped him, and he had somebody that did a little carpentry work for him, otherwise he did the whole thing. I don't suppose I did very much but I thought I did.

He planted some violets and other flowers that he was growing for cut flowers. And I remember, it was early in February of 1923, I had just turned 12, my dad said, "Ted, Mother and I have been taking care of the plants inside the greenhouse. Now there's some flowers coming and we've got to sell those. That's going to be your job. I want you to hurry home from school."

I was in the seventh grade at Whittier School — they didn't have room for me at Crown Hill. He says, "I'll have them packed in boxes and you carry them down to 85th and go downtown on the streetcar. Stop at the first florist and sell what you can, and then go to the next one and the next one, and when you're all through, hurry home with the money. I'll go with you the first time." I'll never forget that. And I sold all the flowers most of the time after that.

Gradually he added more greenhouses, and I prepared the ground outside and we grew summer flowers out there. My dad also planted a lot of lily bulbs to sell to the wholesale trade.

Our very good neighbor, Ed Anderson, who lived across the street, permitted me to put some flowers in the back of his little Chevrolet coupe. Then he would let me off at the first florists, and if I couldn't sell them enough so that I could carry all the rest, they let me leave the surplus there and I could come back after I sold some to the other florists and get the rest of them. There were quite a few florists in Seattle at that time and they were scattered around the downtown area. Lots of flowers were used for funerals in those days, much more so than nowadays. When I got old enough to drive a car, dad bought one for me. "Loud Lucy" was our 1920 Model T Ford that we bought in 1928 for 35 dollars.

In the early days we bought fertilizer mainly from dairy farms and chicken farms, cow manure and chicken manure. The worst thing was, it was so hard to get manure, particularly cow manure, that didn't have a lot of weed seeds in it. Seeds go through the animals as they eat grass and buttercups and quack grass. They were very hard to get rid of, so we finally gave it up.

I graduated in 1928 from high school. I stayed out of school for a year and a half, and then I went to the University. I wasn't ready when I got out of high school. But as time went on I realized that it was important and I took business economics there.

The florists were affected by the Depression, like everybody else. But, fortunately, very few florists actually went broke. Most of them were able to hang on. Some of our customers got a year and a half, two years, two and half years behind in paying their bills, but we got by, and most of those got by, too, gradually. The price of flowers, of course, was very, very cheap. And they didn't increase much for many years after that.

As time went on, we grew more cut flowers and closed out our bulb business. We built more greenhouses and our business shifted from wholesale gradually to retail.

I got married June 26, 1937. My wife Frances came from California. We had an outdoor wedding here. Frances was a registered nurse but she gave up her nursing and decided to work in the greenhouses and flowers. She went back to that about 1966. My father lived until 1946. He was 88 years old. My mother continued to help us almost until the day she died. She died at 92 years old in 1960. It was a nice family business for all of us. We had three children, and they all worked here while they were going to school, whenever they could. They enjoyed it and we appreciated having them there with us.

It was interesting having the school children come through here. One time I saw these little girls coming down. One of them said, "Oh, that smells just like my mother when she's real pretty." There were some heliotrope, very fragrant flowers.

Ted Swanson was born in Minnesota December 31, 1910. His parents came from Sweden, his mother Selma around 1880, age 12, and his father, August Swanson around 1900, age 42. August paid his passage from Sweden with money from a pamphlet he wrote about horticulture. He settled in Minnesota where he started Swanson's Land of Flowers in 1888. There he met Selma, who had her own flower business. After two and a half years in California they came to Seattle in July, 1922, where they established Swanson's Nursery on 10 acres on 15th Avenue Northwest. Ted graduated from Ballard High in 1928. Ted and Frances were married in 1937. They took over the business in the 1950s. When they retired in 1976 they sold it to Wally Kerwin, the present owner. Ted and Frances had three childen: Margie, Shirley and Dick (1950). Ted was interviewed, February 20, 1988. Ted died June 27, 1994.

Ballard City Hall

From 1890 to 1907 Ballard was an independent municipality. The city hall building opened in 1899 and was razed in 1965 due to earthquake damage. The building was draped in black in 1907 on the day of the official annexation to Seattle.

Bergen Place Park

The park honors the sister city relationship between Seattle and Bergen, Norway. It was dedicated in 1975 by King Olav V of Norway and the mural , added in 1995, was dedicated by King Harald and Queen Sonja.

The Ballard Building, ca. 1927

It was built by the Fraternal Order of Eagles and its construction marked the shift of Ballard's commercial area to Market Street. It housed the Bagdad Theater, drug and department stores, and meeting rooms for the Eagles.

Carnegie Libary

This library served the Ballard community from 1904 to 1963 and construction was made possible by a $15,000 grant from Andrew Carnegie.

Maxine Shallow Tuck

"When I was a little girl,
the hoboes used to come."

The bus drivers used to say, "Well, you got your passports ready? We're going into Ballard." Just like Rainier Valley is Garlic Gulch, we're Snoose Junction. My dad's birth certificate said Ballard, Washington. He was born in Ballard, right down here on 50th and 9th. He was Frank Theodore Shallow. He was Polish. He lived here all his life, but his folks came from Winona in Ottawa, above Ottawa, Canada. My mother was German. They met in Seattle, at some picnic. She was born in Seattle, down in East Pine. When they got married, she came to live in Ballard.

We had chickens up until about 1980. Some of the neighbors loved to hear the cackling of the chickens. We were allowed one rooster, but we never kept one. And the Health Department would come out once a year to see if we had rats around here. We didn't.

My father was born in 1895. When he was 11 years old, he was working on lumber wagons, delivering lumber. They went to work early in those days, to supplement the family income. He went to the eighth grade at Irving School. He also attended St. Alphonsus. In those days, they never went beyond the eighth grade, if they went that far, because they had to go to work.

There was very few trees around here at all. We had a garbage dump over here — between Sixth and Eighth and 48th and 47th. And later the people wondered why their porches sunk when they built houses there — the garbage was still settling. The seagulls would get on our roof and my mother would get the BB gun out and shoot them. After they filled the dump in, it was a beautiful place to collect mushrooms. When I was young, we used to pick mushrooms over there and sell them. We had quite a clientele. We hit the owner of the Bolcom Mill, Mr. Bolcom. He always took a big order from us, and Dad would take them to the mill. My dad was general manager there. He was there during the crash in '29. Men who had been big businessmen came there, begging for jobs. He put everybody on that he could. And after the Depression they said, "If Pete Shallow hadn't been so good to us, we would have starved to death."

When I was a little girl, the hoboes used to come. They'd ride the rails into Interbay, camp under the embankments there and they'd come around looking for jobs, like cutting wood, or mowing lawn for a meal. Mama would give them a little job and then a meal. Always very thankful. Very lovely men. They left a mark on the fence where other hoboes could see it. That was in the early '30s.

These guys were out of work, just desperate and they built shacks down there. It was called Hooverville. They built these shacks out of cardboard. They had a real village down there, all those men. And they had walks between the houses.

And you could go down there. Even when we were kids we could go down there, 13, 14, 15 years old. And they'd invite you in for a cup of cocoa. Just single men who had been riding the rails. Most had been farmers and they didn't have any money, so they rode the rails to see the country or to get a job here or there. A lot of them were fathers, husbands. The women stayed home and they'd take in washing, they'd clean house. We had a lot of women around here who did housework for a few pennies a day or whatever they could get out of it. But there was no men around.

After the Depression, I remember the CCC camps. Men from all over the United States signed up for the CCC. They got their food and bed. They built Saltwater Park. There were trails through those woods, but the CCC camp made a beautiful park out of it. They'd put CCC camps in places where they were needed, to put them to work. Instead of giving them welfare, they could take pride in their work.

When my husband was killed, I was left with two little girls, seven and four. I got a pension check from the VA, and I also got my Social Security. Not much, but I never went on welfare. I cleaned houses. I dog sat. I baby-sat until I wanted to scream. I washed windows. My parents were very good to me. They'd take my girls and let me take off for a couple of days, or something like that. And after my kids got to a certain age, well, they'd do the same thing. They'd go out and baby-sit.

Maxine Shallow was born in 1923 in Ballard. Her father, Frank Shallow was born in Ballard of Polish ancestry. Her mother, born in Seattle was of German ancestry. Maxine married Marvin Tuck in 1943. He was killed in the Korean War, 1951. They had two daughters: Eileen (1944) and Nancy (1947). Maxine was interviewed March 5, 1988. She died in April, 1990.

Washington Hall

Excerpted from an article by Otto Brask in the *Nordic Heritage Museum Historical Journal*, Volume 4/Number 2

Built in 1908 by the Danish Brotherhood Lodge #29 Seattle, the "Hall" served the Danish community until 1968. For sixty years it functioned well for lodge meetings, joyful dinners, dramatic plays and neighborhood activities, as well as a home for many Danish immigrants, until the building was sold in 1973.

On March 13, 1908, according to Danish custom, the *Rejsegilde* (roof-raising party) was held on the premises. On May 16, 1908, the first of many grand dinner parties took place. In September that same year a question arose about whether the building was correctly placed on the plat. A surveyor determined that a mistake indeed had occurred, so they had to buy two feet of the lot west of the building.

The wood-framed building included two large halls with a boarding house in 25,000 square feet of space. The fourteen room boarding house was a good place to start for a young fellow who was new in town and a good place to eat. Bachelors, mostly Danish immigrants and newcomers to Seattle, found their home here for a year or two before they got married or found housing or jobs elsewhere.

Meetings of the Danish Brotherhood and Danish Sisterhood lodges took place regularly. Large audiences showed up for special events on Danish holidays: *Fastelavn* (Mardi Gras), *Grundlovsfest* (Constitution Day), *Mortens Aften* (St. Martin's Eve). The Dramatic Club Harmonien (*Dansk Selskabelig og Dramatisk Klub*) was formed in 1911 to produce amateur theatrical plays in the Danish language. They performed on the stage in the upstairs hall but also went on the road with their shows. Revenues collected supported the Northwest Danish Home for the Elderly, war bonds during World War II, and other charitable causes.

Because of its location in Seattle's Central District, Washington Hall became a choice venue for many neighborhood groups. Count Basie, Duke Ellington, Mahalia Jackson, Marion Anderson and Jimi Hendrix were among the many who performed in the upstairs hall.

458

Leo Utter

"This community of Finns had several kinds of organizations . . . going with activities of Finnish Americans. So from the very earliest days I remember the plays, choral concerts, family activities. I was kind of immersed in Finnish-ness very soon. I've appreciated it."

My parents were born in Finland. My father August Utter was born near Jyvaskyla, a little place called Oravasaari. He left for America in 1909 to become a logger in lower Michigan, with his brother. My mother left Finland in 1915 and came to Massachusetts, where her aunt lived. She was planning to go back to Finland after seeing the country. But she came to Seattle in 1918.

My father was already here since 1913, and they met at the Finnish Hall. She decided to stay in America, after meeting him. So that was the way of the romance for their beginning of their life together.

I grew up during the Depression, here in Seattle. We lived on Magnolia Bluff. When I was about nine my parents bought a house on Beacon Hill for $845. They worked on that house for about 16 years before we sold it. My father was a logger, and in the summertime, he would go to Nome, Alaska, to work on the railroad there and in the gold mines. In 1936, he suffered a fall. A limb hit him in the forehead and disabled him for many years.

So it was kind of a tough time for us because he couldn't work. And it was a tough time in general. I became a teacher and stayed at home with them. We bought a newer home on Beacon Hill, where I lived for another 40 years.

We were always involved in the Finnish Hall activities when I was growing up. This community of Finns had several kinds of organizations. Ours was a so-called leftist organization, and we had our activities at the Ninth Avenue Hall on First Hill. That hall existed until 1939, when it was demolished for the Yesler Terrace project. After that our functions were at Danish Hall on First Hill. At the same time there were two other halls going with activities of Finnish Americans. So from the very earliest days I remember the plays, choral concert, family activities. I was kind of immersed in Finnish-ness very soon. I've appreciated it.

[While I was growing up] I was interested in the Finnish language. We got a Finnish paper called *Työmies*, '*The Working Man*.' So I began reading that paper and actually was able to read and write in Finnish very easily without going to school for it. Of course, the Finnish was spoken most of the time with our friends. There were a lot of traditions going on, especially at the Hall, like the New Year tradition of melting lead into fortune taking and telling, dances and songs. My dad was a singer with the chorus, and we had Finnish records at home, for sure.

And there were certain Finnish foods, like pulla. My mother was a good baker and cook. She made things, like liver casserole. I still make pannukakku, the oven-baked pancake, myself.

For over 30 years, I've been involved with the Finnish Community Bazaar. And it's often held here at the Nordic Heritage Museum, on the first weekend of November. So there's a lot of pulla going on there.

As for school, I'm a loyal Cleveland High School Eagle, graduated in 1948. I went to the University of Washington to become a teacher and I went for a master's degree at Columbia University in New York City. I began teaching in 1952, was an elementary school teacher for eight years and then was mostly in middle schools with language arts and social studies programs. And then, at age 55, in 1986, I could retire.

[Since then] I've dedicated a lot of effort to this museum and to the Finnish organizations. It all began about 1974 when there was a bicentennial festival in Seattle and we formed a committee to participate in the Finnish section of that celebration. I've had several positions with Finlandia Foundation, Seattle Chapter, and been president three or four times. I've been chairman of the Suomi Finland Room here at the museum. And I've been chairman of the Finnish American Heritage Committee which started off as the Bicentennial Committee. And I've been involved with the Finnish Folk Dancers for over 30 years, sometimes as president.

I'm very happy and proud about this Finnish community. Twice we've been able to handle the FinnFest here in Seattle, with visitors from all over the country. And I've seen an increase in the use of Suomi Kuolu, the children's school. The Tanhuajat have been dancing in Seattle since about 1974 and I started about 1975. The University of Washington Finnish program has really taken off and looks like it's going to stay there for a while.

I also do some writing. I'm a columnist for the *Finnish American Reporter*. I tell about Seattle news. Another organization is the United

Finnish Kaleva Brothers and Sisters. I've been a member of it since 1967, I think. That group celebrated its 106th anniversary in 2010 and is the oldest organization in Seattle. So we are continuing that lodge tradition. I write for its publication, a bi monthly called *Veljeysvieste*. I hope that someone in the future will read and realize we had activities here.

Here at the Nordic Museum I became chairman of the Suomi Finland Room committee when it started in 1985. Hera Owen was the mainstay in developing the exhibits. We were able to collect things, such as something from the Finnish Hall on Washington Street that was demolished. We got sauna fittings from Hobart where Hera grew up. And we saved a lot of implements from barns and farms. I think that room really represents our parents' generation in many ways. We wish we could have started much earlier to save other things before they went to the dump.

I also was on the FinnFest U.S.A. National Board for a while and it was at that time we got the first FinnFest in Seattle in 1989. And then 10 years later we were able to do it again. Norman Westerberg, Rita Koski, Pirkko Borland and many other people have just been great in getting people inspired for this community effort.

Seattle, especially at that time when my mother moved here, was a place where Finnish people congregated. I guess the city grew tremendously just after the war. She said when she arrived in 1917, they couldn't even find a room. They were sleeping on somebody's floor for a while.

My father had no intention to go back to Finland after he came here in 1909. He came from quite a lot of poverty. It wasn't a pleasant time in Finland when he left. So he didn't think about it much. My mother's father was a tailor. And the family had a place for overnight guests at the railroad station and also the telephone setup for the little town. So I guess they did pretty well. So, she did relate to Finland and became quite nationalistic.

Her parents' name was Hagland, which is a Swedish name. So she and her brother and sisters Finnishized their name to Lehto before she came to America. And my name also is Swedish. Utter, I learned later, was (the name) given to a great grandfather who was in the Swedish army. They just assigned names.

My parents came from near Turku in Southwest Finland. Because my parents were on the leftist side of the political scale, they were very uncomfortable with Finland becoming an ally of Germany during the

Second World War. And later, in 1950, during the McCarthy era, because they were kind of in that [leftist] political group, they were of course subjected to being called subversives. We had FBI agents come to our home in 1950 to question them just because they had that paper called *Työmies*, *'The Working Man.'*

Even in Canada, the Finnish halls were closed after and during the war because they were considered pro-German groups. That didn't happen on this side of the border, as far as I know. But in 1945, when things finally got to the place where we could send packages over there to Finland, boy, our community really sent packages. Not only to our family, but to other people who needed help after the war.

My dad never did go back to Finland, never wanted to. My mother went in 1929 with my brother, who was nine years of age then, so my brother actually did see his grandparents, which I never did.

I've always been proud of my parents' generation. They were honest hard workers and they contributed so much to this country.

Leo Utter was born March 28, 1931, in Seattle to August Matinpoika Utter and Jenny Haglund Lehto Utter. After graduating in 1952 from the University of Washington he enjoyed a long and successful career as a teacher in the Seattle Public Schools. In 1965 he earned a master's degree from Columbia University. Leo also was an avid and accomplished gardener. He was past president of the Seattle Chapter of the Finlandia Foundation, the Pacific Northwest Ethnic Heritage Council, (which awarded him its Aspasia Pulakis Award in 2008), the Tanhuajat dance group, various FinnFestUSA boards and the United Kaleva Brothers and Sisters Lodge 11. Leo grew up bilingual, continued to study the complex Finnish language and taught small classes in his home for several years. For more than a decade he was the Seattle correspondent for the *Finnish American Reporter* and he volunteered at the Nordic Heritage Museum from 1980 until his death in 2010. In 1987 Finland recognized his many contributions to Finnish culture in the United States by bestowing upon Leo the Order of the Lion Medal. In addition he received the Award of Merit from the Suomi-Seura (Finland Society).

Emma T. Vatn

"When I was young I wanted to be a teacher. I wanted to go to Pacific Lutheran University so bad after I graduated, but '34 was during the Depression and it just didn't work out."

Our moving from Astoria, Oregon was a big thing in those days. We had a big van and my old upright piano was tailgated on the truck. My brother Harold had asthma — that was one of the reasons we moved here. [see p. 189] We came to friends [Surland and Petrine Ness] who lived at 319 West 50th Street in Ballard. They found a house for us to rent at 613 West 51st. That was our first house and we lived there for two years. It was a five-bedroom house. I started West Woodland School in the sixth grade right after we arrived.

My mother was the only one of her family here until her brother Wilhelm Haagensen [see Roseberg p. 85], came over in 1924. I think she was very lonely for Norway, but we didn't realize that when we were little kids. Every Sunday she wrote to her mother. She wrote to my dad too, even if he was fishing close by. She'd give my brother Harold and I each a dime, we'd take the Number 19 streetcar on Sixth Avenue to Fremont, then transfer to the Phinney streetcar and go to Woodland Park. The dime was for a little treat. We would walk home down the hill from the park. I went to West Woodland from the sixth to eighth grade, and then went to Ballard High, and graduated in 1934. When I was young I wanted to be a teacher. I wanted to go to Pacific Lutheran University so bad after I graduated, but 1934 was during the Depression and it just didn't work out.

My friend Sylvia was at our place much of the time. She lived close by. She said she felt like she lived up there, but she never called my mother anything but Mrs. Nilsen. We had dresses alike and we always ate lunch and walked to and from school together. And we did our algebra and geometry over the telephone. In those days, we had homework, we had confirmation lessons, and Sunday school lessons. I got two little cups from my teacher for knowing my Sunday school lesson the best for a whole year. And I had a certificate for Rice penmanship and for Palmer penmanship. I always worked hard.

The Depression years were hard times. We had four fishermen living with us. It really helped us. Two were in the downstairs bedroom and two in the upstairs bedroom. They paid $30 a month board and room. That sort of tided us over.

Mama was a seamstress and she had her little sewing machine from Norway, the portable kind you hand crank. She even made wedding gowns on that. Harold made a little sign and put in the front bedroom window that said, "Dressmaking and Alterations." We had an electric stove in the kitchen and our old wood stove in the basement. In the wintertime when my dad was home, he did most of the cooking downstairs — to save on electricity.

Then my mother went to work for William Allen, president of Boeing, as a kind of nanny. They had a little girl named Nancy and lived in The Highlands. She called her *dukke* [doll]. That was all part time — she wasn't there every day. When Mama's cancer took hold, Mrs. Allen wasn't too well either. They went to Arizona for her health, and took Mama along. She was gone a couple months, but she came home very, very ill and lived just three weeks after that. When she was going to come home, Harold and I scrubbed the kitchen ceilings and walls, getting everything all ready. She never even got into the kitchen to see that.

Harold and I were in the first confirmation class at Phinney Ridge Lutheran Church in 1930. We became involved in Ballard First Lutheran in 1941. John and I were married there because it had a center aisle, and Phinney Ridge didn't have a center aisle then.

I started working immediately after high school. I started at Bemis Bag, 65 South Atlantic street. It was hard work — my fingers would bleed. I made $13.20 a week. I cried every night when I punched out. We did wheat bags on a power machine. Then we went on strike, for nine months that year. Mr. McAusland, the manager of Bemis Bag, had a Norwegian housemaid who went back to Norway to visit. So I was asked to work in their home in Broadmoor. That was kind of fun. But it was temporary, just while she was in Norway.

When I was a little girl, I was afraid of the water. My dad had to carry me down the ladder to go on his boat. And I always said, "I'm never going to marry a fisherman," but that's what I did. I knew John [Vatn] from Astoria. He had his own trolling boat like my dad did. The first couple years he kept the boat in Astoria during the winter, and he fished for salmon and tuna. Then every winter he kept it in Seattle. He then sold his boat and became a halibut fisherman here. In winter he worked at the Stimson Mill in Ballard.

My son Jim and I were alone a lot. My husband was gone most of the time — that's the life of a fisherman. I didn't drive, so we took the bus all over. Later, my dad lived with us. He and Jim were really buddies. We did those things when his dad was away fishing.

In 1962 I opened King Paper Company down by the Ballard Bridge. I was there for five years. In those years my husband was pretty ill. He passed away in April, 1969. I was home for a whole year. Then I learned that Olympic Distributors needed someone. I went there and the job was mine. I worked there from June 1, 1970 till I retired June 1, 1988. I still call it my company. Mr. Kildahl was the owner and my boss. The first thing he would asked was, "Is this place convenient for Emma to get to by bus?" I always took the bus.

Nordlandslaget is the lodge for the people of northern Norway. We have lodges in Seattle, Tacoma, Vancouver, B.C., and we had one in Victoria which joined with Vancouver because so many members had passed on. We meet in Ballard at Leif Erikson Hall. I was secretary for 25 years, also secretary for the West Coast lodge for 25 years. I've belonged over 60 years — it's been a big part of my life and still is. At one time we owned our own building, Harmony Hall, but after several years it was sold.

Membership has dwindled because people are older and the younger people just don't seem to come. TV and computers, and parents seem to be more involved with their children now, which is the way it should be. Moms are working and it's just a different era.

Emma Nilsen was born July 24, 1916 in Astoria, Oregon. Her parents, Fredrikke and Halfdan Nilsen, emigrated from the Lofoten Islands in northern Norway in 1915. Her family moved to Ballard in September, 1928. She has one brother, Harold. She married John Vatn February 1941. Their son James Fredrik Vatn was born November 18th, 1943. Jim was very active in the Ballard/Scandinavian community. He and his wife, Joan, were parents to Emma's granddaughter, Elisa (1991). John died in April, 1969. Jim died on November 7, 2010.

Douglas Warne

"Without the International Summer School [in Oslo], without going to the university there, without the Eng family, I would be a completely different person. That experience, spread over 10 years, changed who I am, changed my focus of education, changed who I was. It changed who I married. It changed who my friends are, my social activities. It was a life-changing experience. Because of that and because of my interest in education, I've said that part of what I want to do is make sure that somebody else gets to go. So I've created an

endowment that will fund an annual scholarship with the Norwegian Commercial Club of Seattle. There will be at least one student that's going to be funded with tuition and room and board at the University of Oslo International Summer School hopefully forever."

My dad was a fisherman so we always had fish. In fact, he was a halibut fisherman and I had fish on my plate that was as big as the plate. I can remember saying, "Oh, do I have to eat fish again?" And now, fifty, sixty years later, I go to a restaurant, halibut is 29 dollars a pound. I get this little tiny thing that's smaller than my wallet and more expensive than my wallet and I love to have it.

Another one my dad would make [was] salt codfish for my grandmother. It was a liver can with a tight lid on it and you filled it with codfish and salt and she had salt codfish in the basement.

She would pull that out regularly and de-salt it by soaking it overnight, I think. Let the water drip in the basement sink in the container with the fish in it and slowly it would dribble out. In the morning it would be fresh. She would cook it and Mom and Dad and Grandma and everybody thought that was wonderful.

Of course, we kids thought it was the grossest thing ever. Oh, salt fish. She put chopped eggs on it and cooked salt pork. Oh, it just was gross.

Now, I have a cabin at Norway Park and every so often they have had a salt black cod or salt codfish dinner. It's a hundred mile round trip. I'd be happy to drive one hundred miles to have a salt codfish dinner. Oh, it is delicious.

I was the first person in the family that had gone to college. And I went to Alaska and worked in the salmon industry to make money so I could pay for college. Mom and Dad paid for part, and I paid for part. It was while I was at Whitworth College that I met a number of people that had come back — I was a freshman, I guess — and I had met some people that were coming back from their junior year abroad. I thought, how cool can that be, to be in a foreign country and be exposed to all that?

So I set my sights on, I want to be a foreign student. I'd been reading *007* and those stories, and *Orient Express*. And, oh boy, this would be cool. Anyway, so I listened to their stories. Stan Mumford had a duffel coat with these wooden peg buttons on it, and he stayed in Edinburgh for a while. I started asking around where I might go.

I was a forest guard up in the tower watching for forest fires that summer before my sophomore year. I typed a letter to the University of Oslo and said, "I would like to participate in a junior year abroad program, and what can you do?" A pretty short letter.

Somebody wrote back and said, well, we do not have a junior year abroad program. But for you, we will make one. I thought, wow, that's pretty accommodating. Part of the process will be, you must be accepted and attend the University of Oslo International Summer School. Once you've done that, then you can matriculate to the University and take however long you want for your junior year, and we will endeavor to make those credits transfer. The International Summer School credits will automatically transfer, because that's been handled by St. Olaf College.

I thought that was great. I had to raise the money, and I had some money in the bank, and I got accepted. After my sophomore year I worked a little bit, and then late in June, I went to Norway. My whole life opened up at that point. First of all, I'd never flown. In my grade school class, I remember one or two kids had been in an airplane, but not very many. Even when I was in college, not many people had gone, maybe fifty percent of the people. Flying to New York was a big deal. I was on my own.

I went to Coney Island and that was a big experience. I sat up at a bar, a real live bar, and I could have a beer because I was eighteen, old enough. Oh it was exciting. Then I got on the *Stavangerfjord* with probably one hundred fifty or two hundred other Americans who were headed to Norway to the summer session. There were some other undergraduates, school teachers and people like that. There was even a married couple. We gathered together. We danced every night, every day we had classes on board. We played the children's game Go Fish in Norwegian so that we could practice counting and that stuff, so we'd have a little bit of conversation when we arrived. Though how often you'd tell somebody in Norway to go fish, I don't know.

But that's how we practiced it. Then, it was a ten-day trip across the ocean, so it was a great opportunity to meet the other students from all over America. We made great friends. We had great food, learned a little bit of Norwegian, and great dancing in the evenings, had a band. All of us students were traveling tourist class but we sneaked into first class every once in a while and danced to their little swishier music. We always found somebody in first class who said, "No, I've invited them to my table." That was fun. Then, after the music quit, there was a band of twenty or thirty of these university kids. It was too early to go to bed so they wandered the ship and they sang in certain lounges and then they went down to the crew's mess room and had luncheon with them.

Finally a couple of nights the captain came on the all call [system] at two or three in the morning. "This is the captain speaking. Will the students please go to bed?"

We did, I guess. But no matter what time we went to bed we always woke up in time for breakfast. It was a great experience. We arrived in Norway and had a great experience at the International Summer School, students from all over the world. Back then, this was before the World's Fair. Somebody complained about Seattle being the cultural dustbin of the world. It was a small town. I lived and grew up in the small portion of a small town. Everything that I was exposed to expanded my world. I was exposed to people from India, Russia, and Poland. I never met anybody like that here in Seattle. It was a real experience.

But I did learn things. One of the most exciting things that happened to me was that all the years I was growing up in Seattle, my dad was gone fishing a lot of the time, but he always would send me my birthday a card and he would sign it "Dad." Never a letter.

If I was away or if my grandmother was away, she would send me a card for whatever — Easter or Christmas — and sign it "Grandma." Never a letter.

But when I was in Norway and my father and my grandmother knew that I was beginning to speak Scandinavian, my dad wrote me a letter because he wrote in Norwegian. And that was wonderful.

The people that I lived with in Norway asked me what I wanted for my birthday dinner and I said if I could have fish cakes or fish pudding, that would be wonderful.

So I became accustomed to Norwegian cooking. And I liked it. That dinner in Norway was white potatoes, white cauliflower, white fish pudding and white gravy. It was a wallpaper hanger's paste pot. But it tasted wonderful and it still does.

But back to the Rolf and Wenche Eng family [I lived with in Norway]. I feel strongly that I'm related to them. In Norway I became part of the family. We weren't related, but I feel so. At home I lived in a working class community. My dad was a working man. In this new Norwegian family, it was in a higher economic neighborhood of Oslo. He was a businessman, owner. They had a whole roomful of books. In Ballard we had a room that had a shelf for encyclopedias and the Harvard Classics my mother bought when she was a secretary some place, before she was married. That was the extent of it. The Engs had all kinds of books, everywhere. He was in the printing business, so he could get books. But they read all the time.

She was learning Italian. She spoke English, Norwegian, obviously, and Swedish. He had been a student in Germany, spoke English fluently, and of course Norwegian. I was really impressed. This is a different lifestyle than what I had learned. They were not the richest people in Norway, but richer than my Ballard classmates.

The Engs had relatives who lived up on Holmenkollen where they had a lot more than these folks had. But the Engs had a beautiful house. They had a cabin out on an island. They had a farm where they could go skiing.

It was different than when I was growing up in Ballard. And being exposed to that, I guess [it] gave me some ambition to say: "Gee, I would like to do some of the things that these people do. They go to the theater. I think I would like to go to the theater, too. They go to symphonies. I think I would do that. They travel. I would like to do that." Anyway, it began to change my world view.

Fortunately for me, I was able to stay with the Engs many times when I went [to Norway]. And they came to America and stayed with me. ... So there's been a contact for fifty years with these folks.

Over my post-graduate years, I've had three jobs all at the same time: I was an award-winning Kent school teacher; I did the weekly radio program ["The Scandinavian Hour"] and I also owned a company that did repairs, remodeling and rental of housing. So I did all that for thirty years.

My father's fishing career impacted me too and, I think, probably a lot of other families had the same experience. First of all, my mother and my grandmother were Swedish. Scandinavia – in the early 1900s – wasn't necessarily feminist and wasn't a matriarchal society, but the women were strong. You lay that onto a fisherman's family – a fisherman who was gone to Alaska all summer or down fishing tuna fish off of California. Mother is left alone. She has to make all the decisions, financial, discipline, everything. She was already a strong woman. This makes her stronger. I have grown up around strong, strong women. I'll tell some of the people who aren't Scandinavian about my friends and their wives and the family. They say: "'Wow, you just don't understand. America's not like that."

Well, my America is. The women are strong and dependable. Father comes home and they share, at least in our family they shared.

Mom said, "Oh, by the way, I bought a car."

"Oh, I didn't think you were going to buy a car," Dad said.

"Well, we had to have a car, so I bought one."

My daughter inherited that strength and I am sure my granddaughter will also.

Douglas Warne was born September 15, 1938, in Ballard to Hans Kristofferson Warne, who had emigrated in the 1920s from the island of Karmoy in Norway, and Dorothy Nelson Warne, who was born in British Columbia to Swedish parents. Hans Americanized the double "V" originally in his surname to a "W." Similarly Dorothy's family Americanized their surname, Nilsson, to Nelson. Dorothy spoke only Swedish when she entered Adams Elementary in Ballard. She made lasting friends at the school and was the last of the "Adams Girls" when she died in 2008 at age 99. Doug has produced and aired "The Scandinavian Hour" on Seattle area radio stations since 1959. For many years the late Ron Olsen was his partner on the program. Doug met his future wife, Lena Malmberg, when she was attending Seattle Community College on Broadway. Lena and Doug were married in Eskilstuna, Sweden in 1967. Lena, who was born May 6, 1940, and raised in Eskilstuna, Sweden, died in September 2007. Their daughter, Krista, is married to Charles Grinstein. Doug has one granddaughter, Elise Hannah Grinstein.

Margaret Olga Welch

"They brought my grandmother back with them. . . . She never learned to speak English, but there were enough Norwegians around Ballard that it didn't bother her."

My father's father was a fisherman and had a fish-drying business. They lived on a small island near Kristiansund. Three children were born to them, Ole, John and Annie. Their mother died in childbirth with the fourth child. After trying for a time to raise them himself, their father moved them to his sister's place in Tømmervåg, on Tustna, northeast of Kristiansund.

When Ole, my father, was about nine years old, his father drowned. Ole always dreamed he would come to the United States. When he was old enough, he had to serve in the army. Also, he had to wait until he was 21 for his inheritance. He came to the United States in 1894. My mother was born in 1872, on a small island in Hannasvik, Tustna. Her father was a fisherman, and on one of his fishing trips, he and her eldest brother were drowned.

My parents lived close together My father told my mother he would send for her, so she could come to the United States, also. Three young men came from Norway. They crossed Canada by train, and then to Blaine, Washington. They built a boat and rowed to Ballard. When I asked my father about that, I said, "Gee, that must have been a big boat," and he said, "Well, she was staunch." When they passed Whidbey Island on that trip, he looked over and said, "I will have some land on that island someday." Which he did. My father wasn't a very big man, but he had a lot of determination.

It was some years before he sent for my mother. During that time he saved enough money fishing to buy a boat and then he fished for quite awhile and invested in land. Then he learned how to build houses. He was aware that property was very valuable. He sent for my mother, and she came, and they were married in Ballard, shortly before 1900. Then he started buying property in Ballard, 74th or 75th and 34th near the bluff on Sunset Hill. He also bought other property and built houses, probably about 30 houses in all during his time. And in 1911, he built Woog's Lodge Hall, where they all had their Lodge meetings.

We had lots of company, young men coming from Norway, if they needed a place, there was a place for them there. In the big front room, as we called it, we had a wood stove. The kitchen always had wonderful smells in it, because my mother was a wonderful cook. Beef stew and roast beef. My dad really liked meat and potatoes and my mother's pies, especially apple pies, were wonderful. We had a peach tree and an apple tree and, oh, yes, homemade bread. She made wonderful bread. She didn't have a recipe written down, but she made the best bread in town. And she made lots of goodies, cookies and *fattigman* and spritz, and we had *sildbol* and *rømmegrøt*, and all those goody things. Many Scandinavians were in the neighborhood. We all shared and had coffee parties. It was like a little Norway there.

We went down to the beach. There was no road or street. We went through the woods, and over the hogsback. That was dangerous and the kids didn't want me to go with them because I was too small. Once in awhile my mother would say, "You have to take your sister to the beach." They didn't like it, but they did it. They just loved swimming in the Sound, even as cold as it was.

We all went to Webster. I was not quite six years old when I started, so I was pretty shy. We walked through where 30th would be later, but it was just a wooded area then. Outside school we lined up and when the music started, we would all march into the school.

My mother took us regularly to Ballard First Lutheran Church. There were services in both English and Norwegian.

The opportunities here were almost overwhelming for my father. He always read all the newspaper. He learned to read English quite quickly — so did my mother. And there was a time when he didn't want Norwegian in the household. He wanted us all to speak English.

I can hear Norwegian and remember it because my grandmother always spoke Norwegian. When my sister was five, she and my mother went to Norway. They brought my grandmother back with them, and she lived with us from then on. It was just a joy to have her, all the children loved my grandmother. She always had goodies in her pocket. They all called her *Bestemor*. Yes, she was so special. I think she took care of me a lot because Mother had a lot to do. My dad said, "The best thing that happened was that we brought Bestemor here."

All the men wanted Bestemor to knit socks for them, but my dad came first, and she knit plenty of socks for him, big heavy socks, really warm for a fisherman. And she'd knit when she wasn't tending the chickens and milking the cow. She never learned to speak English, but there were

472 - Margaret Olga Welch

enough Norwegians around Ballard that it didn't bother her.

My dad joined the Sons of Norway and the Scandinavian Fraternity. My mother joined the Daughters of Norway and was very active there. Woog Hall [17th and Market] was built, the year that I was born, in 1911. I remember at Christmas we went to the hall and got a box of goodies, and we could eat them all if we wanted to. And we got to dance with our fathers because there was lots of music and that was great. It was always Scandinavian dances, you know, the waltz and the polka the schottische, all those dances.

Dad's brother, John Woog and his wife, Severine came to Seattle and lived in a house Dad built on 34th Northwest. Severine and her spinning wheel were quite famous. A picture shows her in Frederick & Nelson's window spinning, wearing her beautiful costume.

My dad was always proud to march in the 17th of May parade.

Woog Hall on Market Street

Ole Woog

Margaret Woog Welch was born in 1911 at home in Ballard. Her father, Ole Anderson Woog, was born in Norway November 25 1867. He emigrated in 1894. Eventually he sent for his bride. They were married circa 1899 in Ballard. Their four children: Albert, Agnes, Jennie and Margaret. Ole built Woog Hall in 1911. The family lived in Ballard until 1921 when they moved to Cashmere in eastern Washington for Ole's health. Margaret married Elmo Welch in 1938. They had one daughter, Beverly Irene (1943). Margaret and Elmo were divorced (1952). Margaret worked for the City of Seattle, went to Seattle Pacific University and in 1990, received a BA in Biblical Studies and Psychology. She died in 2007.

Benton G. and
Rachel Daniels Williams

RACHEL: "After we were married, we boogied on Saturday night and listened to Bach on Sunday morning."

RACHEL: My mother came from Norway all by herself when she was 15 years old to Burlington, Washington, where her sisters and brothers had farms. She was going to farm. I think that was quite a feat for a 15-year-old girl who couldn't speak English to come, in steerage, then all the way across the United States. She'd never been away from home.

My father did all kinds of work. He was a carpenter and went to sea. By the time my mother had four children, he gave up the sea to be a laborer. When I was very small, it was such a wonderful community. We lived in similar houses, and families grew up together. We went one block to the grocery store. The grocer stood behind the counter and we'd ask for what we wanted. On the other side of the store was penny candy. If we ever got pennies, we had only a block to run to the store. They had living quarters in the back. And we could go a block the other way and be at the meat market. Whenever we went there, the butcher'd give us a wienie to eat. The butcher store was on 63rd across 15th. And then another grocery store was there. He'd put your purchase on a book if you didn't have any money, and then you'd have to pay up later.

I'd go with my girlfriend's family to pick berries in Puyallup to earn money for school. We'd live there for the summer.

Mom used to take us to Alki Beach. We'd go over by streetcar, over those trestles to Alki. And we'd pack a lunch — that was quite a trip. We loved that. And she'd take us up to Woodland Park. We'd go for walks, make candy, go to Green Lake, go to Golden Gardens. It was tough times but we had fun. We didn't suffer, except it changed the way we look at things now, because it stays with you forever. My folks had a place on Lake Goodwin, which was very nice. My dad worked for a man that paid him with property on Lake Goodwin. He built a house out there and we went there a lot.

We had the 10-cent store down in Ballard, with a lunch counter. You could go there and have a little lunch, or soda, or something. A lot of little drug stores had soda fountains, and you could have a soda for 10 cents. There used to be a drug store right on the corner by our house on 15th and 62nd.

Sometimes we would take the street car to Golden Gardens. We could walk over to 24th to catch it, and it would go up to 85th and 32nd. We'd get off there and walk down. We never thought anything of walking up and down all those steps. We were at Golden Gardens almost all the time in the summer.

We used to go to the old library down on Market Street. I think we read every book in the library. We just loved to go down there. We'd walk both ways. Sometimes the boys would come along in a car and honk at us. Of course, that made our day.

When we were real little, a woman from the Woman's Christian Temperance Union had all us kids come to her house after school one day a week, and she would give us something like Jell-O with whipped cream on it. The big thing was, we were supposed to stomp on cigarettes. We would have to say how many cigarettes we had stomped on. Well, anybody that said a number, the next person said one bigger. We were real little when we did that.

Salmon Bay School was just a block and a half away, and James Monroe and Ballard High were just a couple blocks. I could go home every day for lunch, I lived so close, and I loved school.

I took a business course at Ballard because of the Depression; I thought I had to go to work. I worked for the school district as a secretary in schools. When I had my children, I stayed home for 20 years, then I went back.

BENTON: I was the organist at Northminster Presbyterian Church for many, many years. When I met Rachel, that's when I started to be organist there. And I played in dance orchestras around the city after we were married, to earn a little extra income. I was also working at Boeing at the time.

I recall the opening of the Ballard Bridge when it was first built. The Musicians Union decided to furnish a marching band. I not only played the keyboard, I could also play a baritone horn. So I was in the marching band that opened the Ballard Bridge. There was a rather large man who was playing the baritone next to me. He blew so loud that I couldn't hear what I was playing. And Rachel and her mother were standing on the sidelines waving me on.

Benton C. and Rachel (Daniels) Williams - 475

After graduating from the Forestry College in 1939, there were no jobs available, so you had to take anything you could find. Boeing was hiring because of the bombing of Pearl Harbor. When we started we only had 19 bombers, and none of them had guns in them. One of my most "intelligent" decisions was that Boeing would never go anywhere after the war. So I quit, and went back to school at the University of Washington to get an education degree. I discovered on my transcript that all my grades were pretty poor except for mathematics. Maybe I better teach that. Then I began teaching science at James Monroe Junior High School.

I first started of teaching in 1951. I was teaching physiology in science class at James Monroe and I passed out boxes of human bones. Before I knew it, the kids were throwing them all over the room. That was one of my first downfalls in my teaching.

After James Monroe, I taught mathematics at James Madison in West Seattle, at Wilson Junior High in the north end, and McClure on Queen Anne Hill. I broke my collarbone at James Monroe in 1951. The principal was named King and my mother knew him. She came to pick me up with my broken collarbone, and they sat there talking because they knew each other. And I sat there waiting and waiting.

RACHEL: The boys and girls were separated when I went there. Boys went up one stairway, the girls went up another. They also had hall monitors who stood in the middle of the hall with their hands out and the girls went on one side and the boys on the other.

We went to the First Presbyterian Church down in Ballard. It used to be on Market Street and 17th when I was little. When they moved up to 27th, they renamed it Northminster Presbyterian.

BENTON: When they moved to 27th, I became the organist.

RACHEL: After we were married. We boogied on Saturday night and listened to Bach on Sunday morning.

Rachel Daniels was born in Ballard, March 16, 1917. Her mother was from Norway and her father's parents were Scottish and English. Benton Williams was born June 4, 1914. His father was Welsh. They were married December 5, 1941. Their three daughters are Sandra (1944) [see Johnsen, p. 197], Jill (1946) and Melissa (1953). Benton died in 2010.

Louise Moen Wylie

"And then I sang at the fair on children's day, June 5, 1909. They got a thousand voices."

I was born on West 58th. It was called Times Street. Ballard was separate, not connected to Seattle. Well, the house we lived in? Let's see, five rooms — and the bathroom was built on the back porch later and plumbing put in it. Of course, we had an outhouse. I think maybe my dad had help from a friend of his, but he did most of the building. That's where we lived till I was five years old. So, 1901 he built the house at 111 Eighth Avenue [now 6513 32nd NW]. He bought that acre of land when we were living on Times Street. When we moved, they had a wagon and a horse and Henry sat with the driver carrying the cat.

I was five then and I had to start school in Salmon Bay School way over on 20th and 64th. My two older brothers took me to school and they put me in this room and left me there, and I started to bawl. I cried — never been away from home. That's a long ways to walk. When they took me over there two, three times, then I knew the way. But one morning I was going to school and this flock of geese came running over to the fence and scared the daylights out of me, and here I was going to school all that distance by myself.

I just went to the first grade at Salmon Bay. They built two houses on 67th and called them the Bay View School and I went there to the second grade. They were across the street from Webster School. They built that about 1908 when I was in the fifth grade. I moved into it when I was in the fifth grade.

And then I sang at the fair [the Alaska-Yukon-Pacific Exposition] on children's day, June 5, 1909. They got a thousand voices, so many from each school. We formed a flag. They took red, white and blue bunting, and made gowns with drawstrings that we slipped over our heads. Had so many blues for the corner for the flag, for the stars and so many stripes for red and white. So, we must have looked nice down in the amphitheater.

It was on a Saturday night [around 1909]. We didn't have plumbing in the house. We were taking baths in a galvanized tub in the kitchen in front of the stove, and there was a knock, knock at the door. Here was a whole gang on Saturday night, a surprise party on the folks. They gave the folks a living room floor rug. They collected so much from everybody, and they brought all this and brought food with them. Surprise.

When I finished the eighth grade at Webster, I walked for four years down to that Ballard High School, which was right where the hospital is today on Tallman. The janitor rang a bell when nine o'clock came. Sometimes he'd be standing out there, and looked to see if anybody was coming. And if he saw you coming, sometime he'd wait till you got up to the building before he rang it.

I'm the only one in the family who went through high school. I took a general course. We had to take English, and history. and then a foreign language. To graduate you have to have that. I took German, because that was closest to Norwegian. I took four years of German, and after I got through with that, they took it out of the schools — the war came along.

Pa worked most of the time down at the Stimson Lumber Mill. He was tallyman at the mill. Tell how much lumber there is in the piles. Later he got on for the city, digging sewers. That's when Mama had him quit working. She said it's killing him, digging by hand with a shovel. Pa wasn't very big, and Mama said he'd never make it if he didn't quit.

Every summer he'd make good money selling raspberries, and even vegetables. And chickens, and he sold eggs. He used to sell fruit. We had every kind of a tree you could think of — pear and apple and plums and cherries and pie cherries and blue prunes.

In the summertime the grocery would buy the berries, crates of them. And all us kids had to pick raspberries.

Ballard had wooden sidewalks made with planks that wide. They were awful to walk on. And dirt streets and horse and wagon. There was even horse and wagons when my son Jim was little. We slept upstairs, and they had horses in the fire department. And poor kid, it just scared the daylights out of him when they came up 32nd.

We had a cow. They put the cow out with the rope to eat grass, and sometimes I'd have to go get her. The cow would hurry up and scared the daylights out of me. We had a barn down at the end of our property. We had a fence out there and a gate. We'd open up the gate and let the cow come in. Milking is something I never did do. My dad and my mother, but I never did. I think they had a pig one time, because we had a pigpen out there. We had chickens. We had geese.

478 - Louise Moen Wylie

We had our own milk, but we didn't drink milk. We sold the milk. I'd have to walk way down to 60th and 30th to deliver milk; some people named Startup and Peterson both took milk from us. I was maybe 12 years old.

My dad sold potatoes. I was delivering a sack of potatoes for my dad on 30th, and on one side of 30th was a gully — 30th and 64th. I had Ed's wagon and I had Agnes and Harold besides the sack of potatoes. It got to be going kind of fast there, and I tried to steer it onto the parking strip. I was afraid I would go down the bank. It tipped over, and I fell off. The sack of potatoes fell on top of me, and this finger got crooked and it never did straighten.

We had a couple of wells. One well was right there on our porch. When we first went up there — the Asmervigs moved in just before we did, and they lived right below us on 65th — we had to carry water home from there. And we had an outhouse down by the woodshed. Jeepers, think of going out there at night.

It's hard to say when we got electricity, because I remember we had lamps for a long time, When I was still in Webster School we had lamps, because I used to come home and clean the lamp chimneys and put oil in the lamps. That would be in 1910.

After I graduated, I worked at the American Can Company for quite awhile — where they made cans to send to Alaska for canned salmon. Down on Western Avenue and Cedar Street. Then I worked for awhile at Sears Roebuck on Sunday, just mail order in the shoe department. That's what I did before I went and got married.

We had three boarders. The three men had the front bedrooms. We had four rooms upstairs, and my mother and dad's room down-stairs. Mr. Worley, Mr. Nolan and Mr. Sharp. Mr. Sharp and Mr. Worley were from England. Mr. Nolan came from Brooklyn, New York, and he worked at Frederick & Nelson doing the fancy draperies, hanging drapes for people. And the way we got them, Mr. Worley and Mr. Nolan were rooming in Ballard in a hotel. And they were down there walking on the railroad tracks one Sunday. And Henry took pictures of them, and then he says, "I'll meet you here next Sunday," and he sold the pictures to them and he invited them out to the house, of all things.

I used to sew everything under the sun. Now, I don't even touch a needle. My mother had a machine but she didn't want me to sew on hers. Matilda's mother, Mrs. Asmervig, let me sew on her machine. I made my own clothes even when I was going to grammar school. Later on Mama let me. Mama used to sew. She made clothes for the children.

Louise Moen Wylie - 479

These boarders sometime gave her clothes and she'd take them apart and wash them and use the material. She used to do those things when she was young. Of course, my dad was always handy with doing things. We never went to shoemaker; he fixed all our shoes. And then I got so I'd do it, too.

Louise Moen was born in Ballard July 6, 1895 to Ole Moen, born 1858 in Eidsberg, Norway and Anna Henrikson Moen, born 1869 in Hof i Solar, Norway. Ole came to Seattle in March 1889, he sent for Anna in Fergus Falls, Minnesota. She arrived June 30, 1889. They were married July 1, 1889 and moved to Ballard in 1892. Their children: Henry (1892-1983), Ed (1893-1976), Louise (1895-1990), Albert (1896-1975), Elmer (1898-1985), Agnes (1900-1973) and Harold (1902-1992). Louise married James Hill in 1919. Her son, James Hill, Jr. (1920-1969) pioneered the survival suit. She later married Bob "Scotty" Wylie. For many years they owned and ran the popular "Scotty's Fish and Chips" on 84th and 8th Avenue Northwest. Bob died 1982. Louise died 1990. This interview took place January 17, 1988.

Solveig M. Lee

"On January 1, 1934, a celebration was held at the Joe Hillaire ranch near Sandy Point to recognize all that the Lees had done for the Lummis. The Lummi Reservation is where my sisters, Anna and Onella, and I grew up."

My great-grandparents, Peter and Ingeri Egtvedt, emigrated with three sons from Vossestrand, Hordaland, Norway. They came to America in 1846 and settled on Koshkonong Prairie in Wisconsin Territory where there was a community of Vossings. There, two more sons and and a daughter, Anna, were born.

My grandfather, Ole N. Lee, from Lie, Raundalen, Voss, arrived in 1856 and made his first home in America at Stoughton and Koshkonong Prairie. Like many others, he caught the "gold fever" and, in 1859, put together all of his belongings, and took off for the goldfields of California. He made his way to the Sierras, an area – Silver Mountain, first known as Kongsberg – that was founded by Scandinavian miners in 1858. Ole is said to have been head of the crew and to have found many mines. He traveled to what is now Southern California and bought two lots in Old Town, San Diego. In 1868, he squatted on land east of San Diego where Lee's Valley – one end of Lyon's Valley – is located and named after him.

Ole returned to Koshkonong Prairie where he wooed and married Anna in March of 1874. Ole returned to California. In November of 1874, Anna, accompanied by her brother, Peter, joined Ole in Sacramento Valley. There, Ole was employed as head of location of mines and supervisor of new diggings. The family lived in California until they heard that gold had been found along the Fraser River in Canada and Mount Baker near the Canadian-American border. They, with others, took the ship, *Dakota*, up the coast to Seattle. Her population was 3,600 or so.

Ole and others searched for a place to call home. After a time, Anna boarded the Fanny Lake steamer to search for them. When she found them, Ole and other members of the group had built a rough cabin on the South Fork of the Skagit River. A week later, my aunt, Nellie Ida Prizella

Lee, was born. They found that the gold rush was a bust and farmed. They had two other children, Peter and Oscar, all born in Washington Territory.

My mother, Petra, and her sisters, were daughters of Ola and Toline Brenden from Lesje, Oppland. She was born in Eau Claire, Wisconsin. The family moved to Stanley, Wisconsin, then west to Everett, Washington, and then north to Mount Vernon. My parents, Oscar Lee and Petra Brenden, married in Seattle.

Shortly after, my father was asked by Native American friends to go to the Lummi Reservation in Whatcom County to assist getting the land under cultivation. Our family had draglines as well as other equipment and much hired hands to help at Lummi to do what was necessary – diking and dredging of ditches – to prepare the land for cultivation. Bridges needed to be built; the land needed leveling. My father managed the Lummi acreage.

On January 1, 1934, a celebration was held at the Joe Hillaire ranch near Sandy Point to recognize all that the Lees had done for the Lummis. The Lummi Reservation is where my sisters, Anna and Onella, and I grew up. Cousin Peter Egtvedt also lived with us.

Our Indian neighbor, Mae Kinley, was like a grandmother to us. She often picked blackberries with us.

We went to school in Ferndale — six miles away — and church in Bellingham — fourteen miles away. I studied violin during those years and became concert mistress of Tri-County Orchestra and played in the first All-State Orchestra in Yakima.

It wasn't an easy time, what with World War II and the shortages and the worries. How to get crops in with the shortage of manpower! A truck was driven daily to Lynden to pick up Mexican help at the labor camp. My father went to the Bellingham Chamber of Commerce to get help. After regular work, several lawyers, bankers, businessmen and other professionals in Bellingham came out to work in the fields. We provided evening meals.

After high school, Anna, Onella and I went to Pacific Lutheran College. I got my education degree there, and was hired to teach in Georgetown in Seattle. I moved to Brighton, Crown Hill, and then Viewlands.

In the classroom, it was fun doing projects that led to understanding. Once, we sent gas-filled balloons with the school address in them, then waited for responses. We received a few replies from the Midwest and were so impressed they went so far away. Each Memorial Day, the student council had a Memorial Day program honoring the veterans.

Children brought flowers which were placed on the stage in the morning, and, after the assembly, carried by student council members to Crown Hill Cemetery and put on grave stones. Our Christmas programs were based on the scene of the nativity.

A fellow teacher tried to get teachers to sign up for a photography class. I was persuaded. Developing the pictures, black and white, grew on me. Later, I took first place for my photograph, "Coventry," in the national Lutheran Brotherhood Photography contest.

When Hal Ryan was chairman of the 17th of May parade in Ballard, he asked Crown Hill School to participate and I was put in charge of the group. We made paper flags for several countries – Norway, Finland, Greece, and more. One year we had an exchange teacher from Trondheim, Norway, as our guest. She talked about her native land, and then we had refreshments that included Norwegian cookies. Crown Hill participated in the parade until the school closed. We studied nutrition, then with mothers' help, prepared a well-balanced meal that we ate at mealtime. During the Centennial Year, the children colored red, white and blue pictures. Pictures were submitted and three were printed in a book. After teaching at Crown Hill for nineteen years, the school closed. I transferred to Viewlands and there I received the Golden Acorn award.

During my work in Ballard I became active in the Norwegian community. I joined the Sons of Norway, Leif Erikson Lodge #1; gave countless hours at the Nordic Heritage Museum in Seattle; contacting people to be docents for the "Dream of America" exhibit as well as being a docent; served on the Norway Room committee; gathered histories and photos for the Museum's archives, as well as interviewed people around the state, and worked in the Museum store. Though my main interest was Norway, I also obtained information for other Nordic rooms. I represented the Museum on 17th of May Committee meetings and was in charge of the Bergen Place program on the 17th of May for many years. When Ballard was writing its centennial history, I co-chaired with Bonnita Peterson the writing of one chapter of the book *Passport to Ballard* and I became a charter member of the Ballard Historical Society.

Solveig Lee earned her degree in education from Pacific Lutheran College. She also studied at the University of Oslo; Augsburg College, Minnesota, and the College of Ripon and St. John, York, England, the setting for the "Vikings Discovery of Great Britain." She attended a Pacific Lutheran University Study Tour of China in 1979; Penn State for a class on the Revolutionary War; Loyola Marymount for a class on Spanish-America in California, and attended the World Conference on Reading in Kowloon. In 2006, she was Honorary Marshal in Ballard's 17th of May parade. Ms.

Lee is in-house photographer for the Skagit County Historical Museum, and in 2011 she was chosen Volunteer of the Year. She is a member of Vosselag; the Scandinavian Cultural Council at Pacific Lutheran University; Sons of Norway Leif Erikson Lodge #1; Northwest Historian's Guild; Skagit Genealogical Society, and the Retired School Employees' Association; Vesterheim, Decorah, Iowa, and the Seattle-Bergen Sister-City Association. She also is a member and secretary of the Territorial Daughters of Washington, Chapter Two. She has served as a correspondent for *The Western Viking*, now *The Norwegian American Weekly* for many years.

Index

Symbols

488

492

495